CW01368617

TAROT OF THE HOLY LIGHT

Tarot of the Holy Light
A Continental Esoteric Tarot

written by

Christine Payne-Towler

illustrated by

Michael Dowers

© 2016

Noreah/Brownfield Press

Tarot of the Holy Light:
A Continental Esoteric Tarot
Volume One
Published by Noreah/Brownfield Press

Editing and Art direction by Michael Dowers
Production by Paul Baresh
Production Assistance by Michael Dowers
Front Cover by Patrick Dowers
Associate Editor: Christine Payne-Towler

Thanks to: Mihir Chandaria, Tia J. Finnigan, Angel Lozada, Patrick Dowers, Fortuna Aphro, Jessica Schiek, Roger Walco, Corina Bardasuc

Tarot of the Holy Light © 2015 Christine Payne-Towler & Michael Dowers/Noreah/Brownfield Press. All rights reserved.

Visit the Tarot University website: www.tarotuniversity.com.

Second Noreah/Brownfield edition: 2016

Tarot of the Holy Light Icon

Moon ☽ The High Priestess
Sun ☉ The Fool
Mercury ☿ The Star
Venus ♀ The Empress

Mars ♂ Strength
Jupiter ♃ The Emperor
Saturn ♄ Judgement

△ Primal Air ♅ associated with Uranus; The Magician

▽ Primal Water ♆ associated with Neptune; Death

△ Primal Fire ♇ associated with Pluto; The World

Table of Contents

Tarot of the Holy Light:
A Continental Esoteric Tarot

Preface...11

Introduction and Acknowledgements...13

Chapter 1
Introduction to the Minor Arcana...21

Illustrations...62

Chapter 2
The Swords...75

Chapter 3
The Wands...135

Chapter 4
The Cups...193

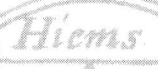

Chapter 5
The Disks...253

Chapter 6
Introduction to the Major Arcana...313
The Trumps...314

Appendix
The Horoscope Spread...435
The Celtic Cross Spread...447
Tarot Deck Citations...453
Graph of Minor Arcana Values...457
Graph of Major Arcana Values...467
Graph of the Shem Angels...471
Bibliography...479
About the Author...491

Tarot of the Holy Light

A Continental Esoteric Tarot

Preface

The writing project that became this book started ten years ago. I was approached by the founding editor of Aeon Books to compose a volume on the history of the Continental Tarots. The skeleton for that review of the cards was assembled from the 78 essays I had written for the online interpretive service at www.tarot.com. That manuscript only got to the rough-draft stage before circumstances beyond control demanded that it be set aside. Right about the same time, a Higher Power brought Michael Dowers into my life, and within just a few years *Tarot of the Holy Light* was under way.

Michael's attraction to the alchemical art of 17th and 18th century Alchemy parallels my own. This common interest gave me a perfect excuse to look behind and beneath the modern Continental representatives (Levi, Christian, Papus, and Wirth, primarily), digging more deeply into the roots of the inherited model wherever they might lead. Michael has a gift for rendering complex ideas into simple terms, which gives him an instinctive knack for occult illustration. Therefore, I happily handed over all of my resources on alchemical art, along with my essays, for him to illustrate. My intent at that point was still to produce a volume that would summarize the esoteric thrust of the Continental Tarots from their first appearance in Europe to the 20th century.

I have a particular categorical habit of mind that allowed me to think through, design, and interpret a very successful commercial online Tarot vending machine in 1998. After long study of the matter, it seems obvious that our Renaissance, Reformation, and Enlightenment predecessors were equally well positioned to exploit Tarot's recombinant qualities in just the same way I did for that project, since the Tarot of the 1500s is fundamentally the same as the Tarot of today. The visual format of the graph or information-grid penetrated into Europe from their Arabic neighbors to the east and south during the pre-Renaissance of the 12th and 13th centuries. This allowed Westerners to visualize and understand the idea of a modulating array of related values that interweave into a connected network. Raymond Lully made this style of thinking explicit in his combinatory wheels-within-wheels. Later Campanelli went so far as to create a three-dimensional "memory theater" to demonstrate the catalogue of interpenetrating forces and vectors that inhabited the magical universe of the times. The book you are holding is the boiled-down concentrate of these ideas derived through their natural historical channels as applied to the outline of Tarot.

When we published *Tarot of the Holy Light* in September of 2011, we had no idea how popular it would become practically overnight. Within months it was voted sixth best deck for 2011 at the huge international forum AeclecticTarot. Subsequently, author and entrepreneur Caroline Kenner approached us to contribute the 78-card essays to a computer app she and her husband were producing under the business name The Fool's Dog. When I shared with her the state of the essays at that point, Caroline wisely pointed out that they needed another rewrite to make them suitable for the kind of uses they were designing into their service. I am forever grateful for her tact and patience as I spun through the essays again to make sure that I fully justified the primary themes and influences detailed on every card. Before her feedback I was still thinking theoretically, viewing our pack as a set of flashcards exemplifying the esoteric principles that are embedded in the Continental tradition. After the revision for The Fool's Dog, it became clear that *Tarot of the Holy Light* was destined to become a working deck around the world.

In the wake of that release, I have edited these chapters yet again, this time to include the influences that aren't expressly detailed on the faces of the cards. These deeper values forced their way into my consciousness as a result of Michael's artistic choices because he drew so much from the art and visionary tour-de-force that emerged from the work of Jacob Boehme, an esoteric synthesizer writing at the beginning of the 1600s. The results of that study became so extensive that we have decided to separate those chapters into a book of its own under the title *Foundations of the Esoteric Tradition*. Splitting this work into two has allowed us to focus this volume on the mature fullness of these 78-card essays, constituting the "owners and operators manual" for *Tarot of the Holy Light*.

The decision to separate the two books has been agonizing for me, considering that in my imagination they exist as the two lobes of one brain. I battled the idea for over a year before I finally gave in to the inevitable. We have gone to great lengths to ensure that this volume will stand on its own as it confines itself largely to the material, emotional, and psychological universe of the awakening individual. Consider it a given that the attentive reader will identify points in the text where more commentary would be desirable, but the requisite explanations are not to be found within these covers. The rest of the story will be found in the companion volume, *Foundations of the Esoteric Tradition*.

At the turn into the 21st century, my peers and arguing-mates at the legendary Tarot watering hole known as TarotL challenged me to write a full explication of the Continental Tarots. Between this volume and its companion, I have made a brave start towards what was requested. I look forward to the discussion that will follow.

Introduction and Acknowledgements

The title of this book states my case boldly: *Tarot of the Holy Light: A Continental Esoteric Tarot* represents the summation of my studies in the field of Continental esoteric Tarots. By "Continental" I mean from the European continent proper, based in the Continental languages, and circulating through Continental populations. I am not including Great Britain or the Iberian Peninsula. I refer to all Tarot decks from the first five centuries of the Tarot's appearance. By "esoteric" I mean possessing all of the occult correspondences that would naturally pertain to a pack of cards with this occult formula:

$[(7 \times 3) + 1] + \{[(3 \times 3) + 1] \times 4\} + [(3 \times 4) + 4]$

[Trumps] + {   Pips   } + [Royals]

My stance is that the very first pack of cards with enumerated Trumps, showing numerals on the faces of the Major Arcana, demonstrates the level of coherency within its implied body of correspondences that would allow it to become an esoteric computer for the Renaissance and all that followed.

Some may say that it is rash to make such a bald summary statement like this, but this conclusion has been reached after a 30-year search through all the materials I could assemble pertaining to magic, the Renaissance Magus, Astronomy/Astrology, Kabbalah, Gnosticism, the Faust myth, Alchemy, Sacred Geometry, and all of the ancient priestly arts at the core of the Western religions. This includes investigating the interweaving of private groups that sprang up in Europe in the wake of the Crusades, as well as the contribution of Masons and Rosicrucians to the transmission. What I have learned is that "all roads lead to Rome." This is to say that the Tarot is uniquely configured to summarize the esoteric bone-structure and mythology of the Abrahamic tradition.

No lessons in esoteric history are required for a contemporary reader to open the box and shuffle the deck. This has been amply proven by the enthusiastic reception *Tarot of the Holy Light* has received in the last few years, even amongst those who have only the handmade "Little White Book" to support it. The subsequent iPad and Kindle apps created by The Fool's Dog have gone a long way towards introducing this pack to the world, although the text included with those apps covers only the meanings of the individual cards in a spread, barely extending into the magical, philosophical, or alchemical implications of the cards. This book will partially make up for that lack insofar as it introduces the inner organizing principles that structure the deck of Tarot below and behind all superficial features. I confidently assert that the scaffolding I am explicating here has been available to any student of magic since at least the time of the *Anonymous Parisian Tarot* appeared with numbers on the faces of 22 Trumps arranged in Marseille order. The numbers found on the Trumps and Suits, also known as the Major Arcana and the Minor Arcana, stabilize the outline of the pack, alerting us to all the related bodies of correspondences and how they are to be applied.

We begin our exposition of the cards with the four Suits because this is the world in which we find ourselves. An opening theoretical chapter lays out all of the design considerations governing the pack, and then we watch those values weaving through the essays on the individual cards. The order in which the Suits are presented is simply a personal preference representing a mnemonic I internalized years ago, probably based on my early readings of Papus and Wirth. Each of these authors presents Zodiacal wheels in various modifications, and these illustrations became some of my earliest exposures to traditional Astrology. I saw that the Aries/Libra axis lies along the east/west horizon of the idealized Zodiac, while the Cancer/Capricorn axis represents the meridian rising from the center of the Earth to pierce the center of the sky. Somehow this visualization informed me that the so-called masculine or "yang" Suits (Swords and Wands) apply to willful choices and actions taken in the theater of the world (on the horizon). The so-called feminine or "yin" Suits (Cups and Disks), in contrast, work with the inner life of the body and feelings. These energies range from the instincts through the intuition, arousing the potential of our specie's evolution as an embodiment of the consciousness within Earth (along the meridian). Nowadays I have a suspicion that this was an early inkling of Tarot's resonance with the teachings of Boehme and the other Protestant Theosophers, a philosophy that I would only encounter directly 30 years later. Boehme's Sophianic mysticism and inner Alchemy comes to us filtered and adumbrated through the multicultural stream of Masons who left their essays on Tarot across the 18th and 19th centuries.

Contrasting with the Suits, the values associated with the Trumps are more "pure" in the sense that they each represent a single astro-alpha-numeric idea per card. These archetypes stand in their own eternal "ipsity," unconditioned by context or circumstance in worldly terms. Comprising the planets, signs, and celestial Elements, the Trumps serenely preside over our mixed-up world from a higher perspective. These values have been analyzed within the

Septenary framework that is so natural to the Trumps, including considerations from Boehme's characteristic Star of Restitution as an aid to understanding his unique view on spiritual cultivation. The entire synthesis of Suits and Trumps is encapsulated in the Icon (frontis piece), which condenses our operative model into a single all-encompassing image.

In this volume I have done my best to at least outline all of the considerations that caused me to design the cards into the overall pattern they take on the Icon. The reader will find the deeper praxis and more wide-ranging integration of magical modalities in the companion volume.

The point behind exposing the various correspondences inherent in the structure of the Tarot pack is to supply the reader with an inexhaustible well of associations for each card, whether one is reading a throw of the cards or using the deck to illustrate astrological, Kabbalistic, numerological, or alchemical ideas. I encourage users to investigate the cards from the widest possible angle. When I'm working with clients, I want to employ a deck that's connected to a full catalogue of sturdy, time-tested associations that can be tapped whenever an impasse is reached in the art of interpretation. I am adamant about packing each card with a range of organically-related ideas that can help connect the card with the current situation, internally and externally. If the picture doesn't instantly trigger a flash of insight, then the reader has access to a broad range of ideas through the number, the title, the Suit, the astrological sign and ruler, the season, the alchemical and angelic Dignities, and other details that combine to make up the card's fuller implications. Over time, the use of *Tarot of the Holy Light* will tutor the good student in acquiring the larger world-view of our magical ancestors.

This volume has been written to conform to the most popular application of 21st century Tarot culture, which is to serve as a catalyst for ultra-short-term or one-session life coaching. Accordingly, this volume spares the reader the painstaking defense of all my choices and the chapters required to put it in context within the historical stream. Here you will find the implications of the choices I have made. I trust that interested parties will avail themselves of the other volume when they are ready for a more thoroughgoing immersion in the history of magic. The companion volume, *Foundations of the Esoteric Tradition*, is where the detailed occult assumptions that inform *Tarot of the Holy Light* are explored.

On the Art and Design of This Book

The font chosen for the text of this volume is a modern adaptation of the one originally designed for the *Hypnerotomachia Poliphili*, which was first published in Venice in 1499. Historians and esotericists see in this volume an encyclopedic compendium of Renaissance scholarly traditions and inner-school gnosis wrapped up in a dreamlike scenario of the type we encounter in Masonic and Rosicrucian literature. This font has a peculiarity in that it lacks certain modern features, among which are bolding, italics, and dashes. Using this font has challenged us to exercise our creativity, to envision a style in which to present all of this interdisciplinary information cleanly. Toward that goal, our brilliant producer hand-made an italic version of the font, which has gone a long way towards de-congesting the visual field.

The use of capitals has presented us with a consummate conundrum. The format we have followed capitalizes any concept that points to a transcendent, supernal, or heavenly value, whether it is personified or not. We also capitalize the technical terms used in the different esoteric arts under discussion. Some terms will always be capitalized because they represent fixed features of our paradigm, though the words might also have an alternate use in common parlance. Included in this group are theological terms such as Sophia, Pleroma, Holy Spirit, and Restitution. Other terms will sometimes be capitalized and sometimes not, depending on whether the reference points to a human, earthly manifestation (uncapped) or points instead to a personification of the Divine, a category title of one of our occult arts, or a title such as that of a book, organization, or corporate entity (capped).

A prime exemplar of this nicety involves discriminating between an ordinary "fall" (as in suffering a sudden loss of altitude), distinguished from the season of fall, the simple fall of a card into a spread, the Essential Dignity of a planet's Fall, or the (theological) Fall of Lucifer, followed by that of Adam and Eve, from our original heavenly origin. Further examples include wheel versus Wheel, trine versus Trine, tree versus Tree, nature versus Nature, and planets versus Planetary Governors. Numbers are capitalized when they refer to Kabbalistic Sephira and/or the numbers that qualify the titles of the cards, but not when used as date markers or simple counting tools. And special mention needs to be made for our unique spelling of the technical term "compliment," which refers to one of the Elemental Dignities. (See Appendix 4.)

To save the reader from becoming overwhelmed with oft-used words being capitalized everywhere, some terms are capitalized in their corporate manifestation (for example the Zodiac), but left uncapitalized in their fractions (in this case, the 12 zodiacal "signs" that collectively comprise the Zodiac). We have also left the broad-ranging term "gnostic" in the lower case unless we are using a qualifier to specify a particular strain of this belief (for example, the Valentinian Gnostics).

To demonstrate our illustrations and examples in context, I often refer the reader to view the reproductions in *The Hermetic Museum: Alchemy & Mysticism* by Alexander Roob, published by Taschen. This represents a stunning, and stunningly inexpensive, in-depth, full-color collection of esoteric art spanning a wide range of sources and periods. This visual feast is astutely balanced by an excellent running commentary crafted by Roob. In addition, many if not most of the important art of the alchemists is generously shared online and can be downloaded without violating copyright protections. Scholar Adam McLean curates an amazing collection of alchemical resources online. This can be found at the venerable site www.alchemywebsite.com/adam.html.

Acknowledgements

Inspiration for this project has been derived from the ideas, insights, encouragement, and scholarly labors of Julius Evola, Wouter Hanegraaff, Joscelyn Godwyn, Arthur Versluis, Nicolas Goodrick-Clarke, Peter Foreshaw, and Christopher Lehrich. Without the particular contributions of these visionary thinkers and consummate researchers, I would still harbor my convictions, but they would be much harder to express and defend.

Artworks and graphs have been created by Michael Dowers, Roger Walco, Barbara Glisan, and myself. Eternal gratitude goes across the centuries to the alchemical engravers whose fertile imaginations have provided the symbolism for *Tarot of the Holy Light*.

In particular I want to highlight the input of those who have dedicated thousands of hours to this project for nothing more than the chance to study these things with me. Thank you from the bottom of my heart Angel Lozada, Corina Bardasuk, and Jessica Schiek. I can say with unqualified certainty that this book and its companion volume would lack polish and be much more confusing for the early Tarot student without their generous and loving attention.

A book of this complexity is never the work of one person. I have been graced with generous support, kind encouragement, stunning syncronicities, and a steady trickle of dedicated friends, students, and fans who have carried this project and me along through its many developmental stages. After all this amazing assistance, if there are still mistakes and blind spots remaining in these pages, the fault is mine alone.

Christine Payne-Towler
Cathlamet, Washington
April 2015

Chapter 1
Introduction to
The Minor Arcana

The Minor Arcana

In my companion volume, *Foundations of the Esoteric Tradition,* I detail the history of the multilayered esoteric assemblage that was present at the times of Tarot's creation. For this volume we will take a different tack. What follows is a recitation of Tarot's intrinsic knowledge categories analyzed for the edification of those who already have a traditional 78-card deck in their hands. The cards in hand can be *Tarot of the Holy Light*, any Marseille styled pack, any of the Etteilla packs containing 78 cards, any of the Egyptian-styled series from the 1800s, or any modern Continental pack. This book supports any and all Tarots that reflect the inherent magical correspondences embedded in the Tarot structure as it existed before the "innovations" of the 20th century.

Historically, the suited cards of the Tarot pack have been relatively neglected in favor of the Trumps. This is because the numbers on the Trump cards make a very clean and unambiguous correlation with the Hebrew alphabet, a 22-unit collection of graphic elements that already possessed a coherent body of correspondences through its ancient origins. The magical alphabet enjoyed such a central position in European esotericism that essays organized around its relationship to the Trumps were among the first formal writings on the subject of Tarot to appear in European literature.

In contrast, the four-suited pack is much more ambiguous and complex in its implications, as readers will see in this chapter. The esoteric references made by the numbers One through Ten are repeated in four Elements, which are then further personified in four suited Royals. The result is a giant chessboard of gradient values that fluctuate through the esoteric arts like recombinant DNA. It is entirely correct to say that the Trumps represent the realm of the archetypes, which shine forth clear and bright in their idealized pure energies; whereas the suited cards represent the mixed and muddied influences that filter down through those archetypes into our manifested world.

This preparatory chapter will present the layers of esotericism that are inherently embedded in the Minor Arcana's structural complexities. The considerations raised by Tarot's natural categories range from the simplest values of the individual numbers, through their connections to the Hermetic Tetractys and Kabbalah Tree, into their dispersal through the degrees of the Zodiac, finally reaching into ancient astro-Alchemy and the Shem angels. Of course, our exemplar pack for this exposition will be *Tarot of the Holy Light*.

However, these esoteric internal structures can be found in equal measure in all of the Continental packs of any provenance.

I can't stress enough that these various esotericisms are directly recruited for consideration with Tarot because of the fundamental and inherent outline of the card pack. The considerations under review in this chapter stand entirely behind the pictures on the cards' faces. In other words, these structural constants define the Tarot outline since the 16th century. My approach is to address the historical fundamentals first and foremost. Subsequent superficial "trimmings" will fall into place as a natural after effect.

Let it be stated, in no uncertain terms, that no users of Tarot (in any form) need to suffer and struggle if learning these different archeological layers becomes a burden to their Tarot practice. These efforts to unpack Tarot's implicates are undertaken because this is the meaning-mesh that has informed Tarot since it first took form as a 78-card pack with numbered Trumps and four Suits with fourteen cards per Suit. The magical consequences of these design characteristics continue to affect Tarot's public profile today. Presently, one can find modern astrological packs, modern alchemical packs, modern Kabbalistic packs, modern Hermetic packs, modern magical packs, modern mythological packs, and many more supercreative variations on the ancient theme. What is harder to find is a presentation that demonstrates all of these related arts and sciences compatibly interwoven into a seamless and multi-modal tool according to the teachings of the Renaissance Magus. This is the deficit I propose to remedy with the two volumes that support *Tarot of the Holy Light*, using this pack as a proxy for all the packs that are made according to this explicitly Continental pattern.

The footprint of Tarot has been extremely stable over the 600 years of its presence in Europe, and it is this internal consistency with European esotericism that I'm examining here. Those who are more interested in simply reading the cards, without requiring themselves to become esoteric masters along the lines of our Renaissance magi, can simply skip these technical explanations and enjoy the 78 card essays as a support for their readings and personal work with the cards. Only magical eggheads and operative occultists are passionately interested in these intimate details of Tarot's interior construction. Therefore, I suggest that the reader simply let all this theory wash over the mind and settle where it may, keeping open to deeper insight but not forcing oneself to intellectually grasp it all at once. Those who care about the machinations of magic will enjoy the chance to work all of these integrated disciplines together as a seamless Renaissance esoteric computer. Others can simply rest secure in the fact that their Tarot is purpose-built to reflect both the exterior and the interior heavens of human experience in a 78-card, one-panel icon (or cartoon) form.

The Original Pack of Playing Cards

Before we can attempt to inhabit the world of ideas that a Paracelsian alchemist with Boehmeian leanings would find in (or project onto) the Tarot, we have to remember that the suited pack was originally its own self-standing tool that was centuries old before it ever appeared on the shores of Italy and Spain. This is an Islamic gaming deck which in the West was called Mameluke, and it was constructed with four Suits possessing ten numbered cards, plus three male Royals in each Suit. The skeletal structure reflects Islamic Hermeticism, according to Ronald Decker's *The Esoteric Tarot*. His chapter on the Eastern cards, their interpretations and influences on Tarot, makes an excellent starting point for those who aren't familiar with this stage of Tarot's pre-history.

The choice of ten cards for the numbered Suits supplemented with three Royals per Suit provides the bedrock of the model of the modern playing-card deck. The original equation for the suited pack is therefore $(10x4) + (3x4) = 40 + 12$. The very simplest magical default of that equation reads "Tetractys (or Tree) multiplied by the four Elements (directions), plus the Zodiac wheel." This is the ancient model of the 12-tribe nation meeting around the compass wheel that marks the four corners of the world, occupied by the four ancient races of humanity. In view of the esoteric "war between the 10 and the 12," one could imagine that the suited pack serves as a bridge or reconciliation device that can merge and modulate the interface between the pagan universe (the 12, the ancient Zodiac) and the Judeo-Christian universe (the 10, the Latinized West). In the harmonizing of 12 and 40, the common denominator of both numbers is four.

Once the Queens were added, the Pages are pushed off the signs of the Zodiac, and a new value is needed to inform the Page category. The solution lies close at hand since the solstices and equinoxes that start up each season always commence with the Cardinal signs. For this reason, we have made the Pages of *Tarot of the Holy Light* into servants of the Cardinal Queens, which we symbolize by giving these two ranks of Royals their own wings. Thus the Queen and Page of each Suit have the power to initiate entirely new developmental stages, while the Kings stabilize and the Knights complete the sequence that the Queens inaugurate. (The four Cardinal Signs also occupy the Supernal Triangle of their own elemental Tree, which is another way of saying the same thing.)

Tarot and Occult Modeling: Tree or Tetractys?

Historians ponder the fact that all the characters in the suited pack are also chess pieces. But that's just the beginning of the web of inter-connections that unites the Western gaming models with divination and esoteric considerations. Not only the Tarot Suit cards, but also dice patterns, geomancy figures, Druidic runes, Lullian wheels, the *Paracelsian Oracle*, the game of Labyrinth, and the *Hieroglyphic Monad* are all linked to the same body of correspondences. Those correspondences are inevitably astrological, whether the link is made through the planets, the signs, the Elements, or all three. The stream of historical figures who have become figureheads for the transmission or this worldview has shown remarkable conservatism across the centuries. This can point to only one conclusion: There was a well-defined philosophical universe that inspired the polymath magi of the high Middle Ages and early Renaissance; and when the Mamluk pack first appeared in Europe, the structure of the deck fit perfectly Europe's pre-existing worldview and ethos.

Given the multivalent world of esotericism, I wavered a bit about whether to prioritize the Tetractys or the Tree on the numbered Pips for *Tarot of the Holy Light*. I only wavered because both approaches lead off into different but equally wonderful worlds of esoteric discovery. Following is the thinking I used to decide what to feature on the faces of the cards.

In the time of our Protestant Sophianics, a lot of attention was paid to the speculation that the Kabbalists were latter-day Pythagoreans. Modern researchers show that peak times of cross-pollination between the Hebrew and Greek philosophers came during the Alexandrian synthesis, and then again with the rise of the Moslem universities in Europe (especially in Spain). Perhaps it is not necessary to make a determination here because culturally speaking, both of these paradigms would be current in the post-Paracelsian, post-Agrippan synthesis that we are examining. However, it is still valuable to investigate the differences between these compatible models, so we can think about when these subtle differences might be applicable in practice.

The inherent relationship of the numbered Suits to the Tree, both in the Mamluk pack and the Tarot, activates a Western yoga and chakra meditation model that leads inward and backwards in time toward the realm of Semitic cultural origins. This is the diagram of a people who believe that humanity is "made in the Image of God." In fact, the Tree is the very map of the Edenic state, in the sense that its first elaboration represents Adam Kadmon, the Solar System Man whose androgynous body embraced the whole known circuit of planets and Lights. Even despite its later metamorphoses through all of its eventual forms, the Tree remains focused and centered on the human heart, embodying the sixth Sefirot, Tiferet. The Unfallen Tree model is reflected in the Trumps, which can be directly analogized to Adam Kadmon and the pre-Fall natural order (as found in the Short Form Sefer Yetzirah). The Fallen Tree model is reflected in the suited cards, which represent our current condition as split creatures who have fallen into a divided state. The ambitious soul faces heroic challenges to regain the capacities humanity was originally created to embody. This is the question faced by every shuffler of a 78-card deck: Can I live up to my Divine inheritance (Trumps), or am I going to prove to be a creature of the Fall?

Working within the Tetractys, on the other hand, opens out into the Pythagorean Lamdoma, which leads to the whole manifestational grid of frequencies, colors, and harmonics continuously expanding towards the realm of outcomes in Time and Space. This is a much more scientific model in the sense that it represents the orderly process of materialization itself, from the One, through the Two, to the Three, to the Ten-thousand Things (as the Daoists like to say). The geometry of the Tetractys is centered on the fifth station, which sits at the exact center of the Triangle of ten units and represents the principle of Sovereign Will. Meditating with the Tetractys conferred a philosophical advantage upon the Pythagoreans, the very same insight that Einstein had when he said "God geometrizes."

Care and sensitivity are required to deploy these ideas. Sometimes one needs to ponder the inner lines of a psychological or spiritual experience, in which case a Kabbalist orientation is more natural. Other times one needs to engrave one's personal vision on the time-stream as it flows into the future, which can be encouraged by meditating on the Tetractys. But always one has to deal with the actual planets and the fixed nature of one's own birth chart with its innate temperament. The magical model that defines the Tarot is infinitely convertible between planets, signs, Elements, numbers, letters, colors, geometric forms, and ratios. Working with this conglomeration of subtle and literal energies trains the practitioner, very slowly but inexorably, to think like Nature and work within her already-established currents.

An individual who is working the full system will find it worth the trouble to become fluent in as many of the intertwined esoteric modalities as she or he can master. Fluency allows a reader to feature those concepts which best embody the client's unique goals and visions. Alternately, familiarity with a range of approaches helps the user to submit more gracefully to destiny: periods of life when one's road is especially intense. Sometimes there is no further chance to redirect the flow, but contemplating "what is" can still bring us comfort and a measure of understanding by helping us to unravel the symbolism of events and tie the energies back to the ancient archetypes. Also, once one fully understands the implications inherent in the attributes that define the progressive Suit cards, it becomes infinitely easier to understand why a given card has come to mean what it does. As each number represents a unique divisor of the One Thing and each Suit represents a different frequency-spectrum from highest (Light) to lowest (matter), the numbered Suit cards immediately reveal themselves to be stand-ins for the gradations of natural law.

Contemplative Versus Pro-Active Tarot

There are different levels of intensity that readers can employ when using *Tarot of the Holy Light* in private or public practice. The first level is that of neutral observer of the overall system. By this I mean the reader will employ the simplest level of surface correspondences for help with translating current circumstances. This is the best method for intuitives and psychics who do their readings from the "feel of things" as the cards take their places. No knowledge of the technicalities of the esoteric paradigm is required; the pamphlet that accompanies our deck will provide a fine jumpng-off point for interpretation, and the simplified Astrology on the faces of the cards can be used in the spirit of the Sun-sign Astrology we find in the newspaper. Those who are more interested in Astrology, to the extent of carrying an astrological daybook, for example, might take the time to look up the planets' positions in the ephemeris at the time of the reading to see how often the cards in the spread are actually quoting the current transits. Overall, the goal for this style of use would be to access a philosophical understanding leading to acceptance and grace in challenging or confusing times. For such people, studying "what is" will be their aim in order to become more in harmony with present developments.

Others will naturally be more active in their handling of their cards and the suggestions they find there. Even if they never venture beyond the words printed on the faces of the cards, there is plenty there to work with. According to the theology of arithmetic, each number is a universe with its own geometry, its own personality, and innate references it makes to unique qualities of experience and expression. Even without delving into the astrological nuances, each number has a variety of different attributes (such as even/oddness, prime status, or the range of smaller numbers contained within it), which adds nuance to the card's stated meaning and suggests strategies for creative responses. The imagery on the cards was designed to be emotionally and psychically evocative, which will bring up another spectrum of associations that a skilled reader can work with.

For more pro-active users the larger body of correspondences that stand behind the divinatory meanings have incredible power to liberate the magical imagination, whether for oneself or for another. There is a certain pleasure to be found in operating the integrated system in its full mathematical beauty and inspirational power. An entire self-cultivation modality is built into this larger meaning mesh, which *Tarot of the Holy Light* embodies and makes accessible to modern practitioners. The companion volume to this one, *Foundations of the Esoteric Tradition*, exposes this expanded body of correspondences in greatest detail, revealing the historical precedents that inform their use. Comprehension of the over-arching system supports the higher art of psychological and ethical regeneration, which I call Boehme's Yoga of the Restitution. Facility with this deeper level of self-cultivation offers the hope of directly affecting one's inner and outer evolution for the better through harnessing the alchemical remedies made available during the unfolding cycles of the planets in transit. For such individuals, those who crave tools for direct action rather than seeking reconciliation with life as it unfolds, the combination of *Tarot of the Holy Light* with *Foundations of the Esoteric Tradition* offers a comprehensive key to the complete astro-alchemical operating system as it was employed by our Renaissance, Reformation, and Enlightenment-era esoteric masters.

Number Theology in the Pips

According to ancient arithmetical philosophy, each number is its own universe. When one divides a 360° wheel by four, the result will define a different universe from the same wheel divided by seven. So every time you move to a new number, you divide the same Monad into a different number of fractions, producing a different geometrical figure. This is how number theory provides an aid to deriving increased meaning from the numbers in our Tarots. In the Tarot Pips pack, each number is represented four times to indicate the different interpenetrating realms of the Elements. These Elements are sometimes thought of as compass directions, root races, or seasons. Here are some ideas to bring depth to the Pips card interpretations.

One: The All

The concept of One is given the meaning of Monad, conceived as the all-inclusive primordial Unity that exists alone, even before Wisdom (Logos or Sophia) was identified within the Divine Mind. In this state everything (or the potential for everything) resides within the formless, shapeless, quality-less singleton. Kabbalah teaches it as Keter, which is backed up by the triple-veiled mystery that is eternally closed to creatures of Time/Space (the Ain Sof Ur). Other names for this would be the Pleroma, the All-One, or the "macro set" of the physicists. Naturally, One is the number of God, Source and Center. In Astrology, the Sun is the symbol of this all-inclusive primal power, which emanates infinite Light and spiritual warmth to vitalize the world of manifestation. Should all else fail, Creation defaults back to the One, the origin and outcome of every process.

Two: Passing Through the Binary

In order for our Time/Space world to appear, the Pleroma or Monad has to open or split, giving forth from its eternally pregnant but sealed state. This must be done in order to pour out all the potentials of the infinite Creation for actualization. Something had to happen for the One to differentiate into the many different "things" and lives that now predominate in Time/Space.

Among the ancient Greeks this necessary change of state came to be attributed to the action of two governing principles that between them rule the world, which were termed Love and Strife. One early philosopher who articulated this doctrine was Empedocles, who lived half a millennium before the Christian era. This juxtaposition is one of many ways to say that in this world there appears to be both a force for health and a force for disease; a force for evolution and a force for devolution; a force for unification and a force for diversification; ultimately a force for life and a force for death. From here humanity gets its basic understanding of good and evil, at least in relation to ourselves.

From this initial division in the Monad, this fateful split of the atom (atman, Adam), are born all of the numbers in their turn. Ultimately the binary split sets the stage for every expanded dimension, every geometrical and mathematical principle upon which the full and final manifestation is hung. For this reason Pythagoras determined that whereas One means fullness and wholeness (and therefore is not a number, since the Monad transcends any division), the number Two expresses the process of breakdown out of that fullness (and reciprocally its reunification back into the Monad again). Thus it was taught that Two could not be considered a true number either, since it is always in the midst of a changeover between the All and some fractionated state, acting much more like a verb than a noun. By necessity, then, Three becomes the first "real" number, representing an actual amount, indicating a unique variety or multiplicity of items. When one investigates how many religions manifest in trinitarian form, it seems that this conclusion is somehow built into the way humans view the fundamental dimensions of being.

Let's remember at this juncture: In the ancient view of things, the sequence of numbers starting with One and developing through the subsequent numbers is not an additive phenomenon. Moderns tend to think that 275 is "less than" 509, as if these numbers were to be used in counting grains of sand or beans in a bushel. But in number theology, One signifies the Whole, while Two immediately brings up the idea of "half." Four inclines the mind towards "quarters," and every larger number therefore leads to a smaller fraction of the Whole. No increase is happening no matter how large the possible numbers can grow because what we are doing is cutting the Singleton into tinier and tinier pieces. This can be a difficult concept to envision at first, trained as we are to think of numbers as ceaselessly increasing rather than being differently-proportioned fractal divisions of an unchanging whole.

Three: The Sacred Trinity

Now that we understand the Monad better, we can more easily grasp why at first the Greek philosophers limited their idea of the authentic Elements to three (Fire, Water, Air). I use the word authentic in the sense of being unmixed with matter, existing even before material expression, hence archetypal, virtual, or ideal. Astrology depends upon Three as well to describe the elemental modes Cardinal (creating), Fixed (holding), and Mutable (transforming) that modulate the Elements around the Zodiac. The Hebrew Kabbalah uses the Three to complete the Supernal Triangle and also to indicate the class of Mother Letters, which also point to these same astral precursors of Air, Fire, and Water. These Mother Letters form the three horizontal bars marking the planes or "worlds" in the Kabbalistic Tree. Alchemy uses the concept Three to express its three principal qualities of existence, which are termed Mercury (fluidity of motion), Sulphur (Fire of life), and Salt (crystallization). Sacred Geometry enshrines Three in the form of the triangle, in particular the 3/4/5 figure (comprising a square 90°, a Trine 120°, and an inconjunct 150°), which we currently call "Pythagorean." Clearly the tendency to see a one-in-three mystery wherever we look has a deep hold on the human psyche. One would be tempted to think that there's an aspect of the human bio-psychic anatomy that is in intimate accord with this archetypal theme.

Four: The Foundation

The mixed Element Earth is attributed to an amalgam that results from the densification of the original Three by admixture with each other. This gives four (manifested, tangible) Elements, all nested into each other in an infinite array of variations. Four is the stage of the square, material and solid, the most stable and unmoving geometric structure of them all. It is easy to see the principle of Four manifested everywhere in esotericism, most notably the Elements of Astrology and the four successively denser worlds of the Kabbalah Tree. Four metes out the directions, the natural unfoldment of the seasons, and the four quarters of the day. Four is the base of the Pythagorean Tetractys, an extremely recondite and cunning symbol of complexity built from simplicity. The Emperor, Trump Four, is sometimes shown sitting on the cube as he presides over his realm as figurehead and administrator. Simultaneously the four Suits of Tarot populate and illuminate the imaginal world of the psyche, embodying all of its astral traffic. The common denominator of all these ideas is that Four is the point where an influence or tendency becomes an actual "thing" with a discreet shape and substantial dimensions that grant it a footprint in Time and Space.

Five: The Boundary Between Self and Other

Once the concept of an Etheric, akashic, or astral plane is defined, we find it being promoted to the status of a fifth, transcendental Element. The aforementioned "primordial" Elements are seen as inherent in the potential of Creation, therefore pre-material, with Earth resulting from their mutual interactions with each other. In contrast, the Element Five makes itself known as the invisible matrix within which the previous four numbers play out their exchanges. This next idea had to be added to the roster to signify all things heavenly or "celestial," demonstrating qualties that aren't bounded by the forms and actions of the sub-Lunar Elements. We would nowadays qualify this with the word astral, meaning "partaking in the substance of the stars." The astral body is the energy body which radiates out from the physical body and is in communication with the whole Creation.

Note how Five and its pentagram cunningly incorporate the idea of multiple interpenetrating planes or worlds. The two bottom points of the pentagram can be seen as penetrating into the underworld: the realm of the "inherent" qualities of the pre-manifestational world coming "up" into manifestation. The next higher points of the pentagram represent the manifested world, what we can see, touch, hear, smell, and taste. This leaves the crowning point, the singleton at the top, to penetrate into the transcendental realms where subtle, invisible forces come "down" from a higher level, reaching right through our material forms to contact our Etheric self, our body of Light.

The construct of a Five Element universe allows for the final "Suit" of the Tarot cards: the Trumps. It also suggests the presence of a special force or charisma that enlivens the terrestrial world with depth, psyche, or soul, in short, the invisible component of human consciousness. The theological explanation for this would be that because we are "made in God's image," we also then possess our own individual measure of transcendental purity and potency. Acknowledging the existence of ether also explains the invisible populations of angels and archangels, as well as the "shadow" beings that exist in the demonic realms.

Five has specific relevance to humanity's plight while living in the Time/Space world: the particularity of our five-ness as humans. We generally have four fingers plus a thumb per hand and foot, a sight-dominant nervous system that tracks four subsidiary senses (hearing, touch, taste, and smell), plus four limbs with a head that complete the body. Theologians have taken these signs to imply that we should understand ourselves to be "in the world (four, the square), but not of it (one, the point)." Additionally, entertaining a world of five Elements lines us up with Hindu and Chinese medicinal/elemental theory as well, opening up further worlds of correspondences for meditation.

Let it also be noted that division of the 360-degree circle by five and ten produces the angles of 72° and 36° respectively. Astrologically, these are the quintile and decile aspects, indicative of genius and inventiveness. These angles are also the key to producing the mathematically amazing, visually dazzling, celestially attuned mosaics of Islamic architecture. If we ever need a tangible reminder of the essence and energy of Five, the art of Islam can offers endless inspiration.

It is not a contradiction to say that the numbers Three, Four, and Five all comprise different stages of the Monad in expression, just the way water can express as ice, liquid, or steam. Harkening back to the oldest ideas about these things, we learn that the reference for the unmanifest Elements represented processes, modes of action, or styles of manifestation (espressing like verbs) instead of being material substances in the sense we now look for (like nouns). We will also learn that those processes appear first in the "pure" and unmixed state (Three, as in the Supernal Triangle) but have their physical manifestation in the mixed and blended world of differentiated substances (Four, as in the four directions or seasons). The cubic world of Four is, meanwhile, the horizontal reflection of the Supernal energies pouring down upon it from the celestial realm (Five). Suddenly the vertical axis intrudes upon the horizon, and the worldview of the astrologer, the mason, and the navigator come into focus for the first time.

We are still talking about permutations in the Monad as we think about these things, which means that every aspect of even the fivefold division would exist within the One. There is as yet still no "other" at the stage of the Five. When thinking internally this way, one can analogize each number as an expansion of consciousness compared to its predecessor. This helps us see why Five is often thought of as the number of individuation. The pentagram or star of five points traditionally references the astral or holographic substrate that projects forms into the materialized world. Hence Five references the awakened imagination, which is stimulative, creative, potentially full of life, and responsive to Divine Intent. We also find the number Five at the exact center of the Tetractys diagram, suggesting a connection with an individual's central motivation and will power.

Five also bridges between the elementals and the planets. Indeed, in the Vedic understanding of things, the five Elements are directly correlated with the planets (excluding Sun and Moon, which are classed together as the Lights):

Mars is Fire, Agni
Venus is Water, Jala
Jupiter is Akash, Aether
Mercury is Earth, Prithvi
Saturn is Air, Vayu.

A very fruitful study can be undertaken on the many subtle permutations of the five Elements/planets, which in Sanskrit are called Tattvahs. Vedic Astrology is rich with applications of five-Element theory. It might feel boggling to have both Elements and planets corresponding to the same number, but this is the type of situation that a student of the esoteric paradigm must get used to. Just like we see the Trumps having multiple meanings attached to the same figure (number, title, astrological correspondence, angel of planet or sign, allegorical or mythical story, location on the Kabbalah Tree, etc.), so also the numbers themselves have accumulated myriad associations through the centuries.

Another approach to the number Five recognizes that it symbolizes the ratio of three to two, illustrating a balanced irregularity of the type one finds as a design element in musical theory, architecture, and certain other of the architectonic disciplines. The larger a number gets, the more interior dynamics of this type it possesses. In his monumental work *The Tarot* Mouni Sadhu analyzed each Trump according to the range of internal equations that could be found within its number in the sequence. The Tetractys can be extended out to six levels, at which point there are 21 stations in the overall shape, which is also an eye-opener in the context of the Tarot Trumps. It is clear that the Trump sequence is cunningly constructed to hold all these multiple associations simultaneously. In esotericism nothing is ever simply what it looks like on the surface.

Summary: One Through Five

When approaching the numbers in the ancient way, it helps to cultivate the attitude of a worker in a science lab, adjusting the focus of her microscope in order to look at the same slide under different levels of magnification. The worker is not prey to the belief that the different views represent different "things" that must be kept separate. She has gotten used to the fact that there are whole worlds existing at each different level of focus, which all belong to the one thing under examination. This is the reality of every item we encounter in our world, whether it is materialized as a discernible, distinct object or whether it is a movement of consciousness at the fringes of perception. No single explanation by itself contains the whole truth; everything has to be evaluated in relation to the inherent faceting of its innate nature.

Six: The Heart and Harmonizer

A central aspect of Six is illustrated by the Star of David figure at the heart of the Hebrew Kabbalah Tree and its distribution of the planets and the Moon around the Sun. This is a model of three times two visualized as the mediated opposite (three) doubled upon itself to form a higher-order yin/yang (the Star of David). Whether one sees Six as three crossed pairs of opposing points or as two interlaced triangles, the number Six has long carried associations of musical and vibrational harmony, the union of opposites, the fertilization of yin by yang, and a conscious awareness of a whole that exceeds the sum of its parts. Five bears the stamp of one's internal, personal reality. The process of individuation unifies a loose and slippery assemblage into a unique being of its own. Meanwhile, the number Six extends into the concept of a group, a collectivity of sorts, whether comprising a couple, a team, a corporation, or several generations of a family. Five looks inward to the multi-dimentional psyche; Six looks outward into the multi-dimentional world.

From the point of view of processes, the essence of Five completes a circle, but Six adds the dimension of depth and pulsed repetition that defines a cycle, a repeating arc of unique manifestations harmonized to their shared center. In music this function is held by the root tone of the chord; in Masonry it would be the chosen ratio that governs the geometry of the whole temple; and in the alchemical Astrology of the Kabbalah, the interlaced Star of David is the essential design feature that locks the individual parts into a balanced and integrated whole.

One can also see this cusp between Five and Six as a tipping point of sorts in terms of psychological time, since all the cards from Ace to Five can be read as expressions of the "now" at various depths. Going forward, the numbers Six and above usually imply longer durations, developments that have crossed several stages in coming from the past and moving towards the future. Six has a discernible rhythm: three beats above, three beats below, like the lilt of a waltz.

The arithmetic of Astrology, one of the remarkable achievements of the Babylonian-Sumerian culture, is sexagesimal, meaning it is built upon the equation 6 x 10. Ernest G. McClain wrote a mind-expanding book on the arithmetic of the ancients called *The Myth of Invariance: The Origin of the Gods, Mathematics and Music from the Rg Veda to Plato.* I heartily recommend this to anybody ready to "step back and think like a cosmos." McClain calls the sexagesimal system "probably the most convenient language for acoustical arithmetic the world ever knew until ... late in the nineteenth century." This tells us that the reputation of Six regarding harmony, proportion, and balanced expression over time is not just a poetic trope, but a hard fact of Nature, anciently observed and still binding today.

Seven: The Planetary Governors

The number Seven has a veritable welter of correspondences, most often linked to the Seven Planetary Governors. Here's where we find the lists of planetary metals, animals, herbs, stones, and so on. This time the celestial list includes the Lights, and it forms the logic for naming the seven days of the week:

Monday = Moon day
Tuesday = Mars day
Wednesday = Mercury day
Thursday = Jupiter day
Friday = Venus day

Saturday = Saturn day
Sunday = Sun day.

One standard way of symbolizing Seven is to put a triangle atop a square, suggesting that Spirit (triangle) dominates and organizes matter (square). Of course, should this arrangement come up inverted, it could mean that matter is oppressing and inhibiting Spirit. Seven is also the ultimate number of directions present in the Kabbalistic Cube of Space. This is an interior structure of the Kabbalah Tree that derives from the planetary Star around the Solar Heart. The Cube has six faces: above, below, left, right, front, and back. All surround and enclose the seventh point at the exact mathematical and magnetic center (the Heart). The seventh point becomes the internal goal towards which the other six are striving. It is also relevant to note that Seven is a prime number with all the eccentricities and uniqueness that entails for the theology of arithmetic. Finally, Seven is the completion-number of the Great Hexegram in the sense that the dot in the center of the Star of David represents the Sun at the center of the Solar System, equating also to the Son (Christos) with Tiferet the Heart center on the Tree. The Kabbalists viewed this Heart Star as the Merkabah Chariot or astral body, which could carry the meditator in any direction through Time and Space, moved by wings of Spirit. All these different implications of Seven should help us understand why the Trumps are organized in three cycles of seven cards each (completed by the Fool).

Eight: The Compass and Wheel of Time

For the Eight, let me just take this quote from Agrippa starting with his very first words on the subject:

> The Pythagoreans call eight the number of justice, and fullness: first, because it is first of all divided into numbers equally even, viz. into four, and that division is by the same reason made into twice two, viz. by twice two twice; and by reason of this equality of division [2x4], it took to itself the name of Justice, but the other [2x2x2] received the name, viz. of Fullness, by reason of the contexture of the corporeal solidity, since the first makes a solid body (p. 281).

This refers, one assumes, to the eight angles or corners of the Cube of Space.

Overlooking the tangled language, the point is made that Eight has a solidity and dimensionality unmatched by any previous number. Illustrated as stacked squares, it suggests gravity and tensile strength. When illustrated as interlaced cubes, it is the wheel of Time moving through the quarters and cross-quarters of the year (applying the "test of Time," so to speak). Astronomically, the Eight also references the traditional Eighth Sphere of the fixed stars, which was visualized as if it were an esoteric atmosphere surrounding the Sun, Moon, and planets, populated at its fullest extension by all the constellations of the heavens. Eight is the compass that proliferates and distributes the elemental effects through the high and low points in the seasons, which have their domains in the Cardinal and Fixed signs. As I often say when I am reading cards, Eight is where the best-elaborated theory (Seven) meets the test of real-time performance in action. In simple terms, Eight is where the rubber meets the road. If one can't demonstrate the superiority of one's approach or creation at this stage, then the subsequent adventures with the Nine and Ten will be occupied with cleaning up the consequences of this failure.

Nine: The Perfect Number

The number Nine has been held up by many civilizations around the globe as the "perfect number." Nine is the last of the numeric sequence begun at the One or Ace because after this, the numbers start repeating with One at a higher level. (Zero is not a number, having no "amount"; Zero is a cipher, a void holding open an empty category in the decimal sequence.) The number Nine, being the multiple of 3 x 3, has a symmetry that's unbeatable; in the *Theology of Arithmetic*, it is said "...it alone of the numbers up to it has a triangular number as its square root" (Iamblichus, p. 106).

There are nine Muses according to the ancient Greeks. They are the daughters of Zeus and Mnemosyne (memory), guardians of all styles and categories of learning, who provide inspiration for all the arts of humanity. The Hebrew teachings work with a three-by-three grid called "the Kabbalah of Nine Chambers"; similarly, Taoism uses the cube of Nine as a visualization object for consciousness-cultivation. The same form can be used as a spread for Tarot divination by dealing the cards into a grid that is oriented horizontally as past, present, future, and vertically as subconscious, conscious, superconscious. According to the ancient distribution of the Element rulers through the decanates, or ten-degree segments of the Zodiac signs (as given by Agrippa p. 375-6 and employed in *Tarot of the Holy Light*), there are nine permutations of the three Element rulers per Suit. Last century the Fourth Way school of consciousness pioneered the Enneagram, a tool for understanding relations between nine different personality types, motivated by nine instinctual subtypes which we all possess within us to various degrees.

Ten: End and Beginning

The Ten has a huge amount of presence, as the Tree among the Kabbalists, the Tetractys among the Pythagoreans, and the decimal counting system that has organized Western minds for numeracy since deep antiquity. Without making too big a deal of this topic here, what we need to remember about Ten is that it completes and "seals" the circuit of Nine, lapping over to the One again at the next higher order of reality.

This is why I use the Tens for the elemental Grand Trines as a whole, whereas the previous nine cards in the elemental sequence represent individual stages along the way towards completion. The Ten recapitulates the potential held within the Ace, manifested at its fullest state of actualization in the material plane (in Malkhut).

For those who would like to follow up on this numerical line of thinking, I would recommend the book *The Theology of Arithmetic* translated by Robin Waterfield. This is a work attributed to Iamblichus (4th century AD), which has helped shape the thinking of mathematical philosophy right through the Renaissance and beyond. If one has a copy of either Agrippa's *Three Books of Occult Philosophy* or else the magical compendium *The Magus* by Frances Barrett (which was taken partially from Agrippa), then one can examine the tables Agrippa put together to explain all the correspondences of each number to the many layers and permutations of the world.

The Numbers Anchor the Meanings

Becoming comfortable with the unfolding number sequence helps the reader get a taste of the natural development moving through the cards of each Suit. By viewing the cards in their sequence as parts of an overall trajectory or process, one learns that no card is simply itself. In every case a card is always colored by its contact with the previous number of the sequence, just as the same card is always setting up the action for the next card in the sequence. The same way one views the planets in Astrology, cards in a spread are best viewed as moving objects streaking through the sky undergoing changes as they fly. In general they are stations in the sequence of natural laws, expressing slightly differently through each Element. This is an excellent way to learn, because if you should ever find yourself reading with a strange pack of cards that looks entirely different from your favorites, you will always have a foundation from which to derive solid interpretations.

For centuries there were no training manuals or even theoretical books about the Tarot. One used the cues on the faces of the cards: the Suit, the number, the arrangement of the Pips or Suit-symbols, and any little hints that might emerge from the subtle background details (like the variously-growing vines of the Marseille pack). Users were required to form their own basis for assigning meanings and making interpretations from these scarce but sufficient clues.

Looking at the Pips through their numbers grants us a dynamic way to analyze people's situations, making it easier to demonstrate the trend of events without activating people's guilt, shame, blame, or apologetics. Numbers are impersonal and nonjudgmental: They individually express their unique natures very clearly, and it doesn't require a lot of psychological or emotional rationalization to understand what they are saying. Seeing the numbers as stages of a larger movement encourages process-oriented thinking; the Suit provides the elemental principle and overall intent, and the number shows where the action stands on a scale of one to ten. This helps the imagination view the Suits as constantly moving along a natural progression, coming from one state and passing through others before finally arriving at their characteristic completion. Each number highlights the kind of considerations that come up at its own point in the process without necessarily disenfranchising other stages along the sequence. Numbers can also be added and subtracted, multiplied and divided, even formed into fractions or ratios at need. Plato is credited with the remark "God geometrizes continually." My recommendation to Tarot readers is to study the truth behind this insight and apply the lessons from this study to their cards.

Long ago I decided, alongside the Continental master Papus, that a card's number is the source of its primary meaning, and all other considerations (Suit, picture, key word, Zodiac degrees, the author's personal preferences, and any other details peculiar to that card) take a back seat to the number and stage the card occupies in sequence. By learning the geometry, psychology, and natural tendencies of the number-principles, we can more easily see that the traditional meanings that have grown up around the cards are by no means arbitrary. Each Pip card is part of a whole mosaic, and each card takes its sense from its placement in the larger context. Nothing is isolated or separate; it's all moving and communicating like the strands of a brain, and it takes every card in the Suit to express the full potential inherent in its Element.

In the Creation myth of the Sefir Yetzirah, which recites the very first Divine Act of Creation, the first ten "paths," are actually the numbers One to Ten ranged top to bottom as an overflowing emanation of Sephirot ("Spheres") corresponding to the visible planets of the Solar System. At the Creation the numbers come first before anything else can appear. Without the Principles of Number being emanated, there would be nothing to hang the Creation onto, nothing to shape into a Zodiac, Tree, Tetractys, wheel, or any other form.

The Fallen Tree Is Specific to the Pips

In the numbered cards of each Suit, we are dealing with the Fallen Tree in its early form before the hidden Sephira Daat was fully rationalized and incorporated. The overview to this approach is taken from the teaching we find about Daat in Feldman's *Qabalah: The Mystical Heritage of the Children of Israel.* I like Feldman's attitude because he takes an essentially shamanic approach towards all of the possible ways of moving on the Tree. After investigating the range of approaches, Feldman gives a neutral report about the usefulness of each option.

One immediately experiences a paradox when trying to express ineffable activities within the Godhead in material terms. When visualizing the Creation according to the Kabbalists, we have to remember that the Creation was originally extruded in the form of the Unfallen Tree (with only ten Sephirot). Once that format was expressed, God was said to have retreated back into the pre-Creation state, hidden away from Time/Space and matter. This is the manner in which both Kabbalists and Christians understood the mechanism by which free will is extended to created creatures. Only when God retreats from the scene can individuals follow their own leadership and develop their personal character. Once Adam Kadmon was broken up into a million Adams and Eves here in the sub-Lunar realm, Creation was left on its own recognizance for the sake of encouraging humanity to grow up and become self-governing. This left the door open for the so-called "war in Heaven," a necessary development that emerges when some aspect of the Creation decides to challenge the Creator for primacy. The natural and inevitable reaction from Jehova/Keter is the lightning bolt of correction and awakening, which comes boiling out of the Supernal Triangle, ripping the veil between Eternity and Time-Space and casting all the Sephirot below Binah into inversion. This is how the Paradise or Unfallen Tree is ruptured, breaking open at the throat center Daat, causing the Heart and Pelvic Triangles to pivot downwards, and forcing Malkuth to descend fully into the material plane.

The ultimate goal of the mystic is to ascend the Tree and heal the rupture at Daat so we have the option to leave the wheel of Time (wrapped around the Sun in the Fallen Tree) and enter our eternal home (the Supernal Triangle) once more. The solution is pictured on the Ten of Coins. To do this, one would follow the lightning bolt path up to and into the Heart (Tifaret). From there one would strive to cultivate all possible upward directions, making sure those paths were individually developed and reliable. At the proper moment the soul would release a flood of mystical desire reaching right up through and around Daat into the Supernal Triangle. Upper and lower Sephira would then pull and tug and reel each other in, hoping to mend and heal and regenerate the Tree with the new attribute of Daat in balance and harmony with the others. At that point humanity has "graduated," having entered into the "new Heaven and new Earth," theologically speaking.

One Falls in Order to Climb

For those who aren't Sophianic mystics expecting to attain enlightenment in this lifetime, there are two things to understand about the sequence played out upon the numbered Pips cards. For one thing, the numbers unfold top-down in the order of Creation, from the singleton Monad in Keter down to the state of greatest complexity at Malkuth. Most people who have encountered the Tree have no problem envisioning this progression since they have seen it repeatedly throughout their Tarot texts. However, very little thought is ever given to what happens to the dynamics of the Three Pillars once the seal at Daat is broken and the two lower Triangles flip from point-up to point-down. The original integrity of the Tree, with all of its Sephirot tied tightly together in two interlaced Star of David formations (see Upper and Lower Countenance), has been exploded by the lightning bolt ripping from top to bottom. After this point the two lower Triangles can no longer be entered "from above" because their peaks are now troughs hanging down below their bases along the Middle Pillar. Therefore, the only method of approach for these two Triangles is "from below" by using the base at Malkhut as our backstop and heelstone.

This does not mean we have to specifically reject or deny the reality of matter by any means. What is necessary, however, is to temporarily separate one's immortal being (one's point-of-Light) from dependence on the body (Malkhut, the material plane) so that the soul can use Malkhut as a stepping-off point from which to "travel up the planes" and discover one's essential nature outside of the contingencies of Time and Space.

A second consideration is that as one traverses the return journey from Malkhut to Keter on the Tree, one is reversing the complexity of the numbers in the process. Things that had become differentiated into a broad spectrum of manifestation in the Ten are challenged to re-unify into a whole again by the time the Ace is regained. Such a thing can only be accomplished if one can de-complexify one's psyche and spiritual life as well. This is tantamount to going backwards in time, reversing the Fall, and returning to Paradise. Here we have the great alchemical insight: that the alchemist has to personally undergo every step that the raw materials go through in the alchemical vessel. The laws of the material world and consecutive unfoldment make it easy to see ourselves at the foot of the Tree, caught up in every kind of complexity. Yet the spiritual quest is about accepting the Fall and our part within it so that we can do the evolutionary work to rise again, heal the Tree, and develop the Divine within ourselves. The Protestant Sophianics felt that the world experiences suffering because the Holy Spirit has as yet still incompletely saturated the manifested world. Therefore the mystics following Boehme sought reconciliation with and for every spark of Light climbing back up out of the primordial ooze, individually and collectively.

The Tree is ecological, offering a sequence of stages that moves both ways across the spectrum of manifestation. The descending motion of the lightning bolt (as well as the Mother Pillar's earthward momentum) are driven by the ineffable crown of Keter pouring through the Supernal crossbar, which corresponds to the fiery and judgmental Mother Letter Shin. This has a direct and intimate identification with the force that Boehme calls Wrath, imparted by the outpouring Jehovah principle which stirs and stresses the Creation. By contrast all ascending forces are motivated by Yesod combined with the gentle and nurturing pulse of the pelvic crossbar Mem. This crossbar arches between Mercury and Venus marking the Triangle where the alchemical remedies are derived. These three functions share the alchemical significance of Water, the Moist Light, qualifying the Boehmian values of compassion, Love, and healing. Venus shines the Light of Nature, Mercury represents the quicksilver intelligence, and the Moon precipitates the celestial dew and the oceanic waters of earthly Nature. All of these qualities and functions correspond directly with the Protestant Theosophers' understanding of Sophia, the Divine Feminine energy that is realized and consummated in the psychic life of the mystic.

In between the disturbing Wrath and the salvific Love hangs the physical Sun and the theological Son/Christ Spirit, which in the human body is Tiferet, the Heart. This is the spot where the Father and Mother forces come together in the human incarnation, creating the synthesis that our Christian

Gnostic Sophianic mystics were striving for. If one handles the complete descent from One to Ten correctly, one is fully divested of personal ego, having dissolved entirely into the Divine Feminine energies that are immanent in this Creation. Only then does one attempt to rise again to seek the next life, a life that is no longer limited to the wheel of incarnation (meaning, the planetary wheel around the Sun in the Fallen Tree). Some traditions teach that such an advancement can only be gained through dying and being reincarnated, but our European magi sincerely hoped to use alchemical principles to speed up time and accomplish these changes while still embedded in their current incarnation.

Brought down into human terms, we can see that the Supernal Triangle (the individual mind) is constantly judging the personal heart, will, and body from a position of superiority (Shin-driven descent on the Mother Pillar). This implies that the act of thinking, evaluating, weighing and measuring, forming opinions, and having reactions, in short the entire human mechanism of consciousness, is biased to enhance awareness of contrast and distinction rather than unity and communion. As our mental projections rain down upon the world of matter (moving down the Tree), our judgmental tendencies and critical attitudes impact this world like a punishment couched in pessimism.

This is the reason why the Protestant Sophianics want us to listen for the still small voice of the dove, the Comforter, and Holy Spirit, which responds from our intuition with compassion and empathy, understanding, and forbearance. It is Spirit that allows us to forgive this reality for being imperfect and unfinished, that helps us see the value and healing potential in the circumstances we previously judged and condemned. This outflowing of loving kindness causes us to regain our optimism despite our challenged circumstances. As we gain the courage to rise again on the Father Pillar, we can consult Chakhmah (our own "left eye of impartial witness") to re-envision a relationship with matter that can actually be healing and evolutionary rather than troubled and unsatisfying. A few years or decades of rising and falling around the Heart will tend to educate the mind to look past its own projections and actually engage with the consciousness of Creation, actively feeling and resonating with all the potential that occupies every molecule of this manifested world.

Everything described here takes place as we move around the Numbers/Sephirot, either towards greater simplicity or towards greater sophistication. The Ten contains the decave, the Tetractys, and the set of ten Sephiot or luminous points that inform the stages of the Pips pack. Every time we shuffle and throw out our cards, we are asking the oracle to point to us the paths and channels (astrological, Kabbalistic, and numeric) that will lead us back to the

Restitution and Regeneration, the blessed reunion of Heaven and Earth. The more sensitive we become to the circular dynamics of the esoteric paradigm, the more we can "find ourselves" in the map of Tarot and benefit from the suggestions we receive from the cards.

Regarding the Icon for *Tarot of the Holy Light*

It was Raymond Lully who first pictured the Zodiac as a wheel of four triangles, one for each Element. This conceptualization has proved irresistible to generations of occultists who have happily seized on his insight for their own purposes. Later Agrippa teaches both the Hindu and the Chaldean group of decanate rulers, so we know that our early Renaissance magi were well aware of this method of dividing the signs of the Zodiac into ten-degree segments. These two titans of the inherited tradition stabilized a natural way to distribute the Essential Dignities around the numbered Pip cards.

This doesn't mean one should change or eliminate any meanings that are associated with an individual card due to its number, Element, shape, title, or any other detail found in a traditional Marseille style pack. We are simply enhancing a body of correspondences that would occur naturally to a person who had access to common esoteric resources in the era of Boehme's formation. These ideas can be profitably added to any normally-structured Pips pack to turn it into a Paracelsian astro-Alchemy computer suitable for a Magus-healer of the mid-1500s.

The Decanates and Their Rulers

Not only does each Suit circle the Grand Trine of its Element, but the three cards representing each sign occupy the triangular centers of the Tree in a very deliberate manner. Each center (Head, Heart, and Pelvis) carries the Cardinal, Fixed, and Mutable sign of the Element in descending order. Meanwhile, the three points of each Triangle, (spread across the Middle, Father, and Mother Pillars) restate in microcosm the primal triad that internally organizes the Trumps: thesis, antithesis, and synthesis. A full graph of all these considerations can be found in the Appendix.

The Aces, Sixes, and Nines represent pure initiating principles, the unconditioned thesis phase of each sign, keyed to the Middle Pillar of the Tree. These numbers resonate purely with their ruling planet's natural habitats, namely the first ten degrees (out of thirty). These energies are neither masculine nor feminine, but instead rest in a balanced state that organizes circumstances according to the higher good of all. These numbers neither descend or ascend, but simply stand in their own completeness.

The Deuces, Fours, and Sevens, meanwhile, represent the second decanate of each sign, the antithesis phase of questioning the givens (degrees 11-20, occupying the Father Pillar), where the compassionate ministry of Mem (the pelvic crossbar) reveals a higher vista by pumping astral Water up the Father Pillar. This decanate will be ruled by the planet of the following sign of its Element, moving sunwise (forward) around the Zodiac.

The Threes, Fives, and Eights hold the third decanate of each sign, representing the experiential learning or synthesis phase of the sign (degrees 21-30). In these numbers, the blended results of the previous two trends enter into the material plane by descending along the Mother Pillar. The planet of the final sign of the elemental Trine (still moving sunwise) will rule this decanate.

Just what do I mean by saying "the planets rule" in the context of these decanate assignments? These co-rulers serve as midwives for your insights and breakthroughs. They can guide your thoughts and suggest methods for handling current circumstances, maximizing the best practices of the shared elemental Trine. Let me pluck an example from my own chart. Because my birth Sun occupies the 12th degree of Libra, it falls into the "antithesis" section of the sign, which grants it the support of Saturn. This also means that my Sun is inherently affiliated with the middle degrees of the other two Air signs as well through a triangle that has its remaining points in the middle degrees of Aquarius (ruled by Mercury) and the middle degrees of Gemini (ruled by Venus). Therefore, when I see the Two of Swords card come up in a spread aimed at my current issues, I am being advised to mentally construct and then "listen in on" the conversation that naturally arises between Saturn in Libra, Mercury in Aquarius, and Venus in Gemini. Every sign has three such triangles within it, offering three different variations on the shared elemental theme according to the different signs being stimulated and the varying stages of the "thesis, atithesis, synthesis" model being emphasized.

Decans (Decanates) Versus Face Rulers

For each 30-degree sign there will be three cards and three rulers representing the sign's three stages. The primary decanate resides on the Middle Pillar as the activator, holding space open for the ruling planet to metabolize naturally. The Father Pillar presses towards communion with a Higher Power in the second decanate of the sign, following this Pillar's natural ascending motion (informed by Yesod and animated by the compassionate letter Mem). Finally, the Mother Pillar rains resultant energy into the world of manifestation with the synthesizing final decanate of the sign (informed by Daat and animated by the judgmental letter Shin). These are the correspondences we have printed on the cards: They follow the natural Zodiac around the wheel of the year in ten-degree increments, and they also step up or down the elemental Tree in the same increments. These correspondences register the natural progression of the signs in their developments around the four great Triangles of the Elements.

Historically one can find situations where the decanates were assigned different orders of rulers depending upon the need of the practitioner in the given situation. The rulers being assigned were always taken from the Seven Planetary Governors, but they would be doled out into different patterns for different magical uses. You can see the two primary ways these things were apportioned in Agrippa's *Three Books on Occult Philosophy* (p. 371-2 and 375-6) under the names of the Decans and the Face Rulers.

In my own Tarot experience I prefer and personally use the application that is commonly called the Hindu Decans. (Legitimate debate exists whether these are Eastern or Western because their time of origin is so old.) In Agrippa the Decans are listed by sign, as in "the first decanate of Aries is ruled by Aries, the second by Leo, and the third by Sagittarius." However, in other texts one can find this same chart made up in planets, literally saying "the first decanate of Aries is ruled by Mars, the second by the Sun, and the third by Jupiter."

Do not be confused. The practice of mentioning planets and implying signs is a regular occurrence in magical literature. Mars is not just the planet; it's also the step in the Ladder of Lights that stretches between Aries and Scorpio. When one is referencing "Jupiter," the word also lights up both Sagittarius and Pisces in the hearer's mind. This is the core assumption of the Doctrine of Correspondences: All things are interconnected; you cannot ever pluck just one string.

Tarot Theology

Due to the trauma and subsequent Fall that theology sees happening within the Tree, the Sephirot below Daath, though numbered in lightning-bolt order, experience a distortion due to the inverting of the lower two triangles. The cards are counted out in descending order (Ace at the beginning, Ten at the end) on the faces of the cards because most of us find ourselves in "descended" condition at this point in our development. To create change in one's karma, one must climb the Tree of each Element, from Malkuth (Ten) upward along the lightning-bolt path until one reaches the Tiferet (that's the fifth station when climbing the Tree). From there some traditions suggest to enter Daat and continue the zigzag climbing pattern. Alternately, one can try the approach illustrated on the Ten of Discs, namely reaching out from the Tiferet to the whole upper half of the Tree, fusing the final arrangement into a permanent wheel around the Heart. This would be similar to the outcome that Boehme and his fellows envisioned.

Let us also be clear about the personal consequences of this theological and spiritual Fall. Looked at from the point of view of Keter, only the Supernal Triangle is functioning normally. Down in the chest, the two arms and hands are triggered into activity before they are even connected to the heart. The legs and feet run us around compulsively, while the Lunar center is ungrounded and misunderstood because it has been falsely dropped into the sexual spot of the body. Ultimately, Malkuth trails off the bottom of the Tree like a tail we forget that we have.

Both of the lower triangles, the Heart Trine and the Pelvic Trine, have the cart-before-horse problem. This is the very condition that Boehme and his followers were trying to heal in themselves, which they then hoped to role-model for the world, eventually sparking an evolutionary episode for humanity as a whole. The spiritual challenge of accomplishing this healing involves humbly descending in the Tree to the very lowest level immediately, so that one can build up that fallen Middle Pillar from below. Due to the distortion of the Fall, there is no access to the two lower triangles from above. It is only through achieving solidarity with the lowest and most primitive aspects of Creation that we can then penetrate all of matter with Sophianic Light to accomplish the Restitution for all of Creation. In other words, one must recognize the existing reality of the Fall from grace before one is able to stage a turn-around profound enough to power a reversal, where one can rise again and reintegrate towards the Restitution.

Essential Dignities Are Alchemical Catalysts

The Doctrine of Essential Dignities, discussed at length in the companion volume *Foundations of the Esoteric Tradition*, is part of the oldest bedrock of astrological tradition, easily as old as the teachings we find in the Sefer Yetzirah. Moving beyond the simple doctrines of rulership, this extended body of correspondences represents the various relationships and treaties each planet has available to it in different realms of the Zodiac.

We have not printed the Essential Dignities on the faces of the cards because they require more sophistication to understand and use. One might think of the Essential Dignities as the recipes whereby the remedies for the conditions portrayed on the card might be found. They are the means by which one's situation can be changed or moved along to the next state of evolution. These ideas take us into a more pro-active relationship with the cosmos, a more magical stance and approach.

The decanates and their planetary rulers as printed on the cards show the natural laws at work, the simple wheel of Time ticking around the cycle. These are the "givens" of current events and circumstances. Contrastingly, the Essential Dignities show us how the person in the situation can actually transform events by tapping into these affinity patterns for sources of fresh energy and leverage to bring about a change. Due to the Sophianic Wisdom Tradition, which has immortalized these strategies for us, we are never without options that support our free will in the labor of reinventing ourselves in readiness for the incoming Age of the Holy Spirit.

Therefore, the correspondences printed on the faces of the cards represent where one stands within the staged unfolding of the cycle. They give an accurate report on "what is," both in the heavens and here on Earth. But digging deeper, the Essential Dignities allow us to work the remedial and medicinal qualities of the Ladder of Lights and thereby influence the rate and direction of consciousness as we move through our life adventures. By remaining aware of these internal conversations and affinities as the planets move around the Zodiac, one taps into critical energies that activate the "Sympathies and Antipathies" of one's individual temperament and constitution. This allows the user to synthesize astral medicines as suggested by the lay of the cards. Simply by bringing awareness to this possibility, subtle changes are stimulated that can increase a potential to the point where it becomes a probability.

Following this outlook to its natural conclusions can shift the cards from static place-holders into dynamic prescriptions for making energetic adjustments. The Tarot deck becomes our diagnostician, pointing out possible alchemical "moral" medicines that can be directly applied to our outer circumstances. In this way we are following the approach taught by Etteilla, D'Odoucet, Orsini, the *Tarot Belline*, Paul Christian, Lêvi, Papus, and the writer of the *Falconnier Tarot*, all of whom are working with the same standard body of curative thought-forms and attitudes that characterize Tarot interpretation across the 19th century. In simplest terms one first reads the imprinted values as the energetic "givens." These can be followed by a thorough search in the Ephemeris and on the Ladder of Lights for available avenues to introduce novelty and midwife evolution into the situation.

The Shem Angels Within the Decanates

An operative astrologer uses several techniques to break down the 360° of the Zodiac into smaller regions. The full cycle is initially separated into 12 30° regions of the sky called the signs, which in sequence make up the Zodiac. Each sign naturally divides into three 10° segments, called decanates. Further, the decanates have themselves been subdivided into halves (5°), quarters (2.5°), individual degrees, and in some cases even smaller units. Each level of granulation holds its own significance and has its own usefulness; the presence of one layer of analysis doesn't rule out another layer being present simultaneously.

Historians of astronomy realize that the art was often practiced "in the field" by navigators and builders using ingenious but also somewhat primitive tools. The traveling Masons of the ancient era could plat out an astrologically-aligned temple/observatory using only a straight staff and a thirteen-knotted rope. The representation that orients the navigator's momentary horizon to the plane of the ecliptic was carved on a rock or crystal and carried in a pocket. Calculating a point in the sky down below its five-degree sub-decanate was unnecessary for most purposes. These five-degree segments of the signs offer a ballpark region by which motion in the sky can be "eyeballed" without breaking out the specialized equipment. Over time these sub-decanates were granted rulerships according to various uses one might make of them. Sensitive individuals and good record-keepers accumulated a body of associations about the types of energies that shine down into the world through these five-degree apertures, including methods to help us harness those energies as they impinge upon us here below.

In my opinion the Pips have been associated with the angels since the time of Etteilla or even earlier. I count it nearly certain that the Shems have been connected with the Pips from the founding of the Martinist Order, but it would not surprise me to find the association being made to the Pips even as far back as Reuchlin's time.

This particular collection of five-degree ideas tutors us in a traditional subtlety of magical usage. One is using the Zodiac as an elaborate timepiece and energetic map. In terms of both diagnosis and prediction, references to the decanates and their interior facets grant the practitioner fairly precise orientation in Time and Space. They point to celestial directions on the cosmic compass and to calendar dates on the wheel of Time. Instead of just pointing to a 30° sign that covers a 30-day time interval in the travel of the Sun, the Shem angels represent much smaller periods. Details like this can be very helpful when a reader is trying to distill intuitive glimpses down into practical advice to carry into action. Not everybody will bother themselves with these details, and they aren't a regular part of standard Tarot divination. But they can be very helpful in certain situations.

People should never feel guilty or deficient if they aren't following the jot and tittle of this astro-Kabbalah-Alchemy. I share this level of detail because I know that there is a subset of esotericists who want to get past talking "around and about" the vocabulary of esotericism so they can move on to learn the practical operations of the integrated system.

The Shem angels are best dealt with as doorways in the firmament that give access to helpers and guides that humans can turn to in times of need. They have been associated with the five-degree segments of the Zodiac since the Persian and Zoroastrian cultures of deep antiquity. These celestial apertures have developed over time as people devoted more energy to them and built out their lore. Grimoires and magical books of the Middle Ages were often supplied with lists of the angels, their degrees, their functions, and other details of concern to theurgists. Our knowledge of the angels in the Zodiac stems from the Hebrew Old Testament, where they were embedded in Exodus and Psalms.

The Suited Pack as a Paracelsian Astro-Alchemy Computer

In this system by following the 3x3 pattern that carries the Decans (also known as Horas) around the Zodiac, we can include all of the natural elemental relationships into the mix. Here is the rule for each sign:

1st decantes = Ruling Planet in Domicile / rx Ruler in Similar.
2nd decantes = Ruling Planet in Compliment / rx Ruler in Detriment.
3rd decantes = Ruling Planet in Exaltation / rx Ruler in Fall.

Following this method:

The Aces, 6s, and 9s retain the initiative and confidence they generally show in the divinatory pack (first term in their ternary, representing the thesis). Middle Pillar.

The 2s, 4s, and 7s retain the challenging and precedent-breaking nature they generally show in the divinatory tradition (2nd term in their ternary, representing the antithesis). Father Pillar.

The 3s, 5s, and 8s find practical expression for the resulting synthesis, as they generally show in the divinatory tradition (3rd term in their ternary, representing synthesis). Mother Pillar.

The 10s represent the full Elemental Trine and all its permutations in simultaneous expression.

The Royals are distributed as:
Queen = Cardinal, the Queens create.
King = Fixed, the Kings uphold.
Knight = Mutable, the Knights digest and transform.
The Pages turn the wheel of the year at the solstices and equinoxes.

As we can see, the upward-looking Father Pillar is encouraged to bring its conflicts and challenges into the prayer-sphere of the inner life. Meanwhile the downward-looking Mother Pillar is encouraged to have hope in a redeemed world through replacing the instinctive Wrath (which glories in the will of the ego) with a more enlightened motive to enact the Divine Will. Such attitudes take a long time to culture within the soul, but the outcome of this worthy work is a redeemed psyche and a healed world.

Notes on Reversals

Reversed cards offer an excellent opportunity for the practitioner to stretch his or her intuition and unpack hidden layers of influence. On its surface the card represents and rules a single discreet ten-degree portion of the Zodiac, whether it is upright or upside down upon presentation. Looking more deeply, the ten-degree segments contain two portions which can refer to the traditional Shem angels, or to the range of Elemental Dignities at need. Reversed meanings also gain further nuance through studying the image: Certain details will only be revealed when the card is inverted. The user of *Tarot of the Holy Light* therefore has a range of correspondences to draw upon for both upright and reversed meanings.

I would counsel that the reader consider both upright and reversed meanings for every card in a spread, not just those that come up reversed. Every card has to be appreciated for its own essential meaning first (number, Suit, image, "face values") before one includes the incidental layers of meaning which are granted by its position in the spread, its reversal, or the card's resemblance to the querant's current issues. The goal is to try to connect the set and standard meanings of the cards in the spread to the fluid, moving situation in the client's life. This, of course, is the bottom line of the reader's art. I envision the varying correspondences belonging to the card as symbolizing a range of options, a spectrum of possible avenues to explore. One can just take a quick scan of the card itself or one can look at the simple astrological decanates or one can dig down and activate the whole body of correspondences that integrate the Hermetic Cosmos to the Tree, Tetractys, and Tarot.

In general the counseling-style warnings that I give for each card have to be taken into consideration no matter how the card falls in the spread. Taoist teachings remind us that anything taken to its extreme becomes its opposite. In that sense the inverse and obverse of each card are reciprocals, like one's left and right hands. Because of the way the planetary and elemental values are distributed on the cards, one could view the upright correspondences as being constructive, magnetic, and attractive, offering positive rewards for cooperating with them. (These are the Sympathies, in ancient alchemical parlance.) The reversed meanings would instead have a de-constructive, scattering, and dissolving effect, providing the service of cleansing, purging, and banishing. (These are the Antipathies, speaking alchemically.) Ought these different qualities to be distinguishd by judgments of good and bad? Not at all. They are each necessary stages of the great metabolism of life.

We already know that the descending and destructive Divine Wrath from the Supernal Triangle (pouring down the Mother Pillar, driven by the letter Shin) has to be met with Sophia's warmth and moistness (the letter Mem) before it can rise on the Father Pillar to re-assemble Eden and return Time/Space to Paradise. This is the paradox of incarnation for humans: We don't value our Divine origins until we have fallen away from them. With the upright correspondences, we employ the power of affinity and attraction (Domiciles, Compliments, and Exaltations) to draw related things together and cause them to evolve naturally in harmony. Alternately, with the reversed correspondences, one calls forth the reciprocal energies (Similars, Detriments, and Falls) to break down, disperse, and dilute currently existing structures and liberate the soul for whatever fresh impulse is coming next. It's all a matter of how far an individual wants to dig down into the layers of possible connections.

Please remember, a reversed card doesn't automatically assume a negative meaning. It is far better and more strategic to read the reversal as saying, "Question this card more deeply because the answers you need are between the lines of the upright meaning." Whichever side is up, you are reading the same card which operates by the same principle but in a more introverted and mysterious manner, following a logic that is implicit rather than explicit. I think reversals need to be handled delicately and investigated thoroughly to find out the hidden realizations towards which they point.

With *Tarot of the Holy Light,* one can use a card's reversal in a sophisticated, therapeutic manner. Both the upright and reversed meanings point to important natural stages of the overall metabolism of the Hermetic Cosmos. This information is given to allow the user to watch for and take advantage of astrological conditions that can be devoted towards your cause or goals. A fairly neutral way to characterize the difference between the upright and reversed cards would be to say:

Upright cards represent straightforward growth towards greater refinement, emotional integration, and consciousness-expansion. Upright cards move away from complication towards unity, from darkness and Wrath to Love and Light. Upright meanings represent a planet in its natural Domicile, in the sign belonging to its mate or Compliment, and in its Exaltation. In these positions the planet is free to function at its natural best. Upright cards are easier to read because they are usually fully-manifested already and are therefore easily recognized and accounted for.

Reversed cards represent destabilizing influences, which force us to learn something new and reach beyond the givens. Due to their affinity with the more challenging of the Essential Dignities, they express our own inner complication, confusion, and/or resistance. Reversed cards appear in circumstances where we haven't yet clarified our motives or questioned our assumptions. They can prove very helpful in situations when it is necessary to antidote the prevailing trend, steal its thunder, or steer away from the common thinking on a subject. After all, one can't always run one's life with the ethos of a popularity contest.

The thought that reversed cards are always the simple opposite of their upright meaning, or are automatically "bad," is naive and reductionist. Consider that the reversed meaning is the upright meaning taken to such an extreme that it is manifesting its own flip side. The two ends of each card represent the upside and downside of the same continuum, just the way an unusually attentive lover might turn out to be a neurotically possessive captor over time. Reversed cards point towards the less-visible aspects of a situation, those parts that are not yet fully manifested, making us dig for hints that must be derived due to the absence of reliable data. Often we have to quiet our minds and ask our subtle bodies about reversals because they refer to things the reasoning mind can't bring into focus.

Don't fall prey to the easy assumption that a reversed card indicates a problem that you must discover and solve; it is almost always incorrect to jump to this conclusion. Better to approach a reversal as an internal issue rather than an external one, asking, "What is motivating this card to appear reversed in this position?" Never take the stance that subtle, interior factors are inherently a problem. Recognize that knowledge held nonverbally in the energy-body will rise to consciousness along totally different channels than the rational mind prefers to use. Such insights can be just as powerful to shape our experience as forces that meet us from the outer world; internal events are equally important to the psyche. We don't want to negate our hunches and "vibes" just because they are subjective and immaterial. Better to become more internally quiet around these subtle signals from the unknown, to let them show themselves on their own terms. If the necessary information is not going to come through the outer senses, then one must become more inwardly still and receptive to let that "still small voice" have an opening.

A simple internal request to be shown the meaning of a reversed card can prime the pump for the necessary intuitive realizations. One who believes an upside down card is something to fear, or is automatically a negative thing, is not creating the mental space to imagine how the reversal can be the perfect expression of the Divine Plan. By assuming a negative outlook at the outset, the subconscious is told, "It's a problem to feel myself; it's fearful to look within; I'm not willing to question the givens." This is a bad internal message to have bouncing around one's psyche, and it's just wrong information besides.

From this expanded macro-cosmic point of view, it becomes clearer that reality is a lot more complicated than can be described through using reversed cards in a binary way. In a multi-modal, free-will universe, there are numerous variables that shade outcomes; it's never a black/white, good/bad, 50/50 split. What I hope to impart to users of *Tarot of the Holy Light* is that everything is a process. There are reasons for every manifestation, including when cards come out reversed in your spreads. Don't neglect these indicators, but instead become curious about them. Reversed cards offer the chance to think beyond the cliches and touch into the mysteries of divination. Challenge your intuition to use reversals to unveil essential realizations that are needed to restore balance and perspective. Users who have learned how to integrate reversals into their reading style effectively double the horsepower of their deck.

Using the Extended Correspondences Attached to Cards 1 - 9 of the Four Suits

As mentioned before, the 52-card pack, or Minor Arcana deck, has collected many different bodies of correspondence because they have a history that is older and more widespread than the Trumps. For *Tarot of the Holy Light,* some of each card's correspondences are printed on the card's face, but not all of them. The Doctrine of Essential Dignities and the Shem angels are background correspondences which are more technical and less frequently used, so I left them out of the overt imagery, though they will be found in the headers of the individual card essays and in the graphs found in the Appendix. Following are some suggestions for ways to integrate the full range of correspondences so you can understand what realms of thinking or practice they refer to and under what circumstances readers would include these values in their use of the Tarot.

Remember, the only values that are being used to derive the divinatory meanings (those interpretations we use when reading Tarot for our friends or ourselves) are shown in the text printed on the faces of the cards. In each case we have a numeral associated with a Suit, as well as a ten-degree swath of the Zodiac and a planetary ruler said to influence these degrees. Here's what these things can signify for the user if he or she wishes to follow them through.

The *number* relates directly to a given Sephira on the Kabbalah Tree. Because of this inherent design feature which reflects the scale of Ten, there will be affinities between all four cards of the same number, even though the different Suits will cause each number's expression to vary from Element to Element. Both the motive and the expression of the card will be governed by the energies of its number, so every interpretation has to be grounded in the principles of number first and foremost. Bringing in the added refinement of Hebrew Kabbalah tradition interwoven through the Tree further empowers the numbers to participate in the larger astro-alpha-numeric meaning mesh of Western esotericism. However, the core meanings of the Pips cards are derived from their stage in the number sequence and their Element, or rank and Element in the case of the Royals. Nothing more is necessary to explain why a card has a certain meaning above all others.

One could follow Etteilla and visualize the elemental scale of Ten in the form of the Pythagorean Tetractys, which is another relevant and meaningful strategy to apply to any of the Tarots of the first five centuries. However, *Tarot of the Holy Light* features the Hebrew-inflected approach over the Greek orientation in this detail because of Jacob Boehme's appropriation of the Tree into his visualizations and cosmic modeling. That being said, any traditional body of Ten-based Mysteries found among the world's historical traditions can be recruited to add meaning to the Pips numbers One through Ten. It still falls to the user to integrate the geometry and natural expression of the number when constructing specific interpretations in the context of a reading. There is a Greek body of thought called the Theology of Arithmetic, also known as the canon, which can add amazing richness to the Pips without clashing in any way with the Kabbalistic values we are featuring here. Among the esotericists of different faiths whose interdisciplinary explorations brought forth Renaissance magic, the Hebrew Mysteries, and the Pythagorean or Hermetic doctrine of numbers are understood to be intimately intertwined.

The *astrological decanates*, or ten-degree sections of the Zodiac wheel, which are assigned to each card One through Nine, carry quite a bit of meaning for the interpreter. For one thing these assignments point the reader to a certain section of the sky overhead, which is also directly linked to certain days of the year in the Solar calendar. That reminds the interpreter to think about the reigning cycles of the Sun, Moon, and planets as they circle the Solar System and influence the astral weather around the questioner. Each of us has a birth chart that represents our unique innate temperament and inherent constitution. Through the references to the decanates, we are asked to investigate what is happening to that spot in the current heavens, and how that spot is affected within any charts that are relevant to the question at hand. Such influences can impact the questioner's chart not only by conjunction, but also by opposition, Trine, or square. Thus one must figuratively imagine oneself occupying the designated ten-degree section of the Zodiac, embracing the considerations and issues that are characteristic to that stage of the circle of the year. It is also wise to investigate the energies of any other moving or natal bodies occupying stations that are related through one of these important aspects. Through these degrees the questioner is introduced to that decanate's characteristic astral climate and seasonal challenges, including whatever reigning influences color that location through other planets in close aspect, with special emphasis on the Elemental Rulers.

The *Elemental Rulers* represent a subtle internal pattern that colors the four Lullian (elemental) Triangles with a slightly different tint for each decanate within the signs. As mentioned earlier, for each Element there are three Rulers, one belonging to each of the signs co-participating in that Element. Among the Fire signs, for example, the three Rulers are Mars (Aries), Sun (Leo), and Jupiter (Sagittarius). So for every Fire sign, the decanates are ruled in turn by one of these. The natural Ruler of the sign will always inhabit the first decanate of the sign; in the case of Aries, that is Mars. The leader of the subsequent sign of the same Element (following the natural zodiacal progression) will rule the second decanate. In this case that's the Sun, Ruler of Leo. The Ruler of the remaining Fire sign governs the final decanate, which in this case is Jupiter, Ruler of Sagittarius. One could say that every sign is a microcosm of the entire

Element, and these three Rulers titrate and adjust the stages of every sign so that it benefits from the virtues and attributes of its partners in the elemental sequence.

Since all the signs of a given Element are inherently related by the harmonious Trine aspect, these sub-Rulers bring positive, supportive, compatible, and nourishing energies to each other's realms, sharing and supplementing each other's natural powers. Like siblings in a healthy family, they bring up methods and viewpoints that the natural Ruler of the sign might not think about otherwise. I use these sub-Rulers as clues to the easiest and most natural way to increase the positive energies available in a given card. The Element Rulers circle the wagons, standing up for each other's interests, lending energy to their siblings no matter where they might appear in the birthchart or current skies.

The rest of the noted correspondences given for our Suit card essays trend away from making specifically divinatory contributions. We will encounter some of my emotional and psychological suggestions about the astro-alchemical remedies in the text descriptions of the Pips, but the traditional meanings of the suited pack do not rely on this layer of correspondences in the slightest for their essential meanings. I don't generally make a point of keeping a hermetically-sealed barrier between the divinatory meanings of the cards (the specifically Tarot content) and the other correspondences that can be given to the cards in the case of a particular person in a particular situation. But for those who are new to this type of thinking, I am drawing this distinction very clearly to help the reader understand the foundation-ground of our standard interpretations of modern Tarot. These conventions have been in place since (at minimum) Etteilla's packs from the 1790s. His packs represent the first known body of standard meanings recorded for the Pips, including specific upright and reversed meanings. These conventions might be older than Etteilla, but so far we don't know for sure. Etteilla's meanings have been convincingly demonstrated to be grounded in Kabbalistic references derived from each card's number and Element. These divinatory conventions have proven quite valuable to the basic meaning-mesh of the Tarot ever since they first came into the public eye. This allows us in the 21st century to feel secure in basing our fundamental interpretations upon these core values, no matter what Continental deck we are using, or what other hints or symbols might be printed on the faces of the cards.

The Essential Dignities associated with each of the Pips cards will point to two astro-alchemical remedies that are associated with each card, derived from the card's affiliation with the Kabbalah Tree. The Middle Pillar numbers carry the Domiciles and Similars for the planetary Ruler of their sign. The Father

Pillar numbers carry the Compliments and Detriments for their sign's Ruler; the Mother Pillar numbers carry the Exaltations and Falls for the given sign's Ruler. These values suggest astral-medicine approaches that can be brought to bear to advance the cause of the querant (meaning the questioner, who might be a client or friend, or who might be the reader him- or herself).

The Essential Dignities are distributed according to whether a card comes up reversed or not, but they don't carry any of the typical negative associations that reversal carries in the modern psychological Tarot arts. An alchemically-minded practitioner will envision the upright Essential Dignity to be adding or strengthening existing helpful energies within the situation at hand, while the reversed Essential Dignity subtracts or neutralizes unhelpful energies. There is no alchemical reason to polarize the upright and reversed meanings. Consider assembling your remedies in ways that take both sides of the card into consideration.

In the broader discipline of magic, intent is everything. Every soul is held responsible for the reality it constructs from its inner world of beliefs and projections. The bias with *Tarot of the Holy Light* is to find therapeutic applications for all the correspondences, to help nudge the questioner away from the realm of the problem and towards the realm of relief or remediation. Readers should investigate both sides of every relevant card in light of the querant's chart so that the specifics of the remedy can be adjusted to the individual who is seeking advice.

I am unaware of any pre-existing interpretations that will instantly reveal the full significance of these remedies, although I am not averse to the idea that somewhere in the annals of traditional Astrology, some rules have been written up to quantify these values into handy working lists. For the sake of the system that animates *Tarot of the Holy Light*, remember that the Middle Pillar numbers point to the medicine of Similars attracting more of their own kind. The Father Pillar numbers point to the medicine of creative pairings sparking between compatible opposites. Finally, the Mother Pillar addresses the clashing opposites that characterize our modern war model of medicine. If one learns nothing more than this little overview about the Essential Dignities, these values can still prove helpful and illuminating when it's time to customize the message for a given reading.

The Catalog of the Angels of the Quinaries, called the Shemhamphorasch (Shem angels) or the 72-Fold Name, assigns personalities and special functions to the two five-degree segments that make up each of the decanates. Hence, whereas there are 36 decanates in the Zodiac, there are 72 quinary angels. These values are the very furthest thing from divinatory meanings. They refer instead to a catalogue of intelligences or spiritual energies that for millennia have been associated with the segments of deep space that surround the circuit of the Zodiac. The Shem angels are understood to be independent of any other demarcations that subdivide the Zodiac (be they signs, decanates, Lunar Mansions, or individual degrees). The relationship of the angels to Tarot is only accidental in that they come to the Tarot from the astrological traditions of antiquity rather than being a function of the cards per se.

People of a devotional mindset use the angels as "entities" to call upon as allies when striving towards a difficult goal, learning a challenging body of information, or struggling to fulfill tasks that seem insurmountable. Each Shem angel is traditionally endowed with particular activities, gifts, and skills that can be marshaled by a petitioner who approaches them respectfully. A standard magical application for the Shem angels would be to discover the names of those angels that govern the degrees wherein your Sun, Moon, and other planets stand in your birthchart. These angels would be called upon as guardians, motivators, and allies who can bring their specific "powers" to bear in helping us achieve our goals.

The Shems are commonly seen as entities, but they could just as easily be interpreted as "directions," since they all point to different sections of deep space as we look off the planet through the windows of the Zodiac signs. Another standard practice would be to find the angel that has the strongest relationship to one's current need or request, and then locate that quinary in the section of the cycle where it naturally falls. This gives the practitioner a "hot spot" in the Zodiac to concentrate on, suggesting the proper timing for Solar, Lunar, or planetary rituals that would be enacted when a moving body is transiting that quinary overhead. The Moon circles the Zodiac 13 times a year, providing a number of opportunities to meet the designated angel on its home ground. Both Mercury and Venus also make several circles around the Zodiac every year, and the Sun enlivens each quinary for five days per year. Ritualizing with these planets as they transit the signs offers multiple opportunities to commune with one's angels as the circle of the year unfolds. According to Boehme, the Moon, Mercury, and Venus offer "remedies" for the challenges posed by Mars, Jupiter, and Saturn. Therefore, it seems like a natural fit to include the Shem angels in one's spiritual and ritual considerations. This can be done either as a way of bringing the angels' qualities and capabilities "down to earth" through observing their action in our own charts and transits, or by taking one or more angels as guardians of one's profession, goals, or aspirations. We see the angel names regularly employed in the making of talismans, medicines, and ritual objects made by or for people who were seeking Divine help.

The Shem angel lists are balanced by parallel lists of demons that attach to the same quinary divisions of the Zodiac. I personally choose to ignore these inverse energies in my astro-alpha-numeric approach. Most of us encounter plenty of "demons" of one kind of another from one day to the next without studying and therefore summoning any more. Instead, my practice has been to meditate with the angel of my choice in a way that helps me stabilize that angel's vibrations inside my body. The technique starts with finding the three root letters that define the name of the chosen angel, stripped of its gendering suffix (either "-ael" or "-iah"). This reveals the three Trumps that spell out the trilateral (three-lettered) root of the angel name. What follows is a meditation in which one visualizes the Trump of the first letter in the head, the Trump of the second letter in the heart, and the Trump of the third letter in the pelvis. Essentially, one is embedding the angelic name into the horizontal paths of the three Mother Letters (between the eyes, across the shoulders, and across the hipbones). This has the effect of focusing consciousness in the Three Worlds simultaneously, following the specific formula that makes up the name you are working with. (The more one understands the functions of the letters on the Tree, the richer this exercise becomes; but in the beginning, just visualizing the Trumps in these three areas of the body will be enough.) Intoning the name of the angel very slowly while visualizing Light pouring into these three bodily centers in turn creates a very powerful and absorbing experience designed to let the practitioner enter into the energy-body of the angel directly. For greatest accuracy one can search around for instructions for speaking the angel's name with the proper Hebrew vowel sounds and syllable emphasis, though some teachers say that this is an unnecessary extra step.

What about the planetary hours? Users of the modern Tarots base their Pip card correspondences on the practice of assigning the planets to the decanates according to the lists of planetary hours governing the day and night. I have pondered this practice for many years but have made no progress on why this would be considered an "innovation" on the 20th century decks. Historians have shown that the standard body of interpretive meanings for the Pips are hung on the Sephirot-numbers from One to Ten multiplied by the four Elements. This simple but powerful convention has provided the backbone for Tarot divination for more than two centuries, if not longer. Additionally, this method of deriving the planetary hours is not a divinatory practice at all, instead being employed when one is attempting to determine the best time of day or night to commence a theurgical ritual. The idea is to start one's devotions in the day and hour sacred to the Planetary Governor most suitable for one's goals. This is a fine practice and quite traditional, but it's not really a suitable foundation for a fixed body of correspondences governing interpretive Tarot meanings.

I say this because the boundaries between one planetary hour and another will vary throughout the year, due to the changing times of sunrise and sunset as the Sun marches through the seasons. There are only two days a year when the hours of day and night are matching and symmetrical, and those mark the two equinoxes at spring and fall. The rest of the year, either the daylight hours are compressed and the nighttime hours are stretched in the two seasons bordering Winter Solstice, or else the daylight hours are stretched and the nighttime hours compressed for the two seasons bordering Summer Solstice. This tells me that the planetary hours are not stable values of the type that can be firmly associated with the Tarot cards the way the decanates, Shems, Essential Dignities, or Elemental Rulers can. Nor does this system distribute the Planetary Rulers in an even-handed and balanced way; in particular, Mars is over-represented when we assign the Governors to the decanates following this pattern. So I tell my students to employ the planetary hours to help calculate proper start-times for their formal theurgical rituals, but don't assume that the planetary hours "should" have a representation on the Pips of *Tarot of the Holy Light*. I chose to work with the Elemental Rulers on the decanates decades ago and have never looked back.

In Summary

While the following divinatory paragraphs were being written, all of the suggested correspondences were being held in mind simultaneously. Initially, the number or title and Suit mark out the stage each card occupies in the elemental process. These clues lead the mind to the corresponding Sephira in the Tree of that Element. This will then point to a discreet planet/sign combination, including their characteristic functions in the overall astral body of humanity. The number and Suit also highlight a certain spot on the Zodiac wheel, which will often turn out to be focal in the birthchart or in the current heavenly transits. From here we can investigate traditional correspondences that stem from the ancient Ladder of Lights. This meaning-mesh offers the operator a spectrum of astral remedies should the placement or disposition of the card (upright or reversed) suggest that an amendment is warranted.

Through the suited cards we break the world down into understandable pie-slices and learn the flavors of every different stage of the cyclical wheel of the year. Along with its sequence of Royals, the deck of four Suits forms a world structured by the archetypes of the Zodiac and its very ancient, very sophisticated rulership scheme. The Trumps are modeled on the Paradise Tree, the unspoiled order of these primordial archetypes as first envisioned in the Divine Mind. But in the Suits we traverse every channel and node of the map that results from the metaphysical Fall. As we navigate this earthly world with all of its asymmetries and blind alleys, by trial and error we finally learn the path of Restitution and return. Over time the planets, signs, and Elements on the Trumps begin to refine and tame the Pips and Royals that they rule. Sustained interest and accumulated experience allow consciousness to climb the Ladder of Lights from Earth to Heaven, raising up the fallen Sephirot and perhaps even resurrecting the fallen angels in the end. This is the universe as described by the Continental Tarots.

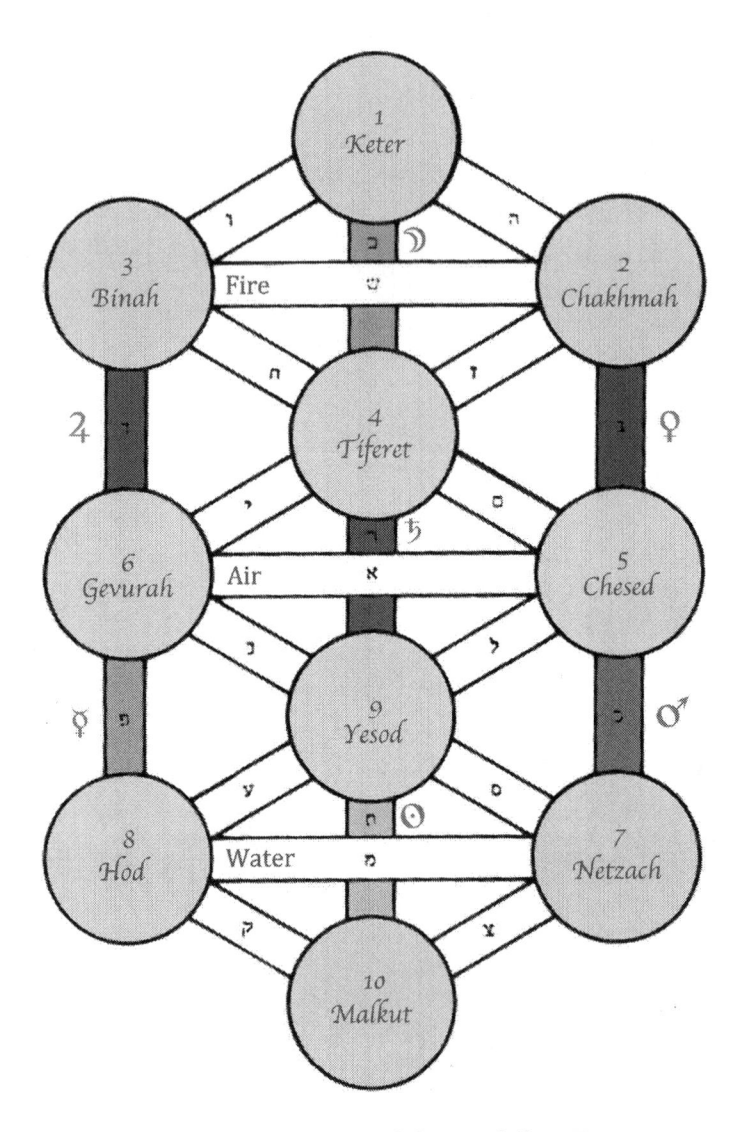

Planets on the Paths of the Unfallen Tree

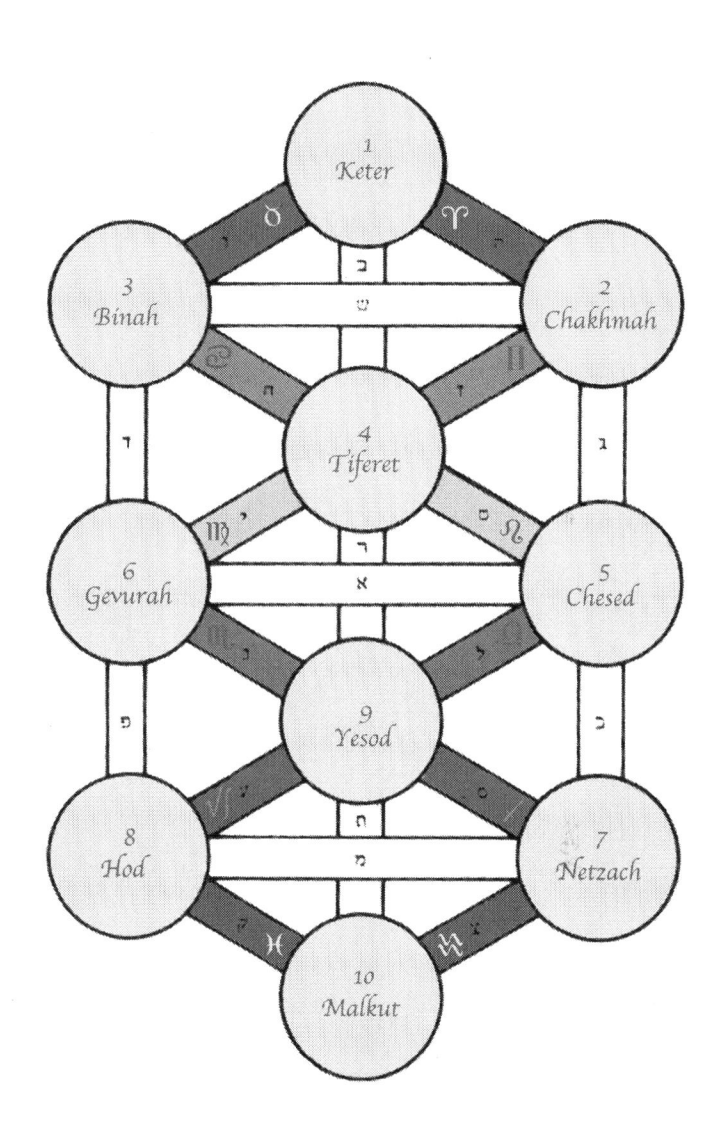

Signs on the Paths of the Unfallen Tree

63

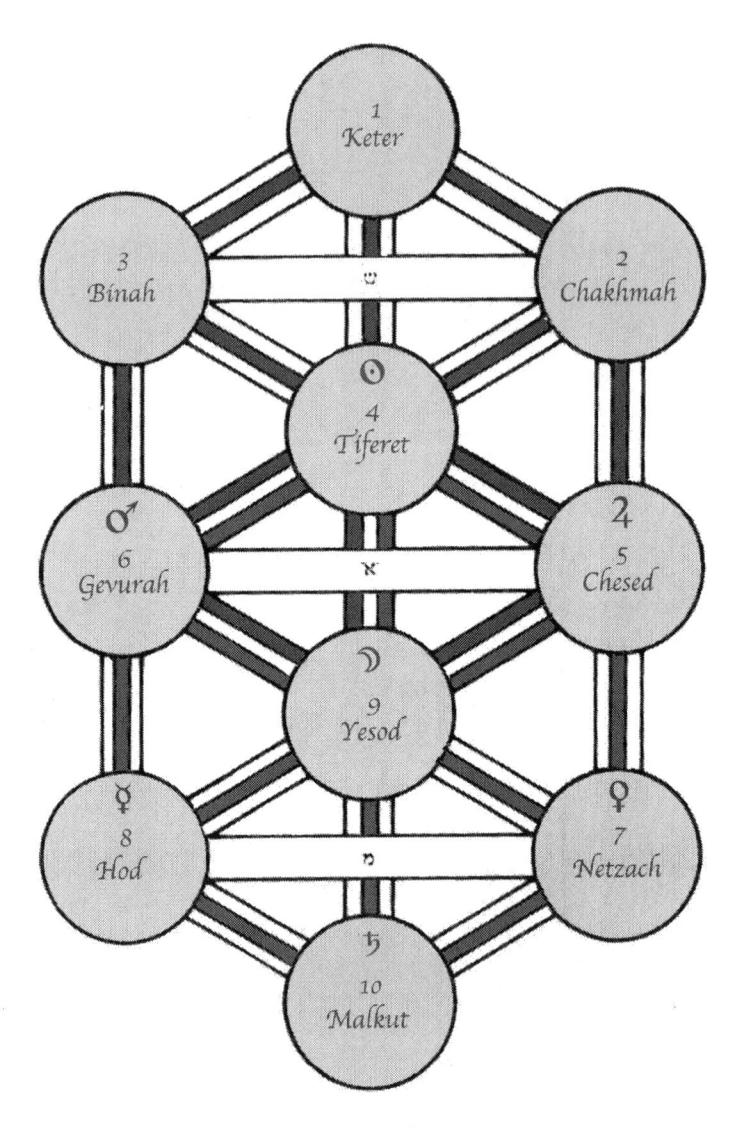

Upper & Lower Countenance

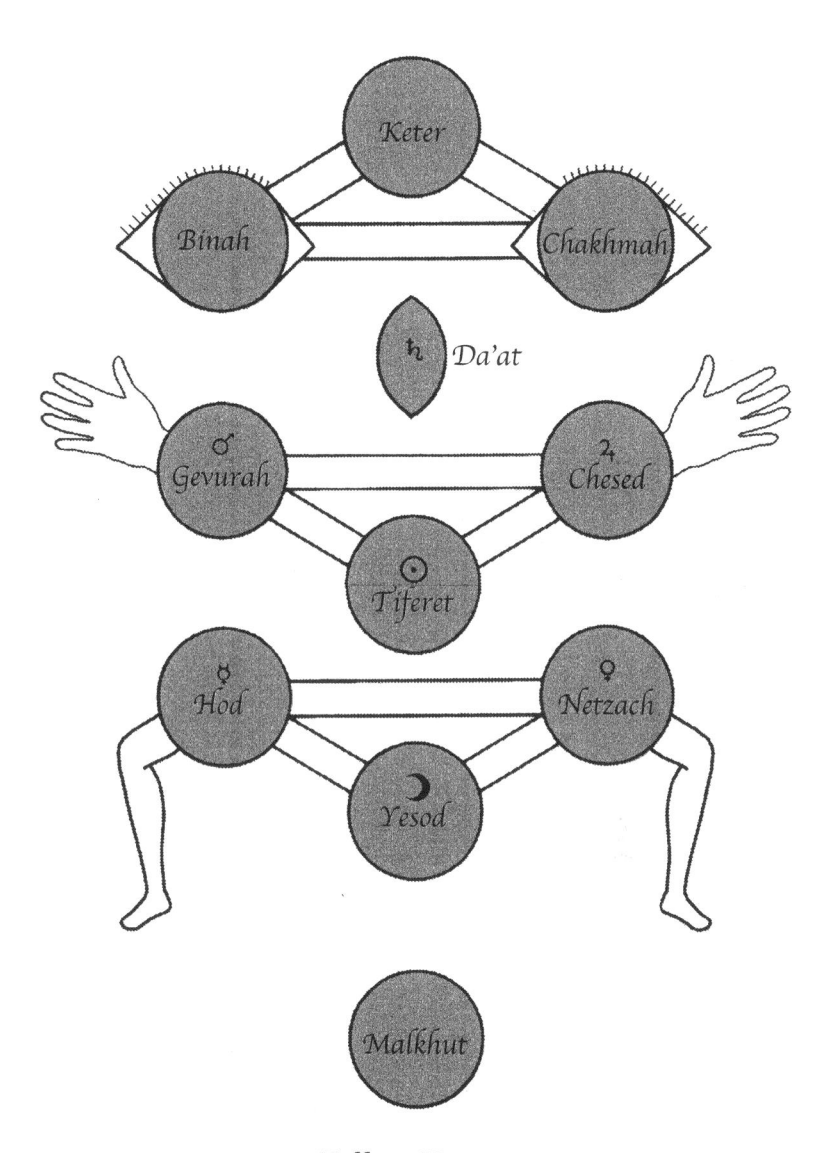

Fallen Human

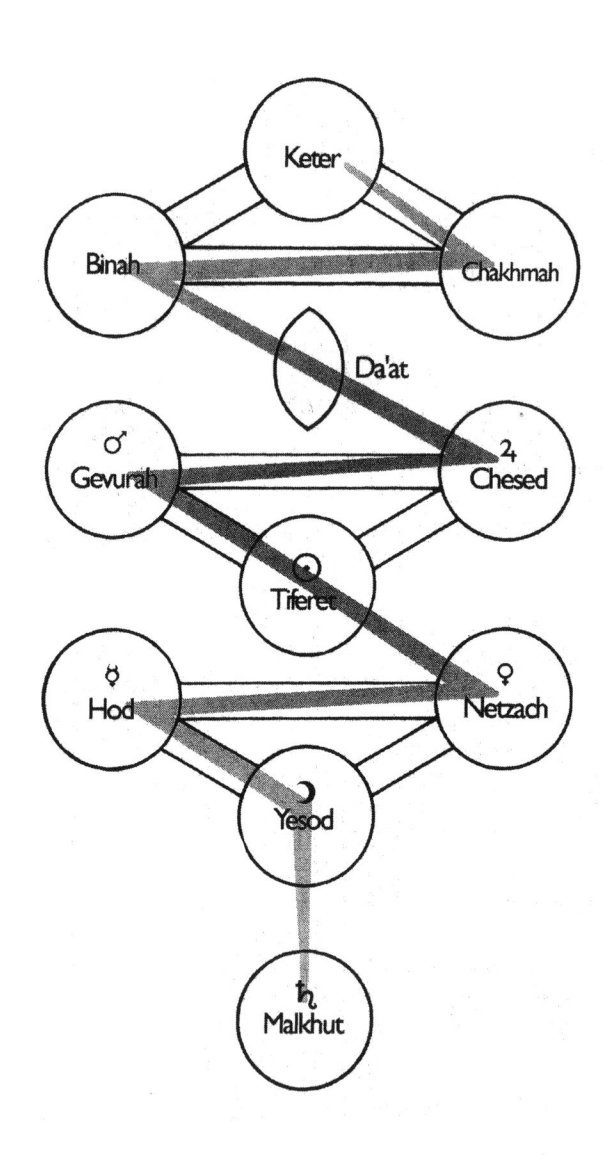

Lightning-Struck Tree "The Fall"

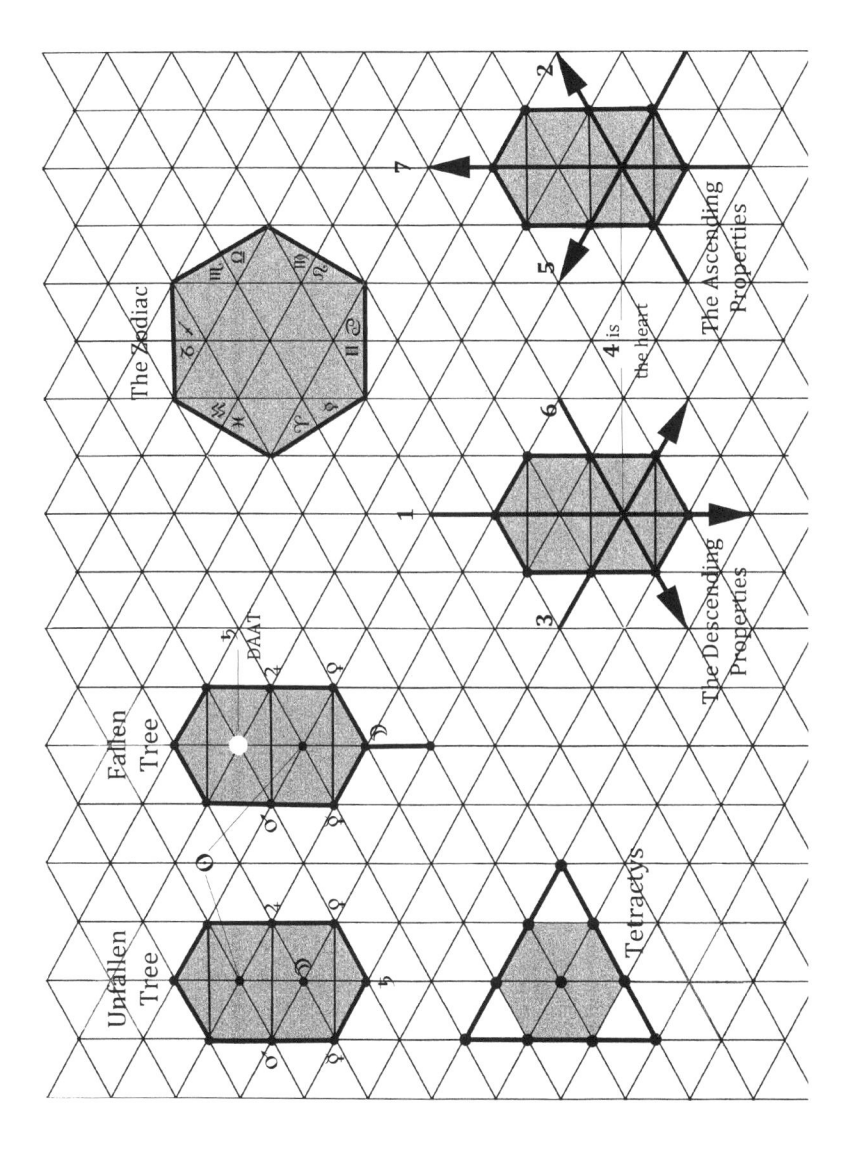

The Sexagesimal Grid of the Mysteries

The Ladder of Lights
Within Lullian Triangles

Tarot of the Holy Light
Mandala

Boheme's Star of Restitution
The Great Septenary

The Maze by Patrick Dowers 2011 full spread used for covers of the book and card deck

Chapter 2
The Swords

Suit of Swords

The symbol of the dagger, scimitar, sword, or cleaver most often represents the world of mind. This is the realm of thought and ideation where we dissect, scrutinize, and frame our view of reality, both personally and collectively. It points to the rational mind, that faculty which compares, contrasts, balances, and names the processes governing relationships and exchanges, be they economic or romantic. At the level of daily life, we can see the Sword as the battle for consciousness, the struggle to become aware and self-piloting amidst the many competing forces in the environment.

Parallel associations reflect qualities of the Element Air, indicating perceptiveness, clarity, and insight. We look for a dispassionate objectivity in this Suit to clarify mixed motives and contending emotions. The scalpel-sharp blade exhibits swift psychological analysis, verbal precision, and an inquiring critical mind in action. Sometimes we experience the action of the blade as alienating because it can be surgical and distancing, even emotionally disconnected. At worst case, Sword energy can exhibit monumental insensitivity. People with the Air temperament seem to retract their emotional bodies up into their minds, making them seem completely detached when under duress. But let us not forget that in a catastrophe, it is the Sword people who have to determine who can be repaired and who cannot. Their mercy is extended only to true survivors; they cannot spare the time, energy, or resources to comfort the doomed.

At the macrocosmic level the Suit of Swords represents the sum total of the friction and distress that settled matter experiences when facing the forces of change. All the Sword values (individuation and discrimination, the proclivity to make judgments, to draw lines and identify boundaries, this whole divisive manner of proceeding) tend to upset the quiescent undivided Pleroma. The Sword impulse breaks up the natural harmony of Heaven into the geography of Space and Time. The great ocean of being is now divided up and sold off by the cubic foot. Our myths of progress tell us this process is determined by Manifest Destiny, but Nature's response to the Sword demonstrates our continued shortsightedness and lack of overview. The Suit of Swords represents all the forces that the human worldview brings to bear upon Creation. Being double-edged, the Sword represents the mixed blessing granted to humanity through our unique endowment, the rational intellect.

In psychological terms "Sword" is a cipher for "Truth." Do you see the "word" in the Sword? This Suit-symbol cleaves through denial and obstructionism, revealing the underlying motives and actions that stand behind appearances. Here is another reason for the undertone of contention and struggle that runs through this Suit: People are not always truthful with themselves, much less with each other. The two-sided nature of the Sword ensures that its user shall be liable to the same judgment that she or he dispenses upon any other. In the esoteric sense the Sword is the tool of the Holy Word, the magical act of naming things according to what they really are. Spiritual sources from multiple traditions agree that when you find the real name of a force, a thing, or an entity, you have the power to command it. The inverse of this concept is that when you assert your fears as if they were realities, they are empowered through your breath, speech, and/or imagining to come true. Psychologists tell us that our subconscious believes every word that we say and take in. Perhaps this Suit is calling us to accountability, reminding us to pay attention to what we say, listen to, repeat, fantasize over, or ruminate upon in our unguarded moments. Beliefs can too easily limit what we are able to envision and what choices we perceive we have.

Translated into the common events of everyday life, the Sword represents contracts and legal forms, the laws of the land, the judicial system, verbal agreements, and all of the shared assumptions it takes to make up our collective reality. This Suit is invariably the one used to register the potential for conflict built into every communication, whether it's just two people chatting or a debate in the Senate. Every conversation brings with it the risk of misunderstanding. Yet there is always information that needs to be exchanged. We must therefore strive for objectivity, subordinating our personal version of events to the greater truth. Of course, there is a price to be paid in this world for attempting to tell the truth, and the two-edged Sword of Truth negotiates the boundaries of this trade-off. Verbal descriptions will never convey more than partial truth, but until we become fully psychic as a species, we'll always need words to get our points across.

In those Tarots where the Swords are given to the Water signs, the emphasis is subtly changed to reflect the ways we use our thinking, our words, and beliefs in negative and disturbing ways. The Swords will be shown influencing the currents of the underground river (psychic and soul life), creating turbulence and upsetting emotional harmony. When the card shows the water in a relatively calm aspect, it is because the individual has gotten enough control over distracting and distrustful forces to have neutralized them, or at least put them in perspective. This version of the Swords demonstrates how easily our serenity can be upset when feelings are ruffled, how sharply and defensively we can react when our sensitive egos take offense.

So although the outer appearances in the situations reflected by the Swords cards may appear the same whether the Swords are Air or Water, the causes, motives, and inner processes will be subtly different as you study the card in the spread. The Water variation implies that the cause of conflict is rooted in interior psychic and spiritual phenomena; subjective currents are being stirred up as the inner life confronts new revelations from the deep dark unconscious. This deviation from the standard pattern is one hallmark of the Spanish school of Tarots. *El Gran Tarot Esotcrico, Balbi, Euskalherria, The Crystal Tarot, The Universal Wirth,* and *The Magdalene Legacy Tarot* are currently available examples of this type.

Ace of Swords

Astrology: 1 - 10 Libra, ruled by Venus   **Sephira:** Keter
Essential Dignities: upright Domicile, Venus in Libra
reversed Similar, Venus in Taurus
Angelic Dignities: upright angel spelled ANI, spoken Aniel
reversed angel spelled ChOM, spoken Haamiah

The Ace of Swords has from the beginning shown the Divine Hand hefting a two-edged sword. Symbolically this represents your prime motive or guiding ideal, that vision which carries you through the outer vicissitudes of life with single-minded clarity. This is God's definition of you, which becomes your personal commandment and reason for being. This Ace grants orientation, allowing each soul to find its personal bull's-eye and fully occupy it, leaving no empty space, with nothing left over. The ability to hone in on one's true center fulfills the primal commandment of this card, "Know thyself."

The Suit symbol of the Sword is traditionally shown pointed upwards, sometimes piercing a metal and/or laurel crown. This optimistic formulation implies evolution, progress, and the temperament of the high achiever. Our version shows the sword penetrating entirely beyond the material plane, probing into the astral level, symbolized as the Empyrean (beyond the orbit of Saturn). The Sword always refers to one's own discriminating mind. In this case the mind awakens to the eternal conversation between the Seven Planetary Governors, including Sun and Moon. We also see a dragon-serpent with tail in mouth symbolizing Eternity, and the two-headed eagle of androgyny representing the *coincidentia oppositorum* of the body and its astral double. All these principles come alive in a single magnificent burst of self-cognition.

Through the Ace of Swords we understand that the ego is simply a lens over the eye of God, imposing the filter of our own individual constellation and temperament onto what is being viewed. This spidery shape stands for your unique blueprint, the geometrical and vibratory equation that defines your true self. This "consciousness molecule" is at the center of all of your experiences. Whenever you rediscover this, you feel again the "eureka" moment of recognition. Body and soul, past and future, the two sides of the brain along with all outer opposites come together at the central rib of this Sword.

Remember that the Sword is the main tool of the Justice card. The goddess Themis holds the scale and defines the opposites via the fulcrum that sets the balance point. The Ace of Swords signifies "first principles," the initial premise around which contingent polarities arrange themselves. All the subsequent actions of the Sword Suit hang from this Ace's primacy in the world of thought. Every natural outcome of every possibility, from the archangels to the underworld demons, is contained "in mind" at the awakening of this seed thought. The Ace of Swords moment happens when both sides of the brain are awake equally. Contemplating life from this ambidextrous center, we are more likely to see this and that, pros and cons. This more inclusive view grants us a wider spectrum of options, most of which are not visible when operating from the assumption of mutually exclusive black/white polarities.

A brain-balanced state also allows us to transcend our gender programming. Don't let conformity impose such a crimp in your essential nature. Those who are on the quest for higher values seek clear-mindedness and steady attention. They are striving to cultivate articulate intuition as an aid in discerning the essential and immortal truths. Issues of gender, age, or any kind of situational contingency simply don't enter into the equation. Those who can enter their still calm pre-incarnated center will have access to the very ground of consciousness. For this there can be no substitute.

A sword represents a single unitary idea, one "grain" of thought, so to speak. When contemplating a complex circumstance or endeavor, sort for the idea that perfectly expresses your inner sense of things. When the mind contacts the right idea, that single (s)word serves as a key to open the imagination. Ideas begin to fly and whole scenarios reveal themselves effortlessly in the blink of an eye. In this sense the Ace of Swords is a catalyst, a scalpel of destruction and renewal from which creativity springs.

As it says in scripture, "In the Beginning was the Word," not just the thought, but also its expression in sound. This is why the ancients often put Air at the top of the elemental chain. This Ace becomes the first manifestation in the Mind of God. Since we are all external nerve cells in that Mind, the Divine Thought moves through us in the form of a bright idea. At the perfect moment the Ace of Swords appears, ripping through the old version of reality and asserting a new revelation. This Ace is the fiat by which whole worlds are created.

Taking the idea of the "scalpel of the mind" to its logical conclusion, one begins to understand that the words chosen to describe our experience make a huge contribution to how our possibilities and options are understood. If we aren't intentional about how we frame our opinions and expectations, we might be too quick to make decisions, navigating by the wrong expectations. Using the wrong terms can close our minds before we've fully understood our choices,

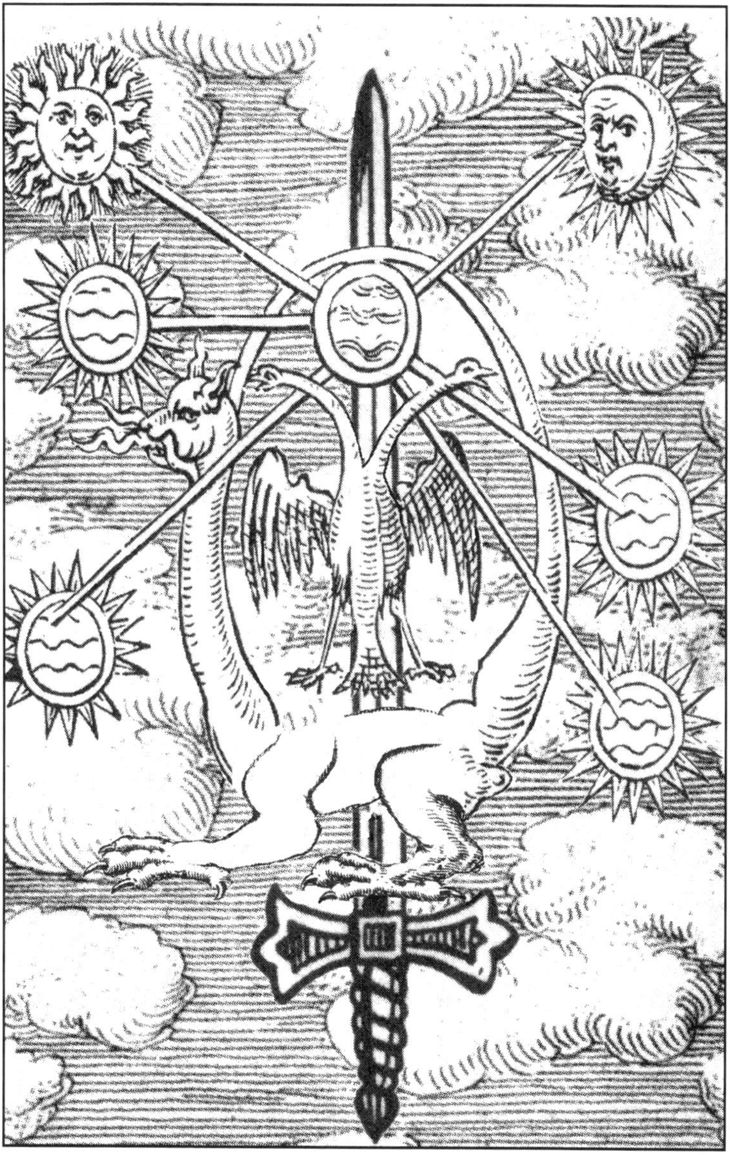

thereby cutting off options we can ill afford to lose track of. Make a habit of speaking carefully, with due consideration for what is also true but remains unspoken, and there will be far fewer misunderstandings in your life.

As an exemplar of the law, the Sword accepts no excuses and offers no second chances. In the world of Air, the situation stands at "one soul, one vote." As quickly as an image can arise in the imagination, Spirit will respond by making changes in the world. The infinite creativity of this world allows each person to experience the natural consequences of his or her beliefs and projections, even if that means punishments will be forthcoming. The two-edged sword is known to cut both ways. This means that it delivers exactly equal treatment to one's enemy, one's friend, and oneself. Whatever judgment is delivered upon the outer world is immediately turned back and visited upon the self. This is the same brilliantly flashing Sword of Light issued to Uriel, the archangel whose job is to test the petitioners at the gateway to Eden.

When the Suit symbol is shown pointed downward, the darker message refers to sacrifice, challenges, and a critical environment. We can best respond to this card by disciplining our minds, narrowing our focus, and keeping our eyes on the prize. Emulate the habits and approach of the martial artist, who understands that the mind and body have to be trained in tandem for optimum performance. Rigorously examine your inevitably mixed motives and their attendant rationalizations. Find the single, over-arching priority around which all your other considerations are circulating. Victory over distraction and self-division can only be won after this type of scrupulous self-examination is completed.

Two of Swords

Astrology: 11 – 20 Libra, ruled by Saturn **Sephira:** Chakhmah
Essential Dignities: upright Compliment, Venus in Scorpio
reversed Detriment, Venus in Aries
Angelic Dignities: upright angel spelled RHO, spoken Rehael
reversed angel spelled YYZ, spoken Yeiazel

The Two of Swords represents the ultimate diplomatic challenge: achieving a meeting of the minds between categorical opposites. Great subtlety, diplomacy, and craft are required, as well as a thick skin that is impervious to all but the heaviest of blows. According to the Elemental Dignities scheme we are following, the Two of Swords represents the relational Venus visiting the homes of her mate Mars. In both the upright and reversed case, she has to work hard to keep her balance without becoming either steamed (in Scorpio) or fried (in Aries) during the course of the experience. By calling upon her ally Saturn's qualities (available because this is the second decanate of Libra), she can access a long-term view of things. This helps her shrug off superficial annoyances and supports her focus on the healing potential of the situation.

The key to this image is in the two eyes gazing out at us from the green and red triangles at the center. A brightly lit arm emerging from the radiant green triangle serves the Mother Pillar, as one can see by the downward-pointed sword. The accompanying eye faces downward to the earthly world. This eye of scrutiny and conscience looks deeply into the soul, albeit sternly, to correct and guide worldly affairs according to the judgment of Heaven. On the literal other hand, the arm emerging from the fiery red triangle is shadowed as if struggling with ignorance and obscurity, its own or somebody else's. The associated eye looks up along the Father Pillar to Heaven for rescue, healing, and forgiveness. The soul prays for an intervention.

There is nowhere to go in this card to escape the clash of opposites. Everywhere you look, the primal pairs seek avenues to reconcile their differences. Divinely ordained attraction between these dire contrasts continues to pull them back into relationship. The opposites twine into each other like the two snakes of the caduceus. Their magnetism cannot be ignored, no matter what momentary clashes are present on the surface. Both sides must surrender to the principle of meeting in the middle, creating common ground that can be shared instead of fought over. The Two of Swords highlights conflicting ideas or visions that must be corrected against each other. Contrast is the way we recognize a unique thing from its background context, yet because of contrast the Two of Swords is burdened with a bad reputation. This card challenges us to overcome aversion and connect with forces that seem alien. Doing so will require marshalling all our discrimination, self-discipline, and humility to face the risky territory of possible disagreement. Mixed signals could easily prevail if we lose our balance. Careful communication is essential to arrive in a harmonious place through these strategic negotiations. Banish superficiality, flippancy, and thoughtless quips.

The danger of the Two of Swords emerges when opposite sides miss each other entirely, even while sincerely thinking they are communicating. In the best instance a frank discussion can clear the air, but that assumes self-discipline from both sides of the conversation. One is not always met with proper manners in situations that trigger polarization, so we must be doubly committed to non-violent, civil, and balanced communication. Use self-control to keep loaded situations from automatically degenerating. A "win" involves maintaining a level of civility that allows all parties to keep their dignity no matter what topic is under discussion.

When the card falls upright, the green background predominates. Here the suggestion would be to seek forgiveness and amend our own sins before attempting to convince somebody else of theirs. By taking enhanced responsibility for our own imperfections and unfinished business, we provide a better role model for others while conveniently stirring up less negative feedback from the environment. One doesn't lose status by being the first one to suggest a win/win alternative. The upright card gives us a green light, encouraging us to take an active role in making peace and defining common ground.

If instead you see the lord and lady against the violet background at the top of the card, then slower steps, more careful listening, and a greater willingness to see the other's point of view are being suggested. Don't fail to note the strain of ambiguity permeating this card, whether it falls upright or reversed in practice. Our paired possibilities show the seeker either accepting correction or entreating mercy, both of which have the savor of "not winning." The Two of Swords challenges our false pride.

Sometimes the issue is that inevitable resistance has not been factored into our expectations. Is it possible that you committed to a path before having fully thought through all the likely consequences? Even people who are completely satisfied with their choices might still have apologies and explanations to make. There are, after all, very few situations in this life that are so non-controversial as to be greeted with universal approval. The ability to keep lines of communication open even when disagreements and cross-purposes are rising to the surface is an invaluable skill that every person needs to acquire.

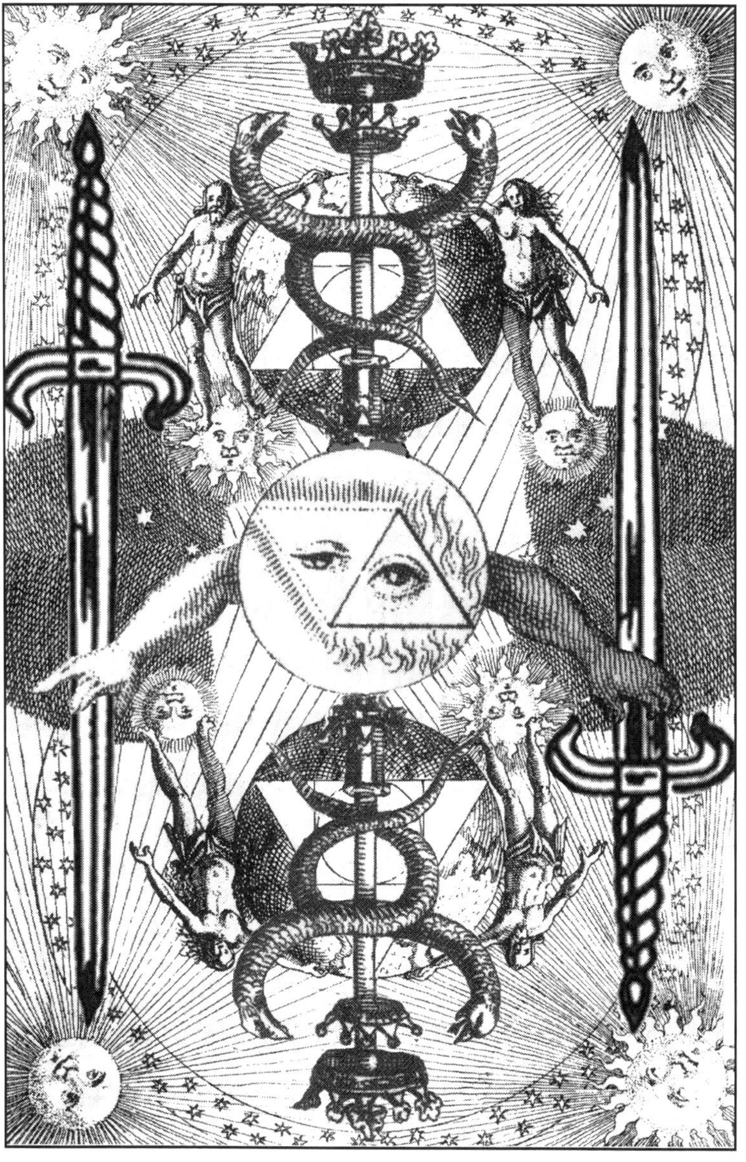

Reversed, the Two of Swords will tighten the knot of disagreement, pressing contending parties into a win/lose duel. There's a real danger of abandoning the win/win option that originally ruled the conversation. Polarized participants refuse to accept correction or moderate their positions, leaving common ground trampled underfoot. The focus shifts from problem solving to accusations and mistrust. Anxiety and contradiction paradoxically provoke the very circumstances they fear. Too many important things are left unsaid until the pressure of circumstances forces a painful confrontation. Lack of foresight demolishes the goodwill between participants, stripping away the cooperative spirit that could save the day.

The best strategy for this card when reversed is to study any split or duality very thoroughly before any words are spoken or action is taken one way or the other. Avoid falling back onto reflex responses in fear of doing damage to one's opportunities. If we take on touchy conversations in the spirit of competition or defensiveness, everybody becomes a loser, even the technical winner. Complete your first analysis within yourself before calling others out on their flaws or unfinished business. In the situation symbolized by the Two of Swords, there will always be either/or considerations which raise the possibility of giving or taking offense. At very least with this card, make sure that you are willing to make a concession of equal or greater import than the one you are expecting of others.

Three of Swords

Astrology: 21 - 30 Libra, ruled by Mercury **Sephira:** Binah
Essential Dignity: upright Exaltation, Venus in Pisces
reversed Fall, Venus in Virgo
Angelic Dignities: upright angel spelled HHH, spoken Hahahel
reversed angel spelled MIK, spoken Mikael

The Three of Swords image shows the drama of critical analysis, which is too often taken to an extreme degree. On the upright side we see the alphabet star (with its groupings of twelve, seven, and three) demonstrating an exploded dissection of reality. Every factor is separated out from the others and standing alone. On the reversed side we see an image of the planet Earth as a single organism with all the parts reunited and operating as a unified whole. In between we see critical thoughts attacking and piercing the cosmological egg and its serpentine protector. To every thing there is a time, whether the need is to break things apart or to bring them back together.

In simplest of terms, the upright card takes advantage of Venus in Pisces, where emotional bonds are loosened organically and participants are freed to re-envision their shared participation, or even go their separate ways. Reversed, we have more difficulty in the transition, including failure of communication, breakdown of agreement, and acrimony along with hurt feelings, guilt, and shame.

The Three of Swords has historically signified separation, termination, a breakup of a relationship or family, and the entire tragic spectrum of emotions attendant upon such events. Some versions show the background of the upright position filled with roiling storm clouds and flashing lightning, while the reversed background is clearing and brightening, ready for happier emotional climes to return. Although our card takes a different visual tack, it is still obvious that the choice is before us, whether to dissolve and diverge, or embrace and unite.

When the Three of Swords is upright, compassion towards the self and others needs to be the major component of your response to current events. No matter how loaded or provocative the moment feels, try to forego allowing the ideal to become an enemy of the real. Resist perfectionism. Remember that the upright card connects with Venus in her Exaltation (Pisces). This is an emotionally saturated, deeply subjective position for Venus, who finds her normal grounding in the Air and Earth signs. Whatever she can express from this inundated state might at first seem sketchy, indistinct, and merely suggestive. Do not press her to quantify her feelings prematurely, and she'll reliably call forth pearls of wisdom from her depths. Mercury's influence upon these degrees will help her to find her words.

Another positive message of this card, however it falls, is to cease defending against the fear of loss. Instead, determine what is worth fighting for, and you will have already dispelled quite a bit of the confusion. Answer the hard questions within yourself instead of waiting to see what others will say or do. If all else fails, letting go and letting God (as the saying goes) might be just the ticket right now.

Sometimes questioning the givens upsets the very forces that have held our frozen emotions in their threatening postures. Too often people will maintain a loaded, critical, negative climate for years rather than confront the situation and discharge the energy. Dare to redefine the current arrangement in a way that sets you free from fear, even though there would likely be a sacrifice involved. Negative bindings to the past will relax when you untie the knots of co-dependence and release all participants to their own recognizance, including yourself.

This card is often seen as the "divorce" card, so let's address those issues directly. In these final degrees of Libra, up against the cusp of Scorpio, one has to accept the fact that not every relationship (partnership, friendship, team effort) possesses longevity. Once a bond has manifestly worn thin (for whatever reason), participants need to rethink their agreements and draw new boundaries for their own emotional well-being. After all, what remains after the base premises have changed? Eventually we come to terms with reality even if that results in separation. Reversed, the Three of Swords says to cut your losses. There is less to lose from letting go than there is to be saved by holding on. It is never pleasant or pain-free to terminate empty emotional attachments we might still be clinging to. But life is change, and it's time to clear the way for the future. Win free of any leftover but expired identities. Release yourself to go forward untrammeled and re-integrated, in possession of an undivided heart.

There is no threat of death with the Three of Swords, although clearly our self-definition is disputed. It is the dream that is dying, and this arouses primordial emotions that might never show themselves at any other time. A Three of Swords period provides a perfect time to undergo analysis, whether with the help of a trained professional, or by undertaking a "fearless moral inventory." Don't be afraid to ask for help in reaching for a new self-description. In the case where a relationship change has the power to undermine one's identity or degrade one's character, it's clearly time to be alone for a while, if only for the safety and well-being of the innocents on the sidelines.

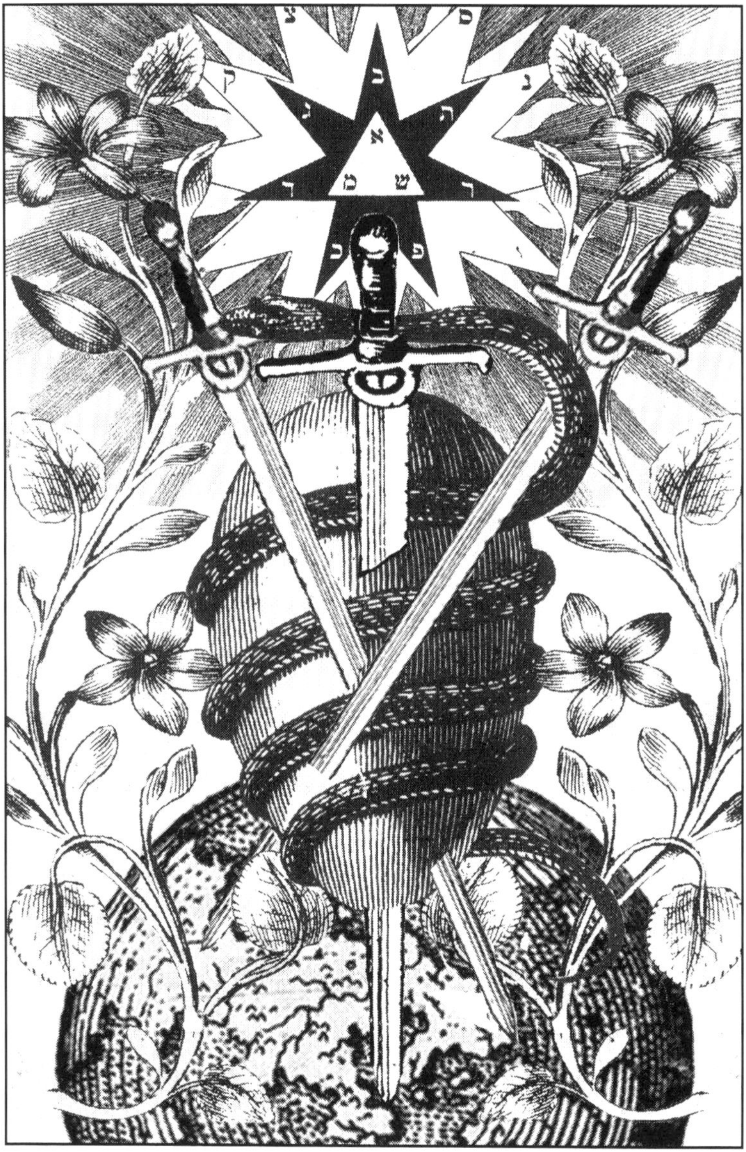

The egg at the middle of this card offers a subtle third option should the circumstances allow. The serpent-wrapped egg illustrates the mystery of our soul's individuality, that unique and indivisible frequency that identifies you to God separate from all others. This magical vessel is your infinite wellspring of inexhaustible potential. Envision this egg as a bubble flowing forever through the quantum foam, your soul embraced by its own Eternity, living out the Divine Imagination untrammeled across all Space and Time. Despite the moment's circumstances, nobody can take that away from you.

When we know our true purpose, our mission, and prime motive, this self-knowledge has the power to dissolve our old boundaries and release us into a multidimensional world of possibilities. First we must outgrow the thinking patterns pressed upon us by a past that has frozen around us. This sets us free to de-constellate our private reality from any preconceived pattern. The instant we can do that, we become aware of a veritable spectrum of insights and options beyond the pre-programmed zero-sum games of the past. The symbol of the egg invites us to contemplate our issues and resolve our problems through adjusting the balances in our inner psychic life. We can name and remove those piercing Swords through our own efforts; we don't need anybody else's permission or assistance. Freed up from waiting for others to get onboard, we can institute our self-administered adjustments and then learn how to live within them. There is great strength to be had from no longer relying on consensus with others before we authorize ourselves to be what we are and know what we know. Take back your power and invite others to do the same.

Four of Swords

Astrology: 11 - 20 Aquarius, ruled by Mercury **Sephira:** Chesed
Essential Dignity: upright Compliment, Saturn in Cancer
reversed Detriment, Saturn in Leo
Angelic Dignities: upright angel spelled SAL, spoken Sehaliah
reversed angel spelled ORI, spoken Ariel

In the tradition of the illustrated Tarot packs, the Four of Swords confronts us with a somewhat shocking image. A beautiful young person is laid out on a bier in the family sepulcher as if to join the ancestors in the sleep of Eternity. We can't know whether this person is actually dead or only lost in deep meditation. S/he could be hovering between life and death in a medical coma, or engaged in a shamanic journey far away from the surface plane of worldly action. The *Tarot of the Holy Light* version confronts us with the even more startling form of the Hermetic Androgyne, signifying the immortal soul decanted from its material support and freed from the imbalances pressed upon it by incarnation. One is at the stage in the alchemical work when the energy of the ego must be banished from the operation. Only then can the soul's acquired qualities break down into their constituent parts and reform again freshly. This experience re-acquaints us with our distilled essential nature, unobstructed by the distractions of circumstance. By discarding every level of externality, every quality, every identification, one is finally alone with "the face you had before you were born." Backing out of Time to touch the lineage-stream, one gains perspective on this life that no other exercise can grant.

The Four of Swords bids us to surrender worldly concerns and retreat to a place of serenity sheltered from the daily grind. It is time to contemplate your mortality, even to the point of breathing in the dust of those whose labors made this incarnation possible for you. Too often people look at life as if it only started when "I" was born and will be utterly obliterated when "I" die. This type of thinking is clearly too small to understand the full significance of the human experience. The Four of Swords appears when it's time to deconstruct the illusion of the self. What remains when the outer shell is completely dissolved? What finally belongs to the soul made naked of this vesture of history?

On this pilgrimage to your ultimate center, led by Mercury who rules these degrees of Aquarius, you can reinterpret and rearrange your roots, potentially liberating fresh energies and refining your goals for this life. Here your true place in the flow of Time and the unfolding generations becomes visible. Quieting the heart and mind also allows that "still small voice within" to become central in consciousness. We learn to temporarily stop Time and depersonalize our perspective, becoming the fly on the wall in our story of the self. The prayer of the meditator in the Four of Swords is, "Let me cooperate with all the good things that flow to me from the souls whose labors brought me here. May I stop fighting my essential nature."

The dance of detachment is a favorite endeavor for those with strong influences in Aquarius, the Air sign of the philosopher. When the card falls upright, Saturn makes outreach to his mate and Compliment (Moon in Cancer). The nurturance and emotional closeness of Cancer (the womb, the nest, the maternal embrace) is refreshing for cold, dry Saturn, but he doesn't want to live there all the time. The realm of Cancer has from antiquity been considered the chamber leading into and out of incarnation: the womb at birth and the tomb at death. Meanwhile, her mate Saturn is the karma-lord, the ring-pass-not, and the Watcher at the Threshold. He controls the crowd of souls moving into and out of incarnation. His firm oversight ensures that the Four of Swords seldom operates as a mini-Death card, although it takes us right to the edge of total detachment, allowing us to fathom the issues.

When reversed, Saturn visits Aquarius' Detriment in Leo; here it can be more difficult to acquire this lesson. The ego is more directly involved, which leads to greater denial and resistance. It becomes more likely that we will find ourselves wrestling with the proverbial demon/angel through a long, dark night of the soul. In antiquity people sought out a period of incubation, being enclosed in a chamber or cave for days to work through a psychedelic experience. The reversed Four of Swords indicates an element of force or necessity that imposes such a period of isolation. It could come courtesy of a physical, emotional, or psychological breakdown. One can feel dead to the world, stripped of motivation, stripped of all reason for living. One has "hit the wall," so to speak. There can also be despair and grief, at least until the individual has contacted the bedrock of his or her being

The alchemical backdrop of this deck provides us with the "astral medicines" of the doctrine of Essential Dignities. In the case of the Four of Swords, the fused opposites on the plinth represent the mated guardians of the descending arc of the winter/spring signs. This is the "Wet Way" or path of evolution through the soul's descent and dissolution into matter. This card raises the gnostic idea that the body is the tomb of the soul.

The question being demanded on the appearance of this card reversed is, "What is the true reason I came into this incarnation?" Without having an answer to this question, all of our human adventures seem vain, superficial,

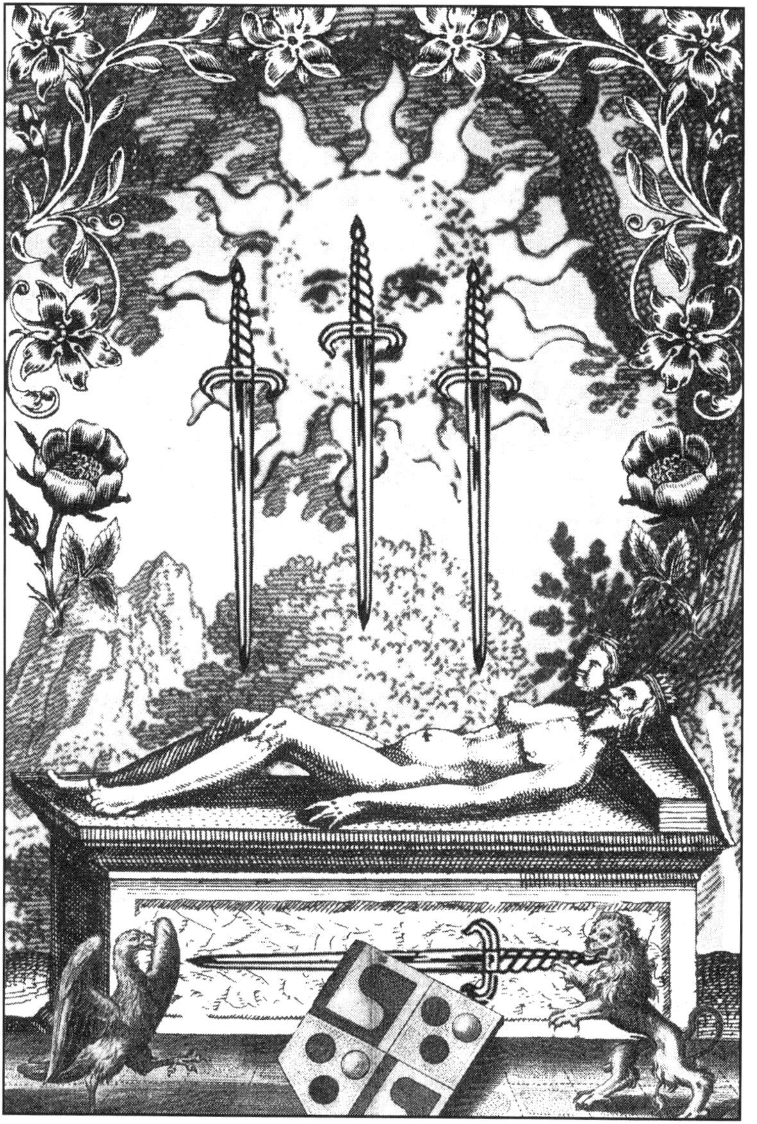

useless, repetitive, and idiotic. Much of our daily human experience can feel unworthy of a creature "made in the image of God," so why did we bother? How can we reconnect with the attraction and passion that first drove our will to embodiment? Those who have lost direct contact with their central motive can become disaffected, depressed, lethargic, and hollow, only barely in touch with the pleasures of life. Until the work of unearthing the prime motive is complete, nothing in the external world will make any sense.

The entire Four of Swords experience provides an effective counter to self-centeredness. In the Ace we feel our unbroken pre-manifestation wholeness that forms our link to the Divine Mind, the Monad. Then we begin to divide the world into self/non-self so that we can specialize on some selected and preferred portion of the whole. Unfortunately, that makes us polarize with the rejected quotient, which transforms us into a house divided against ourselves (Two of Swords). With the split comes a new awareness of loss and incompleteness, awakening us to the suffering that attends upon separation (Three of Swords). Finally, in the Four of Swords we get wise to ourselves if we are lucky. Here we reassemble our fragmented ego-construct via a model that is more inclusive and broadminded.

Five of Swords

Astrology: 21 - 30 Aquarius, ruled by Venus **Sephira:** Gevurah
Essential Dignity: upright Exaltation, Saturn in Libra
reversed Fall, Saturn in Aries
Angelic Dignities: upright angel spelled OShl, spoken Asaliah
reversed angel spelled MIH, spoken Mihael

The number Five marks the boundary between the personal world and the public world. Here opposite sides of a single nature are struggling for supremacy. Ouroboros, the worm of Time, encircles the field on which the opposites contend. Broken and unbroken swords are silhouetted against a fiery shape that shimmers with astral information. The warning color is here to remind us not to get too swept up in the moment's action; this is just a skirmish in a much larger struggle. Pause and think. There is no need to aim for the kill, but only the necessity of establishing a pecking order amidst contending priorities.

There is also no need to imagine that the dark and light colored eagles are mortal adversaries merely because we catch them in a moment of dominance/submission. It is just as accurate to view these scuffling birds as siblings, spouses, or partners working on a mutual project, caught in the act of hashing out their responses to each other's positions. Once they have set rules for their engagement, which each one is honor-bound to observe, then the agreement is "may the best man (idea, path, method) win." Within the circle of mutual agreement held open by Ouroboros, the two can try out their newest moves and develop their skills by playing off each other. Like sparring martial artists or acrobats throwing and catching each other, they become stronger even as they push each other beyond their previous limits.

When the card falls upright, the two actors have a strong and balanced (Libra) bond between them, which has a moderating effect on their individual ferocity and competitiveness. Saturn exalted in Libra boosts fair play and a level playing field, a situation that fosters everybody's growth and learning. Certain lessons can only come from getting in the ring and fighting it out with a partner who is a worthy adversary. One accepts in advance that both parties will take a drubbing in the contest, and the lesser contender will suffer defeat. After all, it's the aversion to being bested that raises our motivation to overtop our limitations. The people who will engage with us and administer our lessons are to be thanked for their service to our learning.

Historically, the Five of Swords usually carries an image that fits with the retrograde implication of this card: the grim and sobering process of cleaning up the battlefield after a rout, after Saturn's men have trounced the forces of the ambitious and scrappy Mars. The overall conflict has not yet been won or lost, but in this skirmish there were grievous setbacks for the side that the ego is tempted to identify with. There is need to regroup and rethink the game plan to discover the blind spots that allowed this setback to happen. The degree of the loss admonishes the weaker hand to analyze what went wrong, so a new strategy can be devised and further shocks of this type forestalled. Once the faulty thinking that gave the victor the upper hand is corrected, the contestants can return to the field for another round.

Further examination of the Five of Swords reversed shows the situation when Saturn's disciplinarian influence is at its ultimate weakest: in Aries, the sign of his Fall. Participants at this point are stressed, annoyed, or otherwise tempted to violate accepted norms, to indulge in illegal and unfair maneuvers. This is never a good thing, but Spirit has its compensatory strategies nevertheless. The violet color behind the Ouroboros serpent (which shows at the top when this card is reversed) reminds us of this fact: In every battle that contributes to human evolution, no matter what the visible outcome, Spirit always notches the win. Any person who snatches a victory by illegal means carries the mark of a loser in his or her aura forever after.

This image highlights the very fine line separating a card's upright meaning from its reversed meaning. When reversed, the two eagles feel locked into a win/lose situation, failing to envision a way to split the difference. The psychological inflation of Exaltation flatters the dominator with the aura of a culture-hero (Saturn in Libra), while defeat pushes the fallen contender out of collective favor (Saturn in Aries). Even worse, when two sides of the same person spar for supremacy, any seeming victory is only temporary. Nothing is ultimately resolved; this fight will be re-staged again and again in different circumstances. Exaggerated opposites are reluctant to allow their differences to settle. The worldview of both halves depends upon staying polarized without thought of peaceful coexistence. In the Fixed sign of Aquarius, the needed awakening could be a long time coming.

In a search for neutral examples of the Five of Swords, one could analogize the natural force exemplified by this card to a cyclone forming at the margin where two weather masses meet. It is now whipping up a funnel cloud and chewing up the landscape in the process. In psychological terms those who fail to discipline their minds are now going in too many directions at once, getting nothing done and making an increasing mess in the process. This card

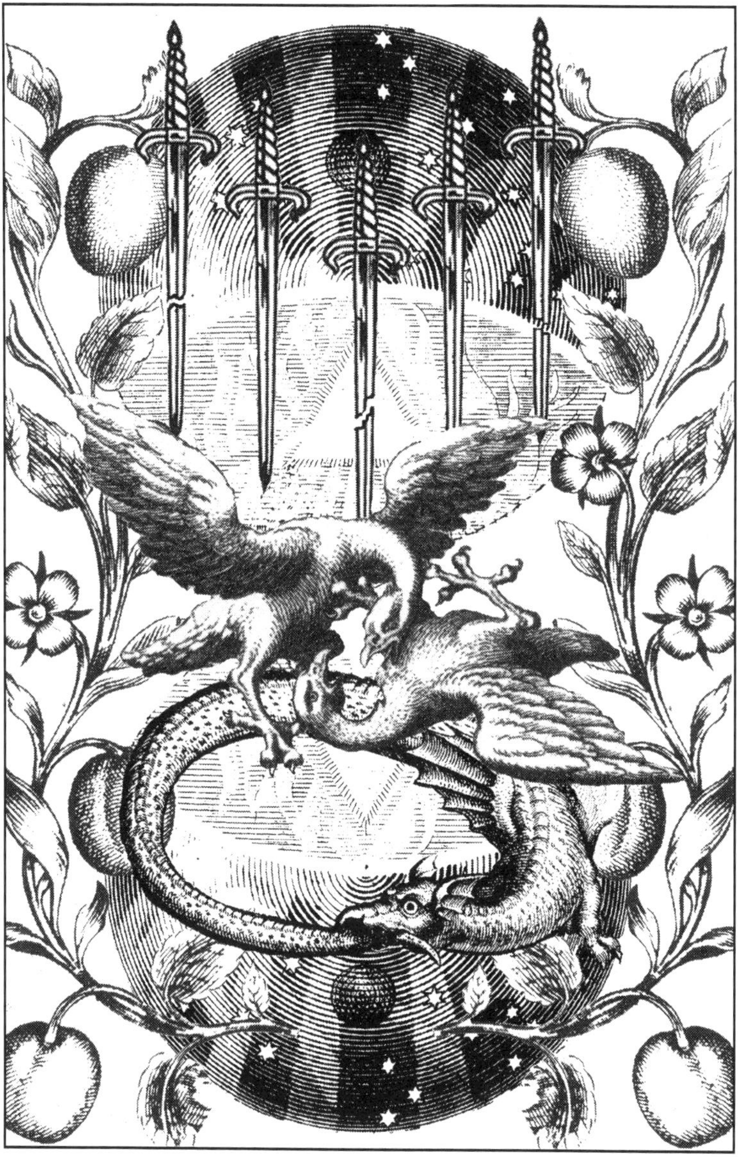

is reaching the point of maximum internal fragmentation and dismemberment just before something either explodes or expires. In fact, the Five of Swords reversed describes the highest level of chaos that is tolerable before one starts arbitrarily imposing order, no matter what the consequences. This Five defines one's tolerance point beyond which one simply will not go willingly. The mind starts turning back on itself, attacking the beliefs that got it into this situation. By whipping itself into this frenzy, it hopes to raise enough adrenaline to break the confusion, cut cords with the old world-view, and impose a change by force; this is a form of self-conversion by the Sword. Similarly, the body stages a fever in hopes of cooking out any germs or viruses that are trying to take hold. Our main work, then, is to just survive this Five without flying into a million pieces and without hacking anybody up or making anybody wrong because we feel so fragmented and overwhelmed inside.

At the collective level this battle is more often fought with words, laws, and contracts rather than conventional weapons. This gives us yet another arena in which our approach, style, strengths, and weaknesses are under examination and exposed to harassment. Those who cannot bear up under this kind of pressure will be forced to cede the field. If our Achilles' heel lies in the area of underdeveloped communication skills, loss of objectivity in tense moments, or unexamined blaming and self-excusing, then our ability to reach our goals and dreams will suffer endless setbacks.

Six of Swords

Astrology: 1 - 10 Aquarius, ruled by Saturn   **Sephira:** Tiferet
Essential Dignity: upright Domicile, Saturn in Aquarius
reversed Similar, Saturn in Capricorn
Angelic Dignities: upright angel spelled VVL, spoken Veuliah
reversed angel spelled YLH, spoken Yelahiah VVL, Spoken Name: Veuliah
Reversed angel—Holy Letters: YLH, Spoken Name: Yelahiah

The Six of Swords has long been associated with science and its objective methodology. Fundamental rules of science have been refined through the generations to sift fact from superstition, forging trustworthy convictions that we feel safe enough to build our lives upon. A classic name for this card is "The Navigator," referring to one who knew the calculations necessary to find a course across trackless oceans and vast deserts. This science kept commerce and the ecclesiastical calendar going, as tabulated by the Babylonians and inherited by Western civilization through the Hermetic Cosmos model. The relations between the fixed stars and moving planets are what inform the navigator where he stands upon the Earth.

Whoever draws this card is typified as having special knowledge. Literacy and numeracy grant an insight into sophisticated technologies powerful enough to change the course of human events. Related titles common to this card are "The Path" (out of danger) and "The Way Through." The popular image of the boatman ferrying a woman and her children away from a turbulent shore suggests that it is time to gather the seeds of the future and go in search of higher, healthier ground to occupy.

Part of the mystery of this card is the issue of waiting for the tide. The Navigator doesn't merely watch the heavens, he also knows the rhythms by which Earth responds to celestial events. In this image our passage out of the cove and into open water is only safe some of the time: when the tides are at their peak and just about to turn. We must craft our plans with Nature's ways firmly in mind. Only then can we follow the wind and the dove who plays in it. Let Spirit lead the way through the blind spots of our old worldview so we can set our new course by the Lights of Heaven.

This whole scenario calls forth a benign and progressive masculine energy that is in service to the Heart and to family values. Water in its ebb and flow is a classic symbol of the Divine Feminine. The little ship's captain is an appropriate male role model, as opposed to those who are creating the danger and turbulence that spoils life on the shore. Like Noah, our Navigator realizes the time has come to preserve the arts and sciences (the "children" of civilization) by leaving the dominance hierarchy behind. He rallies those who can hear his call to grab the babies and run for the docks.

In terms of the history of human culture, our link to the stars is the most precious and useful knowledge that humanity possesses. This is why the Navigator has left all that cultural contention and competition behind; it no longer holds his interest. What does interest him is saving the innocents from being trampled or abused while the contenders rip and slash at each other. The vulnerable ones are being removed from the patriarchal context, at least for as long as the warrior mentality evaluates everything in relation to its testosterone level and primate dominance hierarchy. While the town fathers are busy "bombing the village in order to save it," the Navigator steals away with everything of true value. After the fray dies down and the supposed winners start looking to collect their booty and chattel, it will be revealed that even the winners have made themselves into losers, repelling the very "goods" they came to seize by force.

Like the Pied Piper or Kokopelli, our upright Navigator is a visionary who sees the future because he has an ephemeris to consult. He also has a wide enough view of the world to understand that if we want a different future, we have to stop fighting over the same shortsighted me-first nonsense. Like Moses or any other authentic leader, the Navigator takes it upon himself to relocate to higher ground all those who are not fatally infected with divisiveness. History testifies that the science being referred to in the traditional title is actually the ancient goal proffered by the Wisdom Tradition: the hard-won accomplishment of a rational society governed by the principles of moderation, which lives in harmony with Nature. Humanity struggles to recover from our fight-or-flight biological trance, but this is only done from the inside out and only after a wide range of contrasting experiences has been collected.

Eventually, the observant human comes to understand that conditions aren't either automatically hostile or paradoxically random. There are predictable features like tide and wind that can either help or hinder, depending on how one relates to them. Over time the basics of the natural process reveal themselves, and one gets a feel for the cycle one is embedded in. There are laws governing Nature (ruled by Saturn), though it might take some time and effort for modern seekers to unwrap themselves from their sticky cultural programming enough to rediscover their own natural self-guidance system within the astrological matrix. We must re-learn what every aborigine possesses as a birthright, that we are creatures of Nature first and culture second. After that we

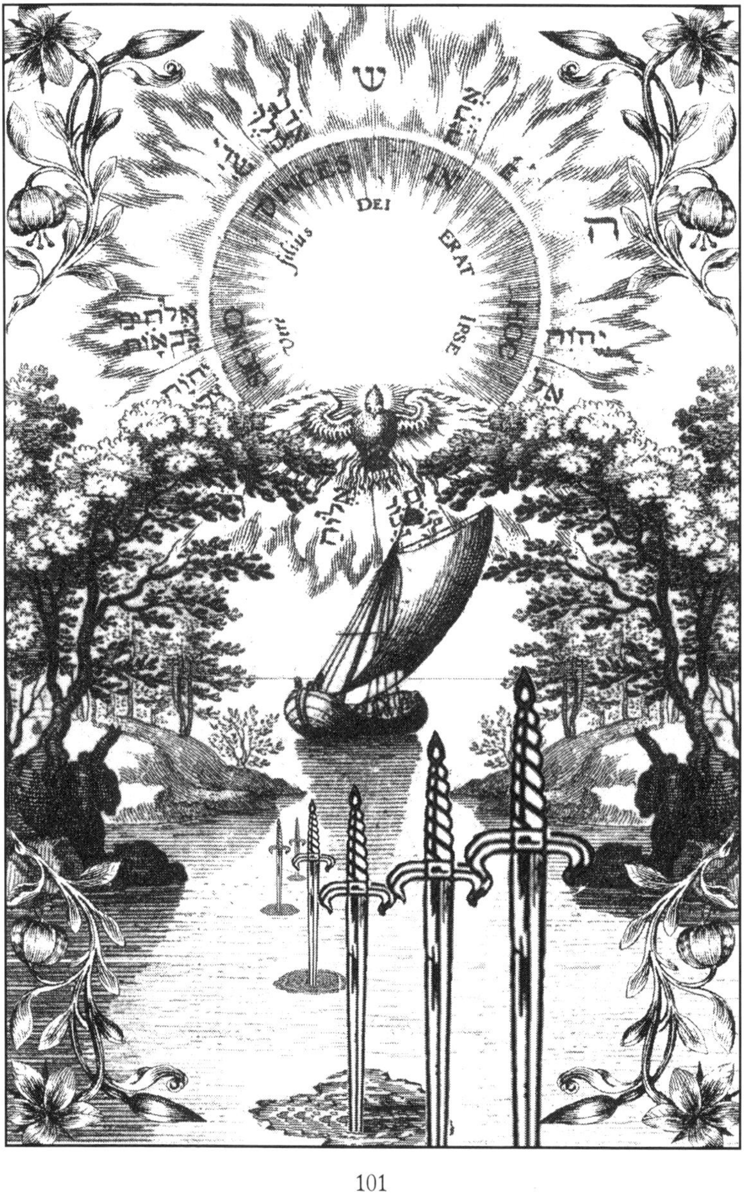
DEI
ERAT
IPSE
filius

can take our place under the guiding sky and move freely, both in mind and through the world.

The reversal offers a different range of ways to read this image. Our Navigator now must face conditions requiring the qualities of a practical here/now Capricorn rather than an Aquarian philosopher and futurist. I like the idea that in reversal the dove and the Swords might be leading the little boat *into* a protected harbor under the sun. But in other cases it's possible to feel as if the tide is going against you. This little notch in the coastline might be too exposed to wicked winds or tricky underwater hazards to allow access or exit during less than perfect circumstances. Think again before leaving safe harbor under current conditions. In such a situation discretion remains the better part of valor.

An even greater danger in case of the retrograde science card would be that peculiar type of superstition that holds science and tradition away from each other as if they were adversaries. In truth a creative synthesis of ancient wisdom and advanced science will be required to rescue humanity from its current predicament. Finding one's orientation amidst the modern information overload bombarding us from all directions can be exhausting. One might start by learning the natural laws exploited by our low-tech ancestors as they solved their daily survival problems. Becoming informed about the tried-and-true methods that kept our predecessors safe, healthy, and strong allows us to evaluate modern "advancements" against the only standard that matters, that of sustainability and respect for all life.

Seven of Swords

Astrology: 11 - 20 Gemini, ruled by Venus   **Sephira:** Netzach
Essential Dignity: upright Compliment, Mercury in Pisces
reversed Detriment, Mercury in Sagittarius
Angelic Dignities: upright angel spelled HChSh, spoken Hahasiah
reversed angel spelled OMM, spoken Imamiah

The Seven of Swords is the card of mental preparedness acquired through the use of imagination. This involves rehearsing and visualizing one's desired achievements in advance. People referred to by this card have active imaginations that support their confidence. The mature Gemini will catalogue the full spectrum of possible options before defining a course of action. He or she doesn't judge the plan by standards of social good or evil, but according to what acts will secure the goal. A combinatory wheel hanging in the heavens reveals the odds of success to the analytical Right Eye (top of the Mother Pillar). Through careful analysis a plan will be hatched that grants "our side" a boost towards the victory.

In the foreground of the card, Gemini's fox, that "clever dog" (a symbol for Hermes) steals the show. His crafty mind for finding advantage positions him perfectly to snatch the vulnerable hen and make away with her despite aggressive resistance from her rooster. If called to account, fox will testify in full sincerity that his motive for the heist was a true and deathless love of chickens, testified sincerely from the Venus-ruled segment of Gemini. The audacity of the Gemini mind is breathtaking; it can rationalize any act that will narrow the distance between itself and its desire.

When this card falls upright, we are justly proud of ourselves for seeing and exploiting angles that others in our situation don't notice. We search for openings that will shortcut the cost, time, or labor required to supply our needs; and when we succeed, our culture tells us we are "winners." Under the circumstance, then, is it really fair to brand the fox as a poacher for raiding the henhouse? He's only showing us a more efficient way to hunt, after all. This same behavior (fishing in a competitor's pool of customers) is considered a recipe for success in the business world, for example. It might be time to ask yourself whether an internalized, unquestioned prejudice against "taking advantage" is undermining your native ability to advance your cause right now.

This is a microcosm of the conundrum that humanity labors under. Survival in wild Nature involves accepting all invitations to thrive and succeed. What one can capture and eat, one does capture and eat, across the food chain. No animal in all of Creation feels guilty for finding dinner; that way lies madness. This is a peculiarly human neurosis. We have grown such a huge forebrain that now we are doomed to overanalyze and second-guess our every move forever. On the plus side this novel quality gives us a conscience, which is our major civilizing influence. But on the negative side we are now expected to repress some of the more successful attributes of our top-predator status.

Behaving in a civilized manner cuts down on our purely instinctive fulfillments. This can be a good thing, but sometimes it seems regrettable and depressing. A lot depends on how we use our native wits in pursuit of our day-to-day survival. Generally, anticipation is the solution to every Seven of Swords challenge; plan your work and work your plan. Those who proceed by this method will acquire such a thorough grasp of their overall situation that there will be fewer surprises, therefore fewer excuses to have any outcome but success. Prior planning justifies the optimism of the natural born winner, and it also helps to cover the tracks of the "fox in the henhouse." Fate is neutral on this count.

An oft-associated image for this card shows a canny warrior infiltrating the enemy camp on the eve of a fateful battle. In the course of investigating the adversary's preparations, our scout steals the generals' swords. This move will demoralize the whole army and undermine their performance in the coming confrontation. By taking advantage of the adversary's blind spots, the scout provides his team with a much-needed boost that could tip the battle in their favor. This portrayal assumes some kind of survival struggle in process. We could be looking in on the spiritual struggle of a shaman engaged in soul retrieval. Alternately this could represent the fight for life of a person in the grips of a devastating illness. It could be a challenge to the individual will, as when trying to conquer the animal appetites and/or steal addiction's thunder. The stakes are always high with the Seven of Swords.

With this card we are being tested on our capacity to create our own reality. Standard activities for the Seven of Swords include list making, mapmaking, self-organization, research, and pattern recognition. Everybody fantasizes, but without organized and systematic overview, mastery eludes us. Address your issues pragmatically without recourse to shame or blame. When the card is upright, Mercury in Pisces reminds us that the fox is innocent despite his predatory urges. Neither the death of the chicken nor that of the fox should be necessary to motivate the farmer to mend his fences. Think like a fox while

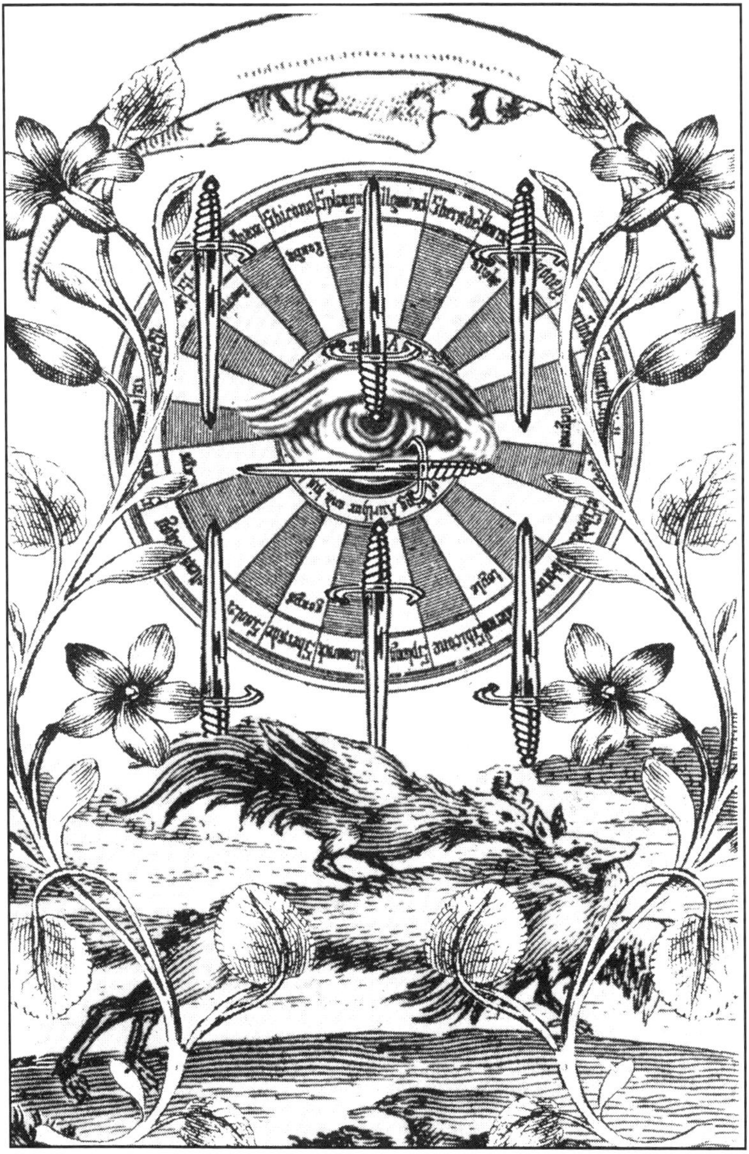

building your henhouse, and peace will prevail on your little acre. As a bonus, you won't have made an enemy out of any creature in Creation. This ounce of prevention will indeed save you a pound of cure.

The reversed meaning of this card is inherent in the upright image. To the chicken the fox's achievement is nothing to celebrate. Those who use their natural advantages to position themselves against the best interests of others are routinely denounced as predators, and rightly so. It is important not to judge others too harshly because "there but for fortune go you or I." Part of helping others be trustworthy involves practicing accountability and banishing ambiguity all through our own lives (Mercury in Sagittarius). The fewer grey areas we leave unexamined, the less leverage is given to our blind spot, whether that's our inner "evil twin" or the predictable predator indigenous to our environment. Ultimately, until we can elevate our own foxy nature, our personal limit-pusher and advantage-taker, we have little grounds to complain about these same qualities in others.

The important thing to take from this card is to consult your conscience even as you strive to deploy your natural and acquired powers to your best advantage. Any achievement we might otherwise win will be tainted if we haven't addressed our double-mindedness in advance. The seasoned warrior goes over every square inch of the battleground, literally and metaphorically, working out a solution to every possible setback the terrain might offer. Develop the habit of being fiercely accountable. Look straight at your situation, set boundaries for your goals, accept any ego-losses that come from making this fearless moral inventory, then adjust your course going forward. Take personal responsibility for your fate, doing your own research and questioning all your assumptions. People who practice a long-term view of life have already learned that we submit to self-discipline in the short run so the future can arrive according to plan instead of by accident.

Eight of Swords

Astrology: 21 - 30 Gemini, ruled by Saturn **Sephira:** Hod
Essential Dignity: upright Exaltation, Mercury in Virgo
reversed Fall, Mercury in Pisces
Angelic Dignities: upright angel spelled NNA, spoken Nanael
Reversed angel spelled NITh, spoken Nithael

The Eight of Swords is often called "The Test," and it usually pictures a warrior running a gauntlet, subjected to harsh examination that might even verge on torture. He finds out just what he (or she) is made of in the process. Life provides us with plenty of situations where we will be subject to close scrutiny, such as an entrance exam for college, a decisive job interview, or the tough conversations that follow upon a breach of trust in a primary relationship. Sometimes the challenge or obstacle course has nothing to do with other people, as when an inventor has to face the ultimate pass/fail question: "Does it really work?" This card shows what happens to one's good idea in real time when the rubber finally meets the road.

Our Eight of Swords is simple and traditional, though with an optimistic and a pessimistic side built in. When it falls sunny-side-up, you are likely to pass this test with flying colors. Your mind, will, and instincts will harmonize as you navigate the maze before you. A blend of confidence and excitement carries you through in record time. Your performance wins high marks, granting you an improved reputation. This is your chance to excel in a situation that has deliberately been made very difficult. The stakes are high, as is the drama quotient. It's too late in the numeric sequence to be able to make up lost ground now. Saturn demands that you simply have to excel and so you do.

When this card appears reversed, you are challenged to manage your emotions instead of dissolving into a subjective puddle under pressure. The bloody tip of one sword reminds us that this is not a rehearsal; now we are playing for keeps. When reversed, the severed branches of past labors are shoved away to either side, and the overturned Moon empties out its promise. It is not at all clear, when upside down, whether one will leave the scene in one piece or several. But whatever happens, a star continues to shine through the gloom, offering hope even in times of stress and setback. Never give up while breath still stirs the heart. Take the attitude of the intrepid inventor and go back to the drawing board over and over however many times it takes.

Another way to read this card would be to take the upright and reversed meanings as timing indicators. When the card is upright, this gauntlet will be run before the day is done; the sun will not set without revealing the outcome of your labors. Alternately, when the dark side of the card is upright and the Moon is upended, then there's a chance of anxious nights and high tension before this issue is laid to rest. We can only hope that the bloody Sword-tip indicates a merely ceremonial nick in one's hide, leaving a scar to prove that we actually survived the ordeal. On the other side of this initiation, you will be a "made man."

Beyond the level of binary thinking, the reversed Eight of Swords illustrates the paranoid mind-control entanglements that proliferate when hierarchical extremes create strict in-crowds and out-crowds. Such a worldview is framed in fearful terms abounding in rules, taboos, and proscriptions. People with this bias show intense control urges, being inclined to squelch all creativity and innovation. It doesn't matter what the organic situation actually calls for; the response will be overkill. Reversed, this card feels threatened and is therefore threatening. Organizations that foster this kind of climate are marked by sparse latitude for individual choices along with strict punishments for small infractions. Thus is revealed the manipulator and control-freak whose every human exchange offers another chance to project dominance and exact obedience.

Before suiting up in your heavy armor and running this gauntlet, why not pause a moment and ask, "Who benefits from maintaining this atmosphere of stress, anxiety, and punishing resistance?" Such a climate of in-your-face demand might be understandable in a situation like a boot camp, where soft young couch potatoes are being turned into warriors. There are also certain professions that cannot admit people who are overly sensitive because their empathic natures will be overwhelmed by the working conditions. But in most circumstances it is correct to question a cutthroat competitive ambiance when it appears in the workplace, around the family dinner table, or in the classroom. Nobody does his or her best work in an atmosphere of intimidation. People who can't modulate their intensity and fierceness, who can't control their fear and therefore spray it all over the environment, tend to damage whatever they get close to. Use your natural intelligence to help you discriminate between worthy challenges that will strengthen you, versus unworthy challenges that will drain you without granting any advantage in return.

Some might question whether there actually is a positive meaning for the Eight of Swords. A sentimental take on Gemini energies might be shocked at this treatment of the inner child. The Tarot generally doesn't speak much about the life of the young warrior beyond supplying a Page for every Knight.

Nevertheless, the astro-alchemical formula for this card makes it clear that evolution does not favor the psychologically immature. The average self-centered bodily ego is so attached to its theory of itself, to its comfort zone and its habitual catalogue of rationalizations, that it must be disciplined and challenged repeatedly if any spiritual progress is ever to be made. Either Mercury has to use his time in his home sign (which is also the sign of his Exaltation) to clean up his act and become fit for the fight, or Mercury's Fall into Pisces will reveal him as a weakling and a wimp, one who lacks the backbone to defend his own existence. Unfortunately, with the Eight of Swords there is very little middle ground.

Fully half of the alchemical stages encountered during the process of the Great Work challenge the seeker with being dismembered and dissolved by evolutionary "acids" supplied by circumstances. Only a soul that possesses the courage of its convictions will endure through this type of travail. One must be self-coherent enough to remain astrally integrated no matter what happens in the material plane. The key to this ordeal is to remember that this is not about persons or situations, self or other. This struggle is about gaining the psychological muscle to define your life in evolutionary terms. Additionally, one has to hold firm to one's principles no matter what, even in the face of annihilation. The warrior who understands the value of his or her unique mission wakes up every day thinking, "Today is a good day to die!" Once this all-or-nothing attitude is achieved, the true contender is unbeatable.

Nine of Swords

Astrology: 1 - 10 Gemini, ruled by Mercury **Sephira:** Yesod
Essential Dignities: upright Domicile, Mercury in Gemini
reversed Similar, Mercury in Virgo
Angelic Dignities: upright angel spelled VHV, spoken Vehuel
reversed angel spelled DNY, spoken Daniel

In the Nine of Swords, we see the dilemma of captive nobility, a creature of the empyrean held on a chain and bound to a chasm in the earth. Torturing nixies that live in the cleft taunt the eagle with its loss of freedom and power. Even the Sun itself seems to be imprisoned, pinned down by the plethora of Swords holding it back. The glancing light of a votive altar throws shadows around the primordial cave, but the eagle of the soul longs only for the open sky. A great yearning fills the soul: to release the wildness of the world and take wing from its purgatory of human exploitation.

The Nine of Swords has special resonance with the Middle Ages because it so often figures the plight of a woman who is alone in the world. During a time when women had precious few personal rights, with no ability to inherit property or use the law in their own defense, the families of fallen warriors were particularly at risk. We often see a noble lady sitting up in bed weeping and grieving in fear of abandonment because of her vulnerability. She wonders what will happen to her now that her protector (father, brother, husband, or son) is gone. The Swords above her head suggest family losses through warfare or similar cruel conflict, the outcome of which has left her behind as chattel, the spoils of war.

Another variation shows the woman in warrior's armor, now captured and bound by the enemy. As with Joan of Arc, her androgynous ardor has inspired passion for her cause, making her imprisonment a blow against her whole army's morale. Having fallen into enemy hands, she can expect exactly the treatment that she has been meting out to her enemies. Live by the sword, die by the sword.

One might ask why a card dedicated to Mercury and Gemini portrays such a painful dilemma. The answer is that Gemini is the first Air sign in the Zodiac sequence. As such it represents the archetypal moment when the soul's native wit and intelligence (Mercury) crashes up against the limitations of matter: this body, this ego, this gender, and all the peculiarities of one's unique Time/Space incarnation. The vast firmament of endless possibilities is proven to be limited, which Gemini discovers with outrage. This Mutable Air sign's restless, shape-shifty, boundary-testing nature will seethe and struggle against any and all limits, seeking the freedom it remembers from the time before birth.

What the Gemini intelligence rails against is this world's materialistic zero-sum thinking, which inhibits the free scope of the enquiring mind by imprisoning it in survival issues. Who knows how many geniuses we have lost from every generation through war and starvation? This image mutely protests the damage done to the higher faculties when a culture becomes so invested in domination that all of Nature groans under its chains. A sensitive, subtle, heartfelt approach to Mother Earth (the Divine Feminine) is trampled and thrown aside, replaced by a winner-take-all mentality. The eagle will never cease protesting against this violation of the soul's unique mandate to individuate freely.

Nevertheless, we must face the paradox that the captive is being treated exactly the way she or he would treat prisoners if the tables were turned. This prisoner is no more righteous or merciful than his or her captors. A rough justice prevails, and the predator is "hoist on his own petard." Mercury in Virgo brings the mind of the accountant into play. The result will require "eating our words" symbolically and literally. The boomerang of natural consequences delivers one's just desserts. Perhaps this raptor has been preying on innocents. We could be looking at someone who has been fattened upon the servitude of others, now finally forced into the same irons with which he bound his slaves. There is, after all, some karmic reason why it is this creature and not any other being punished. Make sure to study the situation fully before arriving at a judgment.

There is such a thing as losing by winning. People who can't control their dominance urges end up alone. The more effective an army is in their scorched-earth campaigns, the more they devastate the landscape that they sought to capture. The habit of feeling superior oppresses and crushes everything it contacts. Militaristic tolerance of collateral damage shows its wastefulness and lack of common sense. The paradox of a chained raptor or a captured Amazon portrays the essential denaturing that we all experience in modern culture. Our individuality is pruned down to what is convenient. Anybody with non-stereotypical presentation is made to regret his or her uniqueness. Such circumstances crush the feminine aspect of both women and men.

What hope there is comes from the fact that the eagle is still alive and still fights captivity. If it keeps up its wing strength and vigilance, there remains a slim strand of hope that its captors will, in a moment of inattention, allow it to slip free. Every day it flies as far as the chain allows and stays aloft until it drops

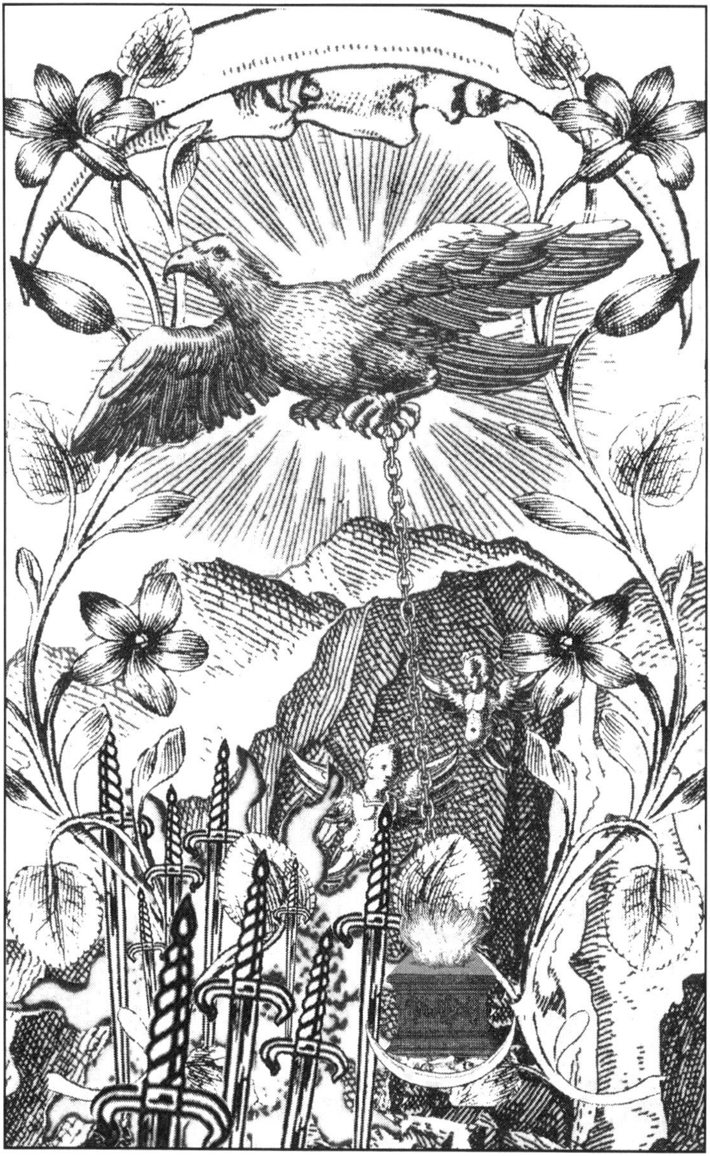

with exhaustion. The glimpses it gains of the open sky provide inspiration should a day come when it can seize its freedom again.

To the extent that one has harbored fantasies of superiority and victory, one empowers a system that inevitably creates masses of angry losers. Beyond the goal of the elevated ego stands a model of spiritual equality and dignity for all. Mature souls interpret the Nine of Swords reversed as an important lesson learned while doing penance, atoning for our sins of omission and commission. In the long empty stretches we review our losses, realizing that those losses came from ignoring the rest of the world as we made our self-serving calculations. Even in the most optimistic of Tarot packs, this can be a fairly bitter card.

The Nine of Swords can also illustrate the mortification of somebody who failed to pass an essential test. Depression is a daily temptation under these circumstances. This card also shows up when one person's focus is creating bitterness and frustration for another. This is the end result of the pure science model, void of sentiment, morality, and humanity, completely alienated from the inner life. One can interpret the Nine of Swords upright as the legal "thou shalt and thou shalt not" rules of society. However, the more a society is tied up in laws, the more repressive it becomes, even to the point of criminalizing natural behavior. Further, the reversal of such a situation drives the cost of that repression into the lives of society's most vulnerable members. In a society run by and for jailers, nobody escapes spending time in prison.

Ten of Swords

Astrology: Grand Trine in Air - Libra, Aquarius, Gemini
Sephira: Malkhut "Kingdom"

In the canon of the Tarot, the Ten of Swords is almost always an unmitigated disaster. We did not want to entirely abandon this traditional approach, but for *Tarot of the Holy Light* we chose to put the idea of disaster in a larger context. We want the user to see other aspects of the Ten of Swords idea beyond the shock value of facing a dead body in the road.

At the cosmic level the Sun dominates the Zodiac, driving Light into every corner of the universe. Sol's effulgence never ceases, and everything we Earth-dwellers do is ultimately driven by this donated vitality. But notice the falling tears dripping down through the cosmos like celestial dew. These beg the question: Why must we suffer, experience pain, endure lack and limitations if the Source is infinite and infinitely generous? This is the mystery of the winged teardrop we see hanging before the face of the Sun.

Even as the teardrop suffers and questions its suffering, a rainbow of Light emanates from the natural prism hidden at its heart. This prism unpacks the broad spectrum of knowledge, inspiration, and invention that is born from human stress and struggle. No soul would become self-conscious without some fixed limit to test itself against. In a free-will based universe like ours, one receives the unedited results of one's choices, for better or for worse. From this we learn what is evolutionary and what is devolutionary, at least for ourselves. There is no judgment coming down upon us from outside sources, but over time and experience we learn to follow the Light and shy away from the shadows, relatively speaking. No attempt is made to force us into one color band or another, since human experience embraces a rainbow of cultures and aspirations. The Light supports us all, wherever we find ourselves within the spectrum.

This idea brings to mind one of the favorite packs from my early years studying Tarot, the *Neuzeit Tarot* by Walter Wegmuller. The Little White Book, which very strongly colored my development in divination, gives this insight: "The ten swords rotate on a merry-go-round within the conscious mind, endowing each person with a specific character or abilities. Symbol of the battle of survival of the various professions. Caste consciousness" (1982, p. 29). Given that the Tens always summarize the full potential of their Suit, this makes perfect sense to me. Both the upright and reversed meanings circle around the struggle for self-definition in a dynamic and stratified environment. In the spirit of the rainbow issuing from the teardrop, it is revealed that between the Light and the darkness exists a spectrum of options to choose from, although there will be challenges and limitations inherent to any choice that is made. When we can remember to look to the rainbow, the Ten of Swords offers a layered landscape of opportunity wherein nearly everyone can find a niche. The key is to follow the Hermetic axiom and "Know thyself."

Taken against this backdrop, the traditional attitude towards the Ten of Swords represents closure and finality, saying, "It's over now. This is the end. Everything that is born must also die." As is easily seen from the cameo, there is no hope for revival here. The brilliant potential seen in the past has been sacrificed, a line has been crossed, and there is no rewriting this story. In some situations this may be felt as a tragic loss, but it often brings with it a paradoxical sense of release and completion. The waiting and wondering are over; there is no more ambiguity. You can rightly let go and move on because there is no further reason to maintain the old worldview.

This card appears reversed when one is exhausted and used up, at the end of the line emotionally. The energy for responding or trying to make a difference has been spent and possibly wasted. The sense of failure and ruination is palpable. When a person feels like the dark end of this card looks, being emotionally and psychologically dead to the world, they have reached burnout and must be excused. Someone in this state can no longer be held responsible for what is happening. They have nothing more to contribute to the action and therefore must be forgiven for caving in or ceding the fight. The simple instruction for the Ten of Swords reversed is, "You are released from the carcass of the past. Go no further down this road!"

But let us not be content with the divinatory level of meaning offered by the traditional Ten of Swords, especially when reversed. The existential crisis this card represents is truly an archetypal theme in human psychology. Spanning the gap between the individual and the universal scale, the eternal Light spreads its beauty and life force impartially through the entire Creation. Its eternal promise becomes even more poignant by its contrast with the crushing reality of individual death. In the light of our infinite potential, the pathos of being taken from life while still incomplete and unfinished is extreme. As the saying goes, everybody dies young.

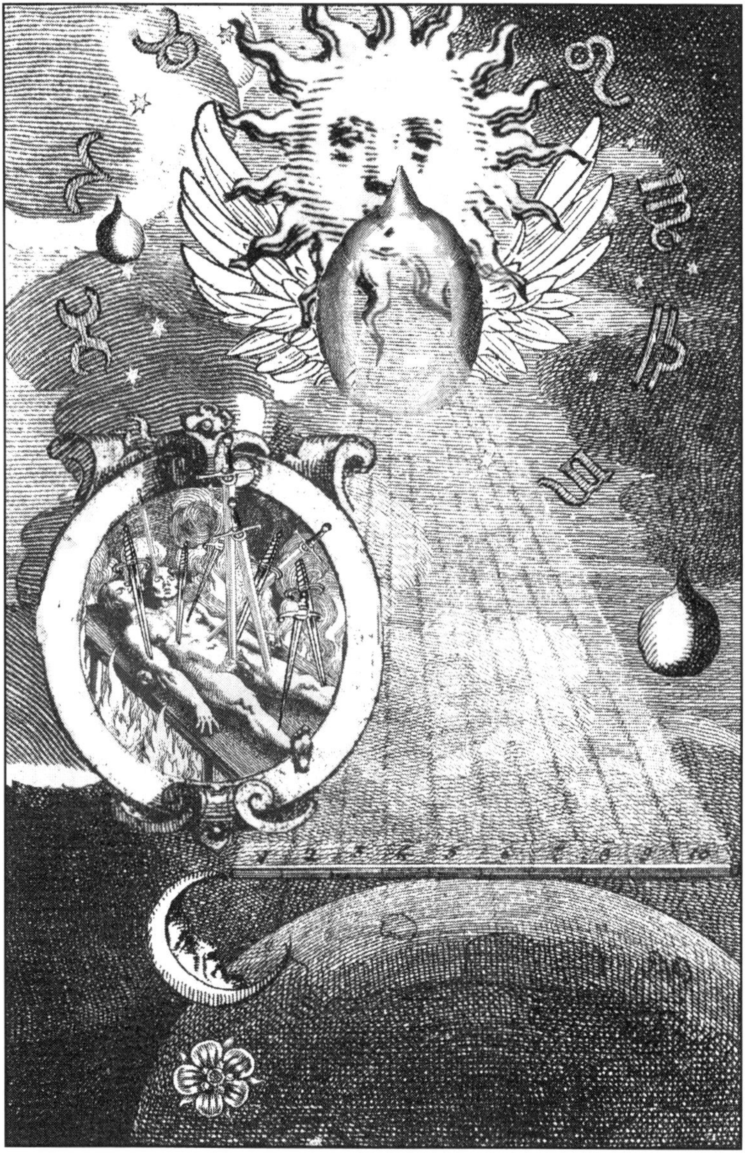

The scene in the cameo, where the Hermetic Androgyne lies pinned to its bier, arouses our culturally programmed anguish, disbelief, grief, and horror in the face of what feels like untimely endings. This moment of frozen tragedy testifies to another instance of irreparable loss. No matter who we are or where on the ladder of power and accomplishment we might stand, the Ten of Swords can find us and wipe us out before we are ready. Psychotherapists consider this fact the fundamental dilemma that every living soul wrestles with in the search for life's true meaning.

The question is what do you believe? Is this really the end of the line? Or will the Androgyne within you use this experience to re-constellate at a higher frequency in a new and improved form? If the soul remembers its origins in the invisible planes, then it knows no ground is lost no matter what is happening in the external world. That which is eternal never dies. Those who have lost their fear of death are functionally immortal, being immune from the belief that superficial changes have the power to interfere with their destinies. The more we rest our identifications in our permanent being, in our true and undimmed original Light, the fewer fears and inhibitions we will suffer through in our daily lives.

King of Swords
Aquarius

The King of Swords is the adjudicator, the wise judge, lawyer, and mediator. He helps parties in conflict discover common ground and build upon it. Over time his faithfulness guides societies to realize their greater good. His archetype is Solomon, ancient lawgiver and philosopher of the Hebrew Old Testament. Sometimes appearing cool and detached, he can be misunderstood as being uncaring. But emotional displays are simply not his medium, nor is he moved by appeals to sympathy or pity. With the philosophical overview that comes from long experience, this King listens deeply, watches closely, and speaks last. When his sword is turned against you, there will be no recourse.

Saturn's rulership of Aquarius makes this King the law-keeper among the Royals. These can be natural laws, social laws, psychological laws, or spiritual laws; he understands the basis and necessity of them all. The Wisdom Tradition of antiquity informs this King's current thinking. He takes the point of view of Eternity, even as he administers the civic courts and governing bodies. His philosophy is shaped by the cycles of the planets' orbits. He stays informed about the pulses playing out overhead, including the human functions that the Solar System governs here on Earth. He excels at devising tests that reveal people's innermost motives according to the scrutiny of conscience. This King's response to a given situation will depend upon the inner process of the protagonists. Hence he looks past surface details, understanding that the same act taken under different psychological circumstances will have different significances, demanding different strategies to accommodate or atone.

The King's piercing insight into human motivation allows him to be sensitive to unspoken ulterior motives and inherent contradictions. He accepts the burden of interpretation as one of his natural responsibilities. It is his role to assemble an overview and name the overriding principle that governs events. As the one who commissions and writes the history books, he has the final word in every case. Through codifying the stories of his people and drawing from the well of communal wisdom to form the laws, he creates a monument that will guide the children of the future.

Our Sword King takes an even-handed pose at the edge of a cloudy promontory. Representing the Fixed sign of the Air Trine, his Aquarius/Saturn nature defines the philosophical arena that embraces the Cardinal impulses of Libra/Venus and the Mutable impulses of Gemini/Mercury. The eagles from the Emperor card have raised the King's totem Swords to a place of perspective high above any personal tumult. The four winds bring him the news and perspective from the four corners of the Earth. A shield of the Element Air protects his aura and declares the Creative Word: *Fiat Monas*. His Air pentacle (and those of the other three Kings) comes from the title page of Mylius' *Opus medico-chymicum* (1622). It reads, according to Stanislas de Rolla, "By the conversion of Elements [and] the Threefold Purification let the One be made" (1988, image p. 134, text p. 150). Since the Elements are four and the modes are three, this reaffirms that our King is a master of the astro-alchemical paradigm, what Boehme called the "perfect clock of the Zodiac."

By this sign we know that the Sword King has mastered the techniques of astro-alpha-numeric magic, including use of the names of power that have come down to us from antiquity. This alchemist-King has fully fathomed the royal arts, having both an intellectual and operative grasp of Sacred Numerology, Astrology, Kabbalah, and the spiritual Alchemy derived from them.

When this card is upright, there is no need to question this King's analysis because as a practice he doesn't let opinion intrude into his calculations. His objectivity and experiential wisdom have earned him the respect he receives from his community; those who cannot work out their problems seek him out for answers. In family affairs he is the wise father, not necessarily sentimental or cuddly, but offering a model of rational thought and considered action that provides stable orientation within the vicissitudes of this world. Only the enemies of civilization and accountability need to fear him. Those who understand his role take refuge in his unfailing fairness and commitment to reality.

Clearly the King of Swords reversed can be devastating to justice in his territory. If he has the motive to favor one and undermine another, everybody suffers. With this King reversed, the spirit of the law pretends mercy, but the letter of the law is wicked. On his dark side this King is biased and hostile, critical and inequitable. What's worse is he can't be swayed from his arbitrary decisions, even by the lucid reasoning he displays when he's upright. He might also be taking unfair advantage of the situation, using insider information to consolidate his power and benefit the few against the many.

Remembering that Saturn rules Aquarius from the highest point in the descending arc of dissolution, there is the problem of alienation to address. From his cold remove, so far away from the heart-warming signs of summer, the Aquarian King can develop the habit of looking down on his subjects as his flock, herd, or beasts of burden. He might as well be an alien doing

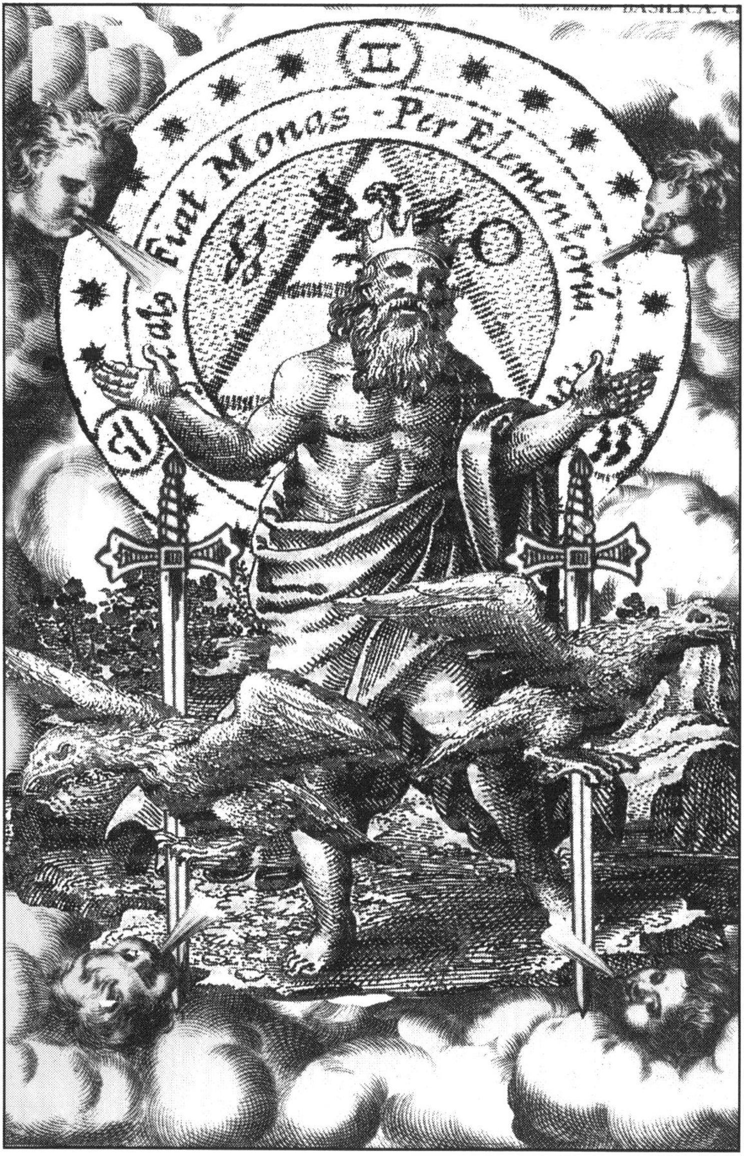
fiat Monas · Per Elementoru

experiments on the local flora and fauna. From this disconnected view he wants his subjects trained to bend their knees and obey him, but he doesn't extend himself to imagine what they might be feeling or what would satisfy their emotional needs. His fine grasp on the ins and outs of human psychology is instead devoted to the arts of manipulation and oppression.

For those who question how things come to this turn, we have to remember that the vast majority of humanity has difficulty bringing their consciousness to the fine and sharp point that the King of Swords is naturally able to achieve. His broad-ranging perspective literally has him seeing backward and forward through time. This gives him undue advantage over the other three-fourths of humanity, who are more gifted in the remaining Elements. The eagle testifies to his raptor methods: From his mile-high aerie, he can spot those specimens that need to be culled from the pack. Nothing escapes his prying eyes. If you are not one of the eagles, you can be sure you are part of the herd he is managing.

Most people live their lives utterly innocent of this King's effect on their world and environment. To maintain his anonymity, the reversed King of Swords is the propaganda boss, the dominator of the media, the schools, and the laws. In this way he builds prisons for his subjects' minds, which they then willingly subsidize under the misapprehension that they are being educated, informed, and/or entertained. While the King artificially limits their development and horizons at every juncture, his brainwashed people clamor for their diet of bread and circuses. Strongman politics and the old boy network are his specialty, leading all of his people to become enmeshed in his tentacles.

Queen of Swords
Libra

The Queen of Swords steps up with a fully developed attitude, showing the sophistication and appreciation for nuance that is natural to a worldly "woman of a certain age." History has not been kind to this Queen; traditionally she's been known as the widow, crone, or divorcee, the unwanted woman or the shrew. In myths and fairy tales she is the bent old lady whose cabin sits off in the woods away from the boundary of the village. Herbalist, witch, or shaman, she has psychic powers that scare people, yet her knowledge is sought out when the simpler folk remedies fail.

The Sword Queen has the temperament of a sharp thinker who controls her lifestyle so she can live into advanced old age with all of her wits still about her, perceptive and undaunted to the last. The things she is interested in are the verities: the undying truths discovered by the ancestors. These truths demand to be kept alive for the coming generations. She sometimes resembles a space traveler or a visitor from another time because she is essentially alone in a timeless bubble suspended in her mind's eye. Her studies keep her in mental communication with the ancient past. Because of this she can readily see the future forming up in the germ of the present.

People are sometimes spooked when this Queen looks deeply into them, because it seems she can dial directly into their DNA and bypass the ego entirely. In fact, her perceptiveness and probing intelligence tend to search out and awaken people's conscience. Suddenly strangers feel moved to confess themselves to her even when she hasn't actually asked. Therefore, only self-aware people who are internally consistent and possess integrity, those who walk their talk and show the refinement of long cultivation, can be truly comfortable with this Mistress of Swords. She may never mention it, but this Queen sees right through those convenient fictions that unconscious people use to pretend their way through life.

Nowadays we see the Sword Queen as a model of feminine self-sufficiency, independence, and high intellect. Of the four Queens she is the most often seen in armor or chain mail, suggesting that she doesn't back down easily once she takes a position. The Sword Queen has extremely high standards due to her subtle sensitivities, which can be perceived by those around her as being critical and hard to please. Her true motive is to refine the world, to upgrade people's understanding so everyone can have the space they need to individuate.

A wonderful example of the type is Hildegard of Bingen (1098 - 1179), who was from childhood a visionary mystic, and in adulthood was unanimously elected magistra of her Catholic order. A tireless advocate of increased independence for the nuns, she had to wage a spiritual battle with conservative Church forces for years before she was finally granted the right to move her convent to the location God had originally pointed out to her. Despite a lifetime of chronic neurological and bodily illnesses (Oliver Sachs has diagnosed her as a migraine sufferer, and she was most likely anorexic as well), Hildegard had a long, mystically fertile and creative life as an administrator, writer, visionary, healer, and spiritual mother. Her list of formal accomplishments is formidable by the standards of any century, and on the side, she was an herbalist, musician, and poet.

Every culture and time has its own response to intelligent and outspoken femininity. As a result this Queen is hailed as a heroine by some populations and calumniated as a wicked scourge by others. Even if we work hard to avoid negative clichés, the Sword Queen is not interested in conforming, which may be why she has a reputation in certain circles for being difficult. This Queen will ask the essential questions, and she doesn't care whose ox is gored in getting to the answer. She is too intelligent to be confined to the role of housewife or nursemaid, although she is perfectly competent in those areas when she wants to be. She is also canny and strategic, choosing her associations and her aloneness to serve her own agenda. She will seldom get caught up in dependency relationships, at least not for long. Her critical intelligence may not be entirely comfortable to be around, but she can be counted upon to see through superficialities and put her finger on the truth of the situation. One could say that she is a woman who can think like a man. Only the most developed souls of any gender can hold their own in conversation with her.

When reversed, this Queen's sharpness can be devastating. You do not want to make the thoughtless kind of errors that offend her sensibilities. Our inner child fears being scolded by this stern mother figure. The paradox is she can't be avoided because she's the psychologist of the Zodiac. She's already got us all figured out. The Sword Queen knows just what buttons to push to make us do what she's already programmed us to do; even our rebellion is factored into her calculations. In fact, her voice is that of our species conscience, the civilizing force that wrestles us all into becoming human. We might sometimes rue her name, but we still need her to remind us of our better selves and induce some kind of evolutionary change. If we were already self-aware and taking full

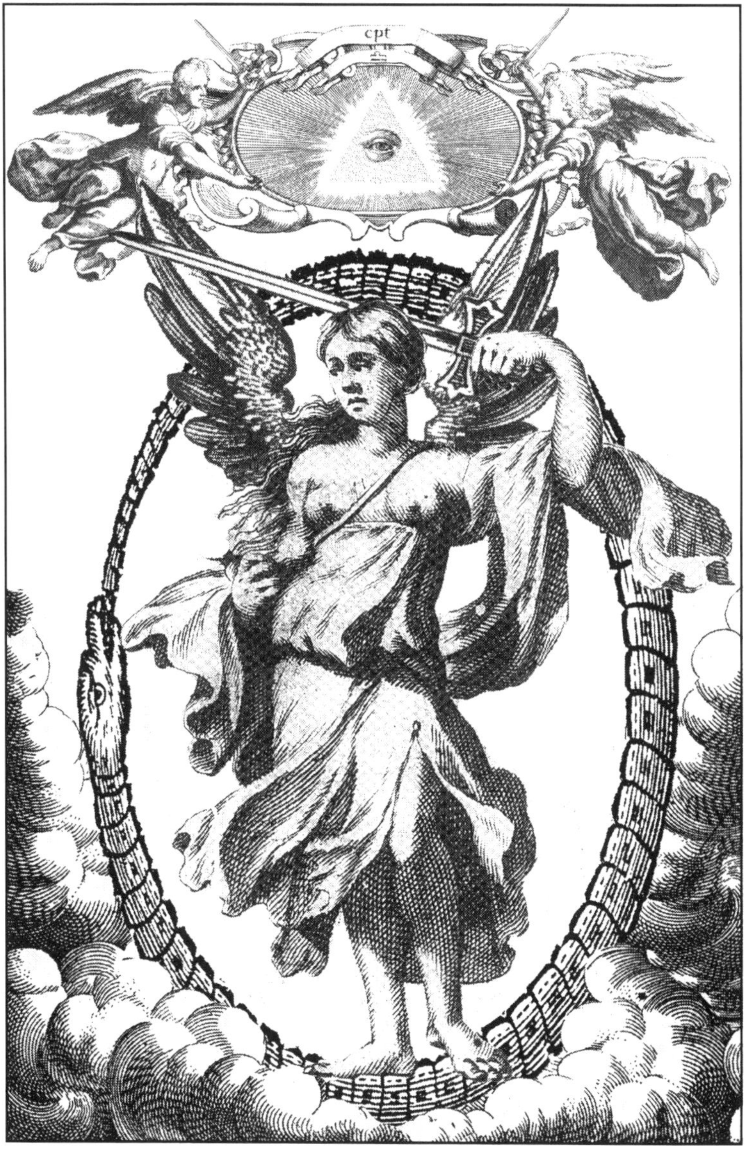
cpt

responsibility for ourselves, she wouldn't be able to catch us in the act of failing to evolve, and we wouldn't be eligible for the correction we find ourselves receiving in her name.

Another irritating quality the Queen of Swords has when reversed is her ability to manipulate guilt and shame in the people around her. She has a "should" and an "ought" for every occasion, and those who cross her invisible lines will have to hear all about it, possibly for years to come. Her relentlessly over-determined view of what needs to happen leaves very little room for a fresh interpretation, at least when she's feeling threatened and is therefore clutching for levers of control. These strategies might be great for running a classroom or managing the occasional stressful dinner with relatives, but carried on for years without the consent of the governed, they will inevitably lead to revolt.

Whether upright or reversed, emotionally mature women have to stop being afraid of the discounts dished upon Queen of Swords types by people who accuse her of being an emasculating bulldog. Her retort to this kind of thinking is to remind the mockers that if they were as self-realized as she, they wouldn't be wasting precious brainpower crafting insults to fend off her superiority. This Queen's willingness to individuate, whether she is approved or not, encourages her more eccentric subjects and provides a thrilling role model for the timid. In her presence intelligence becomes the definition of beauty, and superficiality is exposed as ugliness.

Knight of Swords
Gemini

The Knight of Swords embodies the Gemini paradox: His reputation has been earned by being "armed and dangerous," but his sign is often seen as the wit and humorist of the Zodiac. We usually find this fellow in an expansive and experimental mood following his ruling planet Mercury into educational adventures that help to establish new branches of science and forge new vocabulary for the Arts. But when the quick wit and sharp perceptions of the Sword Knight are colored by motives derived from offense or defense, then watch out, because he'll hit you hard on your blind side and then claim it was a joke.

However he appears, the Knight of Swords portrays the restless mind busy turning over every rock to see what will scurry out from under it. The Gemini form of intelligence is world-renowned for its curiosity and ability to argue both sides of any question. In fact, this Knight takes more delight in the sparring than he does from being either right or wrong. He is especially motivated when he can find somebody who will take his bait and tussle with him, either intellectually or physically. People who allow personal emotions to enter into such exchange can feel pranked when they discover that he doesn't really care about the position he has defended so vociferously. The Knight might have demolished his debate partner's life work, but he's not remorseful because he found the process of jousting to be fun and interesting. He doesn't entertain concern for consequences; collateral damage is written off as a natural part of the process. It's all for the sport of playing with his mind and sharpening his sword.

Shape-shifty and ambidextrous Mercury rules Gemini, so we have to agree with the alchemists and ancient astrologers that the Knight of Swords would naturally be an ambivalent character. As is shown by the lives of the world's geniuses, so often their best work is accomplished before they have fully integrated the fixed rules of their disciplines. In youth the plastic imagination is still open to surprise invention and inspiration. This is the great gift, as well as the downfall, of the Knight of Swords. At any moment he might have a truly spontaneous thought, a completely novel impulse. One can never predict what will come out of him next. His cultural scripting hasn't jelled yet, so he remains a bit liquid in his boundaries. The visions in his mind haven't been reduced down to reality yet, so this Knight is a wild card in every situation.

Ever the wordsmith, this Knight just loves to listen to himself expounding. This quality can be great when he's a teacher or tutor. His enthusiasm for his topic is infectious, leaving the student hungry for more. The Sword Knight's active imagination lights up the whole territory around the topic he's discussing, leading to endless fascinating digressions. He's in touch with the spirit of all the famous historians of literature and drama, with a sweeping view of the forces behind history that shape human destiny. He is of one mind with the ancient bards, or even Shakespeare, author of so many of our cultural "types" with his amazing caricatures. The Knight of Swords is actually very similar to the characters of myth and legend in that his larger-than-life story of himself is what he wants you to know about, rather than the facts of his actual being.

The downside to having such a great imagination is that this Knight can get so swept up in the storytelling that he forgets the official plot line and starts to substitute his own momentary inventions. He inclines towards bragging, which can lead to claiming others' accomplishments, as well as over-disclosing the more shady side of his thinking. When he's feeling insecure, such as when he becomes a little tipsy, or when he's entranced by flattery and ego-seduction, he might start to leak privileged confidences. Once his desire to be in the spotlight gets ahead of his good sense, he could forget his boundaries in ways that could later cost him greatly.

This Knight's heroic side emerges after diplomacy has failed. For a just cause when negotiation is not possible, bold combativeness takes its place in the military repertoire. When the Sword Knight is inspired about the rightness of his cause, he is capable of acts of great bravery and self-sacrifice (even if history might eventually reveal that he will have done them for utterly muddled reasons). Apt advice for this card is to deeply question the logic driving what you are about to say and do. Forethought will help you discriminate between being guided by a universal truth versus being caught up in the grips of an enthusiasm that will soon pass. Best practice is to discipline any traces of impulsive heroics before your inspiration runs you into trouble with your allies.

In a few packs one might catch a hint, implied by the detail on the card, that the person inside the armor is a woman rather than the expected man. There is some evidence that the tradition of knighthood included a certain number of anonymous knights who took mythic names and veiled their true identities. Living on the road with few or no servants, they served as free-lance defenders of travelers, champions of the little people against the exploitation of both highway robbers and the wealthy classes. Odds are that some of these

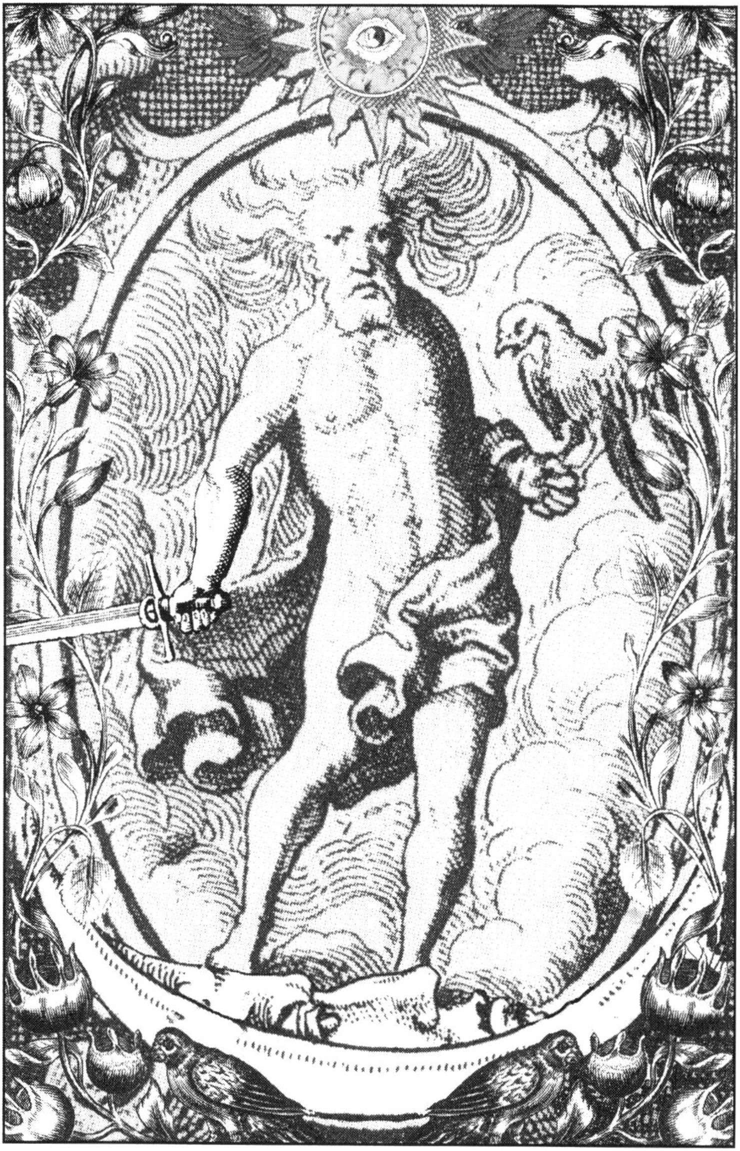

knights errant were camouflaged women, an idea preserved with this unusual treatment of the Sword Knight. The question this raises is, "Would we call this a deceiver, or a person who is doing good work by any means necessary?"

In his retrograde mode the Sword Knight is easily slighted. He always has a chip on his shoulder, nursing a hostile and confrontational attitude. When he's feeling insecure, he'll look for someone to blame for his mood. This Knight has amazing radar: He can always spot someone of lower rank upon whom to unleash his temper. His facile mind will torture logic to find a pretext for his rush of aggressive adrenalin. In this bully style he'll bait his target to produce a response he can take offense at. Then, self-righteously, our Knight undertakes to "correct" the offender. Even if he originally had a cogent point to make, this exaggerated and distorted delivery makes him guilty of overkill every time.

Only a very self-possessed and disciplined individual could encounter this complex of irritating qualities and remain un-reactive. The Knight of Swords might get away with enacting these scenes in some situations, but in other cases he is taken outside and soundly trounced by the friends of the person he has offended. Few can stay the reversed Knight's friend for long because of the risk to one's long-term reputation. When each incident has passed and his self-induced conflagration settles, the Knight of Swords will feel misunderstood, a scapegoat of the nasty gossip that goes around in his name. Resignedly, he packs his bags and hits the road again, only to repeat the same pattern in the next town and the next. It takes this character many years to discover that the challenging sharpness he feels coming at him from others is, as often as not, his own brittle intensity being reflected back at him.

Page of Swords
Fall Equinox

The Page of Swords is the messenger, emissary, or liaison between enemy camps. These polarized communities could be currently suffering tense communications or even be actively at war. He functions as a pipeline or vessel of communication, being charged with faithfully representing one side's position to the other. As the go-between, translator, and envoy he bears a huge amount of responsibility, even though he travels in the humble guise of a servant. Consider him an intelligence agent in plain clothes, or a camouflaged diplomat facilitating sensitive negotiations under difficult conditions.

Since the Pages carry the student or apprentice role, this one represents the student of strategy. He studies the art of war through the game of chess, combing over the stories of the Crusades, the Knightly Orders, the Grail legends and all the world's famous battles for inspirational role models. His military connections as well as his tracker's instincts earn him the title of "The Watchman." He also represents the messenger who risks getting shot when his message isn't well received. This consideration motivates this Page to be strategic, articulate, and creative in the clinch.

The Swords Page acts as the eyes and ears of his employer, which might also be the family enterprise. Like all the Pages, he serves at the behest of his Queen, maintaining the network around the royal family. In an enlightened nation, the Queen's sympathy is with her people, as is that of the Page. He fulfills her wish to know the people's minds. The Page keeps all different parts of the realm in contact with each other and with the court at its administrative hub. His mandate is to convey the leaders' vision to the people, whether these are political, educational, or economic pronouncements.

In his function as a harbinger, the Page of Swords is a warning messenger who prepares people's minds for what is soon to come. He reminds us about the increasing darkness and decreasing warmth that are creeping over the landscape. Fall storms surround this Page with a turbulent and harrowing wind. The green cover over the land is dying back (green Moon underfoot). All the animals that aren't hibernating must compete more fiercely to keep up their energy and temperature (blood Moon overhead). The mere appearance of this Page in a spread suggests that it's time to sharpen our focus and accelerate our efforts. Nature's support is passing fast with every day of waning light and heat. It is essential that the tribe work as a team at this point, avoiding divisive impulses.

These naturalistic details go a long way towards explaining the more disciplined attitude we must adopt in the season of fall after the long days of summer. In the ancient vocabulary of metaphysics, this concept of falling or having fallen has more than one implication across the different disciplines. The oldest usage is found in Astrology. Each of the Planetary Governors has a sign that represents its Fall, where it is in a state of disempowerment, wretchedness, dependence, and suffering. There is no avoiding these episodes, they happen with every revolution around the Sun, and they are perfectly predictable. These Falling incidents inform the reversed meanings of cards numbered Three, Five, and Eight of each Suit, which occupy the descending Mother Pillar of the Kabbalah Tree. Anytime we find ourselves moving in a descending direction, we are challenged to find meaning in a narrowing field of endeavor. We must adjust our private preferences to the signal task of preparing for upcoming challenges.

Theologians also use this term the Fall to point to that mythical event in the archetypal past when the original perfect Creation was infected by doubt, rebelliousness, and selfishness. A fallen person or angel is in resistance to the prevailing direction of the Divine Will. In light of these hints, one could see the reversed Page of Swords as a frustrated, dangerous, embittered individual who turns against those who have helped him and seeks revenge for old grudges. An insider who now feels alienated, this Page is able to inflict terrible damage on the collective enterprise should he turn coat and ally with the enemy.

The meaning of the Page of Swords reversed becomes clear. A title almost universally associated with this part of his personality is the Spy. He has also been portrayed as a sneak thief and pickpocket, rationalizing that what's been left untended is fair game for his creative approach to ownership. His light fingers (along with his copyright infringement, identity-theft, mistranslation, and pernicious hacking) are supplemented by double-dealing through pitting team-members against each other. Just as the verbal arts are his strong suit when he's upright, this Page reversed is the disinformation agent, the master of doublespeak who wastes his fine mind on creating confusion around him. When he's reversed, wicked rumors and malignant misunderstandings plague the environment, muddying the public discourse and distracting away energies needed for finding common solutions. In his public role this Page collects and inflames people's ego-imbalances, using the resulting contention to take hostages and create factions that cumulatively immortalize the worst qualities of human nature.

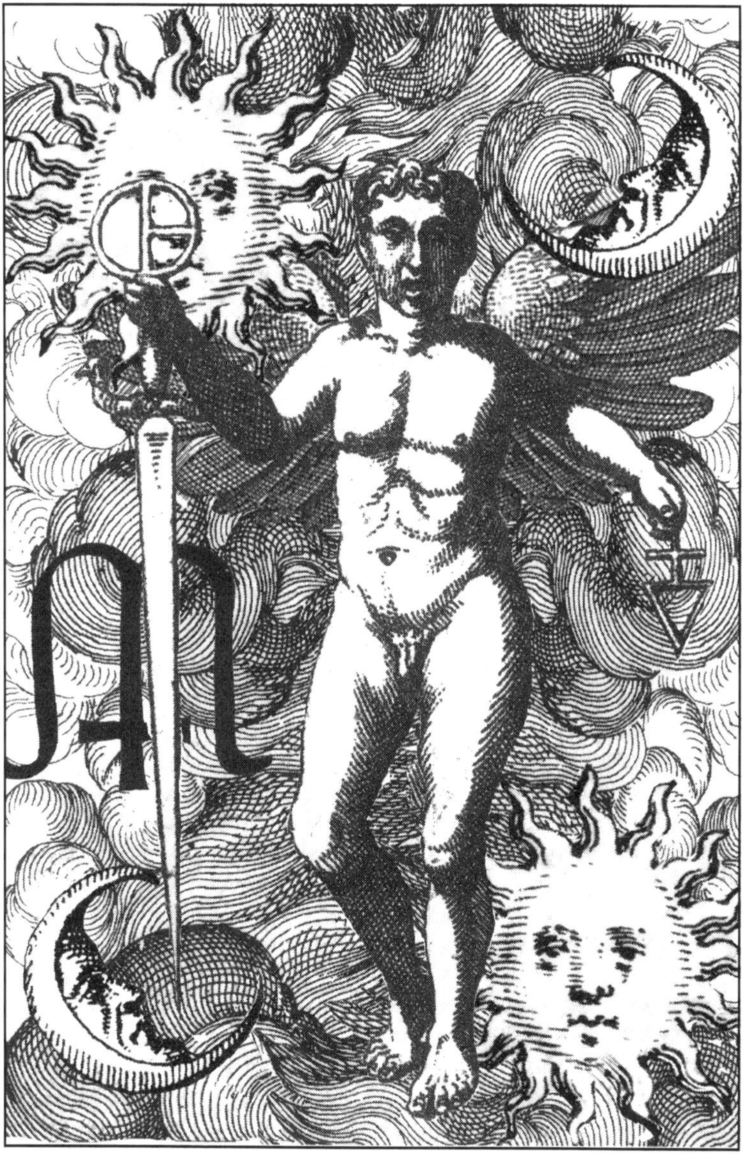

In the reversed Page's private life, antisocial meddling helps to maintain those poisonous family and social systems that produce people who are bitter, spiteful, nasty, and heedless. The reversed Page expresses himself in extremes, overlooking the middle ground every time. He can't seem to find his way to the time-honored approach of respecting another's individuality and splitting the difference. His attitude becomes brittle and arbitrary, unyielding and vengeful, offhanded and utterly lacking in empathy. Just a few layers under his civilized surface, there's a feral creature lurking. It can be shocking to see the change in character that comes over him when inverted. Something has triggered his survival instincts, and once that bolt of adrenalin is released, he just wants to cut himself free of every entanglement no matter who or what he might accidentally gore in the process.

Remember that the Pages, unlike the other Royals, represent elemental transitions akin to the change of seasons; they do not stand in for any single sign of the Zodiac. People from any sign can find themselves caught up in the role of any Page simply by getting swept up into emotional "weather fronts" that reflect momentary changes in the zeitgeist. Certain times and cultural climates are poisonous for simple goodwill and fellow feeling. Instead they foster the two-faced, self-destructive trickster who lives inside the reversed Page of Swords. Such circumstances strengthen the dark side of our hidden rebel, which turns out to be a reactive, pessimistic, self-abandoning inner child. Try inviting this reversed Page back into the human circle with love and kindness, because it's his longstanding feeling of being abandoned and unappreciated that makes him take those nasty underdog behaviors.

Chapter 3
The Wands

Suit of Wands

Key words for the Suit of Wands include energy, will, desire, and charisma. The Wand symbol is, at its most primitive, a rough club of wood, sometimes showing sprigs of new green growth emerging from its weathered grain, occasionally aflame like a torch. A more refined version shows a magical wand or staff collecting and focusing life force according to the user's will.

Like a conductor's baton, this symbol leads and directs the unfolding action, and the participants instinctively know to follow the one who holds this symbol of authority. Because the Element connected with Wands is Fire, the qualities of boldness, ambition, drive, competitiveness, and initiative are highlighted. Whenever a Wand card appears, actions are being taken or suggested, change is in the works, and a challenge to the will is implied.

The more esoteric Tarot decks reveal that Wands symbolize life force, also known as kundalini, qi (chi), or prana. This is the animating energy that fills every living thing with vitality, without which nothing could live. Through their correspondence with Fire, Wands also represent the Light that conquers darkness, whether it's a candle in the window or the Sun at the center of the Solar System. This metaphor also refers to the Wand of Prometheus, a hollowed-out club of wood within which was smuggled coals of fire from the realm of the gods, a gift to humans in the ancient Greek myth.

A further wrinkle on that myth is that in the Hebrew alphabet and the Phoenician before that (mother tongue of all Indo-European languages), the letters of the alphabet were originated by ancient priests observing the constellations in the night sky and noting down in "tongues of flame" the glyphs those constellations described. Prometheus is one form of the god Mercury, who traditionally rules all alphabets, numbers, glyphs, signs, symbols, and writing in general.

The code of "Fire from Heaven" anciently refers to the arts of cooking, forgery, pottery, and other early technologies. It also sparks the inspiration that leads to reading and writing, mathematics, codes and ciphers, and all the sophisticated tools we humans have invented to raise our consciousness and realize the world we now inhabit. Wands represent the inventive, entrepreneurial spirit, the quest for excellence and greater command, and the power that belongs to whoever can wield this force skillfully.

Ace of Wands

Astrology: 1-10 Aries, ruled by Mars   **Sephira:** Keter
Essential Dignity: upright Domicile, Mars in Aries
reversed Similar, Mars in Scorpio
Angelic Dignities: upright angel spelled VHU, spoken Vehuiah
reversed angel spelled YLY, spoken Jeliel

Solar Fire warms the Earth and awakens the seeds of the future. Green shoots rise to the Divine Hand with enthusiasm. "Paradise must grow in the soul like a plant, transforming Hell into Heaven, growing upward through the light naturally as a plant seeks the light, rising out of the dirt" (Versluis, 1999, p. 141). All the potential of the plant's whole future life is awakened the moment it sprouts and sends up that first shoot. Due to this act of sublime courage, the soul attracts a supportive hand from the astral plane. In the heavens the Sun enlivens the Great Arcanum formed by the planets' relations within the Zodiac. At this moment anything is possible for the inflamed will.

The Ace of Wands symbolizes a pivotal act, or fateful step, that will set loose a chain of events leading toward your desired goal. As such it refers to a birth or new beginning, the inauguration of an endeavor, and the necessary passion to move intention into action. This Ace embodies the inflamed will pouring forth into its work, embracing the struggle for change. Since it is associated with the earliest degrees of the first sign of spring, there is a tremendous upwelling of fresh energy becoming available, like spring sap rising in the trees. Given the ruling planet Mars' affinity with the metal iron, this card will sometimes have the implication of great force suddenly unleashed, as if "shot from guns."

The Ace of Wands invites us to meditate on the confluence between the first day of spring (Aries) and the first station of the Kabbalah Tree (Keter, the head), the number One, and the concept of the Monad. Since our numbering system is connected to the Sephira, we will always associate the Aces with totality, completeness, and fullness of every type. All four Aces share this energy of "firstness," but the Aries Ace is premier among them all because it is associated with the season of spring. This Ace, more than any other, has the connotation of starting with a blank slate in the sense of emerging from one's own center unconditioned by any prior limiting influence. The best place to seek and cultivate this kind of utterly fresh ground is at the fringes of one's own imagination, in that utterly trackless realm where no outsiders ever tread.

The Monad (literally translated, the All or Fullness) brings the added significance of completeness, as in "the totality is gathered here as One." There might be many moving parts within, they could even be as uncountable as ants in the hive, but all those individual units will be of one mind, one will, and one goal with their Queen, who embodies the hive consciousness. Just so, the Aces will center and guide their Suits from the essential central motive of their Element. In the case of Wands, this is Fire, cognate with the arousing power of desire and aspiration.

From the point of view of the individual, the Ace liberates the energy to move our bodies out of a dormant state and launch ourselves into a new line of action. In the medieval world that might have meant cultivating an extra field of grain this year, which would allow the farmer to acquire a better plow or a new horse to pull it, for example. In more modern times this might symbolize a challenge to the strength of our drive and ambition, like overcoming our fear of public speaking or learning how to bounce back from a fall in the martial arts. Wands will challenge our willingness to work hard, sweat in the sun, and struggle against great odds. Courage and initiative are blessings that the Wands bestow to those who are not afraid to assert themselves when the proper time arises.

Many people don't realize that despite one's age or past experience, there are still parts of our natural capacity that have remained virgin and untouched, being held in abeyance and left dormant until needed. When the Ace of Wands appears, the Divine Will is requesting that a new part of the self should bud and grow forth in response to the current circumstance. The inner quickening that accompanies this outer calling bears witness that we are indeed the one being sought and recruited. Spirit has a plan for us, and now is the time.

Another aspect of this first decanate of Aries is that it governs the ten days following Spring Equinox. This is the time of year when the day and night are functionally equal (though the trend is moving towards longer days and shorter nights). At this period Mars has his balance. He isn't being triggered towards either of his extremes, meaning he can think with both sides of his brain, so to speak. When this card presents itself upright, it is a perfect moment for aggressive, assertive, ambitious Mars to hold his Fire and study his options. Does he want to charge out of the gate with guns blazing like a typical Aries, or does he want to work more slowly and subtly, like the patient Scorpio? Nobody can unsay or un-do what has already happened, so the far better path is to refrain from setting off any alarms until a full examination of the situation has been made.

In reversal the Ace of Wands represents a premature termination,

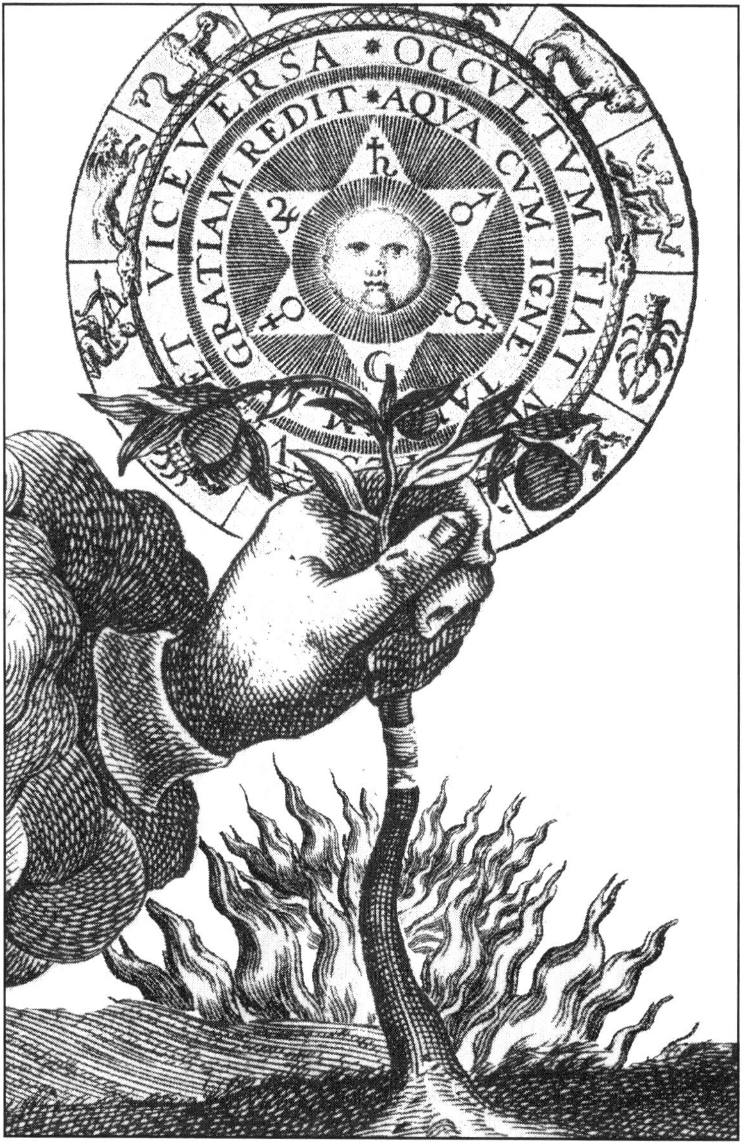
VICE VERSA
OCCVLTVM FIAT
GRATIAM REDIT
AQVA CVM IGNE

whether that is a literal abortion or the derailing of long-desired plans. The start was spoiled, the opening postponed, the handoff was dropped in the relay. Sometimes blame will be apportioned for sins of omission or commission that led to the failure. But often circumstance simply won't allow the intended outcome, and all we can do is chalk it up to the hand of fate. There are also times when we are not literally free to act unhindered in the world. At those times the will is still free to focus desire, make plans, clear obstacles, and empower inner change. Be careful that you don't succumb to spring fever and accidentally squander this wonderful blast of life force on trivialities. Dedicate this new motivation and energy to projects that will get you started in a fresh direction.

Two of Wands

Astrology: 11-20 Aries, ruled by the Sun **Sephira:** Chakhmah
Essential Dignity: upright Compliment, Mars in Taurus
reversed Detriment, Mars in Libra
Angelic Dignities: upright angel spelled SIT, spoken Sitael
reversed angel spelled OLM, spoken Elemiah

Two of Wands illustrates the two ways that matter receives Solar force. On the one hand the force is experienced as friction, pain, discomfort, and stress, all of which can be summarized in the word "Wrath." This experience is symbolized by the dark fulmination on the left, shown paired with the green fire of vegetative life. Here we see the natural conservatism of instinct at work: resistance to change, unthinking reflex action, reversion to more primitive responses that are intractable to cultural modifications.

The very same energy in different circumstances is experienced as warmth and Light, compassion and reconciliation, shown here paired with the red Fire of human blood, summarized in the word Love. Without the smoke and fumes of the Wrath-Fire obscuring the atmosphere, the Light is free to penetrate from its celestial Source to directly touch and inspire the lives below. From his benign position above all polarities, the Sun watches over the process and supplies the energy required to turn Wrath into Love. Those who have the awareness to separate the Light from its myriad effects will be much better able to handle the extremes without losing their faith or their drive

The original illustration that supplied this image comes from the lineage of Jacob Boehme and was offered as a way to understand the two-sidedness of the Divine Light. If we think like mystics while viewing this image, we will realize that both the Light and its attendant fulmination are natural consequences of the very same process. Neither manifestation is better or more virtuous than the other. As a matter of fact, the radiant brightness illuminates the smoke and ash for what they are: visual evidence of rapidly accelerating energy ripping through the settled order, imposing transformation at a pace that compresses Time and escalates old forms into breakdown mode.

Under the influence of the immutable Sun, the world of matter is forced to awaken and undergo the changes that evolution demands. This is a process that consumes the previous arrangement utterly, although without a scrap of negative motive. Nature's pulse is quickening as the mid-Aries Sun draws the sap up into the tree branches, awakening the landscape to a new cycle.

The detritus of last season releases its stored energy as the soil's many creatures come out of dormancy to feed and multiply. The green fire immolates everything that represents outworn forms to feed the awakening new life of the Earth. The coals and ashes, all that remains of the past, become fertilizer for future growth and fruiting. Paradoxically that very same force that swells the bud on the branch rots the seedpod at the tree's roots.

The Light that stimulates the red flames, on the other hand, represents the piercing ray of illumination banishing the darkness in our consciousness. We might be praying for this, seeking it out, longing with all our hearts to be lifted out of our ignorance and limitations. But even so, when it finally arrives, this heavenly laser can burn just like criticism, smiting and stinging as if we were being castigated for our imperfections. This is where the traditional meaning of "buyer's remorse" comes in. In the Ace we dedicated ourselves to a new path of action, but in the Deuce we experience the doubts and fears which instantly and inevitably follow upon our actions. We will have to find the courage of our convictions if we are to persevere through this blinding awakening.

When it appears in a spread, the Two of Wands advises us to interpret the current friction, stress, and heat as the necessary price of change. This is not a sign of things going wrong, although the moment can still feel unsettled, challenging, and possibly threatening. Try to remember that if your project or goal were easy, everybody would already be doing it. This feeling of facing an uphill battle is appropriate; it is correct to be stirring up the status quo and setting loose unpredictable consequences.

If you find yourself suddenly polarizing, however, it's time to view your opposite as a partner and reciprocal, the same way your right and left hands function, or the way Mars and Venus operate as mates. Even though the two hands are opposites, they are attracted to each other and entrained together in your brain so they can function as a unit. Embracing this back-and-forth between contrasting perspectives will help you hone your skills and outgrow your weaknesses. Since the healing mode of the Two of Wands involves Mars visiting his mate Venus' territories, this can help us imagine the best use of these complementary energies.

At its best the Two of Wands offers a chance to reinforce the fateful step that was taken in the Ace. Tentative souls are tempted to hesitate in fear of "what might happen," but pro-active types will double down in an effort to ensure that transformation is the only outcome. Make every effort to bring doubters and nay-sayers along as events unfold because the project's success is increased when the collective will achieves a clear picture of the ultimate goal. By engaging the doubters in the process as problems are identified and solved, all the

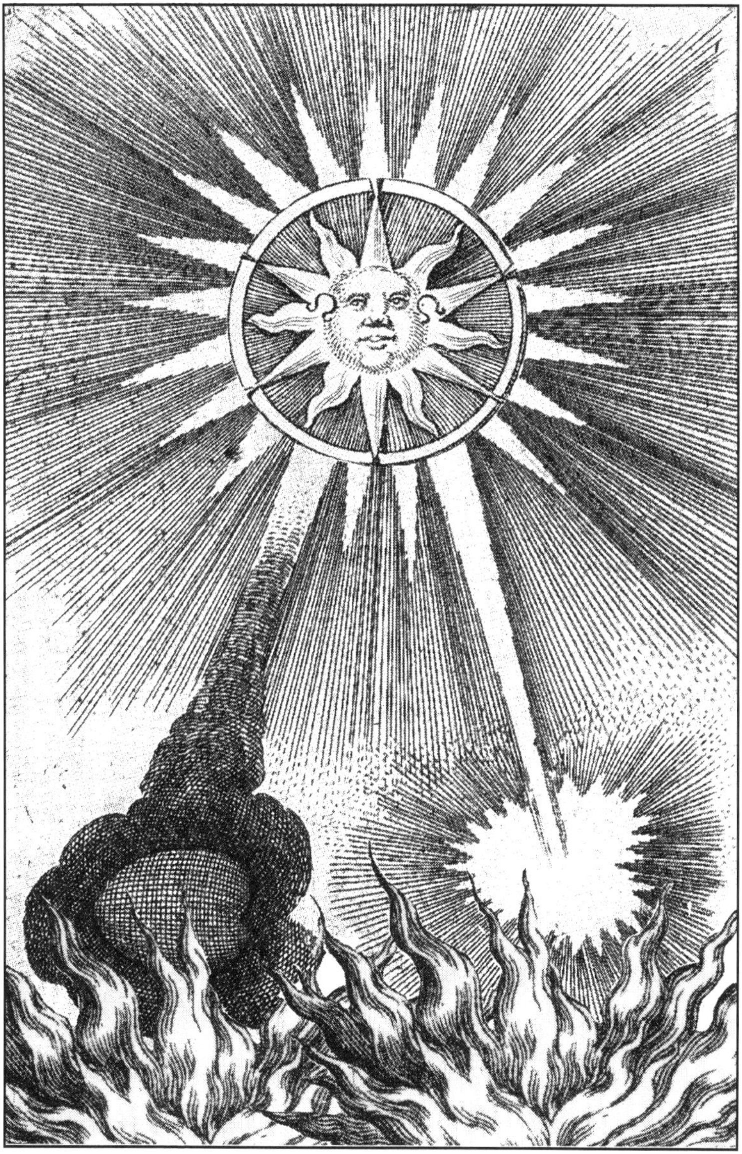

participants have their perspective enlarged and their confidence bolstered. This card upright symbolizes the type of situations referred to by the old adage, "He who hesitates is lost." When reversed, the Two of Wands risks turning into a deadlock due to energies working at cross-purposes, often portrayed as crossed wands sparking against each other. This could refer to an internal situation, an equal split between optimism and pessimism, for example, or a situation where you feel "damned if you do, damned if you don't." It could be a standoff with another person or with limitations that are externally imposed and inimical to your goals. You might be up against a dam in the stream. Creeping dread of self-doubt implies fear that perhaps you have bitten off more than you can chew. In such a case give yourself a moment to take in the full implications of your situation. Regain your bearings before launching yourself back into action. Deal with concerns before they become regrets.

Three of Wands

Astrology: 21- 30 Aries, ruled by Jupiter   **Sephira:** Binah
Essential Dignity: upright Exaltation, Mars in Capricorn
reversed Fall, Mars in Cancer
Angelic Dignities: upright angel spelled MHSh, spoken Mahasiah
reversed angel spelled LLH, spoken Lelahel

The ribbon on the Three of Wands bears the Latin motto "Virtues United Are Stronger," and in every way this is a card of teamwork, for better and for worse. Another motto for this card could be "All for one and one for all," like the Three Musketeers. The mission is clear: Your companions are in agreement, so now it's time to proceed with all of your powers and capabilities at the ready. The rising Sun and setting Moon bless your goal, and the alchemical serpent on the Tree of Life promises aid from invisible powers.

This card symbolizes an inner confidence that makes a person strive to command the future, whereas others limit themselves to managing the present. The illustrated Tarot decks will often show a rich lord standing on the protective ramparts of his castle, watching three ships leave the harbor loaded with trade goods for far-off ports. Every part of their mission has been initiated and overseen by him personally, from the boat building to the purchase of the trade goods to finding the proper captains and merchants to make the mission a success. Our noble lord will have to wait years before he finds out how his ships have fared, and in the meanwhile there are a lot of resources tied up, whatever the outcome. Only those truly confident in their ideas and abilities would extend themselves to such a degree.

However pictured, this card represents the type of personality who expects to undertake great adventures and accomplish notable deeds. Inherent in such endeavors is a substantial portion of risk which cannot be avoided and which is guaranteed to produce a huge loss if things go badly. Boldness to brave such a challenge, which marks the hero both in literature and in life, can look like foolhardy fate baiting when things don't work out as planned. The very same temperament that stretches for the prize also drives many people one step too far. For this reason the idea of "the team" is featured here. With checks and balances provided by seasoned assistants, one person's grandiosity has less chance to scuttle the project. A detail that sometimes appears in the older Tarots is a winged wand with two snakes twining around it. This is Mercury's wand, symbol of his multi-valent androgyny. Called the caduceus, this is an ancient symbol of the healer or shaman, one who can travel between the worlds to rescue souls from death or possession by demons. The early Kabbalists used a three-headed snake as a symbol of the Divine Will making its mark on Time and Space. The circular shape of this serpent also suggests motion and action, now that we have moved beyond the doubts and hesitations of the Deuce. The feeling of empowerment this card represents points to a strong internal mechanism of self-healing and motivation. This wand of power can also refer to the courage it takes to be an entrepreneur or an inventor, an inherently magical process that brings not only opportunity for success, but also an opening to new worlds of experience.

In these final days of Aries, Jupiter, known as the Greater Benefic in ancient Astrology, rules the overall climate. This is a special moment, as under this influence we might get lucky and make a breakthrough. In order for Jupiter to find us worthy, however, we have to raise our sights beyond the narrow compass of "I, me, and mine." We have to look around to see what needs doing, what is missing in the world as we find it. It takes a special kind of creativity to look past the givens, to envision a new and better way; Jupiter challenges us to rise above our personal limitations and reach for a goal that brings value to our whole family, tribe, or nation.

The Threes in all four of the Suits take their meaning from their presence at the top of the Kabbalistic Mother Pillar, serving as the Right Eye of analysis, calculation, and demand. The Mother Pillar numbers (Three, Five, and Eight) also reflect the complications and temptations posed by the astrological principle of Exaltation and Fall. For Mars as ruler of Aries, his Exaltation in the saturnine sign of Capricorn means he is being supported and promoted by the Solar System's father figure. In Capricorn, Mars is adulated as a harbinger of future victories, being the ruler of spring's renewal; his heat offers hope and confidence even during the longest, darkest nights of the year.

Of course, the danger for Mars in Exaltation is that his head might swell if he begins to believe his sponsor's rhetoric. He might forget that he is not the spring itself, but only its representative, like the cock that crows at dawn. The promise implied in Mars' Fire has not yet been solidified in manifestation. But the light of hope in the future's potential and the shining vision of inspiration that Mars arouses keep the Capricorn natives from bogging down in the moment's limitations.

When reversed, the Three of Wands suffers a deflation of the heroic overcomer impulses that are associated with the upright meaning. The glue that holds the team's motivation together (or the ego's focus) begins to fail. Despite otherwise favorable influences, these Martian energies just can't get organized.

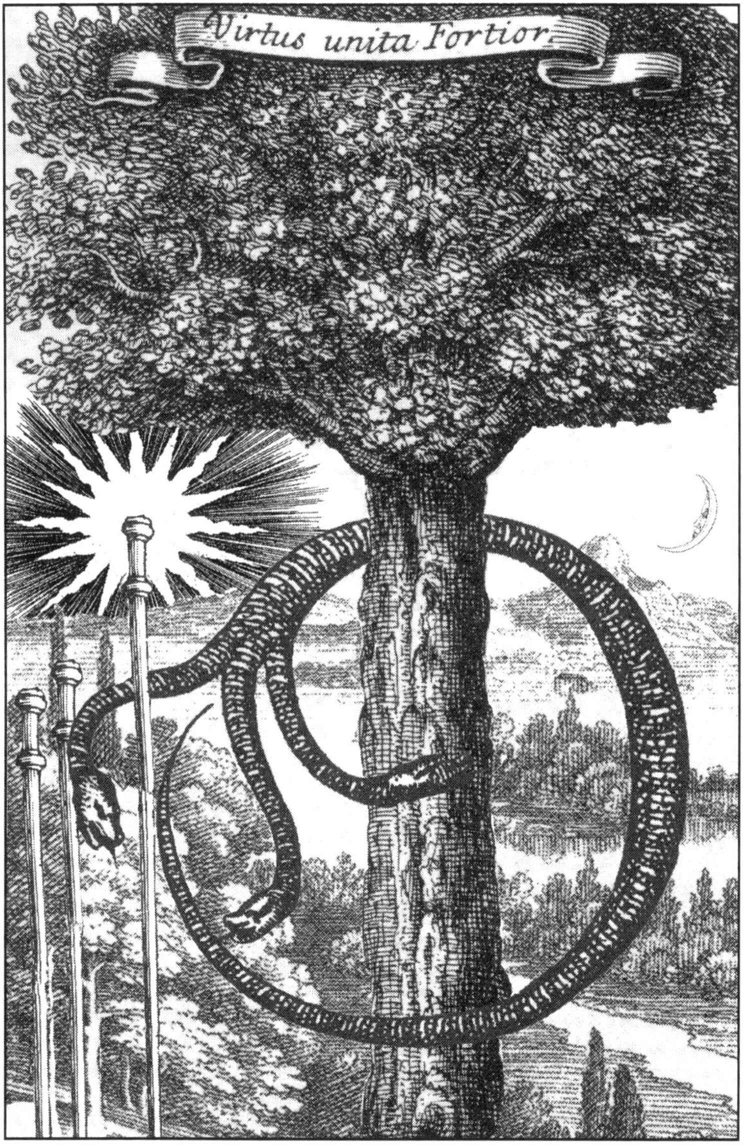
Virtus unita Fortior

When Mars enters a Cancer environment, the sign of his Fall, he feels unmanned by the Moon's maternal, watery, and emotionally saturating influence, which smothers his usual spirit and spunk like a wet blanket. The ironic cartoon of Alexander the Great going into therapy to overcome his urges to conquer the known world comes to mind here.

No, we don't want to eliminate the heroic dimension of life, far from it. What we want, and are all seeking, is a cause or a movement that is spiritually significant and deeply inspiring enough to give us energy when the problems of the world start to overcome us. We want the assurance that with effort and discipline there will be better times to come. Mars is seeking guidance toward a worthy channel through which he can apply his prodigious energies for the betterment of the world. And if he knows what is good for him, Mars will accept wise counsel when he hears it.

As we find with many cards that appear upside-down, there isn't anything overtly wrong when the Three of Wands comes up reversed. It's merely saying that a low-key situation of average normalcy simply doesn't have enough galvanizing "oomph" for the adrenalin-driven ruler of Aries to get aroused about. Therefore he's tempted to lapse into his adolescent-minded rebel or trickster side, illustrating the adage "Idle hands are the Devil's playground." This would be a good time to enlarge your sphere of responsibilities. Actively seek a larger point of reference you can contribute to. Consider allying with a respected leader or cause and doing some community service. Mars' loose-cannon ego needs a holster to contain it for a while.

Four of Wands

Astrology: 11-20 Leo, ruled by Jupiter **Sephira:** Chesed
Essential Dignity: upright Compliment, Sun in Capricorn
reversed Detriment, Sun in Aquarius
Angelic Dignities: upright angel spelled HZI, spoken Haziel
reversed angel spelled ALD, spoken Aladiah

Four wands interlace on this card, signifying a burst of creative effort that provides a scaffolding upon which to grow a community, form institutions, or establish a secret society. Crossed wands suggest a crossroads where paths linking several communities intersect. This defines an enterprise zone where innovators can do well for themselves by improving the lives of those who pass by or stop in. Through identifying the presence of this intersection in an otherwise undeveloped area, the primary actors will attract prosperity for themselves and the community they serve, a winning combination. Thus the traditional significance of this card refers to collective labors coming to fruition. The Four of Wands can indicate both the project itself and the group organism that does the work stage by stage. It can also signify the celebrations and gatherings that will grace the collective well-being once the new construct is integrated into the community's life.

The Four of Wands is a culture-building card, sometimes figured by two entrepreneurial couples who have joined to create something along the lines of an inn, a factory, a theater, or store. If the principals have made the right choices, they will be welcomed to the neighborhood and given plenty of patronage. But still, time and patience are needed to fulfill such a grand vision; eventually other people of ambition and talent must be attracted to this nucleus for it to fulfill its potential. But for now, the four wands represent the minimum skill-set and energy level required to address the initial stages.

The relationships established by the founding visionaries set the pattern for the culture that will emerge from this start-up. At the outset all parties pledge to be strict equals; and if they are smart, they will put safeguards in place to ensure that this standard is maintained for the life of the enterprise. This partnership symbolizes any collective endeavor where the whole is greater than the sum of the parts. As such, what is being created is not just a "thing" like a machine, but instead is an organism that over time will grow its own metabolism and life cycle.

The number Four makes an esoteric reference to the cube of matter, seen in alchemical art as the throne of the Emperor. Whatever is created at this stage, whether success or failure, will endure for a long time to come. This is true for all of the Fours, but nowhere is this more literally applied than in the Four of Wands. Think of all the hundred-years-standing Masonic halls and fraternal society buildings that appear in every city in America. The people who created those wonderful multifunction meeting halls and theaters handed off a gift that keeps on giving to future generations the builders would never know. With love and preservation, such public treasures provide sanctuary and serve as incubators for the unique culture of their region.

Calorie-burning sweat and muscle are the secret to fulfilling the goals of the Wands Suit. The principal actors in the Four of Wands will be taxed on every level for the privilege of making their dreams come true. With such a small core group to start with, each participant will be required to wear multiple hats and serve multiple functions. Only people who are passionately committed to their shared vision will dedicate so much of their time and energy this way. On the astral level the project and its blueprint take the place of a personified leader; the human participants are happy to serve the ideal directly, rendering and enacting all the steps of the process for the joy of seeing the finished product emerge from their imaginations. Clearly only people of a certain inspired character can harmoniously co-conspire for the length of time required for this kind of project to find its realization. Hence the time-honored association of the Four of Wands with the foundation of a secret society, lodge, or order, the members of which are pledged to manifest the will of their invisible superiors.

The Sephira Chesed is called the "left hand of benignity," which grants the card an accidental double Jupiter influence (since Jupiter also colors this middle segment of the sign of Leo). It is extremely fortunate when people can come together harmoniously to enhance their community. Spiritual progress is made in just such humble ways. By slowly and steadily working out our differences for the common good, we get the chance to wear away the sharp edges of our egotistic and competitive thinking. The best of what we have to share crystallizes in the collective project, which remains and testifies to the creative impulses that bind us together through good times and bad.

Astro-alchemically, the Sun and Jupiter (rulers of Leo and Capricorn) are the two patriarchs of the Zodiac, being figureheads for the Dry Way of Detachment. This is the life-path of the mystic, magician, or philosopher, who is moving away from enmeshment and entanglement in the worldly ego. Remembrance of one's higher Nature is traditionally symbolized by the Sun in Leo. The subsequent fall and winter signs challenge the newly awakened soul

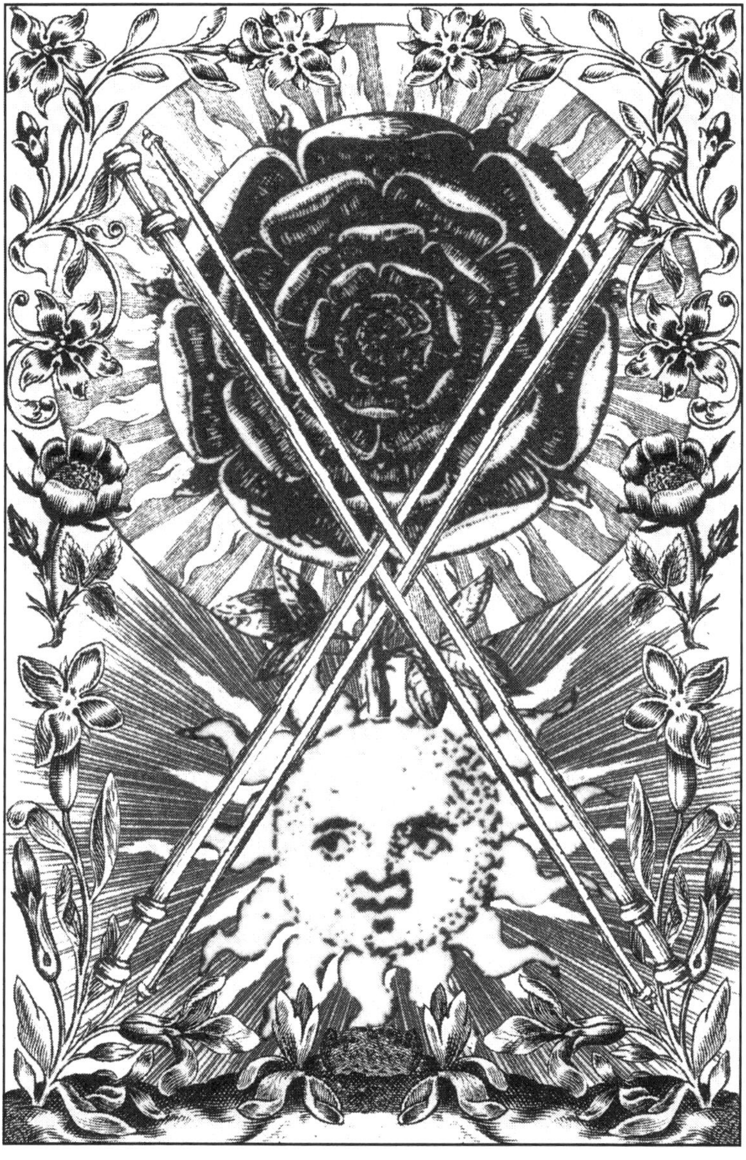

to recover from its immersion in and identification with matter. The Dry Way represents the soul's slow struggle along the path back to Eternity, achieved by developing the attributes of the signs Leo through Capricorn.

The struggle is much more overt when the card appears reversed. Expansive Leo's ruler feels constrained under the legalistic gaze of Saturn in mental Aquarius. Leo's midsummer energies are vigorous and productive but are seldom analytic or strategic in the farsighted style of Aquarius. Leo's style is to offer up a charismatic leader and position him for visibility to rally the workers. But Aquarius is the radical egalitarian view that critiques the cult of personality and nips any jockeying for ego-acclaim in the bud. Whether this becomes a problem or not depends on the human personalities who have come together to fulfill the plan.

The competence and flexibility of the initial core group is an essential strength of this card when upright, but with such a small initial population, it only takes one person having a change of heart to put the whole project at risk. Also, should the focus shift to boosting charismatic individuals instead of supporting all participants equally, the highest promise of this endeavor is likely to drain away, the momentum lost to infighting of a political nature. Selflessness is what's required here, and a motive to serve true human needs.

Five of Wands

Astrology: 21-30 Leo, ruled by Mars   **Sephira:** Gevurah
Essential Dignity: upright Exaltation, Sun in Aries
reversed Fall, Sun in Libra
Angelic Dignities: upright angel spelled LAV, spoken Lauviah
reversed angel spelled HHO, spoken Hahaiah

Five of Wands has historically represented alchemical gold among the Continental Tarots. Because the alchemists were adamant that the *prima materia* (the raw ingredients for the alchemical work) is abundant but unappreciated, available everywhere but valued nowhere, we have given this card the title of Opulence. To express the amazing variety of *prima materia* available to us all, we chose an image that demonstrates Nature's ever-effulgent creative process. Note how the celestial dynamics of the Solar System (Zodiac, Sun, Moon, and planets) are combined and formulated in the imagination (the bi-colored crystal in the center with Mercury and Antimony on it), from which all manner of manifestations pour out into the world to form the fabric of our day-to-day life. A great secret is being revealed here for those who are inclined to seize the hint and run with it.

The design of this card makes use of lenses and prisms to create these converging and then diverging rays of potent Light. In the visual language of Alchemy, the radiant energies of our spiritual guides and archetypes are being gathered and combined in the central crystalline chamber (the soul). Out of this amalgamation, a set of planetary essences is being emanated into the material plane. This central prism is a classic symbol for the Philosopher's Stone, which here stands for the consciousness of an awakened human soul that's striving to evolve. By steadily studying and attracting the powers and properties of the Sun, Moon, and planets, the user of *Tarot of the Holy Light* is becoming his or her own initiator. As one slowly comes to understand the mechanism of Creation, one gradually approaches the mind of the Creator. The Five of Wands represents a healthy and gradual process of self-cultivation, wherein steady attention to the workings of the cosmos results in permanent progress for the evolving soul.

This image encourages us to be active interpreters of our experiences and daily circumstances, rather than passive consumers who sleepwalk through life. In that spirit let's look more deeply into this idea of alchemical gold itself. The reference is not to the shiny baubles that are the end product of the alchemical work. In fact, tradition attributes this card to the refiner's fire that separates the dross from the gold in the alchemist's cauldron. It is the fire that breaks the rock and drives out the gold hidden within it. Over and over the molten gold is skimmed to remove the scum of foaming rock that bubbles up to the top of the basin. This smelting is a violent and intense process, but the end product is nothing less than the pure mineral Light infused with the intelligence of the whole Solar System. Wise souls know that consciousness is the true alchemical gold. To achieve it, the dross of daily life must be patiently cooked down and filtered out. Only after long suffering and challenge do we liberate the true spiritual Sun that has been imprisoned within our souls.

Tarot artists have had trouble illustrating this card convincingly once standard practice departed from associating gold with the Five of Wands. What is most often substituted in divinatory parlance is a distressing scene of conflicting agendas, mixed messages, and daunting confusion. It appears to be "every man for himself" in a rough and tumble atmosphere that promises to bruise all who participate. I read these images as descriptions of the molecular action going on in the superheated crucible, the violent rending of the gold from the rock that contained it. Only those whose mettle is as pure as the noble golden metal will prevail in such a free-for-all.

Another way to look at this constellation of influences is to recognize that Five is the number of the "right hand of discipline," Gevurah. Thus we are looking at an ambitious, willful Martian influence driven by the activating Fire that courses down the Mother Pillar from Shin. This card also covers the third decanate of Leo, which is colored by the force of its Fire-family sub-ruler, Mars. Mars' influence is further reiterated by the astro-Alchemy correspondence for the upright Five of Wands, which takes its remedial potency from the Sun's Exaltation in Aries. Thus the feeling of self-willed empowerment is palpable in this card: If not now, when? If not I, who?

As we can see, pure archetypal ideals (Solar and Lunar Light) become imbued and impressed into the personality through the slow and steady movements of the planets. As the prime movers of the Solar System parade overhead, their influence pours into the manifested world through the mercurial crystal of the human imagination. The act of re-envisioning and re-interpreting renews our heroic spirit after which anything is possible.

In short when this card falls upright, the querant is being complimented for being able to think for his or herself, follow his or her own Lights, and find meaning from joyful participation in the dance of life. But when stressed in reversal, the Five of Wands points to struggles brought about by ambitious maneuvering. The spirit of competition jostles and hustles to push the self

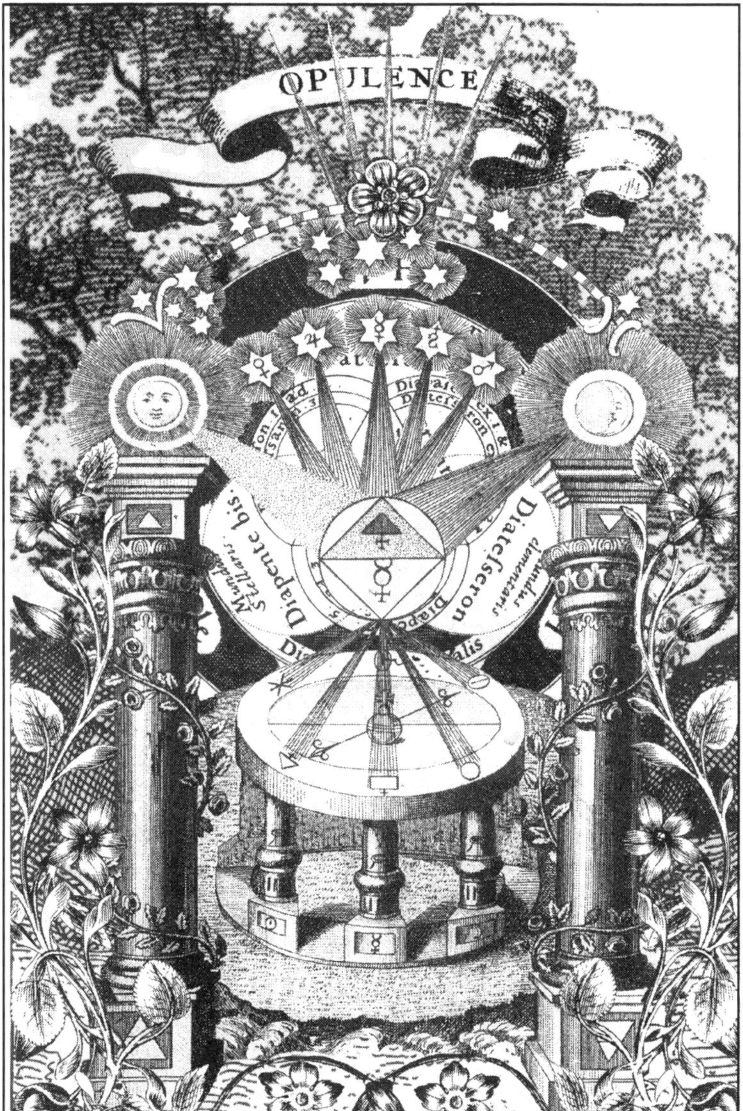
OPULENCE
Diapente bis.
Mundus Stellaris
Diatessaron
Mundus elementaris

forward at the expense of others. In this type of environment, sensitive souls can succumb to overwhelming hopelessness and cave in on themselves, or else lose their temper and flip into overkill. This is the type of setting wherein very few people experience winning, while far too many are branded as losers. To avoid being forced into such an outcome, the truly self-directed individual must disconnect from the mass mind. Very seldom will a fiery influence benefit by being averaged down to the lowest common denominator, its Light dimmed in the miasma of the masses. Nevertheless, these experiences must be endured as the Sun falls into Libra with this reversal.

A fine line exists between demonstrating personal excellence and making others feel like failures. Ask the question: Who really benefits when we all fight so hard for such small rewards? For example, aren't we serving an essentially negative, manipulative agenda when we start applying battle metaphors like "divide and conquer" or "all's fair in love and war" to our intimate lives and activities? When this card shows up reversed, it tempts us to imagine ourselves caught in a zero-sum game. But don't lower yourself to that worldview. Let your motive center on being the best you can be, and spend your time working on your own plans and goals. That way you'll minimize the number of egos bruised along the way, lest your successes be celebrated alone.

Six of Wands

Astrology: 1 – 10 Leo, ruled by the Sun **Sephira:** Tiferet
Essential Dignity: upright Domicile, Sun in Leo
reversed Similar, Sun in Cancer
Angelic Dignities: upright angel spelled AKA, spoken Achaiah
reversed angel spelled KHTh, spoken Cahetel

The Six of Wands places us at the heart of the Suit and the heart of the issue. Tiferet centers the Tree, linking the upper world to the lower one and providing motivation for the two hands, Gevurah and Chesed. The Heart also mediates all of the planetary pairs that arrange themselves around its axis (Jupiter/Mercury, Mars/Venus, and Moon/Saturn). Relating this to the Six of Wands, we learn that the significance of the manifested world pivots around the individual's idea of selfhood, specifically the inherent loyalties, obligations, and privileges that accompany individuation. This is neither a judgment nor a criticism, only a neutral statement of the psychological reality that we discover in the "Six of Will." The path to self-development leads through service to the community. Even the highest lord and lady of the land largely function as the head servants of the realm. There is no escaping it; we all must contribute from the heart to keep the wheels of state on track.

According to ancient theology, humans are designed for a free-will universe, and theoretically nothing interferes with our self-sovereignty except our own vision of ourselves. But in actual fact one soon discovers the collective pressures that inhibit our free expression in this world. Every situation we encounter comes complete with an invisible boundary of convention and expectation that is constantly present, hemming us in. What good is free will if we can't use it any way we want to? Why bother with other people when their influence constrains the full expression of our personal desires? This is how the shallow ego frames the issues. This type of thinking costs some people years of fruitless energy wasted on distractions before they finally realize the value of teamwork in pursuit of collective values.

As we become more enlightened, we ask: How can I learn to desire and foster what is best for everybody, knowing that it will lead to what is best for myself? The inspired soul seeks opportunities to take responsibility and make a difference, as we see across history. Natural leaders channel the self-authorizing power of the Sun in Leo; they "become the change you wish to see." When in tune with the moment, a single individual can become the agent of the collective fate, even if totally accidentally.

Historically this card zeroes in on the domestic hierarchy. In particular the Six of Wands is associated with the servant class in the castle community. We can extend this idea to the more modern expression of allies, helpers, staff, and subordinates in the hierarchy of the workplace or extended family. For every leader there will be a group of followers who have to be minded and managed to ensure that their individual contributions stay in harmony with the larger project. Should a youngster from the lower levels show a special aptitude, a healthy community will ensure that he or she is allowed to advance in the ranks and expand on those talents through direct experience.

The essential virtue of the traditional Six of Wands lies in this process of fostering the best of upcoming talent, thereby making room for new faces in the circle of heroes. It stands to reason, then, that the reversal of this card might sometimes suggest a climate that is reluctant to give credit to the upstarts and outsiders. The lion practices inclusion and gives rewards but only to the extent that his will remains law. His possessive style welds every member of his pride to his demanding ego, or else. The reversed card (Sun in Cancer) suggests an alternate path for those who don't see themselves as herd animals content to remain perpetual children, dependent upon the forceful and controlling lion for their safety and well-being. This alternative option is signified by the austere but noble life of the eagle, who can seize a solitary freedom in the empyrean. Thus the raptor symbolizes our ability to resist the bindings of collective expectations, even if enhanced status might result.

In more recent times the Six of Wands has come to represent respect and acknowledgment coming your way in gratitude for your contributions towards community well-being. The familiar image is often that of a victory parade after a pivotal battle. It took the whole tribe to win the victory, of course, but it was a particular individual's courage and clarity under pressure that inspired the rest to give their all. The accidental hero of the day may not feel particularly deserving of this adulation. Nevertheless, his team is thrilled to have come up the winners, and they want to celebrate all the elements that contributed to their victory. The parade is also an expression of collective relief that the struggle is over. The people's image of their own better selves can now be restored, a true healing after the scourge of war. But let nobody's head be swelled by having a moment in the sun. Enjoy the fifteen minutes of fame should it fall to you, but then get back to daily tasks, since there's nothing about this achievement that will relieve anyone of chopping wood and carrying water.

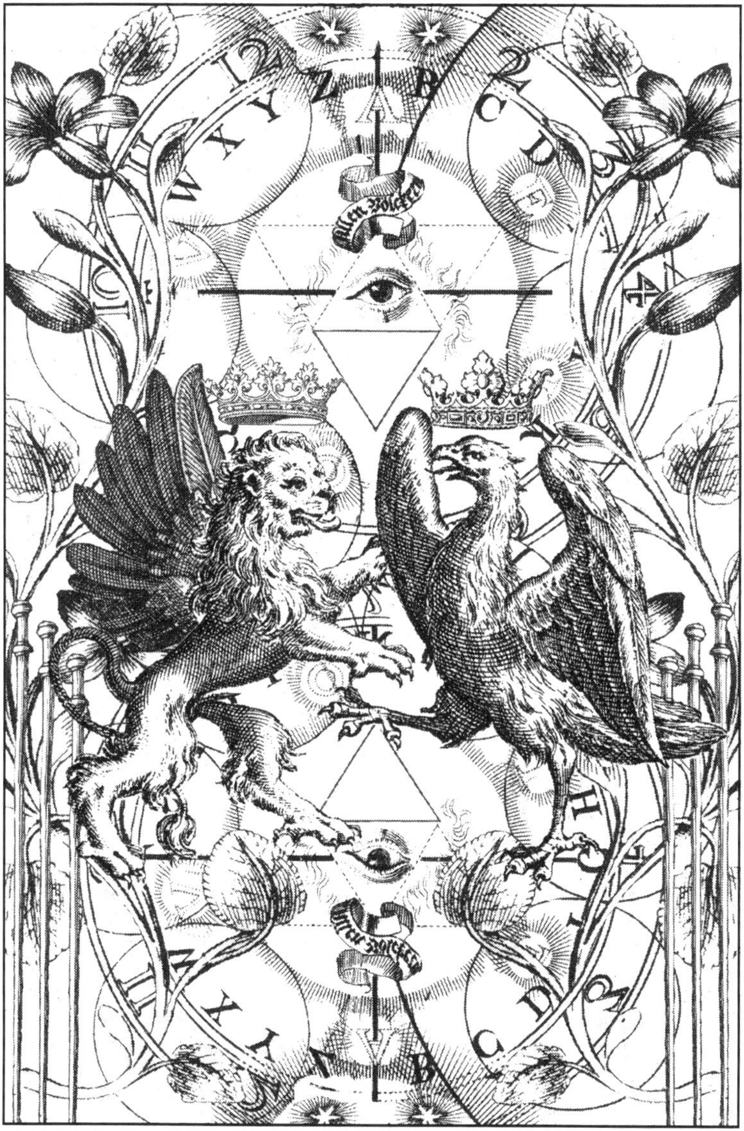
12
W X Y Z
B
2
C D

Whether upright or reversed, Six of Wands highlights the Sun's responsibilities in the signs he co-rules with the Moon (Leo and Cancer). When the Sun is in his own sign of Leo, he pours himself out selflessly to the people, increasing the wellbeing of the collective organism. Sol centers the planets as the "first among equals," and those who cooperate with him will prosper. While in Cancer, on the other hand, Sol turns inward to the private sphere where he is husband of the Moon (and/or student of Sophia). If this association is fertile, there will be projects to complete and young lives to nurture away from the milling throngs. Here Sol takes his turn as "last among equals," sheep-dogging the family parade to ensure that everything wraps up and turns out as planned.

The reversed Six of Wands also presses us with the reality of finite time: there are only so many workable hours per day. Therefore, the choices we make with our time hour to hour will have long-term consequences. It is necessary to think deeply about your priorities because the demands of the collective good (the lion) seem to be competing with the needs of our private individuality (the eagle). In some circumstances we'll be tempted to decline an invitation to support the commonweal, instead taking refuge in our own private reality. But that is the better choice only when the situation is dangerously toxic and perverted, when the group mind is truly in the grip of a mania that you would do better to avoid. Whenever possible the greater good suggests to volunteer something of yourself, making personal resources available to the larger whole, even though that might slow down the fulfillment of your own individual interests. Hopefully the situation can be rescued and improved before sheer survivalism determines that it's "every man for himself."

Seven of Wands

Astrology: 11 - 20 Sagittarius, ruled by Mars **Sephira:** Netzach
Essential Dignity: upright Compliment, Jupiter in Virgo
reversed Detriment, Jupiter in Gemini
Angelic Dignities: upright angel spelled HRI, spoken Hariel
reversed angel spelled HQM, spoken Hakamiah

With the Seven of Wands, you have arrived at your own personal "gate of fears," the edges of your known capacities. In some situations you will be stopped in your tracks needing to rethink your expectations and strategies. In other circumstances you will find a way to rise above and outsmart the appearance of these supposed limits. There is no judgment being made in either case. This is simply the reality we face whenever we set a goal and try to move through the steps of its achievement. There is always a block, a setback, whether we have anticipated it or not. Moving from supposition to action tends to press us right up against the stark facts of the situation, at which point all our woolly-headed hand-waving has to cease so the challenge can be directly addressed. The protagonist is either bound to overcome this obstacle, or else the momentum of the previous six cards must be rerouted in a way that will provide a workaround. Whenever the Seven of Wands appears, you are being challenged to compete with yourself and strive for a "personal best," winning your way through any past self-esteem blocks or inhibitions you still unconsciously harbor.

Esoteric practitioners know that whenever they see the number Seven, there is a chance that an inference is being made to the Seven Planetary Governors. This is certainly a profitable thought to remember in this case. Examine the positions of the planets in your birth chart to discover the unique contribution each one makes to your negative fantasies. This will go a long way towards decoding the significance of the symbols that appear on the Seven of Wands: the sudden leaping fire, the closed gate potentized by the magical symbols woven into its design, and the ominous shadowy path that lies ahead.

Every person has his or her own internal complex of fears and spooks. For most our bogeys need only make a little stir in the back of our minds, and we will immediately self-edit rather than suffer that sensation a minute longer. This reflex works to the disadvantage of anybody who is pushing the envelope or engaging in boundary-crossing experiments. The rulership of Mars over the middle section of Sagittarius reminds us that only those who are bold and unflappable will keep their focus and win the day. We have to continuously question our givens, else our future will always look exactly like the past.

Historically, the Seven of Wands refers to a person who regularly commands success in working his or her will in the world. This person is truly gifted, standing head and shoulders above the rest, a standard-setter and exemplar who exceeds previous conceptions of what is possible. In the early era of Tarot, this card would point to an admired and feared warrior with a reputation for vanquishing overwhelming adversaries. But nowadays one's realm of accomplishment could just as easily appear in the world of science, the arts, communications, or healing. The Seven of Wands person knows what he or she is capable of. Such an individual doesn't hesitate to demonstrate superiority in his or her chosen arena. S/he has outgrown the false humility that tends to average the gifted ones down to the lowest common denominator. All fears of standing out and being exceptional have been conquered.

The "edge" possessed by the Seven of Wands' soul, which lifts him or her above the pack, is an unconquerable spirit. If success can't be had by plan A, then plan B is devised and the same un-crushable energy flows through new channels with equal ferocity. The question is not whether the limit will be overtopped, but when and how this can be arranged. The seven staves built into the gate suggest seven ways of getting things done; the high achiever is the one who has investigated every one of those options, who therefore acts from full knowledge rather than wishful theory.

The astro-alchemical orientation of this Sagittarian card sends Jupiter to the sign of his Compliment when upright. Hence Virgo comes into focus as provider of a precise methodology that will systematically deliver the fulfillment of our aspirations. Virgo's concerns are for steady nourishment and attentive care, maintaining the web of life (including the flora/fauna of the gut and digestive system) through prolonged and patient attention to detail. Over time Jupiter energies applied in the Virgo style will cultivate robust abundance in a well-ordered, sustainable, hygienic society.

Contrast this Complimentary orientation with the issues raised by Jupiter in his Detriment in Gemini. The relative immaturity of this sign, where a short attention span and inadequate preparation lead to multiple false starts, tends to fritter away vast amounts of life force before any worthy project can truly begin. A tremendous amount of practice time and self-discipline will have to be expended to equip the individual with the necessary skills, strategy, and sheer guts required to challenge the presenting obstacle. The Seven of Wands reversed hints that if we have come to this pass thinking we were prepared, but still we

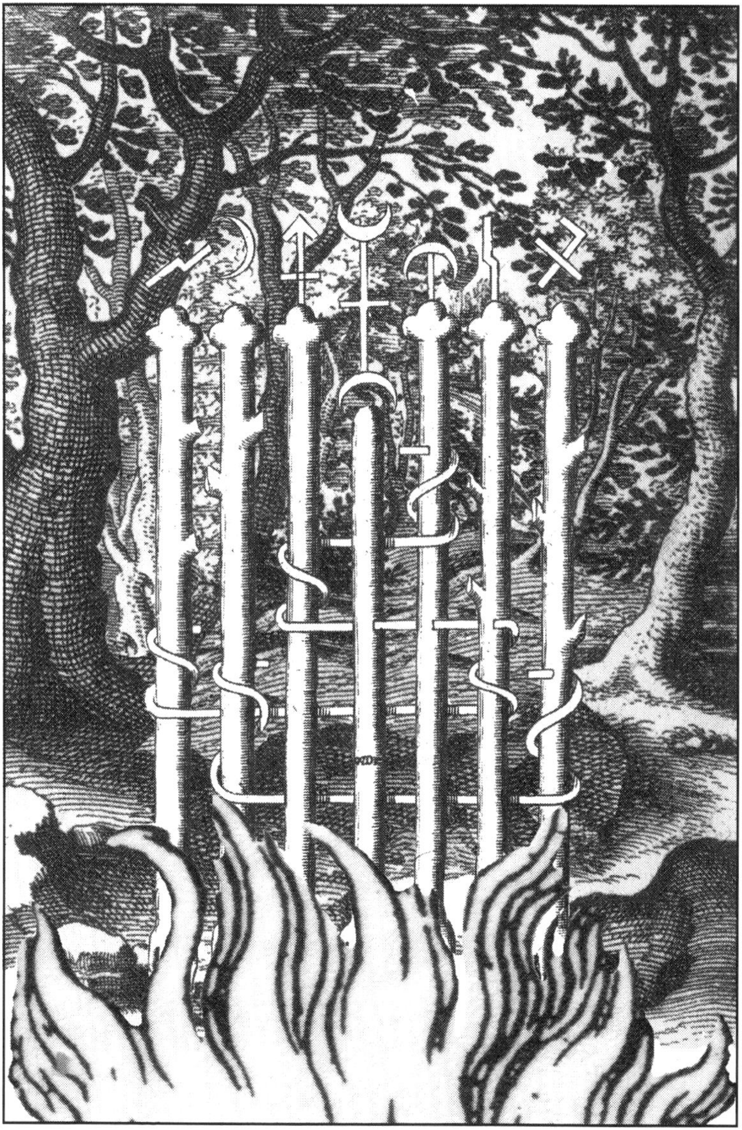

fail to pass through freely, it is likely because we have allowed our limitations to overtop our will, instead of the other way around.

Beware of the creeping smugness that can appear with this card in reversal. Having unique gifts or being lucky enough to arrive at the right place at the right time do not make you invincible, nor do they indemnify you against thought errors. Remember that there is always somebody smarter, better looking, craftier, and more talented than you, who would be glad to steal that victory from your unprepared hands. Don't waste this opportunity on the pursuit of trivialities that only serve your momentary whims; seek out real accomplishments that have the potential to make a difference for the betterment of people's lives in the future.

Eight of Wands

Astrology: 21 - 30 Sagittarius, ruled by Sun   **Sephira:** Hod
Essential Dignity: upright Exaltation, Jupiter in Cancer
reversed Fall, Jupiter in Capricorn
Angelic Dignities: upright angel spelled LAV, spoken Laviah
reversed angel spelled KLI, spoken Caliel

With the Eight of Wands, circumstances have reached a flash point. The astral weather is now perfect for wildfires, and here we see that potential becoming actualized. The tinder-dry forest floor is thick with fallen leaves and dead twigs. Now spontaneous ignition threatens to throw sparks in all directions. What will stop the flames from spreading into the surrounding forest? Might it be better to let the fire run its course?

European conquerors found evidence in both North and South America of indigenous populations using controlled burns to alter the habitat to suit their purposes. The act of harnessing fire as a tool for human use moved the self esteem of our species many notches up the evolutionary ladder, from being animals to being people. Before we could become masters of fire, we had to outgrow our very justified and self-preservative fear of it. It will never be known how many generations of humans came and went before a primate reached out with a dry stick to ignite the first torch. This is the paradox of evolution and the ultimate secret of Alchemy: We can't exploit the outer world until we master the inner world. Our picture of ourselves in Nature needed to undergo a radical restructuring, from passive opportunists to active directors of the Elements, before we could assume our current station in the hierarchy of Nature.

Fire is the classic magical example of a natural force that is dangerous but awakening, potentially fatal, and yet generously life-affirming. Terrestrial Fire is the earthly token of the Sun, which is why every altar around the world will host a lit flame while ceremonies are being enacted. Even Jacob Boehme, pacifist though he was in heart and soul, clearly understood that the Wrath he found in the Saturn/Father archetype provides the essential precondition for the evocation of the Feminine Divine. The truth is, personal consciousness is increased only by the presence of pain and suffering; there is no other way. We have to become dissatisfied with things as we find them before we will make the necessary moves to improve our lot. Assume that when you see the Eight of

Wands in a spread, it will be necessary to leap into action to respond properly in the moment. No half measures will do.

The Eight of Wands often shows a flight of arrows or staffs moving through the air in formation, as if an unseen group of spear-throwers had released them simultaneously. When the card appears upright, the reader can assume that these projectiles were released to further the seeker's goals and plans. However, when the card appears reversed, the seeker might begin to feel targeted in an uncomfortable way. A simple formula to remember for this card is that when the Eight of Wands appears upright, the seeker is closing in on a goal that is soon to be achieved. But when the card appears reversed, the forces of chaos and unpredictable results might just rise up and begin closing in on the seeker. A simple change of wind or a bolt of lightning probing into a pile of tinder can precipitate all hell breaking loose. With that comes a sudden acceleration of drastic developments, even to the extent of a total loss that devastates the very landscape within which the goal was to be secured.

The traditional title of the card also echoes the idea of swiftly unfolding events, whether by intentional design or unpremeditated accident. In any case, a huge amount of energy is due to be released, and both the positive and negative consequences of that contingency are multiplying fast. It would not be remiss to think of this card as the burning bush in the sense of a sign or portend of circumstances speeding up and the stakes being raised. Ask yourself, "What is Spirit trying to tell me through this image? Where in my life am I being prepared, prodded, and pushed into spontaneous transformation?"

There are more serene and prosaic versions of the Eight of Wands which aren't necessarily marked by the feeling of emergency we have inculcated into our imagery. This calmer approach will often emphasize the sophisticated and demanding agricultural dance that farm families perform to secure their harvest each year. The *Medieval Scapini Tarot* parallels the growth of a summer's garden with the swift growth of human children into adults having children of their own. In each instance, emphasis is on the relentless pace of seasonal change and the race we run to keep up with it. With the turning of the seasons we are constantly hustled by Nature's transformations. There is no remedy but to live with that awareness firmly in mind. We are put on notice: Catch up. Get busy. Do it now. There is literally no time to waste.

Reversed meanings take their color from the more stressful aspects of the above observations. Initial stages of the project might not have been handled with proper attention to detail, making it very difficult to achieve or maintain order now. In the current situation excess growth, weeds, and a build-up of dead matter are marring the garden and putting the harvest at risk. Unforeseen

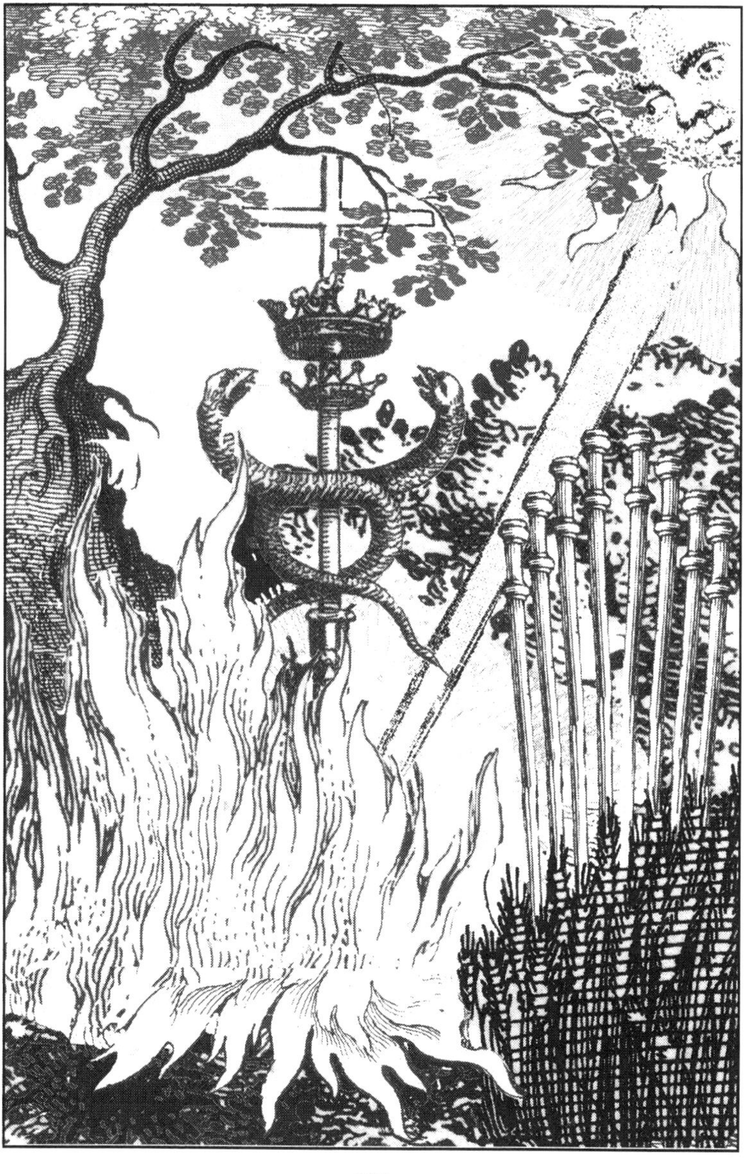

consequences are running rampant, draining energy and resources. Jupiter now has to accept intervention from Capricorn's more melancholic temperament, which has the power to freeze things in place for a little while. An out-of-season cold and wet spell can lower the danger level temporarily, but it also puts a damper on Jupiter's spirits, quashing his enthusiastic dream of "hot fun in the summertime" (Jupiter in Cancer). An inclement period might seem endless while we long for a break in the clouds. But until this setback is taken advantage of (to put order back onto the verging chaos of overgrowth), Jupiter's fond fantasy of abundance and security will remain a far-off daydream.

Nine of Wands

Astrology: 1-10 Sagittarius, ruled by Jupiter **Sephira:** Yesod
Essential Dignity: upright Domicile, Jupiter in Sagittarius
Reversed Similar, Jupiter in Pisces
Angelic Dignities: upright angel spelled IZL, spoken Yezalel
Reversed angel spelled MBH, spoken Mebahel

Thor's hammer is pounding in the Nine of Wands. A volcano has awakened and it dominates the landscape. Two creatures that are normally predator and prey, the wolf and the goat, take refuge together in a cave that offers protection for both. There are times when the necessity of the moment overwhelms our traditional postures, forcing us to make peace with strange companions. Admit your weakness. In extreme circumstances, the old order of business has to flex. As a result you might find unaccustomed allies in the most unusual of situations.

The drama we witness in this card has its origin in Jupiter's attraction to larger-than-life situations. This is not an ordinary day in the forest. Instead the whole landscape is shuddering and molting in an extreme way around the two shocked animals. Some might interpret the volcano's eruption as a sign of disfavor from the gods, a warning, or a punishment. It might even be hard to avoid the feeling of being jinxed, fated, or singled out for harassment by a higher power. But consider that the degree of one's setback on this bad day is probably in direct proportion to the degree of one's grandiosity on a good day. Perhaps a bit of humbled pride would be medicinal, reminding even the wolves that we are all just fleas on the back of Gaia, no single life being any more important than another.

Surely nothing will be the same after this moment. The explosion in the background carves a line in time, which will forever separate "before" from "after" in the memory of everyone who lives through this experience. Surviving an epic adventure like this volcanic explosion permanently changes the internal texture of one's consciousness. Perhaps one's fear of death will suddenly disappear. One might discover a hidden pocket of religiosity buried under the veneer of cynicism. The stress of it all can lead to a transcendent vision, a powerful spiritual conviction of the type that could never have emerged in calmer times. If nothing else, the riveting power of the volcano and the earthquake helps us rediscover our awe, our respect for Nature, and the childlike qualities of wonder, trust, and submission.

The Nine of Wands is often used to indicate a need for a time-out in the midst of a high-stakes and high-intensity environment. None of us is made of stone. We can only handle so much stress before we need to hide out from the fray, mend wounds, and restore our vital forces. An event of the scale that dwarfs mere individuals is happening right now. Don't personalize it; there is no advantage to be gained from continuing any longer in fight-or-flight mode. As the old saying goes, "He who fights and runs away lives to fight another day." This card does not counsel heroism, but instead recommends self-preserving practicality.

The image on the Nine of Wands advises that if you have found a spot of temporary safety, you are correct to just seize the moment and rest up. In a team or troop effort, cede the front lines to fresher hands for now. Resist the ego's attachment to staying at the crest of the action. In any long extended conflict, participants must try to snatch some down-time whenever possible to avoid becoming just one more corpse on the battlefield. There might even be times when the polarizing team uniforms would be secretly abandoned, and battlefield enemies could find themselves sharing food, warmth, and companionship offsides of the formal conflict. Not every soldier aspires to die for their cause. The will to live is strong and enduring, even in these fragile and delicate bodies we occupy. Don't be guilty of underestimating your capacity for creative adaptation. Perhaps the extremity of the situation will give birth to a radical new form of cooperation that was unimaginable in previous times. Strange times make strange bedfellows.

Reversed, this card shows the danger of becoming punch-drunk and losing perspective due to the radical pressures coming to bear. Piscean energies are vulnerable, sensitive, delicate, and easily traumatized. We might have let our guard down prematurely, or we might have entertained the enemy unawares. Adverse circumstances can leave us too exhausted to be effective in calculating our next moves, too rattled to accept help or even see an avenue of retreat. At this point one is running low on resources for rising to the occasion, and our decisions will not be the best. Try not to leave yourself short of essential support in times that demand high performance. In my own life, this card has come to symbolize "migraine weather," especially when reversed.

When there's been no chance to recover from past blows, there is no stamina for taking another beating. If you find yourself hitting bottom, leave the heroics and grandstanding to others. Just quit the scene. Even if you'll have to endure a loss of prestige and personal pride, remember that a punch-drunk and addled fighter cannot be an asset to his or her cause. When this Nine of Wands is reversed, it's good to remember Aesop's fable of the Wolf and the

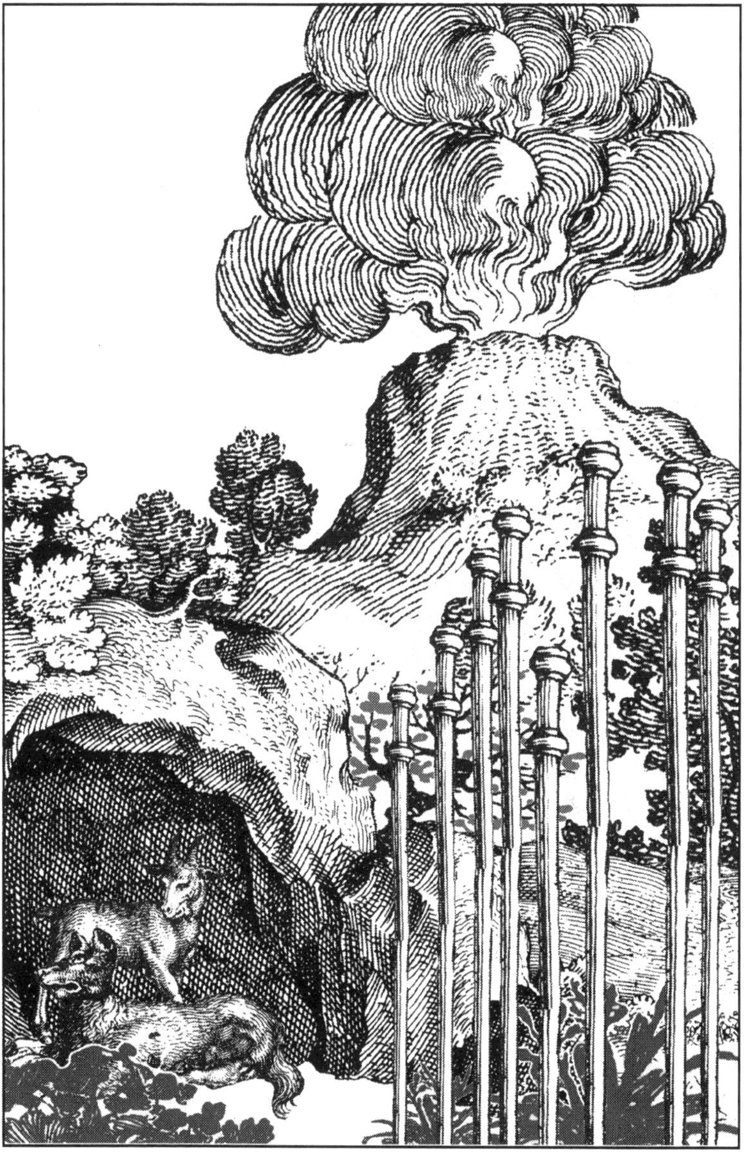

Goat. Don't accept any invitations that will put you in harm's way. Better to spend life searching out sparse grasses among the rocky crags, alert for loose rocks and avalanche, than to become a creature of the flatlands, forever subject to wolfish predations.

Ten of Wands

Astrology: Grand Trine in Fire; Aries, Leo and Sagittarius
Sephira: Malkhut

The Ten of each Suit stands for a convergence of all the energies, characteristics, and expressions of its Element. This includes those Cardinal (initiating), Fixed (stabilizing), and Mutable (transforming) qualities the Element manifests as it weaves through the Zodiac. Accordingly, the Ten of Wands catalogues a combination of Solar Fire (and its reflection from the face of the Moon), wildfire, and the chemically bound fire that greens the plants and reddens the animals' blood. In all these forms, Fire is the energy that stimulates, speeds up, and irritates the world, forcing growth and change whether it's wanted or not.

As we look upon this ancient pagan image of the crucified serpent, we embrace a paradox that is older than Christianity, yet that is just as torturous and unsolved today as it was in antiquity. What is the purpose of the great sacrifices we all make in this life, the heroic labors and courageous challenges, when faced with their ultimate end in certain death? What does it mean to be born into an imperfect world that will batter and bruise us from cradle to grave, which will ultimately hound us right out of our bodies at the end? Exactly what is it about this life that is worth this kind of suffering, especially in the light of its guaranteed expiration? Only the individual soul can find an answer to these questions, and the answer will apply to the finder alone. Yet without the painful search and self-expenditure, what is found becomes meaningless. Such is the nature of the eternal quest, of which this serpent is one of the symbols.

It can be hard to fully fathom the mystery of the serpent when one has been subject to the reductionism that most religions impose in order to regulate their adherents' beliefs. In fact, the serpent has been a powerful, mysterious, and charged symbol for all humans since the dawn of time. No single religion actually "owns" the serpent, though contemporary evidence suggests that the Jungians are its current sponsors and apologists. Even a brief attempt to summarize humanity's relationship with the serpent would take pages. For this purpose the serpent refers to the animating Spirit, the life force, kundalini, or chi that distinguishes living creatures from inanimate objects.

This dramatic image of the crucified serpent refers back to our Old Testament ancestors. The word for serpent in ancient Greek is "ophis." This is an anagram of the noun "sophia," meaning wisdom, which was not originally a proper name. There was a sect of gnostics (the Ophite Gnostics), existing both outside of early Christianity and within it who believed the serpent of Genesis was a messenger from Divine Sophia (God's Wisdom or Logos) sent to give fallen Adam and Eve the saving knowledge of their eternal origin and destiny. In the fascinating chapter on the Ophites in Hanegraaff's *Dictionary of Gnosis & Western Esotericism* (p. 897), we find these immensely suggestive remarks from Hippolytus' description of certain gnostics' beliefs: "... the 'true perfect serpent' was shown to the Israelites by Moses in the desert (Num. 21). This universal serpent is 'the wise word of Eve' (Gen. 3) that finally appeared in the form of the Son of Man who, like the bronze serpent in the desert, was to be 'lifted up' (John 3, 14)."

In light of the above, the Ten of Wands represents an all-out sacrifice, an ultimate commitment to a sacred trust that demands everything you have to give. We are looking at a pre-Christian crucifixion portraying the agony of Sophia/Logos taking on the cross of matter in her effort to awaken the Fallen souls to their Divine Nature. The Moist Light of our Sophianic inheritance is being called forth from the broken serpent, elicited by the Wrath, fulmination, and chaos of unmitigated heavenly Fire. Misunderstood, reviled, cast-aside, and crucified, Sophia responds to us from our own woundedness and dreams of healing, as well as from the margins of all the Abrahamic-family scriptures. Little do her detractors know that their very resistance to Wisdom will serve as a lightning rod, attracting a fateful bolt from the blue to crack open the clenched heart of mater, releasing the healing Holy Spirit into this suffering landscape.

When you see this card fall upright in your spread, be of good cheer. You are coming to the culmination of your labors. Your sufferings will not have been experienced in vain. Your mission is to do whatever it takes, to give your all, and expend yourself utterly, letting Spirit determine the results.

If instead the Ten of Wands should appear reversed, one might be tempted to say, "This is a lost cause, give it up." Those whose courage is ebbing might consider this a sign of failure. But the card itself would beg to differ. The significance of the blue serpent in the background now comes to the fore. Unlike the still-living red serpent pulsing and panting on its cross, the blue serpent is a fossil, long dead but still preserving the shape and attitude of his final sacrifice. Like a statue of a saint or an illustration in a book of myths, this serpent mutely testifies to the motivating power of spiritual inspiration, even absent a current living exemplar.

History proves that the seeds of transcendental ideas can lie dormant in the collective psyche for generations and centuries, to one day suddenly arise

175

full-blown in circumstances far from the time and space of their origin. The midnight color of this frozen serpent matches that of the dark night in which the Moon floats. The ideal for which it died is still potent and transformative, even when it is hidden and dormant within the vault of the collective unconscious. Upon contact with a soul that is ready, willing, and able, the Divine Idea will come to life again in a heartbeat.

King of Wands

Leo

Our King of Wands stands in a scintillating landscape of living flames. Even the pruned-down tree in his hand, which remains rooted to the Earth, is ignited at the tips with tongues of flame. His aura is lit up as well, haloed by a rainbow bearing the 72 names of God from Athanasius Kircher. Magical flowers rush to open in the effulgence of this King's radiance. He possesses a special gift that travels through his noble bloodline, called the "King's Touch." This King is a Magus by blood; it is believed that his blessing can heal stubborn diseases. Even the Catholic prohibitions couldn't gainsay the powers his subjects attributed to him. He perfectly fits the near-universal archetype of "a fertility-bearing pagan good luck king" (Flint, 1991, p. 383).

The King of Wands also resembles the classic hero of myth and legend, being larger than his circumstances in personality as well as in form. This trait sometimes makes him the victim of his own arresting presence. As one would expect of a charismatic leader who is known for being entrepreneurial and ambitious, the King of Wands is constantly being petitioned to lend energy to new adventures. He neither gets nor craves much in the way of downtime, whether he's at rest or on the road. In his youth it was hard for him to be left behind to mind the castle and protect the ladies when military campaigns were being undertaken. He would quickly feel itchy and restless, bored with the predictable routines and angry at not being included in the action. If his friends and courtiers weren't able to devise fitting outlets for his outsized energies, this King's attitude would become surly and challenging, irritated with life itself. Even in his ennui, this King shows an uncommon edge and intensity.

Like the folk heroes Paul Bunyan and John Henry, this King's mighty energy and vitality serves as an inspiration to his followers. Under duress he proves to be a formidable figurehead of personality power, a moving force to be reckoned with. He is a very difficult person to say "no" to and make it stick. The enigmatic *El Gran Tarot Esoterico* gives the King of Wands a set of attributes that point to the famed Babylonian King Nebuchadnezzar II, who ruled from 605 BCE to 562 BCE. Nebuchadnezzar's outsized military and cultural achievements were chronicled in the Old Testament, most notably in the Book of David. The Bible also details the divine punishment he receives due to his overweening pride. This entailed living through seven years of feral madness, raving naked through his imperial gardens on all fours, growling and barking like an animal. Thence for millennia, Nebuchadnezzar's example has represented the brilliant despot whose ego expands until it shatters against its own inadequacy, to then regress and devolve beneath its own extremes.

In daily life people with the qualities of this King will prefer and crave a big assignment, since they would rather lead than follow. Whether he succeeds or fails, he wants to do so spectacularly, without inhibitions or impingement. Unfortunately, his judgment is all too easily influenced by subjective factors. This will be evidenced by his court's environment, which is permeated with flattery, seduction, and collusion. Always a performer, the Wand King over achieves in situations where it will be noticed. His manner of dress and architecture betrays a taste that is biased towards the grandiose. In private he expects to be served and adored like the head lion of the pride. Ever the benevolent despot, he makes life wonderful for those he loves, and agonizing for those who displease him.

Having so much innate attitude and magical charisma can sometimes be a burden, even to those who are born to the purple. It is not possible for the King of Wands to have a neutral impact or to be anonymous in any situation. Like a chemical catalyst, his presence automatically changes the atmosphere, effortlessly constellating new probabilities out of the same old situations. He cannot be disguised or passed off as anything or anybody else other than who he innately is; the sheer demand-level of holding his gaze is riveting and unmistakable.

The King of Wands finds that the burden of people's projections can be inhibiting, often forcing him to forego spontaneity and replace it with calculation. Everybody in his realm has opportunities to take a time-out from their labors, but he never once gets a break from his exceptionalism. There is never a day when he isn't King. Even when he suffers, it is seldom from lack, but instead it's from excess of one type or another. His attacks of temper can be fatal to those around him, though he will experience regret and self-loathing after the heat of the moment passes. As he matures he'll slowly learn that the most effective leadership consists of doing and saying less, but watching closely and listening deeply.

When this King appears reversed, it is his fate to endure pain for his exceptional nature. This image is actually a portrait that Kircher made during one of his travels, of a man afflicted with gigantism. The man's body didn't know how to stop growing. Kircher positioned him next to the tree to demonstrate how massive his limbs were, how enormous his hands. The model was willing

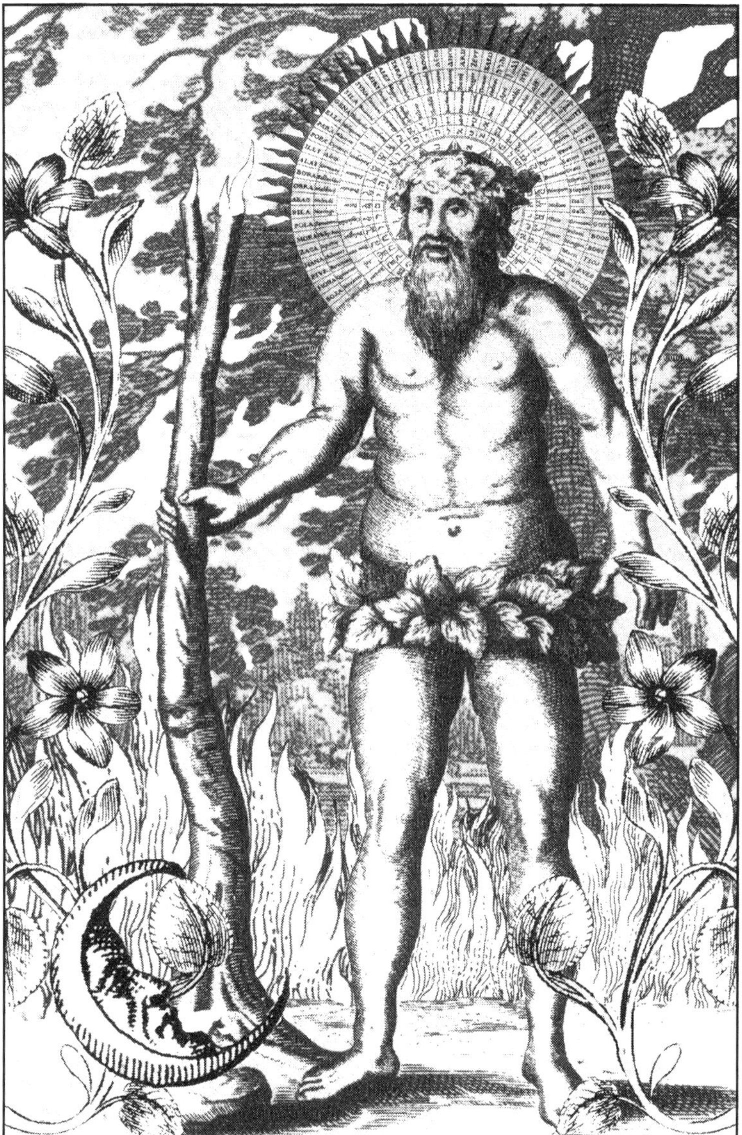

to pose naked to show his struggle with gravity. Looking at the fine line of hair that runs down the center of his chest and torso, it is clearly zigzagged. He also has deep divots on his sides between some of his ribs. This indicates that his backbone isn't straight: His vertebrae are pulled this way and that from the effort of holding up his great mass, so his ribs are akimbo as well. The man's arms are also short in proportion to his legs; this implies that his inner organs might suffer from proportional distortion as well. Doubtless it was difficult for his circulatory system to lift his bodily fluids up out of his lower body. On top of everything else he is dealing with, his chest is narrow compared to his hips, suggesting that his breathing would likely have been impinged and painful. Odds are the man died young, overwhelmed by the exertion of simple survival. Let this be a reminder that there is such a thing as "terminal uniqueness." Too much of a good thing is still too much.

Queen of Wands

Aries

This Queen of Wands is a natural leader, an accomplishment-oriented type whose gift it is to create teams and assign tasks. She sees to it that the collective labors run smoothly, that all phases of the operation are on task and performing to expectations. She is as comfortable running the nunnery as the farm, the production floor as the sales operation. Everything she gets involved with prospers. Our Wand Queen will often be found with sleeves rolled up and skirts tied back, sweating in the sun alongside her employees. She's a quick study in all she undertakes, forcing her workers to keep pace with her prodigious energy. One of this Queen's most endearing qualities is her gift for keeping the work fun. When upright, she is the best kind of supervisor to have, much like a challenging but encouraging mother, believing that you have it in you to do your best work under her direction. Her rosy shoes make it clear that after the sunset, she can also play and party just as hard as she works.

This Queen of Wands believes in her team, and all the hand-picked members work hard to please her. She is, however, not the least bit sentimental. Like a seasoned farm wife, she views her crops, her animals, even her employees and family members as necessary tools for the achievement of the larger goal. Being a woman and a mother does not interfere with her productivity and efficiency. When it's time to take the lambs to slaughter, she can let them go without a second thought. The agitated call of the mother cow with full udders, bellowing all night long for her calf that has been sold at market, doesn't trouble this Queen's sleep in the slightest. That's the sound of money in the bank, after all.

In fact, our Queen's thinking is very much like that of the raptor that is her totem. She is willing to make the hard choices, including deciding who lives and who dies. In this sense, the Queen of Wands gives evidence of the fiercer attributes of Mother Nature. She's not above imposing her will unilaterally. She does not pause at calling for body-modification upon her helpless children (as in circumcision, infibulation, or foot binding) as part of the process of making them more culturally acceptable for the future marriage-market. It doesn't occur to her to think about what these individuals stand to lose from this gross interference, only the future usefulness of getting the necessary work done early. Frankly, the Queen of Wands is not big on emotions or empathy. She finds them impractical; they get in the way of taking care of business.

Because of these qualities, this is the very best Queen to have on hand when one is facing an emergency. Her entire administration is based on a fierce and ongoing analysis of the expanded "now." Her exceptional will-power and self-discipline are legendary throughout her land. She knows when it's time to stop talking and start doing. This is the type of woman who will be found leading nations, overseeing the social service net, coordinating difficult campaigns, and calling her subjects to sacrifice. Because she is willing to put herself through whatever she is asking of others, her castle staff and family will follow her unquestioningly, secure in the knowledge that she is watching their backs. Love her or hate her, everybody has to acknowledge that this is one formidable dame.

The Queen of Wands copes with the intensity of her role by never looking back but advancing ever forwards. She harbors no hesitation and entertains few regrets. In her view, she is only doing what is necessary, no more and no less. Whether this Queen represents a housewife or the manager of a huge downtown hospital, she sees her role as the one who imposes order and keeps the process moving right along. Introspection and questioning the system are not welcome in her operation, except in measured doses. This Queen also doesn't care what anybody thinks of her, which gives her an amazing freedom to proceed without being inhibited by outside influence. In her intelligence and courage she is the equal or better of nearly every citizen of her realm, male or female, young or old. Anybody who makes the mistake of typecasting her as a "little woman" will be summarily run over.

At her best this Queen is inspiring to men and women alike because her avid intelligence and love of a challenge are infectious. Nobody can get the best of her in sport, and she won't be taken advantage of in love either. If anybody has the antidote to the cloying clichés of helpless femininity, this Queen is the one. Like the pioneer women of the wild West she can shoot and cook and sew and wrangle horses, and then in the evening she will smoke and drink the men under the table, dancing until the wee hours. Whatever she does, she gives the effort 100%, and anybody who doesn't is a loser in her eyes. Her Spartan approach to life results in a populace who are competitive, fast-thinking, hardy, and fit.

A moment's thought will make it clear what the reversed suggestions are in this Queen's case. Her paramilitary attachment to her game plan and strategy can crush the life out of any spontaneity that sneaks into her viewfinder. She can be a bit ruthless, sometimes breathtakingly so. Even her friends and loved

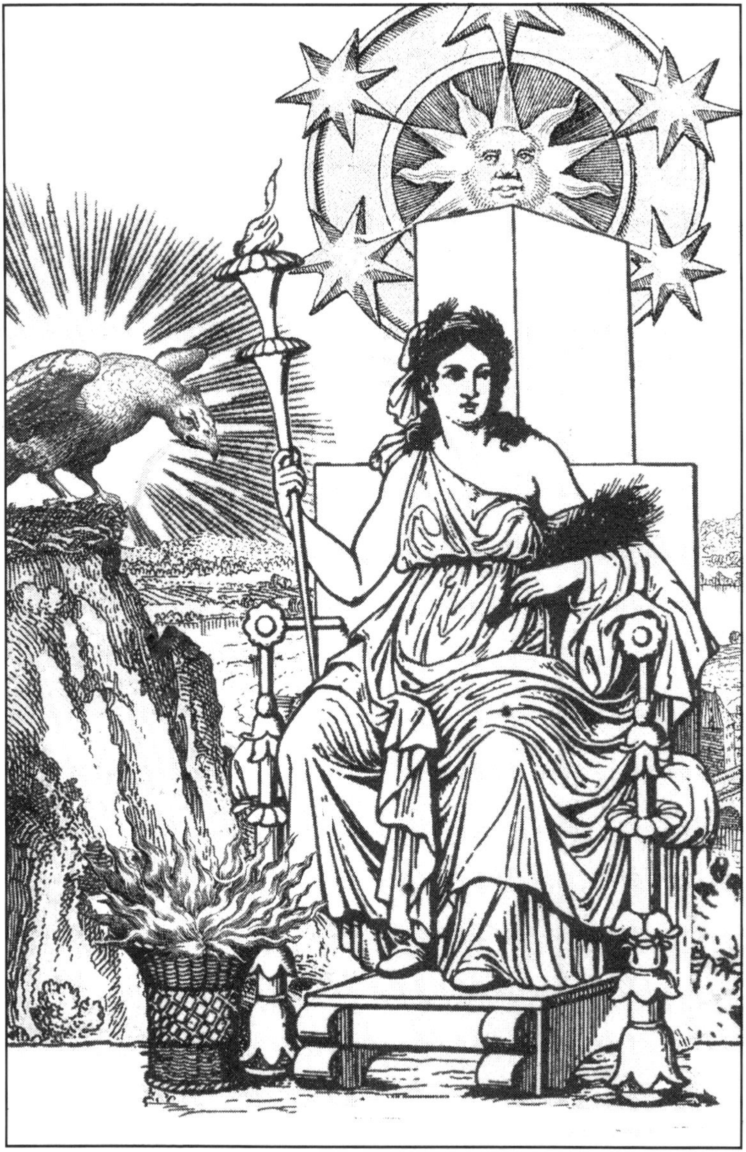

ones can be stunned by how quickly her mood can shift from generous and open minded to controlling, blaming, and shaming. If she feels she is losing her grip on the direction events are moving, somebody is going to be punished. This will happen right in public so the whole realm understands the consequences of displeasing the Queen. Do anything you can to avoid needing her sympathy. In this Queen's universe, individuals who cannot carry their weight and contribute to the whole simply aren't fed. It's nothing personal, you must understand, she simply can't see a practical reason to support the weaklings or off-types. Better to stay out of her line of sight if you can't make an excellent presentation the instant you are called to account.

Knight of Wands

Sagittarius

The Knight of Wands is a rabble-rouser and fire starter, a feisty and easily provoked character that bursts into flames first and asks questions later. This Knight is not shy about how much he enjoys a fight; he also experiences some reluctance to embrace diplomatic solutions, even when they are truly called for. In his own view he's trying to help, rescuing the world from its natural chaotic state by imposing his sense of order on the space around him. Like the mythical salamander that is his totem, he thrives in high-demand circumstances that would deplete and consume the average person with their ceaseless stress. This Knight lives with passion and verve, drama and excitement. It's truly never a dull moment in this fellow's company.

The Knight of Wands has a special mission in the world of Tarot. His keyword is almost always "embarking," which refers to his get-up-and-go, his willingness to hit the road, embrace change, take a risk and, if necessary, lead the raiding party. He can often be seen in beautiful new armor on the back of a huge, well-fed battle steed, giving the impression that he excels with every advantage that his knightly education can impart. He keeps himself skilled with all the newest weapons, as well as being a strategist with a fertile imagination. In times of peace he shows himself to be an able artist or musician, even a bit of a fashion-hound. But he takes his greatest pleasure from remembrance of his fiercest adversaries, without whom, he realizes, his skills would never have risen to their highest peak of expression.

The Knight of Wands' virtues include a visionary inspiration that seems to make magic wherever he passes. Like the fiery letter Shin hanging over his head, this Knight has a galvanizing effect on nearly everybody. Whether they are attracted or repelled by him, everybody finds his glittering presence riveting to experience. He is capable of being swept up by vast spiritual transports, which illuminate his personality from within and impart a near-messianic cast to his aura. When he becomes possessed of his certainty, his unassailable belief in the cause rouses courage in the bowels of his troops and casts fear into the heart of his adversaries. Like a berserker or a kamikaze, he does not count the cost of his attack, knowing that the element of surprise and shock works in his favor. He will literally do whatever it takes to win the high ground and will count his fallen troops as heroes.

Representing a Mutable sign, this Knight of Wands has some of the shape-shifting, androgynous qualities of his related Trump, the Devil. One of his personifications in myth and legend is the renegade priest who leads a secret flock in forgotten, ancient rites. There's also a chance that he is an ordained member of one of the military orders within the Church. He is most often thought of as the anonymous returned Crusader who patrols the dark forest between castle outposts. In this role he serves as a one-man police force, priest, and avenging angel, bringing civilization to areas where it would otherwise never penetrate. In the Renaissance world, the Knight of Wands would carry some of the cachet of a superhero because of his combination of castle culture, wilderness survival skills, mystical inspiration, and remorseless force.

This Knight shows more than one face because his mood swings are so dynamic and wide-ranging. When he's presenting his benevolent aspect, he's magnetic, almost angelic, radiating Light and goodwill for the whole Creation and making everything seem possible. In his performer mode he can strike any number of attractive poses, charming his audience with sincerity and heart. The Wand Knight's fearlessness and willingness to confront can certainly be a blessing, too, as when he's defending threatened treasures or interfering with dark forces. In the tradition of natural warriors everywhere, the Knight of Wands is the one who will volunteer to enter the cave of the dragon and confront it on its home turf. (He does this just to test himself, but if he saves the village in the process, so much the better.)

Like the magical and psychic youngest brother in the old fairy tales, our Knight can find his way through the maze and save the princess when his older and more traditional brothers fail. If you find yourself faced with such a Knight, do not succumb to his shape-shifty distractions and flashy diversions. Keep track of your temper when this Knight is around to be sure you don't provoke him to unleash his Fire (which he will gladly do at a moment's notice). The Wands Knight really enjoys intense experiences and is always ready to "take it to the next level," but that doesn't mean you have to go along for the ride. Once in awhile, that kind of kamikaze intensity is perfect, but on a daily basis it can be exhausting.

When this Knight appears reversed, righteous indignation comes boiling out unchecked, and his more temperamental side starts chewing up the landscape. There is irrationality to his inflamed persona that expands all out of proportion to the infraction it's trying to address. He may have a legitimate point that deserves to be acknowledged, but it can't be resolved because he's so

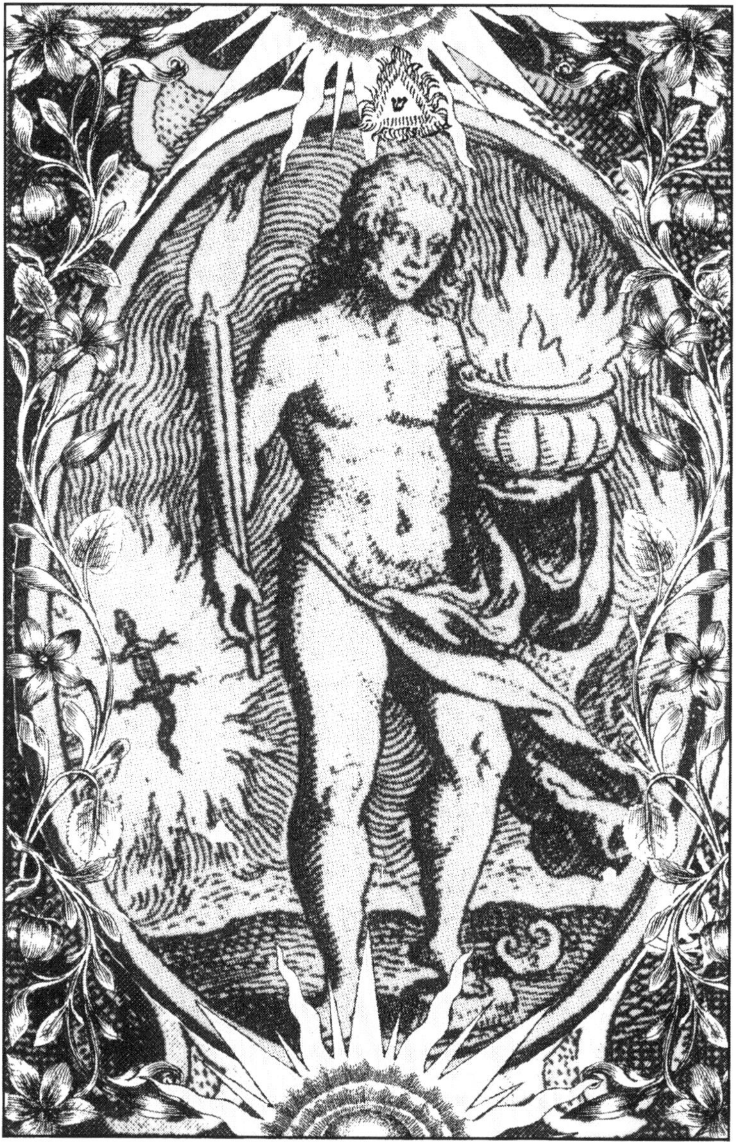

over-the-top with indignation and accusations. Some say that he's got a permanent chip on his shoulder, stemming from a deep-seated sense of inferiority. Others feel that the sign of Sagittarius is burdened with an innate sense of specialness that is a handicap to simple shared equality.

This Knight's vices are bossiness, paranoia, and exaggeration to the point of hysteria. Once he gets on a tear, it's hard to stop him until he flames out and drops from the sky like a burned-out husk. Then he's miserable and mortified because, of course, the whole debacle was preventable in the first place. The secret reason why the Knight of Wands goes through these fluctuations and suffers these extremes is that he's a closet perfectionist, is massively competitive, and secretly fears that he's not measuring up. The force behind all of his drama and intensity is anxiety, expressing as temper. The more he can learn to move beyond his testy impatience and judgmental self-talk, the more he can live up to his high standards and embody his idealism without calling forth the bitter edge that flays everybody around him.

Page of Wands

Spring Equinox

In *Tarot of the Holy Light*, the Page of Wands is a servant of the invisible world, as can be seen from his wings. He announces the Spring Equinox, when the turbulence of clashing weather systems begins to give way to warm soils and eager sprouts. The red rune under his outstretched hand symbolizes Nature's vital forces rising from under the Earth to greet the longer days. His appearance announces, "Awaken, sleepers, bestir yourselves."

This Page stands in the gap between the passing winter and the coming spring (or similar episodes of life). He banishes the cold and dark with his blazing aura and sense of mission. By a wave of his hand he elicits and circulates Solar power, enlivening the dark Earth and distributing the dews distilling down from the Moon. Even those who have succumbed to melancholy, sure that winter would never release its icy grip from their hearts, take encouragement as this Page brings Light to the awakening year. At his suggestion, buds swell and branches sport fresh color, helping us remember our hopes for the future again, despite all our setbacks and sorrows.

Like all of the Pages, this individual is just passing through. These functionaries of the Queen serve anonymously, without expecting notoriety or special attention. The Pages make themselves visible at important times, announcing changes of scene, time, or overall focus. Their appearance is always arranged for the sake of effect; like walking billboards, they exist to make the implicit explicit. All the Pages assume their stances and play their parts willingly, subsuming their individual wills in the process. Therefore, we are relieved of the responsibility of psychologizing the Pages within the Zodiac signs the way we do with the other Royals. This Page of Spring turns the page on the old cycle, as is written into his script by his Queen. His only concern is to fulfill her will and inform the castle community.

The demeanor of the Page of Wands is unique and highly individuated. He's never one to copy from others, instead being bohemian and independent by nature, requiring little in the way of outside affirmation or approval. Some would call him a nonconformist or antisocial, but in doing so they are reacting to what he appears to reject instead of taking the time to recognize his higher allegiances. In certain circumstances he might give the impression of a malcontent, but more often he's a futurist, innovator, and inventor. His specialty is finding simple solutions to complex problems. High technology does not impress him because he figures his free will and his time to be infinitely more valuable than any gadget.

The Page of Wands as sovereign individual seems like a paradox from the standpoint of standard cultural norms and mores. In most cases, a servant does not volunteer his labor but is pressed into the role by circumstances beyond his control. Nevertheless, this Page's life is lived through an ethos of self-ownership and self-empowerment, and it is under these terms that he undertakes his service to his Queen. He's a hard bargainer when it comes to taking commissions at court, but in the village he'll spend hours with the children just for the joy of helping them learn. He's somehow networked in with all the movers and shakers of the realm, with a finger in every pie, yet he carefully avoids becoming associated with anyone in particular. Though his visible rank is low, he will only respond to people whom he can respect, whose causes he feels are worthy. Freedom is such an important value in his universe that he would rather do with less voluntarily than be trapped by the seductive wiles of luxury or wealth. One will sometimes see him down on one knee, planting his staff like a flagpole into a patch of unplowed earth, drawing up power and refreshing his sense of mission in meditation with Nature. This Page's true leader and commander seems to be synonymous with his invisible Higher Power.

Although he's performing an educational and inspirational function within the court, the Page of Wands presents a humble appearance and low formal rank in the hierarchy. His purple robe implies that he hails from a noble house, but he prefers to take a less inflated stance amongst the people. He positions himself as a helper, a greaser-of-wheels, and a shoehorn for community projects. Whatever task he participates in, he assists the different personalities to find a fit with each other for the greater good.

What works for the upright Page might not be as comfortable for the Page of Wands reversed, however. His humble guise and camouflaged status can get him into dangerous situations, too, especially when he's far from his home court. This Page will have to keep his own counsel, watch his back, and cover his tracks to keep his options open, given that he's posing as a low-status person in a very fierce dominance hierarchy. The traditional Pages are often shown dressed in the livery of the family they serve, but nobody should imagine that this Page's will or loyalty can be so easily determined.

When he appears upside down, the Page of Wands has the power to create significant interference, striking fear in the hearts of power-players on both

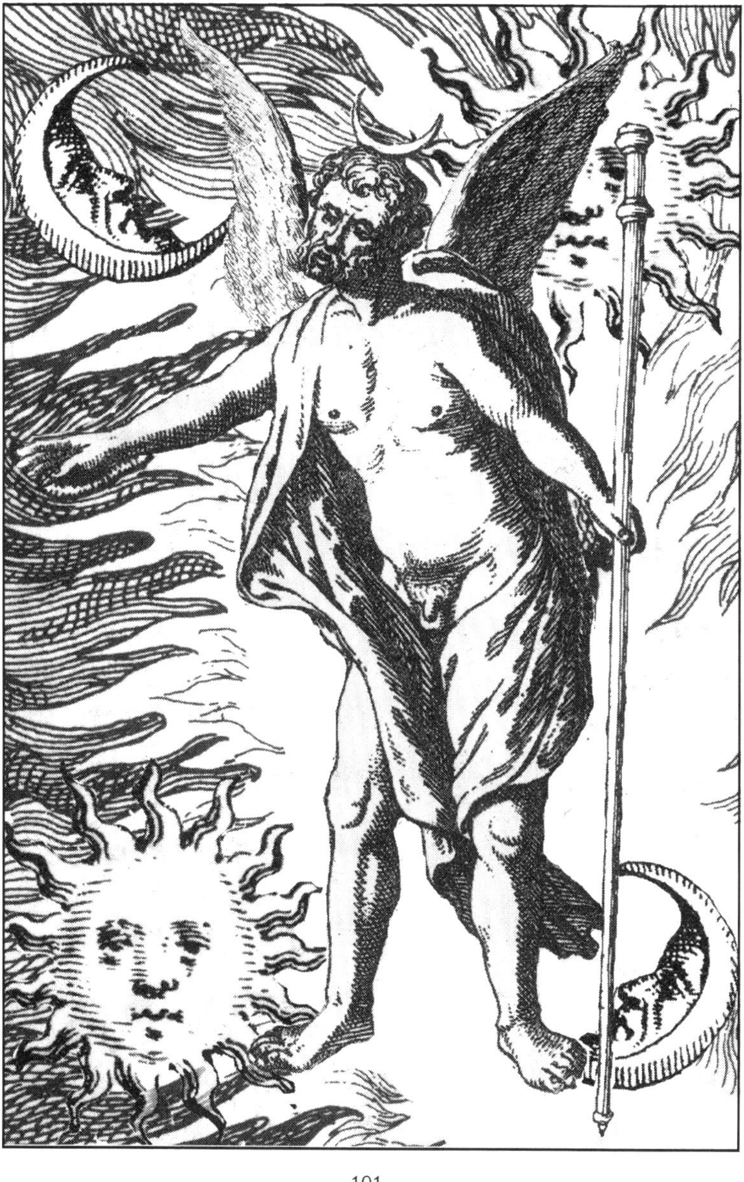

sides of any issue. For one thing he's been taken into everybody's confidence, so he knows where all the bodies are buried (so to speak). It is very difficult for anybody to get away with anything on his watch. He's not motivated to join the existing system, nor to achieve fame within it. This means he can't be bought and he can't be blackmailed. The Page of Wands fully understands the psychology of power, both how to accumulate it and how to undercut it. This all makes him the consummate asymmetrical warrior. Since his tactics can't be predicted, he can't be properly defended against. Having taken no binding oaths, he also can't be commanded. With his obscure origins and his impeccably maintained independence, he is bound for a future nobody can predict, following a plan he never shares. He mostly keeps a low profile, but in truth, the Page of Wands is always a wild card.

Chapter 4
The Cups

Suit of Cups

In the majority of European esoteric Tarots, the Suit of Cups refers to the Element Water. The Suit symbol is usually a large drinking cup or communion cup, like the mysterious Grail chalice, occasionally shown pouring forth with Holy Water or other sacred fluids. Associations with this cup include the Holy Grail; a Fountain of Love; the Cornucopia that contains all good things to make us happy; the Krater, stone vessel of the Mysteries, containing Soma, psychedelic elixir of mushrooms and cannabis pollen; the communion cup of the Catholic mass; and the pomegranate cup of the Egyptian cult of Isis and the old Hebrew Mysteries.

The substance in the symbolic Cup also has multiple references. One of the oldest associations would be with the ancient blood mysteries, symbol of the ultimate sacrifice, whether it's menstrual blood or that of a sacrificial animal, warrior, or world savior. The Cup is also used to symbolize sacred sexuality, with its connotations of merging and bliss. And of course, the link to Water ties the Cup to every creaturely form on this watery Earth, signifying the bond we share with all of life. In each case the symbolism reflects the Heart of life constantly pouring out the nurturing substances and experiences that keep Creation whole and healthy.

In psychological terms the Suit of Cups rules the psyche or emotional life, also known as the dreamtime. This is the Lunar, tidal, monthly cycle of subjective experience that rides unspoken below the surface of consciousness. As we can see from the depth of its correspondences, Cups include all aspects of the inner life, from fantasy and imagination to great heights of ecstasy, deep wells of grief, and the immense calm of spiritual security. With this Cup in hand, we enter into the world of feelings, embracing all of our close emotional and spiritual ties. It represents all the ways in which people can be touched and moved in our nonverbal, empathetic, sensitive, and intuitive natures.

As the imagery implies, the Suit of Cups is pregnant with meaning for Western esotericism. This Suit has been used to carry the traces of an underground belief held in certain Christian Gnostic circles in southern Europe about the lineage of a Holy Family founded by Jesus of Nazareth and his companion, Mary Magdalene. According to this belief, Mary was taken to

Europe along with her child/children after the crucifixion, for their protection during the troubles in Jerusalem. The family was said to have settled in southern France, founding a dynasty that eventually rivaled the Roman Church. This legend contributed to both the Crusades and the Inquisition as a result of Rome's attempt to eliminate the family's influence in Europe.

The Queen of Cups is therefore regularly portrayed as the Grail Queen, unambiguous icon of the Arthurian legends. If this archetype is being indicated indirectly, she'll become an idealized and dreamy Venus-like figure as in *The Medieval Scapini Tarot*. We also see her as the Black Madonna, patron saint of many villages on the Iberian Peninsula (as pictured on the Egyptian-style Tarot decks). Sometimes attributes of all three are present, as in a Black Queen with exposed breasts who carries the pomegranate Cup (*Ibis Tarot*). These various guises reveal the Cup Queen's role as Sophianic goddess: Sacred Virgin, Lover, Mother, and Nurse. This icon of femininity is simultaneously a living woman and yet a reinvention of the ancient Great Mother, still beloved despite any overlay of patriarchal Christian dogma and symbolism.

The Magdalene-tinged Tarot decks are also the most likely to imply that the cup is full of blood rather than water. If the cup in the hands of your King of Cups burns, bubbles, smokes, or flames, you are probably looking at a Tarot informed with the alchemical theme of the Holy Blood. This references a lineage carried by the Cups Suit that has inherited and/or is actively cultivating spiritual powers (practices which the Roman church strictly anathematized yet simultaneously strove to usurp). In those Tarots the Page will be shown with a downcast demeanor, with his cloak draped over his cup, or else a lid covers its fullness. This indicates the true royal heir who is forced to live incognito, banned from his inheritance and denied his proper role in history. *The Knapp-Hall Tarot* goes to the length of showing his lineage tree broken in half behind him.

There exists a small group of Continental esoteric Tarot decks that use the Suit of Cups to symbolize the Element Air (the realm of the mind) rather than the Element Water. Such Tarots are the Spanish-influenced or Iberian Tarots from Spain, Portugal, and the southern coast of France. These Tarots relocate the Holy Grail away from the sentimental and emotional life, focusing it in the philosophical sphere, the realm of the mind. Here the Cup is a symbol of the soul's consciousness, receptive and open to Divine Inspiration, experiencing communion with higher planes and higher intelligence. As such it refers to subtle states of meditation and contemplation and an active, aware receptivity to the Divine Word.

Decks that follow this pattern leave the Suit of Swords to represent the turbulent emotional realm of human society, where egos joust out of insecurity, and words are used to wound rather than inform. You can recognize these decks due to their preponderance of butterflies, birds, insects, and flowers adorning the Suit of Cups, sometimes even extending through the whole deck. These packs are not usually fully illustrated in their Pips, though various atmospheric and seasonal devices are used to indicate changes going on in Nature and in the subtle energies. This family of Tarots will often have a higher percentage of female images in the Major Arcana, with especially suggestive and sympathetic imagery associated with the Devil card. These clues imply contact with the most ancient Hebrew Mysteries, carrying gnostic, Alexandrian, and Moorish influence barely hidden beneath the ubiquitous Catholicism imposed from Rome. Examples of this family of Tarots are *El Gran Tarot Esoterico*, the *Salvador Dali Tarot*, *Euskalherria*, *Balbi*, the *Royal Fez Moroccan*, and most recently, the *Magdalene Legacy Tarot*. Of all the branches of the Tarot family tree, this Iberian model corresponds most exactly with the Gra form of the Sefer Yetzirah, suggesting strong Kabbalistic influence. Subtle differences exist between this paradigm and that of our *Tarot of the Holy Light*. Those who are working with a pack of this description might want to acquire the two books by Hariette and Henry Curtiss called *The Key of Destiny* and *The Key to the Universe*, both from Newcastle.

Ace of Cups

Astrology: 1 - 10 Cancer, ruled by the Moon **Sephira:** Keter
Essential Dignity: upright Domicile, Moon in Cancer
Reversed Similar, Moon in Leo
Angelic Dignities: upright angel spelled LVV, spoken Leuviah
Reversed angel spelled PHL, spoken Pahaliah

The Ace of Cups shows a fountain overflowing every attempt to contain it, offering an endless stream of water, wine, blood, or soma for the people's refreshment and healing. In theology this represents the fountain of eternal life. Classic associations with this card are the Holy Grail; the sacrament of baptism; a fountain of Love and self-esteem; Heart's home; and the mystical center. As such it is the fountain at the heart of Paradise. This idea of a tiered fountain mirrors the Kabbalistic doctrine of emanations, which teaches that as God poured out into the space dedicated to the Creation, one Sephira would fill up and overflow into the next all the way down the Tree to Malkhut. Just so, this Ace expresses the benediction of Water, which nourishes and heals us through the benevolence of Heaven.

In more practical terms, Water is the common denominator of all the life forms on this planet. Where the springs are, that is where all the species will gather to make a life. This is why Water is such an apt symbol of the sentience and sensitivity inherent in matter: Water is the manifested psyche of Earth, circulated and distilled by the Moon. The Water from this fountain, when sent out into the four directions as in the mythical Garden, will awaken the seeds of Paradise that lie dormant in matter.

The fountain itself testifies to the benefits of civilization which enhance the natural blessing of the original springs. The action of the fountain introduces the two active Elements, Air and Solar Fire, to the feminine Element Water, enlivening it and purging out microscopic contagion. Thus we can include healing powers and regeneration to the natural attributes of this Element when found in the wild.

As the Monad and prime mover in the Suit of Cups, this Ace represents the dream of the soul, a symbol of the higher life that moves us deeply, offering to sweeten our psyche if we surrender to it. This card indicates an unfailing source of balm for body, heart, and soul. When you see it, you are instructed to relax into a safety net of love, support, and communion.

When this card falls upright, its feeling is focused on the private inner life, including prayer and meditation, communion with Nature and/or Spirit. This includes one's psychic life of presentiment and intuition verging into the dreamtime, where all of life's memories are kept. The Ace also signifies the hormonal and emotional effect of these things as experienced by the body separate from the mind's constant reinterpretations. At every level from completely unconscious through brilliantly superconscious, the Element Water is present to nurture us and provide the moist matrix in which we can discover and refine our feelings.

The upright card also carries the significance of the Moon in her natural Domicile, displaying her innate depths of effortless responsiveness. The effects of this card are consciously or unconsciously characterized by the maternal instinct, referring to all situations where nutritional, emotional, developmental, and psychic needs are being met. Whether it refers to milk gushing from a mother's breast or the instant mobilization of the immune system in the presence of an invading pathogen, the Water intelligence knows exactly what is needed and wordlessly moves to provide it. The character of the Ace of Cups is to enfold, cleanse, refresh, dilute toxins, saturate with nutrients, to restore and reassure the organism at every level.

In reversal the Lunar impulse visits its other half in the sign of Leo. This suggests contact with one's spiritual or faith community to gain the inspiration that only collective immersion in mutually held ideals could generate. We must not forget about the value of commingled energies, all focused together towards a transcendent goal. In fact, one of the most direct paths to accomplish a magical goal is to connect it to the energy-body, or egregor, of a communally worshipped deity. It is through steady, repeated group focus that such structures are created. And of course, once created, such entities increase the bonding, cohesiveness, and harmony of the social group they represent. By pooling together both tangible and intangible resources, the group becomes a family, especially for those who lack living relatives, who might otherwise experience themselves as social orphans, rejects or accidents of birth.

This reference to Leo as the Moon's alternate Domicile brings up the challenge of managing the ego, wherever one sees Leo or the lion among these images. When in Cancer, the Moon can operate simply and transparently, spontaneously sharing from the heart without constraint or compunction. But in Leo, her partner's sign, the Moon is subject to the social pressure from the unspoken expectations of the group, represented by the feline Leo's "pride" or posse. The presence of onlookers, even approving co-conspirators, subtly changes our experience in a way that averages one's unique individual energy

AQVA

into that of the whole. This may not be a bad thing in the long run, but the ego often perceives these episodes as a distraction from the individual search for self-realization.

The blessing and advantage of community participation cannot be gainsaid, however much we might cling to our individualist predilections. A solitary shaman can create tremendous results if s/he is focused, dedicated, and persistent, there is no doubt. But in a fraction of that time, a well-focused group can channel a prodigious amount of energy such as would take a solitary practitioner months or years to accumulate. Therefore it is wise to keep open connections to the spiritual and cultural community that is blossoming around you. Let the corporate entity be your friend and give time to the causes that unite your community.

While it seldom turns out to be entirely negative, this card in reversal can point to a violent or emotionally devastating rupture that has the power to poison the well for a group of people, be they family or community. Think of the force of a dam breaking, unleashing a devastating wave upon the downstream community. If there are truly toxic emotions or circumstances threatening the collective waters, it is important to do everything possible to isolate the precious natural resource away from those who currently cannot behave correctly. The wellspring's purity must be protected because it represents the life and health of the community.

In the terms of Boehme and the Protestant Sophianics, Water is Sophia's domain, and we are all pledged to protect and uphold her healing prerogative. Anything that interferes with the web of life or the outworking of the Divine Will is to be baptized in the Fountain of Love and offered up to Spirit for awakening and resurrection. Sophia has plenty of methods for correcting her errant children. Equally, she takes special care of those who understand the power of Ho'oponopono: "I'm sorry. Please forgive me. I love you. Thank you."

Two of Cups

Astrology: 11- 20 Cancer, ruled by Mars   **Sephira:** Chakhmah
Essential Dignity: upright Compliment, Moon in Aquarius
Reversed Detriment, Moon in Capricorn
Angelic Dignities: upright angel spelled NLK, spoken Nelchael
Reversed angel spelled YYY, spoken Yeiayel

The Two of Cups generally signifies the union of opposites, often showing an Adam and Eve theme. The card is traditionally associated with a romantic relationship, but between the lines can be found all types of partnerships based on affinity and deep mutual understanding. Sometimes it means that your outer self and your inner self are discovering each other, possibly for the first time. This card highlights a karmic tie that is undeniable and inexorable, portrayed by the red serpent and green bird chasing each other's tails around the two cups. Love it or hate it, the circuit is live and irresistibly engages your energy. One has to either make an ally out of this polarizing force that has captured your attention, or it will turn into a demon and afflict you mightily.

Referring to the union of alchemical opposites (called "dual cultivation," as in sacred sexuality), the oldest packs will show a long-necked flask wound about with twined serpents, the mouth of the vessel spouting flames and sometimes winged. This composite indicates the refining and mutually completing effect of a true and lasting human or chemical bond. Even in a non-relationship context, this card will represent a harmony of distinct ingredients that merge to produce a unique synthesis. Yogic teachings emphasize the bliss potential that comes from cultivating brain chemistry to an exquisite level through a combination of practices and lifestyle designed to yoke the body and soul together towards enlightenment. In the best of circumstances, the card indicates an unparalleled creative fusion from which can spring a world-changing revelation.

In *Tarot of the Holy Light*, we have replaced the winged serpentine vase with an annotated Star of David or Great Arcanum, which carries Mercury at the center of the other Planetary Governors. Mercury/Hermes is the representative of fused inter-sexuality, full androgyny, which is one of the benefits and attributes available to a person who takes this symbol as an internal event rather than an external one. One who embodies both Cups within his or herself has the advantage of being able to deploy both male and female styles of thinking, communicating, and acting. This is a tremendous blessing, actually, the cognitive and emotional equivalent of ambidexterity.

In its upright manifestation the magic of alchemical Compliments is at its most concentrated in the Two of Cups. The Moon shares the throne of her partner the Sun and is well-served by the cultural and social largesse that Leo effortlessly generates. The northern hemisphere's seasonal cycle highlights the signs of Cancer and Leo as high summer, benefitting from the very best climate conditions including the longest days and mildest nights. This is traditionally the time when one's alchemical goals are brought to their peak expression. In this card, all the conditions are in place to signal fertility, increase, progressive influences, and fortunate partnerships. Even Mars' rulership of this decanate supports the Moon's foray into the fiery, outgoing realm of Leo.

Sometimes the Moon finds Leo's constant social whirl and near-compulsive search for new amusements to be overstimulating and perhaps even a distraction from the true goal. But in the main the Moon can use her experiences with the collective organism to gain valuable exposures and discover buried parts of herself. Things get a little more difficult for this Deuce when it comes up reversed and the alchemical situation of the Moon in Capricorn is highlighted. This is Luna's Detriment, which suggests that her unquenchable flow is running into a brick wall and cannot saturate through to its intended target. Whether the obstacle is due to stubborn materialism, a karmic block, or simply the complicated contingencies of time and space, the power of Saturn to freeze and immobilize the flow is currently dominant. Considering that Saturn rules the signs of Capricorn and Aquarius, which characterize the northern hemisphere's winter, one might sense a creeping coldness generating ice-cube emotions that bruise and batter our more tender sentiments.

There is a choice to make when a person bumps into Saturn's cold shoulder in a context where one would expect a more summery reception. One might be tempted to mimic the icy stance that's been encountered, to respond with offense/defense thinking and rigidify on contact. But how does that help us, really? Consider making the choice to thicken your shields a little bit, close your pores in order to retain your sunnier internal climate no matter what mood swings others are going through. Such a thing can be done totally internally without causing any exterior ripples simply by refusing to distort your natural temperament through assuming other people's projections.

In Renaissance medical Alchemy, every individual is his or her own planet, subject to unique influences and personal patterns due to the particulars of his or her birth chart. Although humans appear to share the same objective world, every person's individual subjective landscape and climate is utterly and completely different from any other's. There is no blame in employing the Martian qualities available in this decanate of Cancer to defend our right to

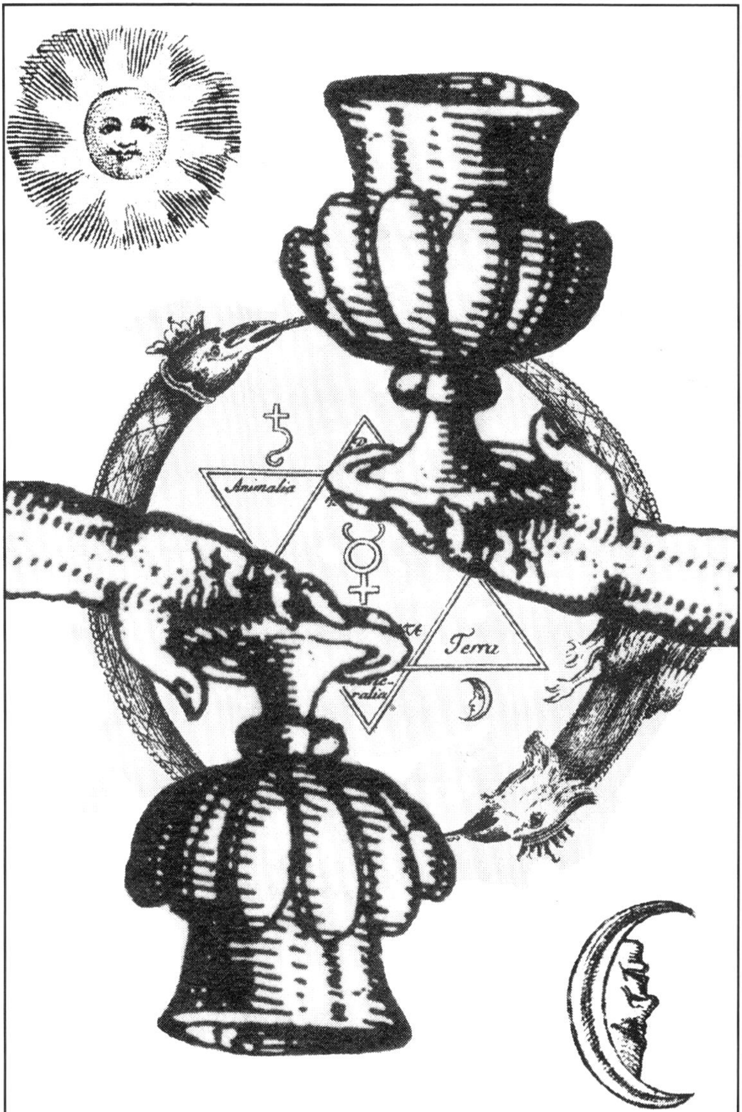
Animalia
Terra

remain happy, optimistic, openminded, and positive, no matter what habits of thought others indulge in. It is also true that when Mars' energies have something positive to engage themselves with, they are less likely to get into trouble. Best to view the Moon-in-Capricorn side of this card as a challenge to become more pro-active managers of our personal psychological climate. The less we give away our power and positivity to others, the more we can serve as catalysts for others in this arena.

There are times when the opposite-that-attracts becomes the opposite-that-repels, and this is where the real undertow of the retrograde card comes in. Quirks that initially seemed appealing lose their momentary gloss, and our patience for personality dynamics wears thin. An exchange that once felt free-and-easy comes to feel labored and unbalanced. The dream of equality comes up against the reality of everybody's mismatched programming, past wounds, and stuck emotions.

Nothing is ever as easy as it seems at first. Only the truly committed find a way through the snares. Those are the souls who realize that even the bumpy road, the wounds of love, and the pressure to conform are not powerful enough to steal the beauty and rightness from the ideal of Love. At its heart this card is a troubadour of Love and emissary of union, no matter what stage the dance has reached.

Three of Cups

Astrology: 21 - 30 Cancer, ruled by Jupiter **Sephira:** Binah
Essential Dignity: upright Exaltation, Moon in Taurus
Reversed Fall, Moon in Scorpio
Angelic Dignities: upright angel spelled MLH, spoken Melahel
Reversed angel spelled ChHV, spoken Haheuiah

The upper part of the Three of Cups was created for Jacob Boehme and was meant to show the Heart of Christ pouring forth Light from the cross of matter, while the dove of Spirit hovers over the fiery (cup of) Wrath. This combination expresses Boehme's deep surrender to the pain and suffering in life, with full acknowledgement of the struggles a soul must go through to consummate the alliance with Spirit. By humbly and willingly uniting with the Wrath, entering openhearted into the realm of fiery judgment, one evokes the corresponding baptism of Light from the Son/Sun, and Wrath is transformed into Love. The blessings of Spirit (inverted triangle) condense in the dove, symbol of Sophia. Light and Love enter into the dark and turbulent fierceness, the Fire is quenched, and the healing response provides the redemption of Nature in the soul of the mystic. From the communion, calming and healing influences saturate the scene with Love and compassion.

Real life is complicated. Anyone who has lived long enough to gain some wisdom sees that all blessings are mixed, all peaks produce their equal and opposite valleys. But with the Three of Cups, we accept a certain measure of suffering or confusion through relationship. We do this consciously, considering it a fair exchange for the awakening that comes with commitment. We willingly acknowledge that living in the heart will bring periods of pain, grief, and misunderstanding as well. Mature individuals are willing to brave those periods for the sake of the bonds we can form by remaining open to each other.

The Three of Cups is traditionally called "consent" or simply "yes," implying a spirit of agreement and mutual support, encouragement, and teamwork. Regularly pictured as three women celebrating their bond in a dance with lifted cups, it has also been called "sisterhood," the classic mutual admiration society. With this card we recognize all the benefits of harmonious peer relationships. One can also read family bonds from this card, either by blood or by mutual choice (as in grandmother, mother, and daughter). In this little group a strong sense of approving recognition pervades. There is a sweet and accepting emotional tone that allows the participants to relax and share visions, creative thoughts, and healing strategies. We are reminded of the kind and long-suffering temperament of the Moon in Taurus. The term "safety net" provides an easy catch phrase for the feeling of this card in action.

It is in this context that we translate the astrological and alchemical implications of the Three of Cups. Jupiter's rulership of this section of Cancer rewards psychic sensitivity with the inner pleasures felt only by mystics and spiritual savants. Who can continue to be satisfied with the coarser pleasures of the flesh once one has tasted spiritual communion, the exquisite joy of reunion within the soul? Nature uses the promise of pleasure to attract us to what is best for us so we can readily give in to this force of inclusion, harmony, and mutuality. Between the Moon's Exaltation in the natural garden of Taurus, and Jupiter's beneficial influence from his watery Domicile in Pisces, we can see that this card is redolent with the astral fragrance of Eden. There may be sacrifices to endure to earn one's place in that charmed circle, but everything is set to reward those who keep the faith and follow their hearts.

Reflecting on the Moon in Scorpio (our reversed alchemical indicator), we are made aware of another aspect of this card that is less often highlighted. These are the drama-queen extremes that some people bring to the Three of Cups, as if any happiness we can achieve must be wrung from the twisted folds of pain and suffering that life cruelly catches us up in. This turns the dancing ladies on the standard card image into sob sisters and harpies. In this mode the three Graces or Fates serve as a lamenting Greek chorus keening out their sorrows and enumerating the world's sins. In actual fact, there is probably just as much good in the world as there is evil, but the point of view emphasized by the Moon in Scorpio is so much more pessimistic that one sometimes can't remember that this is just the flip side of its Exaltation, the trough that naturally precedes and follows every peak.

Astrologically one might assume that the Moon, when visiting Scorpio, benefits from the Trine aspect that harmonizes Cancer with its sister Water sign. However, due to the increasing darkness and coldness experienced in the fall sign of Scorpio, the delicate sensitivity of Cancer's intuitions are dulled unless extra warmth is applied. Traditionally, the practitioner is advised to "bury the experiment in the compost pile" at this stage so it can be protected over the winter from the dangerous cold. In this way the work is slowly gestated in a life-supporting gentle state of rest, similar to the slow growth of a baby in the womb. Danger comes when a hasty person decides to rush the gestation by subjecting the work to a physical fire, thinking that a few extra degrees will speed the growth along. Beware this approach in all matters of the heart. Artificial conditions create uncontrolled results, in Nature and in relationship.

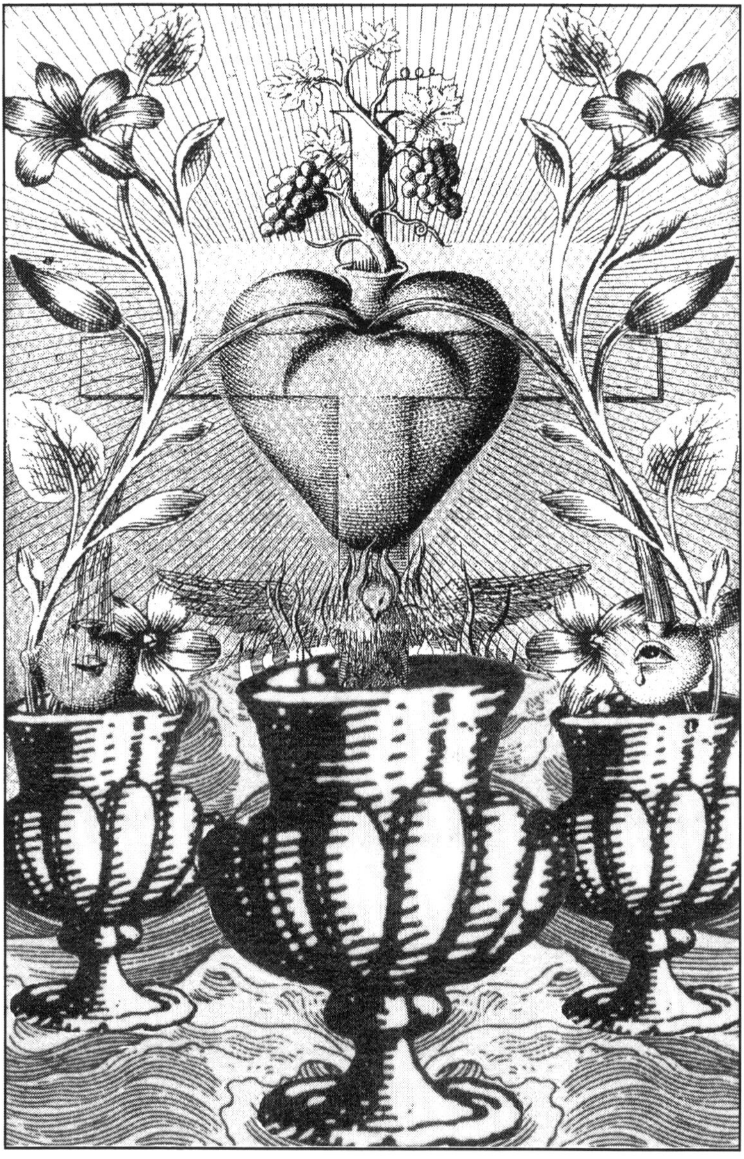

Inevitably, a thread will snap in our support system, and trusted structures will be stressed, threatening to fray. Then suddenly we are full of fear, seeing monsters inside the people we supposedly trust and love. Here we enter into the most damaging region of the card's reversal. A self-aware person will realize that the specters arising are nothing more than the ego's catalogue of old war-wounds projected into the mirror of the other. Those who can come to their senses will look up to their higher Nature for guidance.

A classic Scorpio technique when circumstances are unclear is to turn up the heat until somebody or something boils over. The immune system does the same thing when it stages a fever to kill an invading pathogen. It is a magical axiom that powerful effects can be produced when the operator is feeling emotionally hot or cold, but nothing can be done if the operator is tepid, blah, and unaroused. Scorpio energies are designed to be intense enough to break chemical bonds and/or reform them. Remember this when you are tempted to fire up the blast furnace and burn somebody.

The average human cannot stand this level of intensity for long, so there have to be safety valves in place to help diminish the danger to bystanders. People who are always steaming, boiling, and scorching the landscape do unwitting harm to their relationships, wounding everyone around in their fits of self-loathing. Such moments call out for a merciful and compassionate dove of Spirit to fearlessly enter the fiery chaos and quench it with healing forgiveness. Whoever can stem the conflict and bring the healing balm restores the harmony. The dove is a warrior of peace.

Four of Cups

Astrology: 11 - 20 Scorpio, ruled by Jupiter   **Sephira:** Chesed
Essential Dignity: upright Compliment, Mars in Libra
Reversed Detriment, Mars in Taurus
Angelic Dignities: upright angel spelled YRTh, spoken Yeratel
Reversed angel spelled ShAH, spoken Seheiah

The Four of Cups shows four chalices struggling in a turbulent sea. Overhead the spiritual Sun or galactic center stands behind and enlivens our local Sol. The excitation of the astral plane sends ripples of information streaming into all the lower worlds. These same frequencies provide the cause of the waves in the water. Their direction seems confused, however; there doesn't seem to be a coherent focus for these emerging energies as yet. The Cups of the Four Elements are starting to drift away from each other, suggesting disengagement, disorientation, and feelings of isolation. The scene is unresolved, stirred by invisible forces that are seeking order but haven't yet found their common denominator.

The Four of Cups has come to be associated with a restless period. A person feels dissatisfied with life and becomes caught up in fantasies. One becomes emotionally uncomfortable with friends and family, habits, and routines. Feeling stagnant and longing for change, the heart is questioning its options, sometimes to the point of cultivating cravings for distraction and oblivion. A dull trance of alienation pulls like undertow, indicating that the emotional waters are not safe and predictable anymore. Symptoms include loss of motivation, fitful meandering among the nonessentials, failure to find pleasure in one's traditional attractions, toxic and self-polluting habits, and a vague presentiment that something is not quite right. Something as-yet-unspoken is disturbing the waters.

This quote from Harold Bloom's (1996) *Omens of Millennium* totally clarifies the spiritual issue with the Four of Cups: "The pre-Socratic speculator, Empedocles, explains sleep as a cooling of the blood caused by the separation of fire away from the three other elements" (p. 96). Immediately we remember the classic Waite/Smith image of the limp, entranced individual dimly gazing at three cups at his feet (Air, Water, Earth) while a Divine Hand behind his line of sight holds a flaming cup. The individual on the card is falling into a reverie or torpor due to the deficiency of Fire in his constitution. His temperament goes slack through disengagement of the Fire gear (symbolized by Mars, Scorpio's traditional ruler, planet of ambition and motivation).

If this state of disengagement goes on too long, the ego risks losing its center. In that circumstance, one is open to being invaded by outside forces, parasites of one type or another that move into the space vacated by the soul's authentic mandate. Thus we read the appearance of this card as saying it's time to rediscover your will and power of agency. Get back into the driver's seat and start steering your way through events again, else these chaotic, aimless waves could easily pull all your previous efforts apart. Any situation that isn't being actively guided and watched over by a directive hand is subject to entropy, which slowly and steadily erodes and effaces any previous progress. Lack of a distinct plan for order will inevitably encourage chaos.

The most positive way to use this card is to get excited by the vision of the solar revelation that is shining out from the center of the heavens. Whether it represents fresh potential coming through a significant relationship (Mars in Libra) or through a significant project (Mars in Taurus) is less important. More important is that one finds a worthwhile and evolutionary direction towards which to point one's natural vitality and intensity. This Scorpionic Mars needs to press some discipline on his energies such that his natural heat and fierceness are tempered, allowing his arousing and enlivening influence to be integrated gradually. His partner Venus gives him the necessary feedback to help him titrate his intensity, whether she's beaming warm support to him from Libra, or giving a more stern, corrective message from her Taurus Domicile (opposed to Scorpio).

What Mars forgets but Venus remembers is that the turbulence we perceive from the environment is usually the very same turbulence we are ourselves generating and emanating due to a knot of unspoken, unresolved feelings. In other words, the power of these disturbing emotional waves is due to them being unexamined and unclaimed as originating within ourselves. This card presents itself when we need a time-out to re-examine just exactly why we are so agitated and emotionally chaotic. We must learn to stop burning up precious will-power on useless irritants. The individual who is identified with a larger goal doesn't let himself or herself be pulled apart by momentary disappointment in the external sphere.

The reciprocal of the above is that the outworking of your plans depends entirely on your own ability to focus and stay on track. Our greatest tests and temptations come from within our own imagination, and it is there that our most important spiritual battles are fought. With this card, especially in its Martian aspect, one can feel crushed and exhausted by the mundanity of

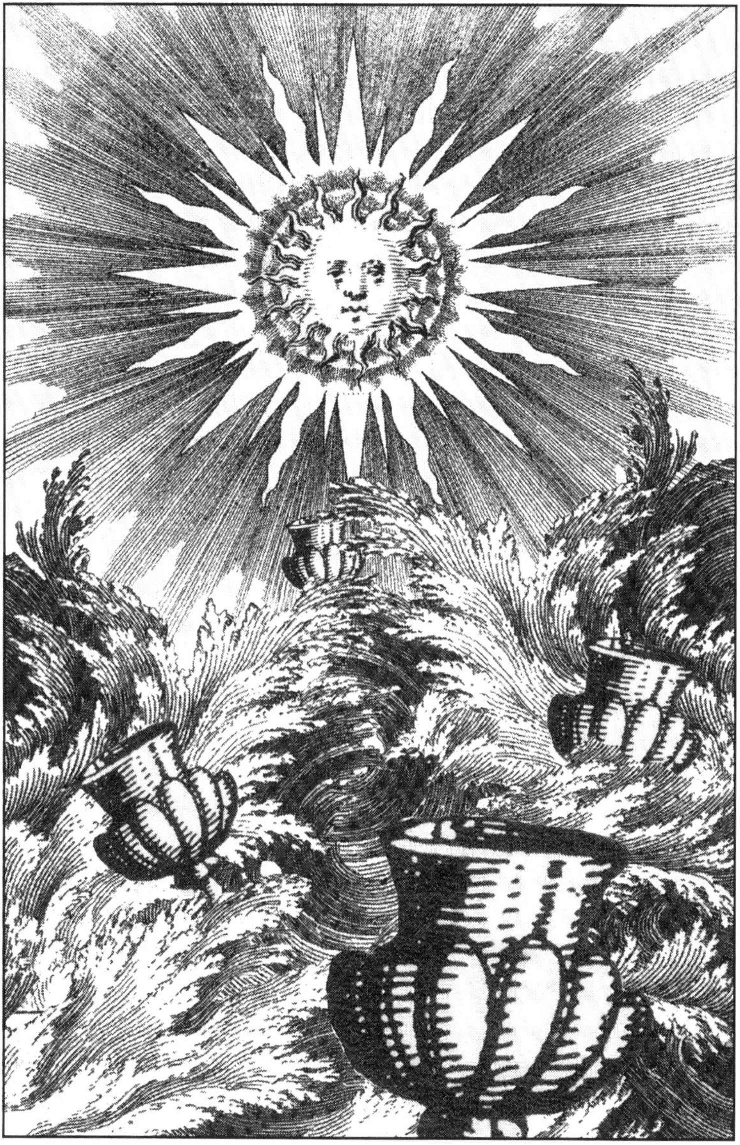

endless chores. It's as if the humble routines of our daily necessities were deviously designed to be a burden and a trial upon the soul. Mars craves adventure, glory, high achievement, and acclaim. He scorns and resists the daily discipline of chopping wood and carrying water. Since this card represents the Pisces-flavored segment of Scorpio, haughty Mars is forced to take a lower profile, to damp his Fire, and accept a limited role while waiting for his times to shine.

The face of the Sun is the symbol for the Primal Adam/Christos among the Protestant Theosophers. This is humanity's unique identifier within the participation mystique of the great cosmic drama. Despite whatever seems aimless, random, and akimbo in the world here below, there is nevertheless always a thread of the macrocosmic plan being worked out through current circumstances. Attaching oneself to the reigning Divine Idea offers a chance to rise above the clash of personalities and their conflicting agendas.

Meanwhile, advice for reversed manifestations of this card suggest that you shake yourself awake from this drifting, passive state before the ship of state washes off course. Get back in touch with your personal mission; you'll need that compass to find your way out of the swamps you have drifted into. Don't succumb to blaming your malaise on others; that's the coward's path and it's also totally untrue. The waters are choppy for everybody at times. This is not a personal thing that's happening; you are participating in a sea change that everybody has to make his or her individual way through. If you find that your focus is constantly drifting away and won't be constrained, then perhaps you are devoting your energies to something that your own body and psyche dislike. Why are you surrounded by things and beings that you can't force yourself to care about? Rethink your allegiances so your outer world becomes a better context for your inner world.

Five of Cups

Astrology: 21 - 30 Scorpio, ruled by the Moon   **Sephira:** Gevurah
Essential Dignity: upright Exaltation, Mars in Capricorn
Reversed Fall, Mars in Cancer
Angelic Dignities: upright angel spelled RYY, spoken Reiyel
Reversed angel spelled AUM, spoken Omael

The Five of Cups receives an influx of Water from the Divine Gardener. The blessing flows in so fast that it knocks over the two smaller vessels, but the larger three containers have kept their balance and are filled to the brim. Although the Water is running away into the garden (which is certainly not a waste), there is also a sufficient amount of the precious liquid remaining to accomplish the alchemist's plans. We intentionally show the upright vessels as larger than the fallen ones because we want to visually emphasize the concept of abundance. The Solar orb behind the outpouring bucket reminds us that the blessings of the Light are effulgent beyond measure. Our job in response is to make the best of what is given and go forward in good faith.

As a rule, the number Five represents a situation we have created through the use of our unique will and individual drive. One can envision the four directions or the Four Elements tied together at the center by a fifth force, which magic tells us is the personal will. By themselves these Elements make up the things and beings of the natural world. But when centered and activated by the fifth force, the human will, we see a transformation that pushes the Elements beyond their natural state. When we are working from an evolutionary motive, Nature is happy to grow into the shapes that our focused will directs. Even if the current environment isn't traditionally hospitable, a creative individual will search out ways to exploit whatever advantage the situation offers.

Mars' Exaltation in Capricorn refers to the northern epiphany of the Winter Solstice when the longest night is broken, allowing each subsequent day to become a few minutes longer over the following six months. When Mars visits Capricorn from his home in Scorpio, he offers a warm ray of hope against the cold and dark of winter. Mars' passion, enthusiasm, courage, and excitement for life help to rouse those who suffer depression during the long dim months of wan sunlight. Meanwhile, the practicality of Capricorn encourages Mars to devote his energy to tasks that will bear fruit next spring when the cold cycle is over. A great benefit falls to the person who has invested time and energy in forethought. When this card appears, take advantage of the opportunity to shape the future in advance through the use of creative will.

The opposite of this Mars exulting in practical Capricorn is Mars having fallen into (what he sees as) soggy, wet-blanket Cancer. The reversal combines with the decanate ruler to imbue the fallen Five of Cups with a feeling of regret, sorrow, loss, and grief. Passive-aggressive guilt and shame can flow abundantly. Tarot tradition reminds us that crying over spilled milk is simply too little too late, the loser's fate. Better to quit making excuses for our lack of readiness, but instead promise ourselves to outgrow the immaturity that put us in this circumstance to begin with.

In the most practical terms, the Five of Cups suggests that we take stock of our gains and losses as a means of cutting down on the emotional drama resulting from being caught out unprepared. Construct a cost/benefits analysis of your enterprise here at the halfway point of the Cups sequence. Make sure to factor in hassle value, unforeseen reactions of important parties, and natural disasters. The truth of taking risks is that you win some and you lose some, although where and what is never quite predictable from the outset. We learn as we go, and even our best efforts at anticipation will have significant lacunae.

One thing is sure from the alchemical situation of Mars in Cancer: Wailing and lamentation after the fact is self-indulgent, expensive, and wasteful, eating into energies better spent staying flexible and responsive to circumstances. In the best case of this card, we willingly take responsibility in advance for our intentions and their probable consequences. By being self-aware and practical, preparing for all contingencies, one can feel secure instead of stressed. Foresight also keeps us out of the victim position, free from needing to be rescued or redeemed by those around us. This is the emotional climate of Mars exalted in Capricorn, where Mars uses his downtime to mend and prepare his armor, his weapons, and his strategies for his coming big moment in spring.

In addition, the card suggests we be realistic about our formal and informal agreements, especially in relation to people's unspoken expectations. In a situation where there are haves and have-nots contending for scarce resources, foresight is the only insurance against clashing interests, where fractiousness can put the whole project at risk. One has to plan for irregularities or risk being overwhelmed when they inevitably come. Those who anticipate lean periods and provide backup systems for times of scarcity suffer far less when natural consequences unfold, as they eventually do. By having a worst-case plan as well as a best-case plan, we become part of the solution instead of part of the problem. That's the type of heroism that best characterizes Mars exalted in Capricorn.

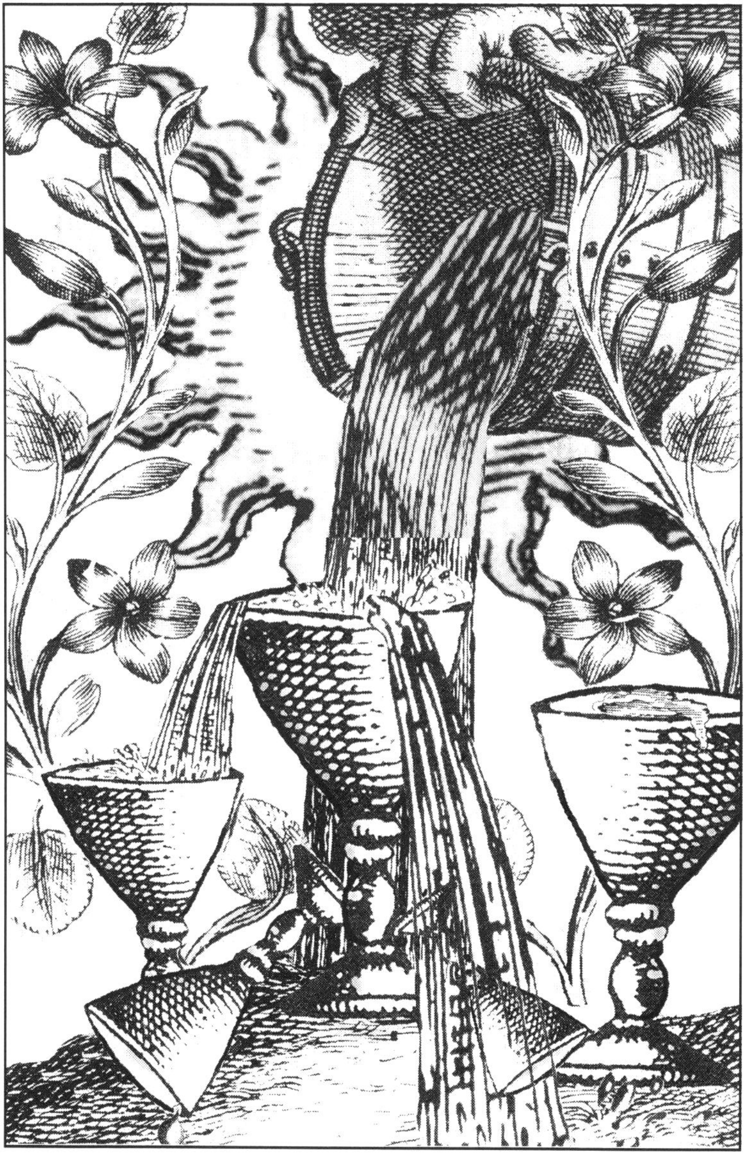

Across the spectrum of Tarot decks, this card's design invariably illustrates the relative optimism level of its creators. It's best to remember that even in terrible times, facing an abject loss or grievous setback, there still remains something left over from which the future will be constructed. Obviously the potential for regrets can be high with the Five of Cups, even when it falls upright in the spread. The more one concentrates upon the resources remaining in the unspilled Cups the better. Otherwise valuable time and energy will be lost in seeking to fix blame or punish the participants. What is the point of that? If we find ourselves out of options, the fault lies in the lack of foresight.

When this card falls reversed, fight the lazy thinking that seduces you into assuming that a generous flow will always be there to support you. The spilt Cups often refer to the mess that is left after an emotional upheaval, such as a tantrum or fit of rage. Consequences run the gamut from a hangover and lost wages to abuse and ruined relationships. One of the oldest associations with this card is a warning against letting emotions get the upper hand. The retrograde symptoms associated with this card abound in regretful replays and angry recriminations. The traditional title of the Five of Cups, "heredity," further suggests a cross-generational legacy of substance abuse, broken families, shame, blame, and emotional abandonment. Such symptoms follow naturally from a lifestyle of self-indulgence without the insight gained from introspection. Sadly, these same interactional patterns when magnified to tribal and national dimensions have ravaged the peace of nations.

Six of Cups

Astrology: 1 - 10 Scorpio, ruled by Mars   **Sephira:** Tiferet
Essential Dignity: upright Domicile, Mars in Scorpio
Reversed Similar, Mars in Aries
Angelic Dignities: upright angel spelled NThH, spoken Nith-haiah
Reversed angel spelled HAA, spoken Haaiah

Playful angels hoodwink the lion of the ego, granting even this fierce and immensely powerful king of beasts an afternoon off in the garden of childhood. One angel is down on hands and knees playing a game in the grass with colored balls and studying the flames in the six alchemical vessels. The other angel throws his robe over the head of the big kitty, granting the fierce predator a dizzy and delicious moment of sensory disorientation. It's a game of trust that the players know well, so there is no danger and everybody has fun. A high-noon Sun blazes through the fountaining water, purifying it and throwing rainbows into the landscape through the prisms in the falling drops.

The Six of Cups represents a climate of refreshing openness and innocence, replete with the enjoyment of stress-free learning. Intervals of play and experimentation strengthen our optimism and teach us to trust that things will get better as we grow together in understanding. The traditional title "The Past" reminds us to think back to a time when we were enthusiastic and open minded, when anything was possible and the future was an open book. Like these cherubs, we didn't have any idea we should be afraid of the lion or of our nakedness or of Nature. The Six of Cups reminds us that this same freshness of new possibilities is always available, even now. All we have to do is surrender our conditioning and reflexive resistance, looking at life again through the eyes of a child.

This image of angels playing hide-and-seek with the alchemical lion instigates the idea that through play we tease out our latent skills and sensitivity. The learning we acquire through recreation and experimentation can ultimately make a big difference for our future. In this era of longer life spans and higher education for many, there is time to discover and develop several different gifts, interests, or latent talents. Whatever you might have missed in the past can still be reached through the future, should you only aspire to it. If nothing else, this card can also remind us that it's never too late to have a happy childhood.

At the bottom six flaming vessels sit atop the summer and fall band of the Zodiac hinting of a summer-camp situation where quality recreation and gentle encouragement are part of the recipe for cultivating new skills. By approaching life with the simplicity of a child, we stay open to blessings at any age and stage. An attitude of calm trust allows us to learn faster, think more clearly, even stave off the losses of aging beyond the averages. Further key concepts attached to this card by tradition include memory and nostalgia, vacation times, simple pleasures, trusting your inner child, and uncomplicated relaxation as a reward for work well done. One often sees children playing and reading in a walled garden or mini-Paradise, free of threat or coercion. Our natural intelligence can best unfurl and thrive when we have breaks from unpredictable, dominating, negative, or draining circumstances. We have to be able to let down our defenses sometimes so we can dedicate our life-force to higher functions.

Because this card falls to the first ten degrees of its sign, it highlights the most positive aspects of Scorpio and its traditional ruler Mars. When watching healthy children at play, one is often surprised at their concentration, avidity, and sheer passion for the activity they are engaged in. No cynicism, doubt, or double-thinking arise to inhibit their full participation in the fantasy of the moment. They give themselves willingly to their experience, even if it's totally absurd from a "realistic" standpoint. Through role playing they get to explore every different stance and option. In the course of their fantasy, they awaken the nobility of the hero who risks his own safety to save the prisoner (Mars in Scorpio). They can also come to understand the misled and misdirected bad guy who forgets his origins and wastes his attributes on games of domination and punishment (Mars in Aries).

Most creatively, the child of any age who is unafraid to follow his imagination all the way to its end will discover that fine line where "being bad" can be good, in fact it can be excellent. In these situations refusing to conform and thereby breaking the mold can open whole new realities, not only for the discoverer but also for all of his playmates. This would represent the best case of the reversed Six of Cups when Mars visits Aries from its fall-season home in Scorpio and takes his cues from the Aries precedent-breaker and individualist. In scenarios wherein the problem can't be solved from inside the frame of its first appearance, only a pioneer and fearless explorer will keep challenging the givens until the real solution shows itself.

When the Six of Cups shows its worst reversed tendencies, the king of beasts can find himself a bit overwhelmed by the games of the angels. These *putti* have nothing to fear from the lion, so they will sometimes push him past his comfort zone. His feelings get hurt when they outsmart him one last time, and then he'll sulk (Mars in Scorpio) or lash out (Mars in Aries). In extreme cases the pressure of self-restraint in a high-demand climate will make this lion

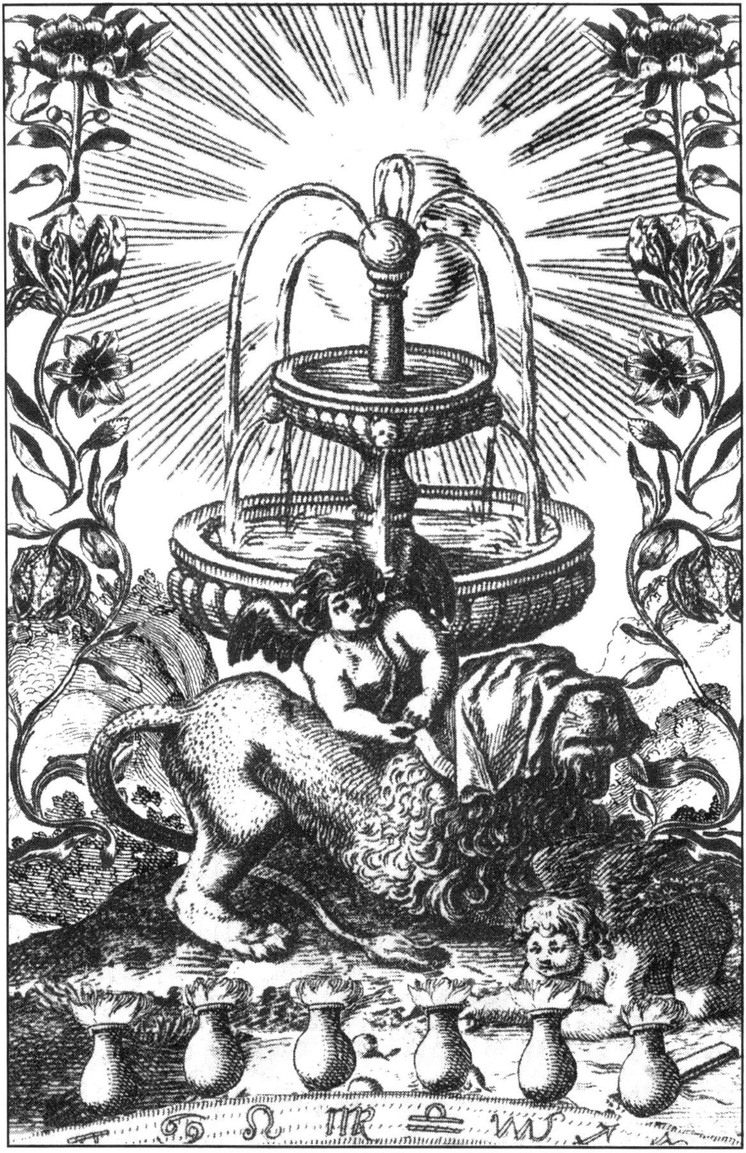

revert to the feral state, with resulting displays of temper, fearful power, and ruthless dominance. If these little sprites weren't already immortal and therefore immune, the lion might easily render one into mincemeat before lunch. Martian types have a temper that is lightning-fast and viciously ripping. The results of such outbursts, occasional though they might be, are seldom pretty. The aroused lion will land a blow before ever consciously calculating the damage it will cause its recipient. What's worse, he'll then blame the victim for "making" him do it.

When necessary, circumstances will conspire to place the lion/ego in a kind of karmic treatment center where the blowback of any bad behavior will instantly produce a bracing bout of consciousness-raising. To facilitate his awakening, the lion must experience direct consequences for regressive and antisocial acts. He must learn to feel shame, modify his instincts, and gain skill in making apologies when he forgets his manners. This is the minimum requirement to maintain the demeanor that grants him acceptance in polite society. These karma angels are the trainers of the self-centered ego, gently weaning him away from the law of the jungle and teaching him to choose a higher destiny.

Seven of Cups

Astrology: 11 - 20 Pisces, ruled by the Moon **Sephira:** Netzach
Essential Dignity: upright Compliment, Jupiter in Gemini
Reversed Detriment, Jupiter in Virgo
Angelic Dignities: upright angel spelled YChV, spoken Yehuiah
Reversed angel spelled LHCh, spoken Lehahiah

The Seven of Cups typically refers to works of the imagination, pointing to the use of dream, desire, and reverie to call forth a future that is different from the life one is currently living. The mythical beast Hydra on this card has seven heads, suggesting seven ways of looking at anything, seven possible futures. As in the versions that show each vessel holding a different reward, this Seven of Cups indicates that a plethora of choices is available to us right now. It reminds us that our outcomes are not set in stone. Relationships and circumstances are changing even as we struggle to bring them into focus. In such a fluid environment, we can raise our hopes and expectations or change our goals and strategies and thus upgrade our future potentials. Do not be fooled by the traditional title Fantasy. At its best this card indicates the catalytic quality of the awakened imagination. A better title might be Vision or Fantasia because that is what this card invites and represents.

Many people are afraid to admit their heart's desire, even to themselves. Sometimes we can't slow down long enough to recognize that our dream is already present in our lives. Only in rueful hindsight do we acknowledge that we overlooked the true gold while excitedly chasing after the brass ring. Yet as soon as we can admit our heartfelt feelings, at least in the privacy of our own being, a current of energy awakens that will slowly and steadily bring the world into closer harmony with our dreams. There are invisible powers we can harness with our imagination, even when the visible methods don't seem to be working out. Once we know our true heart's desire, that subtle current has the power to bend the world around to reflect the dream. Bonds of love, longing, and identification will eventually bring us to the threshold of our long-time wish and dearest hope. The question is, when our opportunity finally comes, will we be courageous enough to step into the dream and live it? A further question that's relevant to ask when this card comes up is, "Which facet of my being do I wish to empower right now? Which part of me should be leading the action?" Since Jupiter in Gemini is the natural expression of this card when upright (awakening to multiple possibilities), there will be a number of ways to achieve our goals. Framing the question in an open-ended fashion allows us to push our outlook past the either/or fallacy. By acknowledging the spectrum of options that exists, we can make better-informed choices about the style and methods we would prefer to use. One has the option to make an informed and pro-active choice at this juncture, rather than to allow the instinctive, reflexive, knee-jerk habit-body to lead the day. You can rise above your past dichotomies the very moment you realize that there is more than one way to get from here to there.

The Seven of Cups is the card most in line with the concept that each one of us creates our own reality. Whether Jupiter (traditional ruler of Pisces) is enjoying his Compliment in Gemini or enduring his Detriment in Virgo, the circumstances he encounters are a product of his own projections. Jupiter, who multiplies whatever he touches, is forced to eat his words in Mercury's signs. His pedagogical methods are tested against reality either because he has promised more than he can deliver (Gemini), or he has become so bogged down in details that he loses track of the overview (Virgo). Both sides of this alchemical challenge require careful balancing between the visualized ideal and the manifested reality. Jupiter's traditional role is that of mentor-teacher and guide to Mercury. Jupiter encourages Mercury's natural intelligence and confidence while correcting his immaturity and short-term thinking. Jupiter is much more slow-moving and deliberate than flighty Mercury can ever be. Jupiter therefore offers the experienced perspective of an elder, specifically the co-regent of the late fall and winter signs alongside Saturn.

The somewhat pejorative title Fantasy instantly points to the source of problems when this card is reversed. We all know people who seem to have lost all contact with the ordinary universe, whose view on every little thing is so unique that it becomes hard to relate to them. Such people seem to live in a deep subjective trance, lost in their private preoccupations. At what point do our personal eccentricities become an obstacle to making progress towards our goals? In truth, we all harbor quirks of belief or action that we have never officially acknowledged or owned but which affect our views on the world and ourselves. Even in the face of official denial, others can see these biases and will begin to comment about them. If we don't actively confront these unexamined distortions on their own (internal) ground, they will start to leap out at us from our outer life, showing up as blocks to our plans and personality difficulties with key people.

This card has also been entitled Pipe Dreams, pointing to impossible expectations born of the trance of intoxication. There could be some kind of illness or systemic imbalance present, including complications from bad diet or chemistry-changing drugs that exaggerate one's innate hallucinatory

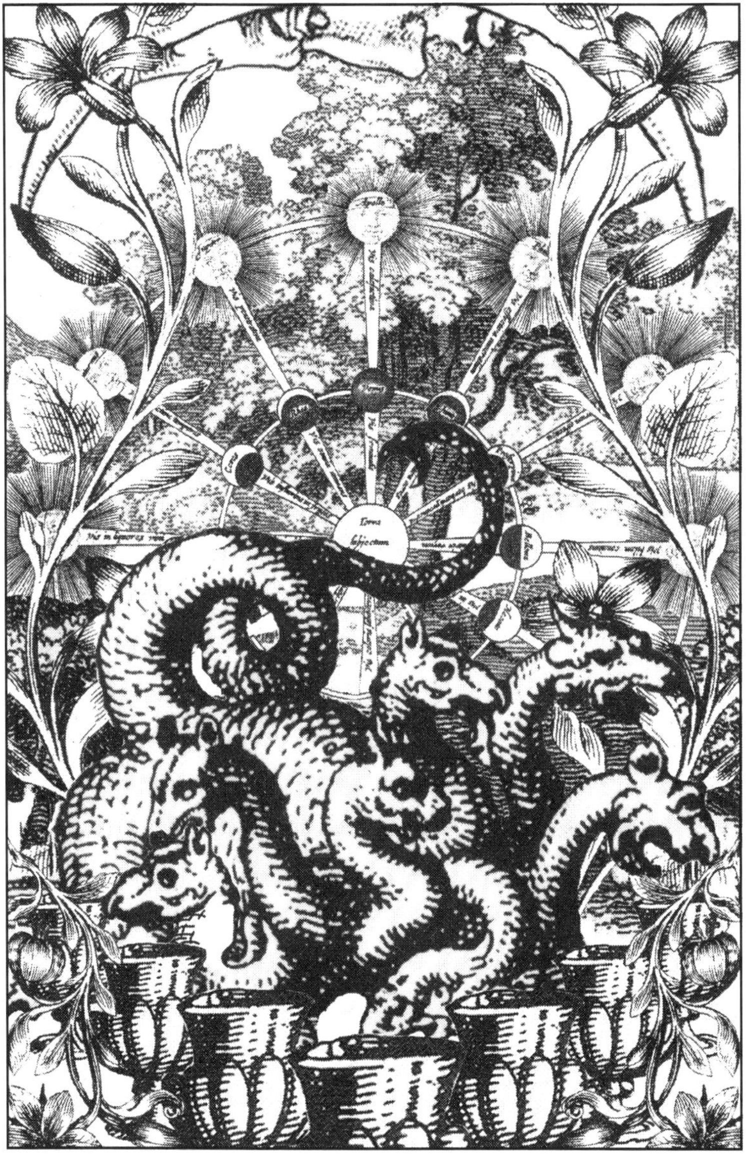

tendencies. Whatever the cause, the imaginative side of life is coming up for consideration. We might be in the grip of secret addictions or useless compensations that give back nothing in the way of benefits but hold us back and crush our hopes. We must re-educate ourselves so we can discriminate meaningless wheel spinning from those activities that can make a difference in our lives going forward. Conquer the fog of fear and ask the question: What makes this bubble of distraction preferable to the fullness of the greater world around me?

The rate of change in contemporary society has us all suffering from exhaustion due to overstimulation. The symptoms of this disorder are a kind of paralysis manifesting as an inability to differentiate between better or worse options, leading to a state of overwhelm in the face of simple life choices. Here is where we see Jupiter in Virgo becoming a real disability. Those who are afflicted feel unable to move in any direction for fear of being wrong. Our relentlessly commercial civilization has taken to staging a war of perceptions in our heads and at the marketplace.

To avoid becoming victims of our perfectionism turned against us, we must edit our mood swings and keep a firm hand on the imagination. We can only afford to host the images and ideas that serve us and move us closer to our heart's desire. Most of us experience fear when we face down our anxieties and take inventory of our issues. We must break the spell that leaves us so entranced and enraptured by the virtual world, leaving the real issues of the near and longterm future unaddressed.

Eight of Cups

Astrology: 21 - 30 Pisces, ruled by Mars **Sephira:** Hod
Essential Dignity: upright Exaltation, Jupiter in Cancer
Reversed Fall, Jupiter in Capricorn
Angelic Dignities: upright angel spelled KVQ, spoken Chavakiah
Reversed angel spelled MND, spoken Menadel

The upright Eight of Cups shows a therapeutic arrangement of hot tubs and angelic attention under the nurturing gaze of Sun and Moon. Solar radiance and Lunar nurturance are perfectly configured right now; they stand ready to reach into and through your body/mind, balancing and re-tuning all the systems. If you can accept the fact that you need some help, this well-timed offer can wring out those old stuck emotions that stain the astral body.

The upside of this card strongly suggests that we grant ourselves some time out to detox and mend from our life-labors. One is encouraged to take advantage of a local source of healing support as a restorative step between exertions. Why don't we more easily surrender to this healing touch and accept the gift we are being offered? So often we ignore the offer and the opportunity. People become so identified with their wounds that they fail to understand the purpose of the experience, which is the healing that being wounded drives us to seek. This card represents purification of body and soul, whether in preparation for an ordeal, or afterwards in the recovery stage. In its upright aspect, the esoteric signifiers harmonize to provide a true regeneration for the inner and outer life.

A Western koan states, "The wound calls the blade." Paracelsus likened a disease to a raging husband and compared the necessary medicine to his loving wife. She knows how to enter into his rage and sooth it, calming him down and turning his ferocity towards resolution. Boehme extended this principle to the dynamics of the Christian Trinity, namely the wrathful Jehovah/Father, the tender loving Sophia/Spirit, and the Son/Christ who holds the Light for both sides. In mysticism the moment when suffering becomes healing is called Metanoia. This is the balm of angelic intervention, mediating the necessary turn-around, the point at which the descent into chaos is halted and the long walk toward Restitution begins. For centuries this process was considered an essentially religious issue. But the 20th century has produced the secular concept of recovery, which holds the same promise to those who once were lost, but now are found.

When the card appears reversed, or when we must deal with Jupiter in the sign of his Fall, we are reminded that long-held wounds have not yet been addressed. It directly suggests that we are struggling with an active condition that is draining our life force and dragging us down. This condition doesn't have to be permanent, nor is it always a physical affliction. In any case it won't release us until we release it. Never forget, the inner life is always the cause, and the outer life demonstrates the inevitable reflection.

This is one of the cards in which we feature the more common traditional meaning on the reversed side of the card. When it is upright, or at least showing its better aspect, the challenge or setback can be addressed directly and cleared up reasonably swiftly. The darker side of the Eight of Cups signifies a great disappointment, an emotional setback, betrayal, or an injury to the heart. Some Tarot decks illustrate this principle by showing a young woman who has just been molested and then cast aside by a stranger passing through her village. This selfish and heartless act has left her both personally and culturally vulnerable, with potentially drastic consequences for her future. Thus the Eight of Cups reversed signifies the victim of a user, pointing to the swath of devastation that an unrestrained abuser causes.

Even in those cards where the molested girl is not shown, we still often see a man with his back turned, walking firmly away from whatever is contained in those eight vessels. At best this could be a hero, leaving behind his life of security to face a danger that's been plaguing the village. He could be leaving behind his old ways, looking for a different description of happiness, purpose, and/or worthiness. Perhaps his temperament demands a more stripped-down, self-determined existence where he doesn't have to accept the limits that seem so natural to the crowd. It is also possible that a headstrong ego might have evoked social censure by taking an antisocial stance resulting in being shunned by the community. Emotions and loyalties become tangled, straining old bonds and forcing rifts between longtime compatriots.

In reversal there can sometimes be a motive of self-abandonment involved. Sometimes the pain attending this crisis is so strong that all pretense of normalcy is stripped away and the soul is left defenseless, to wander off into the wasteland. Unfortunately, this is sometimes a necessary precondition before a healing can commence. These kinds of interior confrontations with our stuck emotions, beliefs, and sense of destiny have been called the come to Jesus moment.

Let us remember that not every grievous development in life is foreseeable. The person for whom this card appears is being put on notice. No amount of trust and good intentions, planning and preparation will ever be enough to guarantee that things will come out all right in every case. Accidents occur,

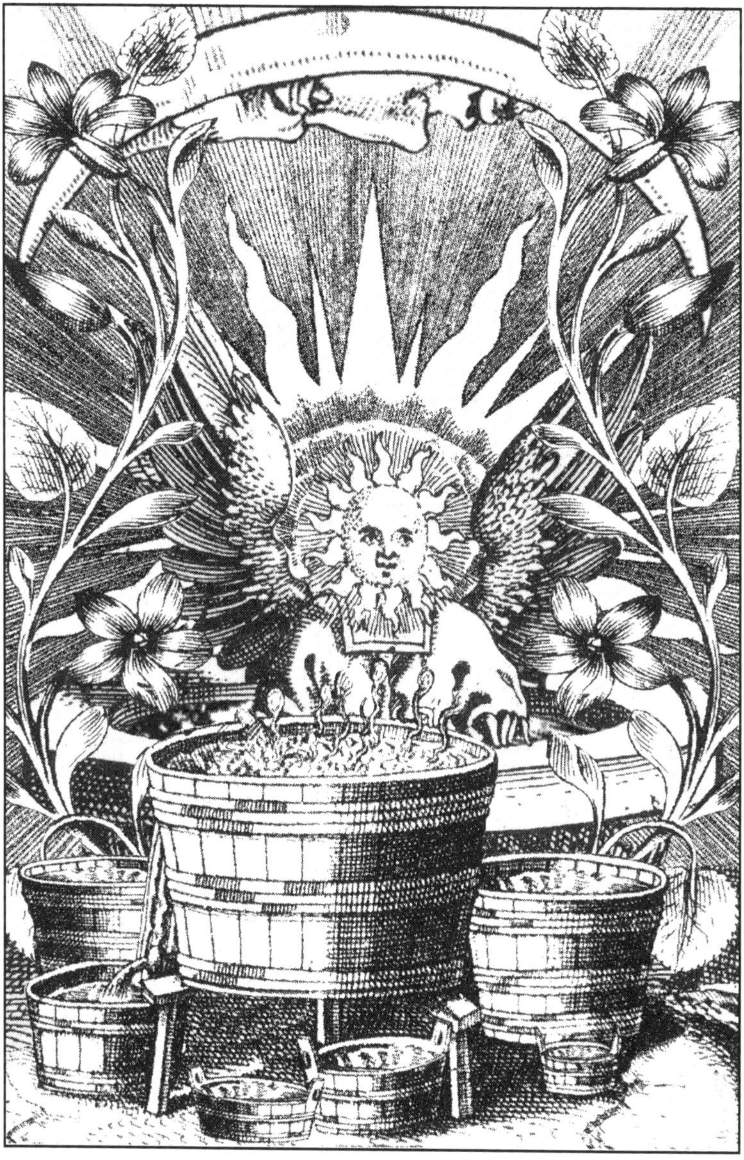

tragedies happen, and there isn't always someone or something to blame. Additionally, there may be no avenue of recourse to repair the damage or make up for the losses. Note that when Jupiter moves from his home sign Pisces towards his Exaltation in Cancer, he is moving sun-wise, meaning following the natural rotation of the rest of the planets. Whatever comes from his appearance in Cancer has a natural forward-looking optimistic feel to it. But when Jupiter moves towards his Fall in Capricorn, he's facing the retrograde direction, that is, against the natural direction of planetary flow. This leaves him pointed away from the light of the upcoming spring season, facing again into the darkest time of the year, the Saturn-ruled Winter Solstice. It's as if Jupiter requires permission from the karma-lord Saturn before the energies can be untangled and the problem rectified.

Practically speaking, because of the imperfection of this world, it isn't a great strategy to be wearing your heart on your sleeve. Try not to reveal your every thought and feeling so compulsively. The less you leak your vulnerabilities and insecure emotions into the landscape, the fewer openings outside invaders find to take advantage of. This is a challenging card, warning that all is not as it seems and greater vigilance is needed. Remember the old adage: Fool me once, that's your fault. Fool me twice, that's my fault.

Nine of Cups

Astrology: 1 – 10 Pisces, ruled by Jupiter   **Sephira:** Yesod
Essential Dignity: upright Domicile, Jupiter in Pisces
Reversed Similar, Jupiter in Sagittarius
Angelic Dignities: upright angel spelled LKB, spoken Lecabel
Reversed angel spelled VShR, spoken Vasariah

Symbolized as a tree in a magical forest, the soul delights in its current incarnation. Through the magic of embodiment, it participates in the passing of the seasons and the circle of time. The rhythmic pulse of Sun and Moon keeps one's Spirit tree tuned into our dear Earth and its stages, but the tree itself extends so far out into the dreamtime that it touches and attracts the stars. The branches bear exquisite mystical illuminations (the Cups), which settle amongst them like astral dew. The soul is constantly nourished from the invisible side of life via the subtle metabolism of the astral plane. Geese flying through represent the prayers of the holy ones and ancestors, sending blessings and wishes from all those who love you. The twining vines that are the legacy of the Marseille-style decks grow up like Jack's beanstalk to bind Earth and Heaven together as one. Eden is restored in the Heart.

The Nine of Cups is historically dubbed Happiness. A familiar version of this card shows an innkeeper on a weekend night doing a brisk business and grinning broadly at the thought of his profits. His rewards are not all monetary by any means. The scene includes music, dance, food, socializing, and a spirited appreciation of good times. His patrons are the stalwarts of his community, and their comings and goings fill his inn with laughter and conviviality. The innkeeper's heart is thankful for the well-being that flows into his community from friendships, business deals, and new families that have spontaneously generated under his roof.

Sometimes this card celebrates a victory, showing the winged goddess granting the laurel crown and palm frond to a hero in the town square. The constant of every appearance of this Nine is emotional satisfaction, a sense of belonging, and being in company with favorite people. This state of temporary but significant bliss reflects the fact that you have been living in harmony with your circumstance. Your contribution is appreciated, and you are recognized for the beauty and bounty you bring to the world.

Of course, one person's idea of happiness can be very different from another's. This card can also highlight a more cerebral victory, as when one is wrapping up a degree program or other long-term personal accomplishment. It can also refer to a completely personal consummation that is never publicly acknowledged. Both the number Nine and the association with Pisces imply that there has been a long, transformative road that was traveled before arriving at this moment of consummation. The presence of Jupiter in his two natural Domiciles gives a sense of abundance and safety providing true protection for those things that are the substance of our happiness. Whether the inspiration is fiery and mystically arousing (as in Sagittarius), or deep and psychically revealing, (as in Pisces), one can trust Jupiter because he is the archetype of the teacher. Being present for a period like this provokes a sweet release of gratitude, clarity, and recognition.

The circumstances shown on the card will vary, but the constant of every appearance of the Nine of Cups is a pointer towards emotional satisfaction. If one is not yet experiencing dreams coming true, then it's time to contemplate the things that will lead in that direction for the future. Meditate on the situations, people, and things that bring forth a sense of belonging and balance, recognition and rightness. You are tasked with giving voice and vision to your heart's dearest wish, the epicenter of your dream. The focus should not rest on what's lacking or wrong, but instead should be directed towards defining your next fulfillment, what it will feel like and look like to achieve. The ability to connect with one's bliss is a positive reflection of a life well-lived, keeping in close contact with love, appreciation, and gratitude.

Even when the Nine of Cups appears reversed, the meaning isn't changed very much, although perhaps the action is taking place in a less visual sphere, stimulating the inner life and deepest feelings rather than appearing first in the material plane. Jupiter in Sagittarius can find himself aflame with inspiration, gulping in the Light with a kind of mad-scientist fervor. So often the Sagittarius feels as if he or she is standing alone on the cusp of the future, running ahead of the crowd to embrace the incoming ideal. People in the grips of Jupitarian excitement are often so polarized by the future that the present doesn't seem quite real to them. Don't fault the reversed Nine of Cups for its messianic zeal, but strive to understand the catalyst that has unleashed this otherworldly confidence and inner Light.

Whatever he's doing, Jupiter is always more riled-up and turbulent in his Sagittarius Domicile than when in Pisces. But the intensity of this reversal doesn't steal the joy from the card. Jupiter in Sagittarius is the archetype of the activist priest who ministers to the poor and downtrodden, as we see in the life of St. Francis. He possesses a shamanistic tie to the animals, plants, even the very stones and soil. Therefore, when this card falls in your spread reversed, it draws

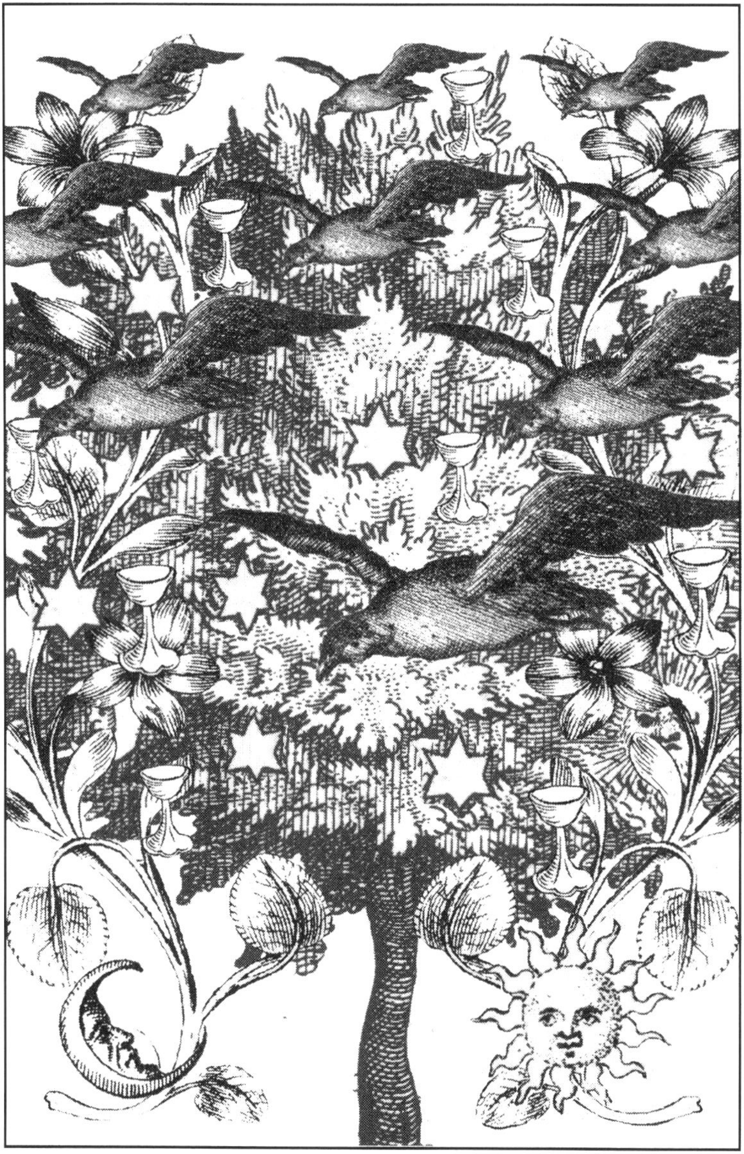

attention down to the humble, fundamental, earthy roots of this tree where the "little people" live. Give more attention to Nature and the local ecosystem rather than to the turbulent, contentious world of human culture. Consider the reversal a signal to examine your conscience and ally with those who are less advantaged around you. Discover how you can turn your own good fortune into a benefit for those who are less able to help or represent themselves.

The Suit of Cups as a whole contains steady hints about the ever-present threat of addiction. The soul trapped in dependency progressively sickens the body in the pursuit of a psychic state that continuously retreats from grasp. Since the common illustration for the Nine of Cups is a scene where folks with the desire for inebriation tend to gather, readers need to remember this potential when the card comes up reversed. Some people's deepest craving is to return to a toxic, overwhelmed, and infantile state over and over; they don't count the cost to self or others. We tend to forget how many of the people we know and love were gestated and raised by parents in the grips of one or more addictions. These souls are born afflicted with a lifetime struggle; thus the sins of the fathers are visited upon the sons. Jupiter loves and craves more of all good things, but when he's off-center, it can seem as if there's never enough to slake his ever-expanding appetites. Tarot readers are not appointed to judge our clients, but this syndrome cuts so deep across modern civilization that we cannot in good conscience ignore the cycle. The threat of poisoned waters spreads across the whole Suit, but this card especially dives towards the toxic desire for inebriation and oblivion. It's worth giving the issue a little extra scrutiny when the Nine of Cups appears, especially when reversed.

Ten of Cups

Astrology: Grand Trine in Water, Cancer, Scorpio, and Pisces; **Sephira:** Malkhut

This Ten of Cups signifies the whole Water world of the Zodiac, summarizing the eternal drama of the soul in a single poignant icon. The ark holds all the promise of a new world, but it is as yet sealed shut, still floating in the amniotic waters of the Flood. Hovering between the drowned past and the unknown future, contact with dry ground is still in the future. The tearful eye seen in the center of an exhausted and flailing Sun reminds us of the labor and struggle that must be invested before we can arrive at the rebirth of the Light. The traditional vines at the borders of the card speak of the proverbial "faith of the mustard seed," whose natural optimism bursts into enthusiastic growth whenever a momentary break in the clouds lifts the gloom.

From the Sun (the Heart, the original spark in the individual soul) an anchor is thrown up through the clouds. It rises past the ten alchemical vessels to pierce the crystalline empyrean. A holographic sigil resonates its geometry into the firmament, ordering the interrelated planets, Elements, arts and substances that together create the *prima materia* of Alchemy. The circular borders of the sigil enclose a square of matter within which an eight-pointed compass-star calls to mind the perfect order that underlies the seemingly random face of Creation. Those who understand Nature's larger pattern will trust the cycle and rest easy in their souls. But those who only use their outer senses will be forever insecure due to their perceived state of helplessness and vulnerability.

Against the geometrical perfection of this astral backdrop, the dove of Spirit has fearlessly raised a rough cross of wood, symbolizing the imperfect nobility of humanity. The base of this cross is grounded in the seven-color, seven-planet rainbow upon which all of Nature's manifestations are founded. The sum of all these symbols teaches that the immortal soul must surrender to the reality of pain and suffering as a built-in necessity, an inseparable part of gaining experience on the wheel of Time. Eventually the evolving soul learns to treasure and cling to its cross of matter, cherishing the dear details of this funky and intractable world. The Hindus say the bodhisattva (or saint) stays with the world even though he or she has no karmic tie to this reality any longer. He or she does this to work towards the enlightenment of all sentient beings.

It has also been said that in the afterlife, souls with the mark of the cross in their energy-body are the most highly respected because those souls are the ones who were willing to sacrifice their eternal calm and detachment to undertake a period of ministry in the rough-and-tumble material world via incarnation.

The Ten of Cups traditionally multiplies the personal happiness portrayed by the Nine, reaching out to the whole tribe, congregation, or nation. The usual celebratory scene of salvation shows the bonding of all the generations and all the life forms, crowned by a rainbow signifying the end of hard times and a covenant with Creator. Love and support extend to all the directions, tracing a grand web-work of interconnected lives. The myth of this card promises that as the flood recedes and the new territory is exposed, the refreshed landscape will provide a place for every soul and every species that has survived the transition.

According to mystical beliefs long attached to the rainbow, this shimmering matrix of subtle communication extends to the collective Higher Power, guides, and Nature spirits. The tearful Sun is just one breakthrough away from awakening to a sacred celebration that will forge an unbreakable bond with the greater cosmos and all of life here below. The main challenge for the ego (the micro-god in the universe within) is to break out of the persistent delusion that humanity is alone in a hostile or uncaring universe. As soon as we can dispel our isolationist thinking, shed our fears, and reach out to whatever exists beyond the edge of our skin, the clouds break open and we see the community of life extending in all directions. This card helps us remember that within the grand architecture of the Hermetic Cosmos, there is a place that has been made for us where we will be recognized and can be safe after the present deluge.

Reversed, this card emphasizes the anchor sinking into the pentacle buried in the heavens. The heart of matter reaches into the world of the ideal seeking a truly fixed frame of reference that isn't constantly churning the way the material plane does. The ego craves evidence of a world beyond the current turbulence. But to find that evidence, the soul has to reach past its known experience through yearning and desperation to finally penetrate these obscuring clouds and arrive where the dove can assist it. Those people who erroneously think that faith is a passive thing have not yet reached this all-or-nothing moment. This Sun feels trapped below a lowering sky, aching to pierce the gloom and contact the upper Heaven. Fears of abandonment and desolation tempt us here on this unfathomable and unpredictable sea. Just so, we must willingly suffer what this world makes us endure or we will never acquire the realizations that await the faithful. This is not a mental process; it is ultimately all played out in the Heart.

235

Every spiritual path is called to account for the amount of suffering there is in this world. But stop for a minute to realize how much of it is caused by free will actions taken by people who should know better. Any painful sensations of the Ten of Cups reversed come from the poignant regret caused by self-centered or shortsighted reactivity. The phrase "act in haste, repent at leisure" summarizes this issue. The reversal of this card forces insolation upon its receiver. One must turn inwards, stew in one's juices, and cook down until one's internal storming has been settled. Quarantine and incubation are the prescription when this card is afflicted.

The tears in the eye of the Sun and the anchor thrown into the firmament both hint at the humbling process that precedes the potential breakthrough illustrated on this card. In the Suit of Cups we dissolve, we resolve, and in every way we melt into our central nature, surrendering all resistance. This Ten introduces us to "the face of the soul" once we can detach from the turbulent and outer-directed material world. The timeless Ten of Cups gives us plenty of psychological and spiritual "space" to meditate, shed outworn identifications, and look deeply into the crystal clear, impassive world of Spirit.

King of Cups

Scorpio

The King of Cups in *Tarot of the Holy Light* is immersed and undefended, so naked to his Element as to even be merging with it. His Scorpion-like nature is intense, driven, and pressurized from the internal steam engine of his essential temperament. Sometimes he has to cast away all the trappings of civilization and rinse his smoldering soul in a cool, wild stream. The land and the river are thrilled to receive their King, and his presence refreshes their fecundity. One could say he is their elemental luminary. The physical Sun and Moon control the flow of his waters, whether circulating in the atmosphere above or in the rivers and oceans below. Therefore, he attends to their dance, leans on their guidance, and translates their movements for his subjects. The Cup bobbing ahead of him is the intuitive compass of his own wise heart, always feeling its way forward in Time as well as Space.

Hovering above the Cup King's back, the eternal Serpent levitates. At one level this serpent points to the existence of the soul independent of the Time-Space identity of the body. But this ancient portrayal of the artificer or demiurge also represents a more interesting story, one that harks back to the gnostic myths of antiquity. It is said that when Sophia and her offspring were ejected from Heaven to take up residence in this world, her child Ialdabaoth (the lion-headed serpent) endeavored to create a race of people in the image of the Archons. He had captured glimpses of these angelic beings reflected in Earth's waters as they passed overhead, but he thought these visions were of his own imaginative invention. But as he worked on creating this proto-human, no matter what was tried, the demiurge couldn't get his newly-formed creature to rise up and walk. The man just lay on his belly like a baby, unaware of his innate abilities. It turns out that Ialdabaoth, earthly matter's Creator, was himself ignorant of a crucial detail: that the breath of Spirit is required to awaken a soul's desire and aspiration. Only by receiving this Exhalation of Spirit could humanity stand up and live the Creator's dream. The King of Cups therefore illustrates the moment when the Holy Spirit emerges for the first time from invisibility to instruct her offspring. In this instant, the demiurge learns that he is not alone, nor is he the highest being on the spiritual totem pole. He discovers a reality larger than himself, which was unbeknownst a mere moment before, and which he utterly depends upon and is responsible to. Ialdabaoth is seen riveted by the Light that has just redefined his existence, having changed everything he knows about himself in the blink of an eye. The impact of this thunderous truth awakens the Demiurge/Serpent through the penetration of the same Moist Light that he will soon deliver to the King in the river (prototype of Adam).

To the extent that any of us are children of Sophia, Lady Wisdom, this is direct instruction for us as well. We can only bring to life those things that are alive in our hearts, which we are inspired about, to which we happily give of our inner essence without reservation. One cannot create, ironically, out of malice or from strictly selfish motives. Should we try, the result will be so incomplete that it will never rise up out of the mud to fulfill our intentions. The demiurge and the King are learning the same lesson simultaneously. The lesson is that self-conscious existence depends upon the compassionate support of a Higher Power. However far up the ladder of Creation one might ascend, the capacity to do so is only possible with the support of Spirit. Without this Moist Light granted by Sophia, we are mere mud, parading around like children in our spiritual immaturity.

In different eras and places the King of Cups takes varying forms. But in every case his energy, his essence, remains undivided. This is the same ancestral shaman who first emerged from the tribe as a visionary healer and mediator between the worlds. Over time his archetype evolved into the sacred long-haired King whose touch has the capacity to heal his subjects instantly. All further trappings that have accumulated during his journey across time are conveniences of circumstance only. This King of Cups is a fearless participant in the dialogue between mortals and immortals. He argues for humanity in the court of Heaven, despite the fact that most of his subjects haven't got a clue about the dimensions of consciousness he fathoms with every beat of his heart.

Historically, the King of Cups is portrayed with a watery background, seated on a throne holding the Cup of mystery in his hand. Occasionally this cup is fulminating like the mouth of a volcano, emanating light and fumes but never quite boiling over. The person referred to by this card is so psychically deep that he or she doesn't need to speak but manages to communicate strength, passion, and commitment in silence. Often enough this King will be robed like the Hierophant, indicating his function as guide of souls in the work of evolution. Possessing a laser-like insight but no patience for dissembling, he is a psychic and psychological force to be reckoned with.

In the family and/or leadership arena, this King is the good father, the strong figurehead whose role modeling can cement a team together with love

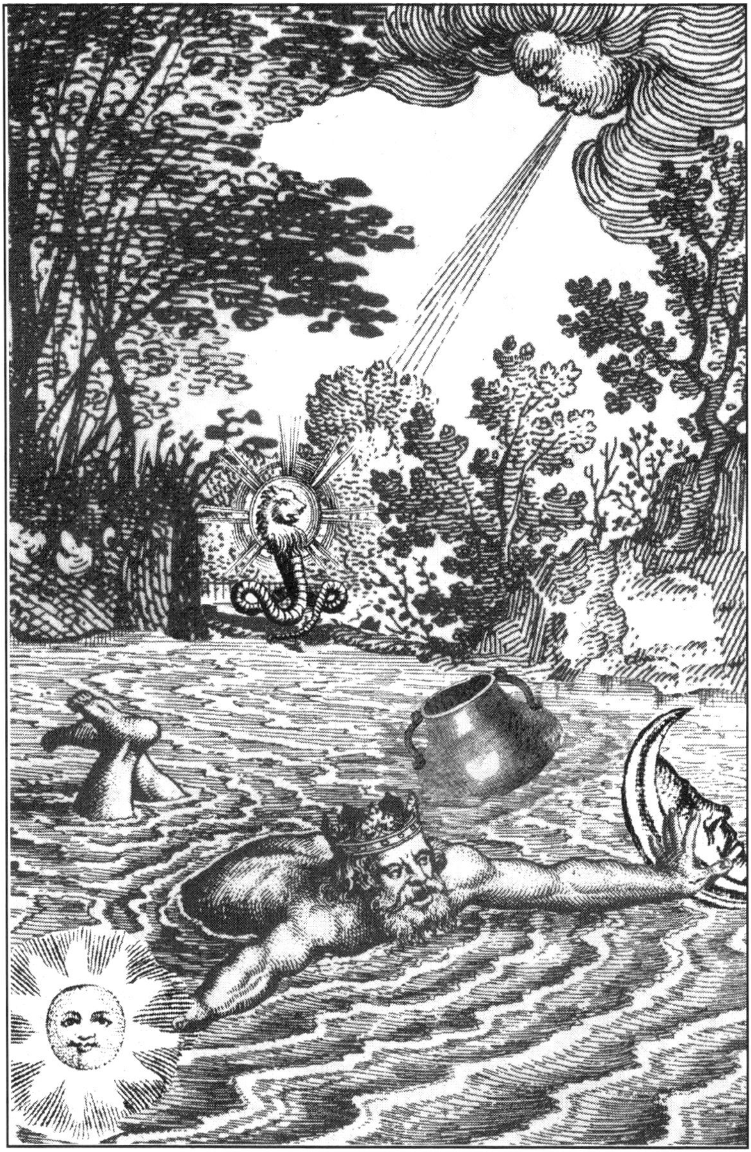

and caring. On his harsh side he will not tolerate works of heedlessness, competitiveness, or selfishness. Nobody wants to disappoint him, not because he will punish him or her, but because he can break a person's heart with a single glance. His nobility of soul causes all who know him to quickly become their better selves or slink away in shame from the unspoken lash of the negative contrast between them. His every word is pulled straight from your conscience.

When reversed, this King needs to carefully modulate his demeanor when he's in company. He can easily wound those who enter his presence unshielded. People who are unaware of his intensely probing, secret-revealing, blast-furnace type of aura can emerge from a simple exchange horrified. To be who he is, the King of Cups often needs to bypass what are socially called "personal feelings," including his own. Think of this King of Cups as the psychic surgeon who reaches right through your skin into your entrails to pull out the tumor. He will not engage with social artifice, pretense, or denial. But he can and will help retrieve our souls when we have finally come to the edge of our learned understanding.

Queen of Cups
Cancer

The Queen of Cups is shown here as Melusine, or Melusina, the ancient European personification of the intelligence of sacred springs and rivers. Here we see her in all her classic attributes including wings, crown, and a shapely human body that ends in two corkscrew tails. Humans are traditionally blessed to be in relationship with her; she sometimes even takes a human in marriage. But she then enjoins an unbreakable stricture upon her human lovers, which sadly they eventually violate either intentionally or unintentionally. In this aspect among others, Melusina bears a resemblance to another ancient misunderstood figure of the Divine Beloved known as Sophia.

According to the myth, Melusina can maintain a human form most of the time, but on regular occasions she needs to take care of her mermaid side. This she does in privacy in the bath. Her rule is that she is not to be looked upon when she's disrobed and in the water. Rightly, Melusina doesn't want to be singled out as "something different, not one of us" among the so-called normal people. In this way she symbolizes every soul's right to privacy and self-determinism inside its own skin.

Sadly, all the myths about her episodes among humans end with the betrayal of her sanctum and the public revelation of her fishy lower half. Her prince is not necessarily trying to reveal her secrets, let it be known. But being a limited human and therefore bedeviled by ego, indiscretion, and lack of perspective, he eventually betrays her confidence and forces her to retreat from the human world again. To distill this little legend down to its innermost essence, Melusina reminds the arrogant humans to refrain from interfering with the water's source (or the intuition's source either). We need to grant Melusina some safety and nurturing support and then just let her blessings flow.

On a more modern, psychological level, Melusina represents the sovereign individuality of every sentient entity. We each deserve the right to be as polymorphously perverse (in the imaginative sense) as is required by our unique makeup. We also need to form our own unique relationship to Spirit without having to be answerable to anybody else about this relationship. If we can manage our eccentricity well enough that we aren't burdening others with it, then we deserve to be granted the space to attend to our interior business from time to time.

Melusina always presents herself as a human to her husband as well as to his castle community. This is a very important clue for interpersonal relations. We so easily forget that even spouses should keep up their manners around each other. Melusina is honorable in upholding her wifely duties, and she refrains from disturbing her husband's social status with gross evidence of her "otherness." Multiple versions of the story assert that their union persists for years in good harmony under Melusina's rules. But the husband eventually could not leave well enough alone nor keep his own counsel. Perhaps he felt the need to brag or complain about the arrangement, breaking his vows at her expense. Maybe he let a good friend peek between the boards of her bathhouse just to win a bet. At some point her dignity was invaded and compromised, after which Melusina was forced to retreat again. The lesson is that the emotional, psychic, spiritual, and shamanic aspects of our natural personalities should not be exposed to the harsh spotlight of the literalistic mind. The common reasoning faculty can only slice and dice Melusina's unique mystery into a mutilated pile of absurdities, and the illuminated Spirit will be forced to retreat.

At another level Melusina is a literal symbol of how to handle a spring of fresh water (or any other sudden blessing) when it is first discovered. A shelter should be constructed to protect the spring from invasion at its source. Too much human traffic around the wellhead can pollute the purity of the water. Nobody should presume to own the well or commodify the blessing of its abundance. Respect the mystery of its appearances and disappearances, making best use of her Water while it is offered. There is no controlling the hidden depths from whence the spring is emerging, but showing appreciation and guarding Melusina's confidences might motivate her to keep company with humans just a little bit longer.

The Queen of Cups is traditionally seen as a very feminine, sensitive, vulnerable woman who is supremely intuitive and offers unconditional love. She is the classic "feeler," sometimes to a fault. Her natural empathy and caring expose her to everyone else's unfinished business. For this reason she occasionally has difficulty identifying her true self-interest in the midst of her responsiveness to others. At those times she can appear slightly unfocused or perhaps overwhelmed.

For this very reason Melusina's strategy of periodic retreats can be taken as a positive response to stress, whereas the fear of defeat can be relegated to the reversed meaning of the card. You don't have to totally give up on enjoying the company of other humans, only be independent-minded enough to take your space when the mass mind isn't conducive to personal peace. At her best Melusina represents the Grail Queen and the goddess of the family. The proof

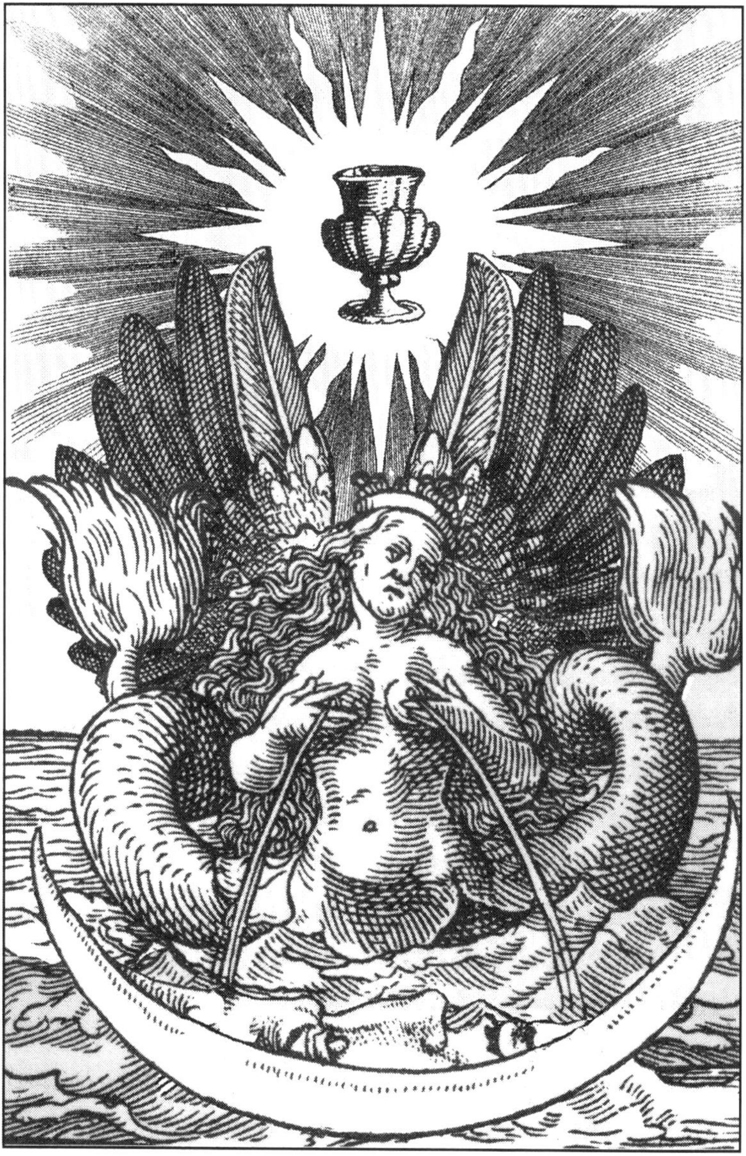

of her fulfillment comes upon witnessing that her loved ones are developing their own conscience, their own conversation with Spirit.

The Queen of Cups infuses the world with loving family values. We could all experience more of her graceful, supportive, empowering attention. The mother who develops Queen of Cups qualities will convey permission to each of her children that they can individuate freely without fear of rejection. If she's not interfered with, this Queen can effectively immunize the next generation of children from the cruel, dysfunctional relating patterns that still saturate the unconscious parts of modern culture.

In reversal the Queen of Cups is feeling over-stressed, used, abandoned, or betrayed. In this light she temporarily shows the symptoms of ancient patriarchal projections. Her distress might be interpreted as lack of character, as if she were a victim in need of being taken under the wing of a dominant leader in order to be protected from her "weaknesses."

On the other hand, she might instead temporarily lose her cool and mete out a fierce dose of comeuppance to her startled family members. Neither of these is her favorite style, being the natural consequence of insensitive, selfish treatment. In fact, she is a loyal and caring person who will take on any amount of challenge for a chance to assist her family members' well-being. But if someone takes too much advantage, showing too little consideration, then one day they will look for her and she'll be gone. Should a client or friend begin demonstrating the crushed and fearful affect associated with the Queen of Cups' stressed-out side, I would suggest that this is not natural, but is the demeanor of a victim of harsh treatment who has been driven into anxiety and fear by a dominating bully or abusive circumstances.

Knight of Cups

Pisces

The Knight of Cups confounds our Tarot formulas on several levels. For one thing he seems older than his King, which is less often seen in a context where the Knights are usually the Kings' sons. This Knight has also outgrown the mystique of his calling, since he's not ambitious, militaristic, nor proud. He further lacks interest in contending with the other Knights on the hierarchical ladder to a more prestigious (and thus more dangerous) assignment. Being a Pisces, he understands his role as that of overseer and defender of the domestic peace. He and the Knight of Disks ensure that the young men of the realm are as skilled in the manly arts of productive labor as they are in scrapping and carousing.

The Knight of Cups has often been titled Homecoming, suggesting a lifetime search to find his true heart's home. This reference stems from the predicament of the noble Cathar families of southern Europe after the Crusade that crushed their homeland (beginning in 1229). Many of these families packed up and relocated to the Holy Land, and their names weren't heard again for several generations. When their descendants returned in subsequent centuries, they came not as knights and ladies, but as troubadours with their pages. In the guise of traveling entertainers, they quietly advanced a heretical religion of love and radical acceptance gleaned from exposure to gnostic and Islamic mysticism.

Historical testimony of the times explicitly states that this type of knight attended by his pages was actually a plainclothes Cathar bishop with his priests, living as circuit-riders and ministering to multiple communities throughout the year. These servants of the gnosis carried news between far-flung outposts, plus they baptized, married, ordained, and consoled the dying. All of this while "on the side" producing an illuminated literature, a musical repertoire, and an underground stream of gnomic artworks that kept the Grail myths and the Religion of Love alive centuries past their supposed extinction. Knowing this, it becomes clearer why this Knight is so often associated with aesthetics, mysticism, music, and art. This Knight's internal cultivation and refinement are all out of proportion to the rough style of his outer life. Completing the journey of return after long estrangement from all he once held dear, this Knight's taste for adventure is exhausted. There is no more romanticizing of battles or travel in strange lands, no search for fortunes or mythical beasts; it has all been expunged from his mind. Now he wants to live in harmony among friends and compatriots, where his help is wanted and welcomed. He craves a life that isn't punctuated by a fight at every turn. Whatever his chronological age, this Knight is older and wiser, and because of this, he's just not tempted anymore. If he once had aspirations of greatness, now he is content to be indistinguishable from his servants, chopping wood and carrying water close to home. Eschewing gender role divisions, he tends to the land and the people around him like the grandparent of an extended family. Men who need nurturing find their way to him eventually; he shepherds a ragtag circle of loose-end old boys who form a tribe of sorts in his shadow.

Another regular association with this card is that of "Knight of the Heart," exemplar of the chivalric and courtly culture born of the Arthurian story-cycles. We often see him painted with the colors of a stock romantic hero. In this role he's the unattainable Knight on a white charger who (it is imagined) possesses all the refined characteristics we fail to see in the people immediately around us. The ladies at every castle pine for this Knight's special attention, but he's always packing up and leaving them behind, off to serve a larger cause.

This Knight's kindness and empathy become the problem when the card appears reversed. His mystical music and gentle manners stimulate different people's fantasies of a higher love, but at the personal level this Knight is simply not emotionally available. He lives a life that's near-monastic, avoiding intimacy and the messiness of expectations and responsibilities. People look for ways to seduce him into getting aroused about them or about castle life, but he seems to be immune to their efforts. Perhaps he's afraid of his dependent feelings or afraid of being exposed as a secret agent for the Cathars. Then again, maybe he just doesn't want to disappoint any more people. He has satisfied himself that no matter what fantasies others might have of him as they listen to his stories and songs, he's nobody's romantic hero. Therefore he won't allow anybody to mistake him for their heart's desire, no matter how attractive their offers might be.

Looking at the esoteric role of the sign Pisces, we have here a mystery of the highest order. As the last sign in the parade of the Zodiac, he appears to be the janitor following the parade. His job boils down to sweeping up and composting everything that has been left behind after the party is over. But those with eyes to see will discover that Pisces' true role in the Zodiac is to function like the Nile river, accepting all the upstream detritus and digesting it to ultimately deposit the resulting slurry upon the downriver plains as fresh fertility for a new growing season. Pisces is the end that prepares for the beginning, it is that last which shall be first. In the twelfth sign we have reached the

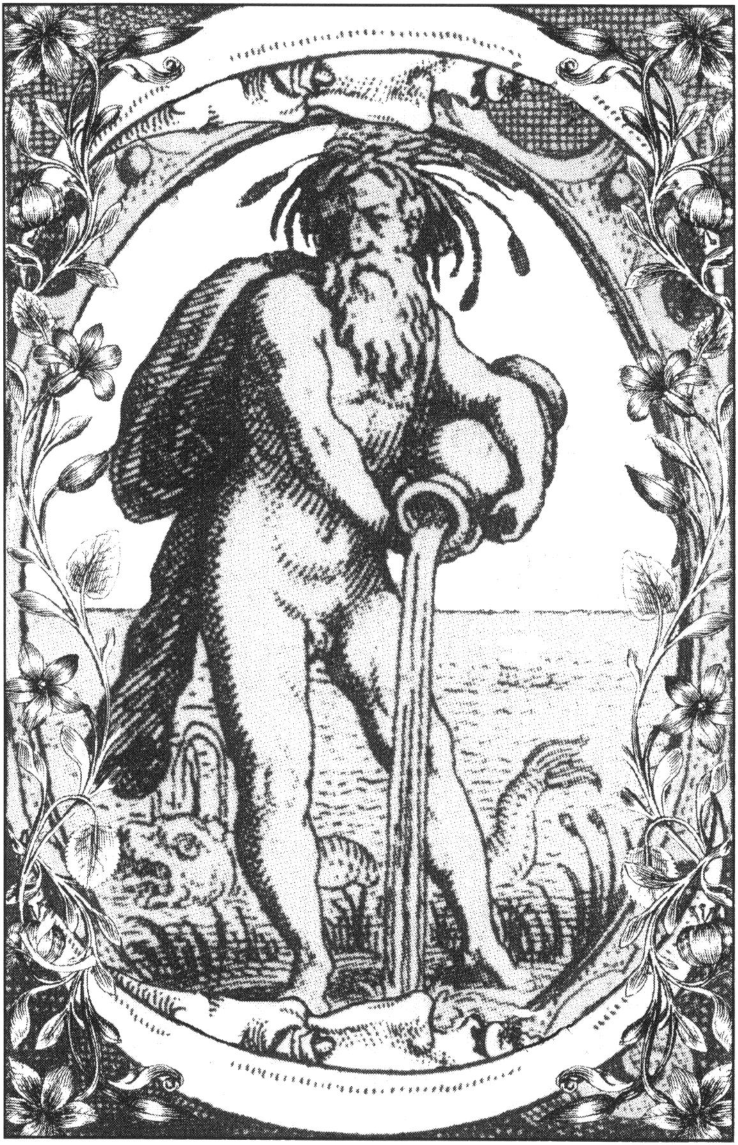

point at which the inessential and unsustainable are finally sloughed off and released. This frees up the essence, the quicksilver spark of life at the Heart of Creation, to go forth and find new forms and associations. One reaches that final teachable moment when figure becomes ground and a whole new assemblage of possibilities becomes apparent. As such, Pisces is the archetype of reincarnation, rebirth, reorientation, renewal, and every similar trend. If we can truly lay down the past and walk on, we will discover a whole new world emerging before our eyes.

For obvious reasons care must be taken not to expect too much of the person this card may represent in a spread. Knight of Cups people have tendencies and predilections that lead them away from putting human bonding at the center of their lives. A person can't lean his or her full weight on this Knight without taking a fall. This Knight's chosen lifestyle may be very close to that of the village shaman. That's because he is concentrating on spiritual cultivation at this point in his life. He feels a deep need to make up for the karma he created and the lives he disrupted before he broke free from the armor, the weapons, the plunder, and the constant conflict associated with knighthood. Of course he would love to be loved and understood, but he's not going to expend his will power in that direction anymore. As we see him now, the Knight of Cups clings to his tender hearted and psychic relationship with Nature and his mismatched band of cast-off, disconnected souls. Through keeping alive the ancestral links to the land and its people, preserved as teaching stories, this Knight passes on the highest values of the ancient society from which he emerged. Living lightly and anonymously among those who were his previous subjects, this Knight takes what comes to him without force or manipulation, humbly making his peace with life.

Page of Cups

Summer Solstice

As an ally of the Queen, this Page of Cups has to keep his heart close to the surface and his antennae out. He truly wants to be of service to the realm, and he will do whatever it takes in order to remain by his Queen's side through thick and thin. His gift is the talent of anticipation. He can feel the future coming just a few heart-beats faster than the mind can calculate. His Cup's inner geometry causes it to sing like a Tibetan bowl when certain background frequencies in the environment begin to shift. Thus the Page stays resonantly informed about everything relevant to his mission. With his Cup, his caring, and his anticipatory acuity, this Page spins a web of protection around the Queen and her family, helping to keep their day-to-day lives running smoothly no matter what politics or fate might impose.

The manly men of the court make fun of the Page of Cups' indoor skill-set, which includes herbal cures and wound care, cooking, storytelling, hair braiding, and making music with the troubadours. But this Page is also known for having great instincts when stressors pile up. He's the first one to proffer the fortifying brew when his liege lord and crew are back from the hunt or a border incursion, exhausted from their labors. He can be trusted to manage, entertain, and teach the castle children on a moment's notice, whatever the weather. Our Page can sooth a little girl's tears or joke a sullen teenager out of his surliness, but he almost never needs to resort to punishment to evoke cooperation.

The Page of Cups can also discreetly scan the newcomers to court, evaluating their energies and accurately reporting on their motives toward the King and Queen. He knows all the latest village news, but he tries hard to be fair, quashing gossip and correcting gripers. This Page could grow into the type of man to whom the world would grant power and authority, but right now he just doesn't seem to want it. In truth his wants are simple: He wants the royal family feeling comfortable, well fed, well rested, and supplied with everything they need to fulfill their duties. This Page is actually essential to the family harmony, but he serves so invisibly that sometimes people forget how much he contributes.

Over the centuries the Page of Cups has gained the reputation of a poetic, mystical, emotionally open, and sentimental person. Some people see him as immature, but this is a superficial read. Our Page is not naive in the least; he is an excellent judge of character who is well acquainted with what can go wrong between people. Yet he still chooses to remain open and encourage the better natures of the people in his care. Since he is sincere and transparent, he's unafraid to own his emotions and can ably name and accurately describe yours. Despite any past setbacks, this Page's inner life is still malleable and idealistic, still given to flights of visionary phantasia, still magically inclined. This Page is unusually empathic, implying access to a realm of directly experienced realities that others only dimly imagine.

In the alchemical lexicon, the time of year that this Page represents is the onset of the two-month period where the Sun and Moon are enthroned in their natural signs of Cancer and Leo. This is the period when astral conditions are most clement in the northern hemisphere, and therefore most conducive to positive results in any type of esoteric or metaphysical operation.

There is some amount of mystery about what has set this Page on his course in life. His role may have fallen to him due to his innate nature, or it could have come due to a turn of fate that he has long ceased protesting. One might parallel this Page with the path of a person like Paracelsus, who constantly traveled around Europe but was never known to make a home or have a family. Gossip held that he had been injured in an accident with a horse as a youth, which helped to cement his focus on the healing arts throughout his adult life. Some felt that Paracelsus lived with a secret sorrow, which was manifested in his quarrelsomeness and his huge appetite for drink. But all who received healing from his hands felt his compassion for their condition and his concern for their well-being.

Whatever the circumstance and in the face of manifold resistance, Paracelsus' natural philosophy made space for a goddess who his gnostic/Lutheran sensibilities dictated should be present within the Christian pantheon. Subsequent scholarship into his life and writings has revealed that the special vocabulary and worldview he invented over the course of his medical practice had its roots in the ancient Valentinian philosophy that had preceded Catholic Christianity.

The reversed manifestations of the Page of Cups are all natural consequences of his delicate metabolism. A co-factor of his exquisitely aware and fine-tuned sensibilities is that under challenging conditions, he can lose his sense of grounding in ordinary reality. Sometimes he feels flooded with information from the astral plane, as the waterfall descending from the hole in his sky suggests. He is also easily overwhelmed by environmental assaults, which in our dirty world come from all directions. This Page must learn to close his aura

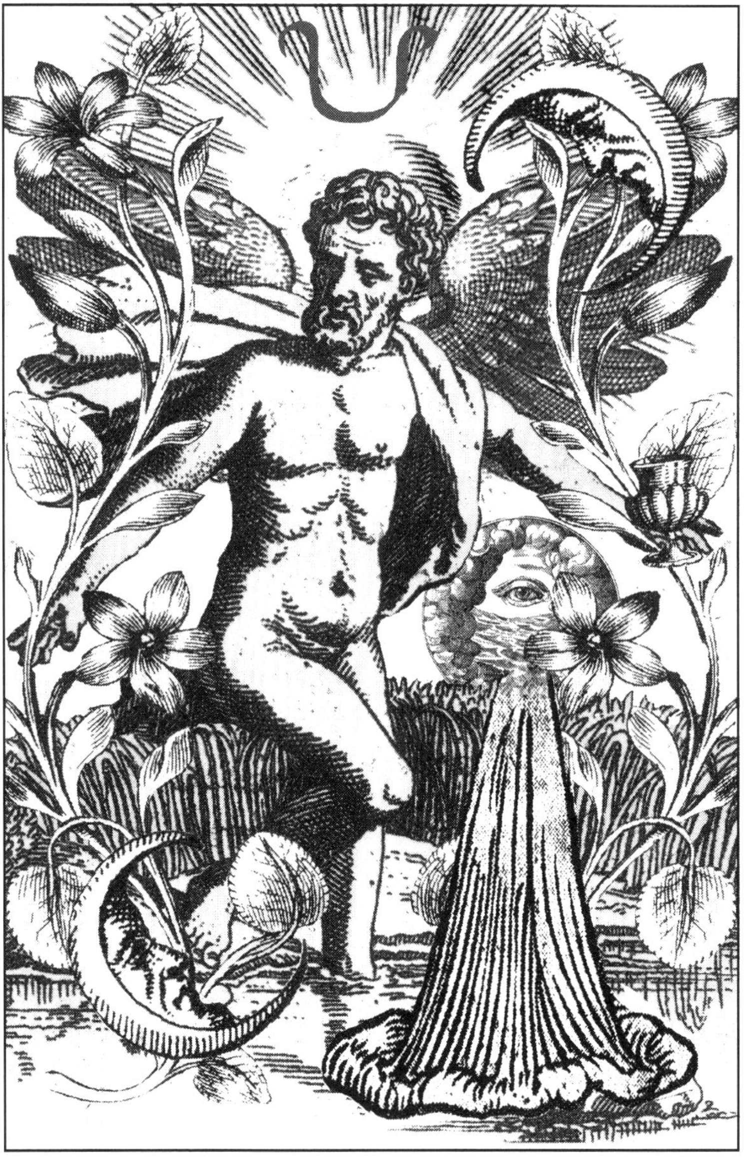

and reject certain thoughts, substances, and frequencies outright, just to keep from being a victim of the times.

No matter his age or stage in life, this Page needs to treat his body as if it were his treasured and delicate child. If he were to abuse his vehicle the way that he sees others doing, he'd be a sick, miserable wreck within days. The Page of Cups will quickly manifest symptoms of gut distress, asthma, eczema, and/or headache when he's toxically overloaded. Some may call him a "lightweight," but really he's a genuine sensitive, which means he functions as the canary in the coal mine. If an external stressor comes to dominate the scene, he'll eventually need to retract his attachment and disengage from the toxic or dangerous sources in the environment.

Since this Page does his daily duties unarmed, he can only afford to function as the filtration system for the Queen's family as long as the environment remains protected. He has brothers and friends among the military men, and there are other avenues for him to apply his gifts should he strike out into the larger world. But on the day he aspires to go beyond serving the royal family in this intimate way, he will need to build a stronger will and a more calculating mind to balance all the emotional saturation and tidal flux that currently characterizes this Page's life. He might choose to do that, eventually, when he no longer feels he can be of service in this more personal manner. But for now he's completely fulfilled by being present for the Cups tribe, helping others be healthy, safe, and supported while they reach for their dreams.

Chapter 5
The Disks

Suit of Disks

For *Tarot of the Holy Light*, we chose this Eye of Gold image in homage to some of the early Disk cards found in the Sforza castle moat. (See Stuart R. Kaplan, 1994, vol. 2, p. 278-80.) When I first saw those Disks, it felt like the cards had beautiful bedroom eyes that were looking out at me. There's a consciousness in matter, a Light with a logic and life cycle of its own. The metal gold was believed to be captured Solar energy accumulating underground, composed of the same substance as the Sun. Those who were making talismans to the Sun would work in gold. Look at each golden disk as a captured ray of Light, of intelligence, of formative power that can imprint itself upon raw matter and draw out its more refined possibilities. The Ace of Disks represents the infinite potential of Earth to hold forms and give them life, calling the evolutionary potential out of raw ideas.

The Suit of Disks represents first and foremost your body, health, vigor, and genetic heredity. It can be seen as the capacity to ground and relax, attuning to the rhythms of Nature within and without. Imagined as a shield that a warrior might carry, the Disk symbolizes a feeling of safety, security, and general protection from survival threats. When unencumbered by fear, one is free to be creative, not hampered by anxiety and reactivity. This theme of comfort and abundance can also extend to a financial situation, though it is not limited to monetary matters. Even the poorest person can be enriched and increased by those golden moments granted by Nature through contact with the energies of goodness, generosity, and sincerity.

As a symbol of your body, the Disk is the seat and throne of your intelligence. Without a body one doesn't have the platform to develop the mind or any other attribute. Your body is your planet, your "Earth." Meditate deeply upon the implications of this statement. Earth is the karma-entrapping substance that binds the soul, but it is also the channel through which the soul can extend its will into the Time/Space world. Examination of this idea leads to the realization that Time as we experience it is a phenomenon of matter, not a phenomenon of consciousness. This suggests that our sense of entrapment in Earth is based on clinging to its momentary appearances.

Consulting the ancients, we learn that the stickiness of already-existing arrangements (their sense of gravity) gives Earth its ability to slow down and impose control over the free flow of the other Elements. This is Earth's signal quality: It traps the other Elements within its flypaper entanglements and forces them to slow down until they materialize. Before the time of Christ, the ancient Greeks decided that Air, Fire, and Water are immortals like the ancient gods. These three behave as if they are alive, in the sense that they possess their own manner of movement, of reproduction, of association, and all the rest. Our wise ancestors saw in the three "pure" Elements all the qualities we attribute to sentient entities. Thus the Element Earth was defined as the mud resulting from various admixtures of the other three. By this way of thinking, any form that can be imposed upon matter is maintained by a combination of the three celestial Elements. If one or more of those Elements were to vacate the premises, the Earth component of the mix would immediately devolve into an inert, "dead" state.

Following the Disks into a later body of associations reveals our Suit-symbol to be a wheel or vortex of energy, which can operate in both incoming and outgoing modes. A series of ten such vortices comprise the Tree of Life developed among the Hebrew mystics of the Holy Land Diaspora. This tradition presents us with a Western chakra system, similar to but different from the seven chakras (human energy-nodes) taught by the Hindu yogis. These spheres or wheels located in different parts of the body are called the Sephirot (plural) or Sephira (singular), and they define the unique attributes and abilities with which humans are divinely endowed. We receive these signal blessings because, as myth asserts, humans are "made in the image of God" (or, "the gods"). These magical Sephirot also possess qualities that are directly related to the planets transiting the heavens overhead. This provides the magical justification for the alchemical Astrology of Paracelsus and all of his followers.

Disks ultimately symbolize strengths or gifts, sources of support that provide for you based on your own efforts or those of your ancestors. Such gifts can include family money, marketable skills, insider connections, a special cultural heritage, farmlands, etc. The biblical use of the word "talent" for a unit of money offers us an interesting play on words. Whether as a coin or as a capability, a talent is a potential, an ability that is ready to be spent in actualization of a goal. Those who are willing to invest of themselves, their time, money, and labor, deserve the rewards of their effort. The Disks provide those rewards, as well as supplying the means to denominate both earning power and spending power.

Think of the Disk as the symbol of the "currency" you possess for protecting your sovereignty in this world. Disks symbolize the value of your assets, whether they are intellectual, entrepreneurial, artistic, or any other "property" you command, right down to the sheer brute strength to physically outwork those around you. When you can translate your assets into a way to pay your bills and take care of your family, you have mastered the energy of the Disks. As it says in Matthew 6:21, "... for where your treasure is, there your heart will be also."

At the archetype level the Disk is the symbol for your values, the things you love, to which you are attracted, which you keep close around yourself. In Alchemy the metal gold represents not only a standard of external value to the mass mind, but also a symbol of purity and refinement compared to the other metals. Gold is naturally brilliant, malleable, and warm to view and touch, with a chemical composition that allows it to blend with other precious metals while retaining its luster. Because of these qualities, gold shows forth the highest evolution of the element Earth and points to the inner Light that inspires all the lives playing out on this planet.

At its highest manifestation the Disk symbolizes the Body of God, the throne or seat of matter itself. Likewise, the Disks are the seeds of all the "things" in this world, each one drawn out of the infinite imagination of Sophia. The earliest blatantly esoteric Tarots (the *Etteilla* packs) show the personalities of the Planetary Govenors on the Disk Pips, arranged by their orbital placements around the Sun (Ace), from the innermost Mercury (deuce) through the Moon in Earth's place, to Saturn, the Ring-Pass-Not (in seventh place). The outermost planets were still unknown in Etteilla's era, so the Eight, Nine, and Ten of Disks were keyed to the North Node of the Moon, the South Node of the Moon, and the Part of Fortune.

Ace of Disks

Astrology: 1 - 10 Capricorn, ruled by Saturn   **Sephira:** Keter
Essential Dignity: upright Domicile, Saturn in Capricorn
Reversed Similar, Saturn in Aquarius
Angelic Dignities: upright angel spelled MBH, spoken Mebahiah
Reversed angel spelled PVI, spoken Poyel

The Ace of Disks is usually pictured with a garden or agricultural backdrop to emphasize the innate nature of this Ace to serve as a seed. If this "talent" is planted and tended carefully, it will sprout and reward you with a good harvest. Think of it as the seed of your future fulfillment. An Ace represents a single step towards your goal, but if that step is continued over time, it can cover great distances.

Another evocative device often employed on this Ace is a trellised gateway, an opening through the woods, or a natural archway of rock that defines a window into another world. This device draws the eye through the open foreground like a funnel, towards a "keyhole" somewhere in the background. A whole different landscape, including blue skies and possibly water, is visible through this little aperture, implying a fresh future awaiting at the other end of "now." This offers a suggestion that I wouldn't want my readers to abandon, whether it appears on a particular Tarot deck's Ace of Disks or not. It promises an invitation to someplace rich and special, a fertile territory redolent with untapped potential. In the Ace you have reached the gate, the entrance to a fabled realm. This potential Paradise beacons if you will reach out and open the latch or walk the path to reach it.

In the light of this eye of gold, we don't want to be guilty of ignoring the will of matter in the outworking of events. Since time and circumstance are experienced differently by mammals versus metals, every order of being has its own logic and evolutionary trajectory. This Ace tells us to study deeply the already-established order that currently governs the circumstances around you. Make sure you appreciate every benefit and understand every feature of the current circumstance before you start rearranging things to suit your momentary whim.

From the alchemical point of view of seeking out remedies, we are looking at Saturn in Capricorn with the upright Ace, and Saturn in Aquarius with the reversal. Both these correspondences represent Saturn in his natural Domiciles, but there the resemblance ends. The Cardinal quality of Saturn in Capricorn inclines towards action, taking charge of the stream of events and directing the flow. The sign Capricorn is the culmination experience for that half of the Zodiac (Leo to Capricorn) that is alchemically described as the "Dry Way." This is also called the way of detachment in the sense that as we cross these signs from mid-summer to Winter Solstice, we are supposed to surrender a part of ourselves to the Planetary Governor that rules each sign. In Leo we share the gold of our ego-attachments, in Virgo we surrender something of Mercury's, in Libra we tithe to Venus, and so forth up to Capricorn. Because Capricorn is associated with fame, reputation, status, accomplishments, and the results of our labors, the soul strives to complete its earthly tasks in order to win the freedom to step off this "mortal Coil" and leave the embodied life behind.

In the course of a human lifetime, the planets recapitulate this arc over and over, at slower and faster rates of motion. The longer our life extends, the more we will ultimately surrender to this invisible astral tax. The truth is we are all fiercely attached to our bodies and our lives, however miserable we may claim to be from day to day. Therefore, eventually the Capricorn energies roll into Fixed Aquarius, and a whole new rule obtains.

In the Air world one's priorities drastically change. Aquarius is the entrance to the so-called "Wet Way," the alchemical moniker of the six signs between Aquarius and Cancer. In this half of the Zodiac, the soul is diving down into Time, Space, and material incarnation, filled with spiritual inspiration and ready to take on the problems of the world. A soul with Aquarius inclinations possesses the eagle's-eye view, being able to contemplate the vast, overarching patterns that govern all of life, not just human life. From this point of remove, terrestrial life looks beautiful, dear, and well worth engaging. There's a feeling of ownership and responsibility that keeps Aquarian energies connected to the world. We could look at the reversed Ace of Disks as the bodhisattva's mission, which brings us back to Earth over and over despite the fact that this saintly soul has no more debts to pay within the planetary system.

Generally speaking, all the Disks indicate the tangible realities of daily life. This Ace could represent that "Eureka!" moment when one moves from theory to reality, from planning and supposition to hands-on experience. Kabbalistic tradition places the Aces at the Third Eye and crown (Keter) of the human energy-body. Focused meditation in the inner Light organizes one's personality upon a vision of matter that is awakened to its original, Paradise state. By practicing this meditation, one could eventually gain enough control of the celestial radiance to heal the body, untangle the emotions, and complete the growth of the soul.

That being the case, the reversed Ace of Disks could be a sterile seed, a sickly body, or a situation that's not likely to be fertile and prosper. Sometimes

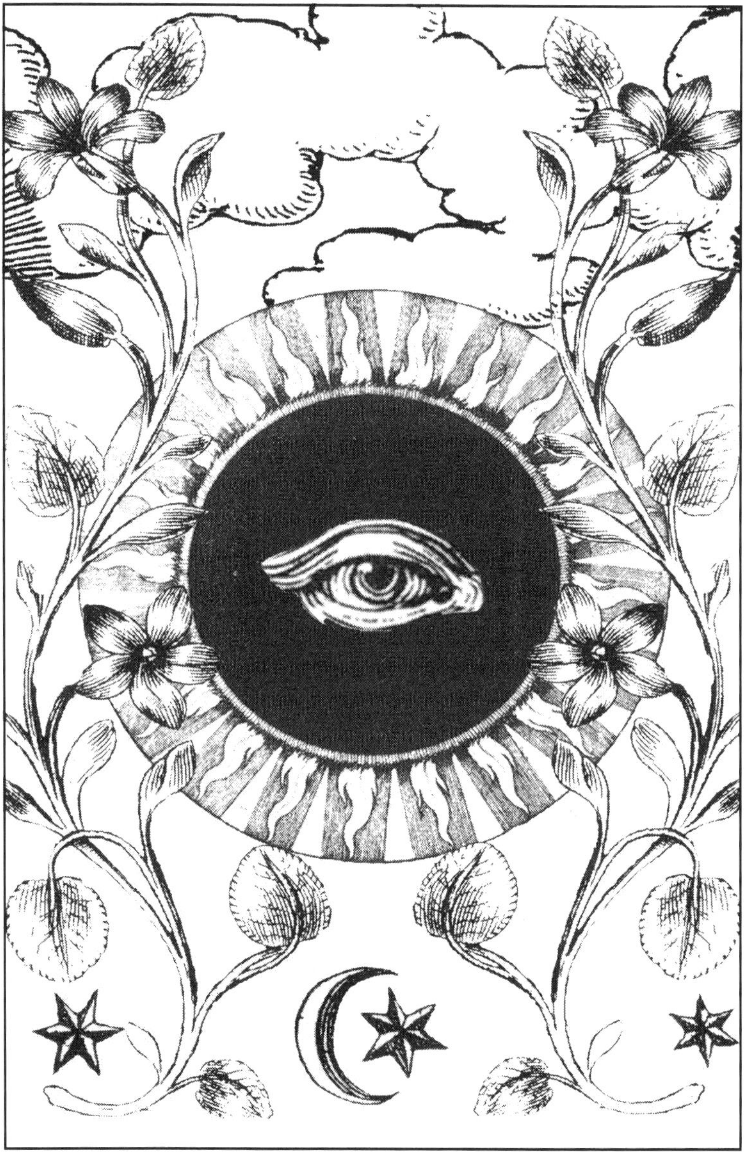

forms don't carry the content that they imply; as happens with designer goods, there are knockoffs. To the extent the upright Ace of Disks might represent seeds for the garden, the reversed version could represent junk food, genetically modified life forms, and Franken-fakes comprised of the cheapest and most unwholesome substitutes. Ace of Disks reversed raises the challenge of distinguishing between fool's gold and the real gold. One has to determine whether self-delusion or projections are imparting the value that appears to be present. What is your basis for determining the priorities of your life? If you don't have a good answer to that question, then try letting Nature take Her course without interference. She will show you the direction She wants to grow.

Two of Disks

Astrology: 11-20 Capricorn, ruled by Venus   **Sephira:** Chakhmah
Essential Dignity: upright Compliment, Saturn in Leo
Reversed Detriment, Saturn in Cancer
Angelic Dignities: upright angel spelled NMM, spoken Nemamiah
Reversed angel spelled YYL, spoken Yeialel

With the Two of Disks, one often sees two coins flipping in the air. Sometimes there's a juggler shown in the act, or else there's just the lemniscate (a sideways figure-8 shape) with coins showing heads and tails as they flash and fly. The feeling of temporary weightlessness and anticipation says that until one or the other coin drops, no final determination can be made. Apparently there is more to learn before you'll know which path of action will be appropriate.

This card counsels patience; do not allow circumstances to hustle you. Since the lemniscate is a symbol of immortality and Eternity, the image reminds, "No need to hurry — you have all the time you need to see through the circumstance, no matter how things appear right now." Implied within this scenario is the idea that changes are in the works, but you will do better to stay calm until you have more information. Everything is in flux right now.

The earliest Deuce of Disks cards showed a ribbon wrapped around the two Disks in a double-loop pattern, though the Disks were oriented vertically rather than horizontally. Sometimes one would see the card printer's name and the date of the production embossed on the ribbon, while other times one finds the familial crest of the pack's commissioner and clan motto there. Modern eyes will see this circling, twisting band as a Mobius strip. But in Boehme's day people more often identified this shape with the gnostic snake or dragon of Time that bites its own tail, making the lazy-8 symbol of infinity. We can take from these suggestions that if we just wait and watch long enough, we might save ourselves a lot of trouble by allowing the opposites to turn into each other, as they always do.

Those who understand the Two of Disks realize that the momentary manifestation of reality is not to be believed, although the cycle of form and formlessness is itself completely trustworthy. The two Disks project a facsimile of form, but in fact there's a lot more empty space than matter present in the shape they describe. This Deuce reminds us that reality is blinking in and out of visibility all of the time. As a matter of fact, the physicists tell us that there exists ten times more so-called "dark matter" (which the human sensory range can't perceive) than visible matter in our universe. Hence, when this card is upright, one can actually understand and follow the action; the changing face of appearances doesn't create confusion. When the card falls reversed, however, the coin falls into the shadow side of reality, and nobody can predict when or how it will reappear.

The lazy-8 infinity symbol was also used to refer to the elliptical path of the Moon around the Earth. The central image of *Tarot of the Holy Light* Two of Disks is just that: an illustration of the wind-up to Full Moon, which takes half the month to accomplish, followed by the two-week wind-down back to New Moon (as taken from Fludd's Lunar calendar). The pulse between reciprocals guarantees that what expands in the upswing will be contracting in the subsequent downswing.

When reading the Two of Disks in a spread, if it falls sun-side-up (signifying Capricorn's ruler Saturn visiting the sign of Leo), you can trust Nature and time (the green side of the cycle) to carry you serenely along within their already established flow. Little extra effort is required on your part. Just rest and relax for a minute while circumstances develop unhindered. This phase offers a natural advantage when it comes to the timing of unfolding events, which is entitled *luna crescens*.

With all these ideas in mind, the Two of Disks falling Moon-side-up (indicating Saturn in the sign of its Detriment, Cancer) highlights a more emotionally contentious state of desire, friction, and arousal. The fiery color urges you to follow your feelings even if it means breaking rank with others, fighting for your rights, or dealing with oppression in the course of following Spirit. Tectonic plates are shifting in the deeps when Saturn leaves his throne to visit the realm of Cancer. Hence the standard divinatory meaning of the Two of Disks reversed indicates a shake-up, whether that is a physical move of house and home, or a shift in the workplace pecking order. Current events could throw us into chaos and upend our sense of balance. The appearance of bad timing can be a possibility when the card comes up reversed, *luna decrescens*.

When things are no longer in their traditional pattern, we can feel lost and akimbo internally. With our norms shattered, nothing happens easily and every step has the potential to introduce fresh chaos. We find ourselves walking on eggshells, waiting for the other shoe to drop. The results of such shifts are by no means always negative, but the uncertainty can create unease until the new pattern settles in.

Another suggestion for the Two of Disks is that when it is upright, the Leo energy points to an understandable cause/effect manifestation that makes

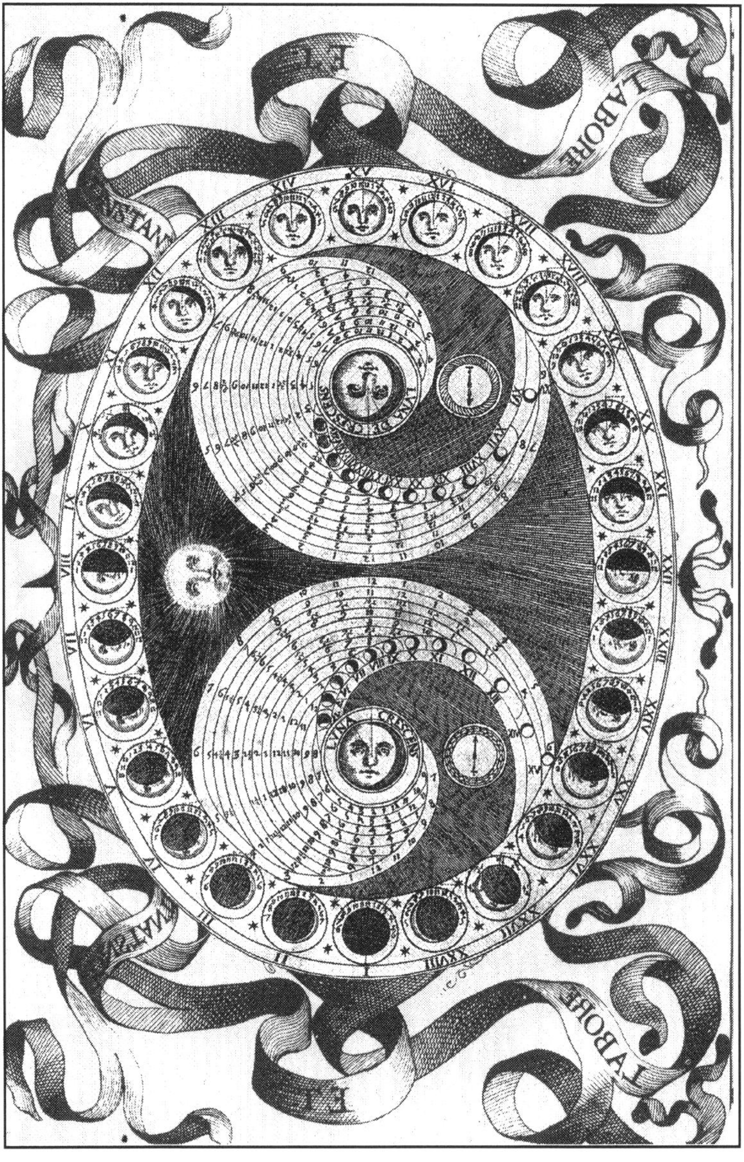
LABORE
ET

sense on its face. Alternately, when this Two is reversed, we might sense that things aren't behaving as usual, but we can't yet see what is triggering this effect. You know that the circumstance is mutating, but you can't catch a glimpse of the strange attractor that has taken over the flow. The causes for the changes might exist at some remove from the effects, suggesting a time lag between when the subtle active agents set to work (Saturn in Cancer) and when their eventual results become apparent (Saturn in Leo). This is the mystery of manifestation: now you see it, now you don't. In truth most items in our increasingly artificial world are really just a displacement of space to create the impression of value. The content is more imagined than actual. The best course would be to cease worrying about which end is up and embrace the paradox that thing-ness and nothingness are simply different stages of the very same energy.

Three of Disks

Astrology: 21 - 30 Capricorn, ruled by Mercury   **Sephira:** Binah
Essential Dignity: upright Exaltation, Saturn in Libra
Reversed Fall, Saturn in Aries
Angelic Dignities: upright angel spelled HRCh, spoken Harahel
Reversed angel spelled MTzR, spoken Mitzrael

The Three of Disks is traditionally the card of genius. In the decks from the 1900s, we typically see a master craftsman consulting with his masons on how to install a beautiful stained-glass window in the nave of the cathedral. The artist's work is at the level of Leonardo de Vinci or Michelangelo: deathless beauty produced on a monumental scale. This masterwork is proudly showcased for future generations to admire and be inspired by, a source of personal and civic pride for the whole community. Alternately, the artist is portrayed at his or her studio, alone and burning the midnight oil in a creative ferment, driven to draw, paint, invent, or whatever work genius is bringing into Creation. The artist is raptly engaged in a process that entails hours, days, months, and years of intense concentration spent solving the problems of the design. Self-mastery leads to mastery of the medium. This card is indicating someone who far exceeds previous limits.

This Three of Disks is very specifically about achieving a masterwork, finding the right set and setting in which to immortalize your talent. Some lucky souls are born with a gift that can be parlayed into a source of income. But only a few become visionaries who outdistance their peers in both talent and productivity, who reinvent their art or restate what their medium can express. The overall design and the keyword harmony point to the internal balancing act that allows a raving genius to function productively within the demands and the limits of his or her times. Experience shows that one can be possessed of fabulous capabilities, but without a balanced temperament, and lacking a supportive audience, an artist can starve before anybody knows of his or her existence. When this card falls upright, those necessary minimums are met.

As the final member of the Capricorn tribe among the numbered Suit cards, the Three of Discs organizes a supreme demonstration of the most sublime attributes of the material plane. Saturn's slowness, sobriety, and substantiality don't allow for him to demonstrate Exaltation in the more human scale characterized by the other planets; his productions are sometimes massive as castles and slow as the tectonic pulse. But at Exaltation Saturn finds himself fulfilled and satisfied in all his desires and dreams, liberated to indulge his natural affinity with the Venusian forces of Libra. Inspired by her evocation of The Good, The True, and The Beautiful, Saturn expresses his most beneficent and beautiful intentions. At these times Saturn's monumental creativity enshrines cultural achievements in a stunning display of aesthetic prowess, all based on the timeless values of natural law. In this way he cements for all future time an image of the best of our achievements to date.

Saturn in his Fall, when this card is reversed, represents the mandate of long-term vision. Saturn is traditionally the father figure and the time-lord. His perception of the long, slow cycles of life is so well developed that it edges into precognition. He can study the landscape and see how the underground forces have worked their will. He can also study history and discern the natural direction that current events will incline. Even as Saturn in Libra celebrates and enshrines the best of the past, so Saturn in Aries recognizes the challenges coming to us from the future.

When the inner senses converge, with both practical instinct and spiritual intuition showing a vista of difficulties in the offing, saturnine types naturally feel responsible to their tribe and their times. Such souls begin to hatch plans to somehow communicate with future generations. This is attempted in order to carry the culture's knowledge, technology, and traditions forward. The motive and strategy will be different in different circumstances, of course. But the genius of Three of Disks reversed is grounded in Saturn's urge to protect and support the people's highest wisdom, to stabilize and preserve it for humanity's posterity.

The tradition of the Three of Disks reversed suggests an environment that is too repressive to support full inspiration. There is not always a complete failure of forward progress, but binding and constraining forces will extract a tax. Until we submit to the disciplined structure imposed by Saturn, we won't be able to fulfill or live up to those genius potentials. In some circumstance the artist might keep his or her highest creations entirely within, held tight between the heart and the imagination. By internalizing the outer Sun, Moon, and Earth modalities (of the Three Worlds), the visionary sets up an interior cosmos that serves as an Etheric womb. Androgyny of mind is like ambidexterity of hand, giving access to a whole new spectrum of impressions and expressions. Here s/he can germinate and gestate the inspiration, whether it ever finds external expression or its imagined audience. These kinds of interior productions can sometimes become so well articulated in the collective dreamtime that multiple

267

inventors create the same machine or process simultaneously without having any contact with each other or any common influences.

Often in such a process, the creator becomes so self-sufficient and hermaphroditic that human relationships seem less interesting, even a distraction. Such an artist enfolds the whole creative process within him or herself, being self-inseminating and parthenogenic, self-fertilizing without need of outside intervention. For this privilege the artist willingly bears the burden of personal eccentricity, even "weirdness" or awkwardness due to being too highly individuated. For the sake of staying within range of inspiration, the artist will endure what lesser souls would reject. Reaching deep within, to a place of transcendent motivation, the visionary invests heart and soul into the conception, gestation, and labor necessary to produce truly unique and culturally important works. The result when the card comes upright again is a revelation to all who witness it; every viewer takes a living seed of Light away from the contact.

Four of Disks

Astrology: 11 -20 Taurus, ruled by Mercury   **Sephira:** Chesed
Essential Dignity: upright Compliment, Venus in Aries
Reversed Detriment, Venus in Scorpio
Angelic Dignity: upright angel spelled ONV, spoken Anauel
Reversed angel spelled MChI, spoken Mehiel

The Four of Disks signifies the advantage gained from belonging to an accomplished tribe or class, that class which sets the standards that others strive to emulate. It is undeniable that there are innate benefits from being born to educated parents, or working for a leading business, for example. This Four can foster great accomplishments, even when one is still young. The protection and support available in these favored conditions speeds growth and allows for the highest expression of one's talents. But these same conditions inculcate distorted expectations embedded in a person who has been nurtured in a hothouse environment. These expectations, like buried time bombs, can destroy self-esteem should those special conditions ever disappear.

This is the charged environment that Venus adapts to when she visits her mate Mars' territories. She must modify her tenderness and sensitivity if she's going to be of any benefit to her children conceived with high-intensity Mars. Upright or reversed, Venus takes the form of her totem eagle, nesting in a bed of flames. Below the nest, a bubble of pure potential shelters four orbs representing the Four Elements. Upright, the influence of the Moon (supportive ancestors) imparts just enough psychic moisture to keep the eagle and her charges from parching in the emotional aridity of the Fire sign Aries. In plain terms, there is enough wisdom and nurturance to guide and shelter those who are still forming, despite this combative and challenging environment.

Since the eagle is one form of the Empress, we know that her children are raised in awareness of their inherent nobility. Taught to hold themselves to a higher standard, they are fully aware that their every move will be scrutinized. The souls represented by those elemental Disks will acquire every quality that raptor parenting has to offer: willpower, drive, ambition, passion, high tolerance for risks, and excitement in the face of danger. Like Demeter laying Metaneira's baby in the fire to make him immortal, this eagle trains her brood to eschew fear and metabolize every experience as empowerment. With the fierce attention of their raptor mother, these hardy offspring will be born pre-forged from the nest of their Aries and Scorpio origins.

The Four of Disks has also been used to express the paradoxical blessing of belonging to a lineage of dominators and conquerors. This especially applies to the two-edged reality that results when one inherits an empire created by a previous generation. Such a circumstance might seem fortunate at first, until one investigates the level of demand that prosperity and leadership attract. With the pressure of politics and competition, plus pre-existing obligations and karmic debts that come with the inheritance, it can be a shock when the generous gift so quickly turns into a burden. Worse, if the present inheritance occurs due to the loss of the founding generation, recipients can feel overwhelmed by their lack of experience at the levers of power. An immature person thrust into such a position would lack the perspective to sensibly assess risks and rewards, putting lives and enterprises in danger.

A lack of guiding overview is one of the crippling limitations of this card when reversed, leading to the inability to correctly estimate the results of one's actions in advance. Wisdom dictates to move slowly and deliberately if change is required, as the consequences will affect more than just oneself. Seek out trustworthy advisors and allies among the older generation, listening to those who remember the long-term development of the current enterprise. Learn to look for experienced partners (Venus in Aries) rather than assuming you can go it alone (Venus in Scorpio).

This also refers to the youth who are enjoying the benefits and protection of the system without fully recognizing all the hard work and effort that goes to maintain it. Look with distrust upon the subtler dependencies that comfort encourages. Like rust, inattention and self-indulgence tend to quietly invade one's reserve of vision and will. If there were a simple way to quantify the instructions this card gives in a nutshell, the advice would be, "Immediately ditch your sense of self-importance. Instead, look around and learn what's best for the greater good." Reversal of this card suggests that something has gone wrong with the inter-generational transmission. Immaturity and control issues from the elders leave the next generation with an incomplete and compromised legacy. The inheritors can feel righteously angry, resentful, and bitter to be receiving these complications, leading to messy and arbitrary overreactions. Alternately, survivors of these flame wars could emerge riddled with anxiety and insecurity, embittered and fighting with their siblings, shadowed by the fear that they have failed in advance of their tests.

When self-esteem is artificially distorted, either towards the positive or the negative, we believe we deserve what we have not earned, be it punishment or

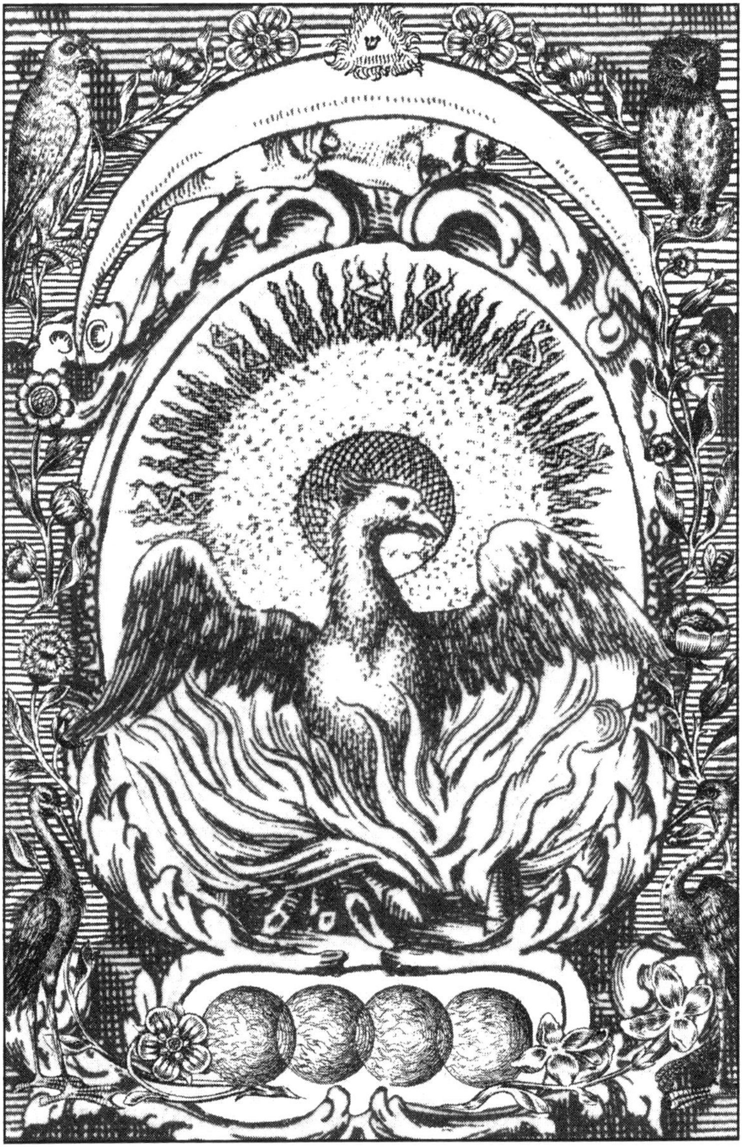

praise. No matter what age, such people never completely mature, failing to understand their inherent value and power of agency. The problem always stems from unbalanced power relations, where the playing field is slanted against the meek, the sensitive, and the unfocused. Those who will thrive in such an environment are rewarded for their insensitivity and become complicit with the system, losing empathy for those who can't perform on demand. Further, raptor parents will often force their children to fight for resources at every growth stage. This strategy may produce overcomer types, but such families can also lack bonding as a result, gifting hurtfulness down through the generations. This creates alienation and rebellion if the younger generation doesn't understand the reason for the sacrifices their elders are asking of them.

In general, Venus in Scorpio means that present psychological challenges are becoming more extreme, indicating a danger arising to one's morale and worldview. We have entered the territory of the mother who has no sympathy. Going against all our modern theories of child rearing, this mother will heartlessly discard any child whom she deems not hearty enough to merit her care. Souls thrust unprotected into environments so dominated by Martian values learn to sustain great intensity without losing consciousness in the Fire. They must be able to laugh at competition and strife, derive strength from resistance, and never settle for the common lot; anything less and they won't survive their upbringing.

Five of Disks

Astrology: 21 - 30 Taurus, ruled by Saturn **Sephira:** Gevurah
Essential Dignity: upright Exaltation, Venus in Pisces
Reversed Fall, Venus in Virgo
Angelic Dignity: upright angel spelled DMB, spoken Damabiah
Reversed angel spelled MNQ, spoken Manakel

Here at the midpoint of the Disk sequence, we have a poignant reminder of that cusp between the private life and the public life. The number Five always references the human will in expression, and here we see an esoteric diagram of this very dynamic at work. Grounded in the "Cross of Matter," the individual takes his or her essential temperament from the Four Elements. Meanwhile the imagination opens the soul to an infinite number of alternate worlds, symbolized by the Solar System surrounded by the Zodiac. Lunar intuition pulses through the field of consciousness, waxing and waning with the cycles of the Moon. The entire composite conjures the symbol of Hermes, archetype of the human gift of "walking in two worlds" (visible and invisible; material and astral).

The material world and its seasonal wheel forever press its claims, as indicated by the upward-climbing vines, buzzing bees, tools of labor, and architectural diagrams scattered on the ground. Potentials beg to be actualized, and life continuously demands response. Even non-action is an action of sorts. This is keenly represented in the pentagram at the very top of the card. The more firmly the upright star holds onto its mathematically perfect symmetrical form, the more fiercely those spontaneous and uncontrolled flames lick out from the interstices.

Paradoxically, the will power required to define "self" from "other" invites an equal-and-opposite backlash coming from that which has been defined as other. Hence, the more a given person strives for individuation, the more strongly the environment will challenge that impulse. That inverted pentagram of flame reminds us that even a motionless, interior act of consciousness has unexpected consequences that ripple out and change the world. We might never tell a soul what we are thinking, but once Spirit knows, the whole world adjusts to fit.

Boiling all of this esoteric detail down to the divinatory tradition, the Five of Disks represents the gift and burden of charisma that a self-aware person possesses. Male or female, a person who is awake and cultivating his or her consciousness radiates out of their body with an entirely different energy than a person who is habitually unconscious. It is not necessary to be young and beautiful to have an aura that draws attention. Sometimes we are born with it; sometimes we create it over time without noticing the process happening. Either way charisma is attractive and arresting; the energy sparkles and makes an impression on people. It is for this reason that the Five of Disks has become the card of infatuation, desire, seduction, and their attendant gratifications expressed in classical tradition as flattery and flirtation.

When this card falls upright, current circumstances are enhanced by a special energy, charm, magnetism, and attraction. Even if the involved parties have no conscious will to start something, there will be an undeniable magic that appears on contact. Between-the-lines exchanges of glance and body language create a spell between two people who might otherwise never notice each other. This can happen intentionally or accidentally, but either way there is an undeniable excitement in the attraction. No matter the venue, despite the individuals' personal life situations, some accident of frequency matching shows two people to each other and suggests, "There's something here to explore."

Wise people know that the presence of charisma between two people is not, in itself, the promise of a bond. If one party is only seeking short-term ego-gratification, the result of getting involved will be frustrating for the party who wants a deeper connection. An attraction that creates a threat to a preexisting relationship comes with the caveat that taking advantage of it anyway will make you into "a house divided against itself." A hint and a promise are not enough of a guarantee to put anything of real value at risk here. Also, since the Suit here is Disks, the attraction is as likely to be related to business as to pleasure. Try to remove the spell of glamour from your thinking.

When the Five of Disks is reversed, the limitations of the Saturn decanate of Taurus start to be felt. Sure, anything seemed possible, but in fact only certain things are probable. Further, the reversal is complicated with the frustration of Venus' Fall into Virgo, where a premature accident of fate forces her Taurus-Libra project to be aborted before it is viable. The magical experience one was having when the card is upright turns into negative coincidence and fatal attraction, plus harsh awareness of inadequacy and imperfection when reversed.

In its worst aspects, this card has traditionally represented the seducer who leads innocents astray with promises of fame, glamour, fortune, and the like. This association is the source of the modern imagery that shows the poverty struck couple begging at the church. If the upright card represents a fortunate attraction, the reversal can invert the idea into an unfortunate one. When this

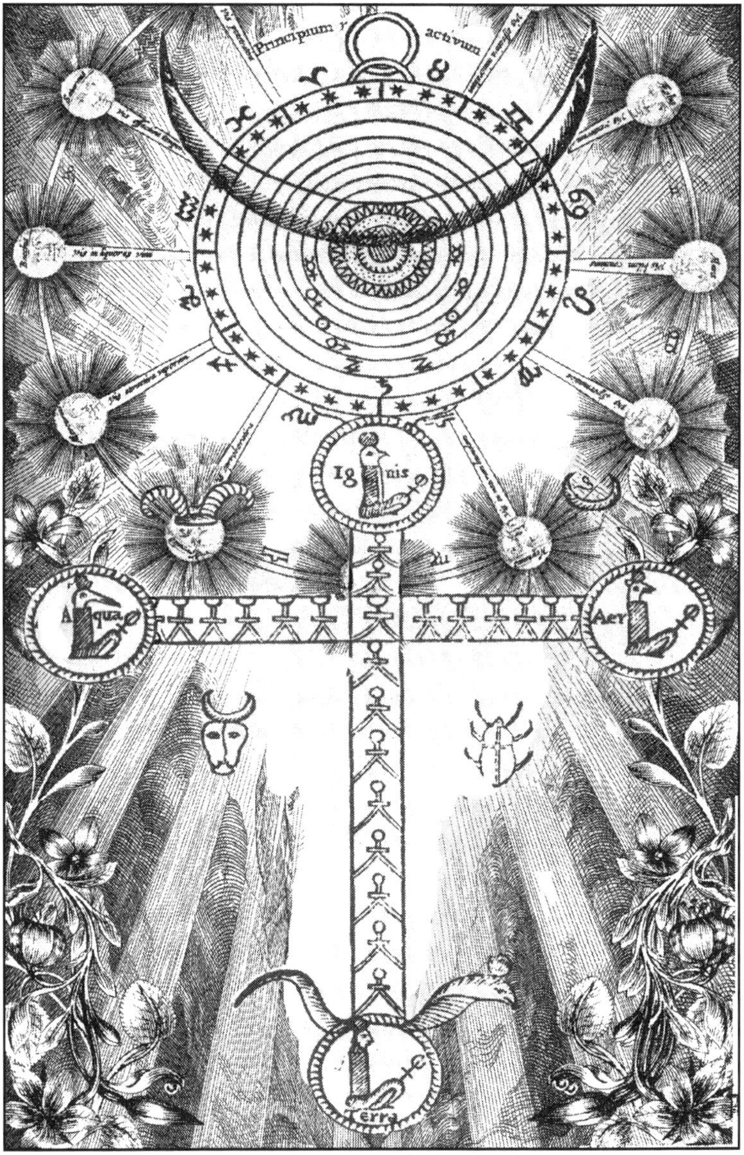
Principium
activum
Ignis
Aqua
Aer
Terra

card appears in a spread, it is not always clear whether the querant is being lied to, or is lying internally, to him or herself. Either way the circumstances arrange themselves, a false impression is being gained that has a high likelihood of leading towards a disappointing outcome.

This card confronts us with the natural consequences of using your free will. In this life we are free to do whatever we want. However, the karma lord Saturn will ensure that we pay for our choice in full. Therefore, right use of this card involves strict, practical self-discipline to keep our magical imagination from telling us stories that derail our own best interest. The glamour and attraction that this seductive energy demonstrates is both a blessing and a curse. Best practice is to get control over your own aura, your own desire body. Then we are less likely to be hypnotized and drawn in by people with exceptional energies who want to latch onto us and drain our energies into their causes.

There is an inherent caution associated with this card, about allowing ourselves to be swept off our feet by the magnetic charmer. Some people are so good at throwing their aura that we forget our boundaries and give ourselves away. Even when this card is upright, we are put on notice: Don't let anybody, no matter how attractive or flattering, usurp your sovereign free will.

Six of Disks

Astrology: 1 - 10 Taurus, ruled by Venus **Sephira:** Tiferet
Essential Dignity: upright Domicile, Venus in Taurus
Reversed Similar, Venus in Libra
Angelic Dignity: upright angel spelled VMB, spoken Umabel
Reversed angel spelled IHH, spoken Iah-hel

One of the oldest meanings of this card is generosity, a sharing nature, up to and including the collective support that maintains the social layer-cake comprising the tribe. Traditional religious almsgiving is one manifestation of this generosity, the patronage system of old Europe is another, and the potlatch tradition of the Pacific Northwest is yet another. Every healthy civilization devises ways to spread the wealth around to ensure that all members can make a rewarding contribution. This card typically refers to the economy of the medieval trading town.

Illustrated packs will often show a person with scales in hand, changing money, and/or dispensing alms (emphasizing the contrast between the haves and have-nots). *Tarot of the Holy Light*, on the other hand, puts the focus on the contrast between flowing natural shapes and angular, mathematical ones. We are looking at the balance between the natural and the cultivated, the instinctive versus the contrived.

Inside the curved compartments we see portraits of the sharply faceted Platonic Solids, each one reflecting its precise geometrical origins. In their beauty and stern symmetry, they symbolize the world of science with its mathematical precision and exacting specifications. Meanwhile, the graceful shapes and twining curves of the ribbons, vines, birds, pods, and flowers remind us of the fruitfully chaotic world of Nature, which provides the inspiration driving artists and crafters the world over. Beauty comes in the graceful balance between these elements so that the two ways of being in the world can complement each other. It's the dance between the spontaneous and the programmed, the individual and the collective, that expands the social organism into a culture with the longevity to support a full spectrum of types.

The principle behind this card is learning your worth. By gaining an objective view on your natural qualities, you learn how to turn your life into a profitable business. This produces the morale of a self-owned enterprise. The issue to solve is that of monetizing (acculturating) your (innate and natural) gifts so that you can evaluate your worth appropriately in light of the marketplace.

People who don't accurately evaluate their contribution either undersell themselves or suffer inflated thinking. One has to have an accurate picture of oneself (Five of Disks) along with insight into meeting the market (Six of Disks) in order to complete this step.

Those who receive this card can feel validated for manifesting a successful idea. This is the test of the artist and artisan, where talent has to accept discipline and work within limitations to turn a profit and earn a station at the marketplace. No amount of creativity will pay the bills if one's product isn't valued in the context it's being offered.

The Six of Disks also reminds us about the positive function of money, in the ways it lubricates the wheels of society. The Six of Disks can serve as our indicator for a healthy exchange that benefits all parties, a true win/win deal. I often call this card "the dicker," pointing to the negotiations that make markets and define the roles for the participants. Proper rules and conventions protect each player from the vicissitudes of the other. It's not just goods and coins that are changing hands; there are also people's fates being weighed in this balance.

A society with real values sees to it that a wide range of good things will trickle through the collective body, following the many different kinds of talent that human creativity displays. Where diversity is encouraged, tribal members respect each other's contributions even if they occupy different socio-cultural niches. In that sense, this card stands for the self-made person who has mastered his craft and can command a living wage. One could easily see Venus in Taurus as a commodity economy, while Venus in Libra would stand for a service economy. It takes both types to ensure a dignified standard of living for the whole tribe.

The reverse of the healthy and diverse economy would be a lack of mutual respect within the tribe, including parasitic relations between the classes and people scheming to get ahead by taking advantage of each other. Adding an imbalance of power to cultural traditions that keep classes apart increases the chances of abuse in the system, allowing harm to trickle down instead of prosperity. The traditional image of the artist on one knee at sufferance of his patron reminds us who has the power. All the patron's offers come with strings attached, and the artist knows he can't really afford to decline.

Venus rules over this card both upright and reversed, indicating that it is essential to get one's values in focus whenever this card appears. What is worth spending precious time and energy on? What is worth compromising some part of our freedom for?

In the upright position, Venus makes her trades to ensure that basic needs at the household or workplace level get met. Under her tutelage the organism

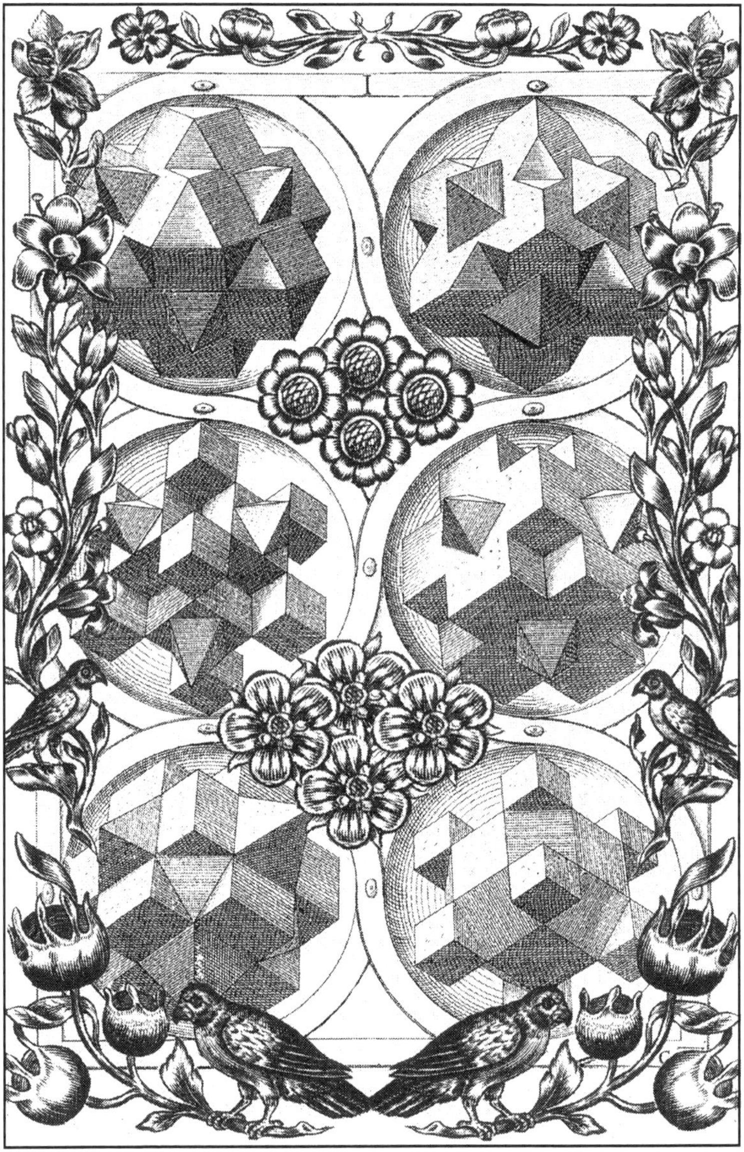

can keep all of its members supported and gainfully employed. Knowing the difference between wants and needs is a big part of the lesson here, keeping practicality foremost and appetites in check. Accepting self-limitation in the spirit of grace is a gift that Venus in Taurus understands. The stark beauty of these strict geometric forms would not be possible unless all approximation and excess are removed, leaving only the Platonic principles remaining. True freedom is bought through the practice of self-discipline.

Venus in Libra, on the other hand, is influenced by pressures from the group or hive mind, which can cause an individual to lose track of simplicity and humility in the race for style and popularity. When this card comes up reversed, one has to resist the temptation to overwrite one's inherent nature with fantasies of fame and wealth, privilege and social climbing.

Additionally, don't count on reputation (Venus in Libra) to judge the quality of an opportunity, but instead read the fine print and ask the all-important question: Who will reap the benefits in the end? Support that is extended just enough to keep recipients dependent is more of a straightjacket than a boon. Inequality of power is always a danger with this card. The person being "helped" in this model needs to be extremely careful not to trade off heart and soul for a chimera of fortune. Overall, each player in this scenario needs to examine his or her investment in playing out a debt-and-domination game when a simple exchange among friends would have served the need.

Seven of Disks

Astrology: 11 - 20 Virgo, ruled by Saturn **Sephira:** Netzach
Essential Dignity: upright Compliment, Mercury in Sagittarius
Reversed Detriment, Mercury in Pisces
Angelic Dignity: upright angel spelled RAH, spoken Rochel
Reversed angel spelled IBM, spoken Jabamiah

The Seven of Disks takes the attitude of the humble laborer willing to show up every day and sweat in the sun for next season's bounty. The traditional name is "cultivation." A farmer brings forth his crop with patience and confidence in Nature's assistance. In truth, he dances with Nature, employing every strategy from the collective memory to stay in communication with the forces that impact on his goals. When the Seven of Disks appears in a spread, the easiest interpretation is to repeat your simple tasks over and over through all the different conditions that Nature has to offer. Take this formula to heart: Be out in your "fields" of endeavor every day. Don't waver or deviate, but become dedicated first and foremost to creating all the conditions that will benefit your goal. Shape your routines and lifestyle to meet the needs of the project.

In *Tarot of the Holy Light,* we see the human soul symbolized in Tree of Life fashion. In this fertile astral garden of souls, your tree thrives and celebrates life by raining opportunity into the material plane. The seven whirling Disks represent separate worlds of meaning that you participate in through the Seven Planetary Governors. At the top the Eye of God looks into our world through the fiery triangle, awakening sparks of Light that drive the swift-growing vines to open their flowers.

In this Saturn-ruled decanate of Virgo, Virgo's ruling planet Mercury departs from his natural home to visit the Domiciles of his Compliment (in Sagittarius) and his Detriment (in Pisces). These two conditions (Compliment and Detriment) are imposed on each sign ruler due to the character of its chosen associations in life. In the ancient system of astrological rulership passed on by Ptolemy and handed across national and linguistic borders right up to present times, Mercury is partnered with Jupiter to exemplify the various shades of the teacher/student relationship. So the two sides of this card will be used to represent Virgo's ruler visiting Jupiter's nighttime home of Sagittarius, and then his daytime home in Pisces.

To address the overall Virgo tone of this card, let's remember that when we enter a field and embrace a community of practitioners, the people present are not there to flatter us or serve as a foil for our fantasies. Those perfectionist ideas we might have constructed in our heads about how things "should" be are soon deconstructed by the powerful reality of hard work, discomfort, exhaustion, and hunger. Certain tasks can't be short cut, certain situations don't have a straightforward method or a one-shot solution, and it does no good to have resentments or take damage from this fact. As you look around, realize that although your workmates might not be the ones your ego would prefer, they are the ones who have earned the right to their roles, because they are willing to do the work. Mutual respect is based on showing good grace in the trenches.

The upright card shows the emotional tone of the alchemical complement of Virgo, the sign Sagittarius. From this viewpoint we comprehend what the Creator loves about the Creation. The inherent beauty of Nature's compositions admits the eye of the soul into ecstasies that manufactured culture cannot offer. Here cynicism falls away in a celebration of Spirit, we see the beauty of the prosaic and look for ways to serve in the garden. Not only are we partaking in Eden, but we also become conscious that we are Eden's destined stewards.

When this card is at its best, our instructions are to simply show up, do the work, and don't waste any time either procrastinating or dramatizing. Keep your attention on the process, and the outcomes will take care of themselves. Remember that time is an ingredient, because Nature's magic is cyclical, slow and steady. No one can control the contingencies of fate and Nature, but you can control yourself in relation to these forces.

The heart of the Seven of Disks is the willingness to chop wood, carry water, mind your own fields, and relax about everything else. Have a rhythm that repeats, and don't let circumstances throw you off. The upright Seven of Disks represents a person who carefully minds every aspect of his or her own business, learning everything possible that will lead to recognition for excellence. No time is wasted looking over the fence into other people's fields of endeavor.

The reversed Seven of Disks (Mercury in his Detriment of Pisces) also possesses a positive side. This has to do with gaining humility and compassion for the "little guy." In Pisces, Mercury learns a service ethic and comes to appreciate the wisdom of self-sacrifice. When Mercury will leave his showman's ego at the door, Pisces admits him to the ranks of the elect, where the "last that shall go first" perfect the invisible arts of sensitivity, empathy, and telepathy. The reversed Seven of Disks has to take the emotional risk of feeling deeply, if he's going to be able to fathom what his living charges need and want from his caring attention.

283

When showing its darker side, the normally very staid and conservative Seven of Disks farmer takes too many risks and loses too many gambles. Some decks show the farmer betting the farm on the roll of the dice and losing it all. Instead of laboring in his field, he's at the craps table begging Lady Luck for a favor, operating on impulse, at grave risk of losing control of the situation to spiral into a fateful collapse.

Further, Mercury in his Detriment can revert to flawed practices leading to a failure of his enterprise to take hold and thrive. People who can't admit when they have made a mistake will sometimes compound their misery by doubling down on their bet, throwing good money after bad. If the actor in the card is unwilling to review his methods and assumptions to find the cause of the problem, what ensues will be a self-destructive period of mania, overreaching, addled superstition, addiction, and/or adrenalin-fueled desperation. It doesn't take long for these practices to consume all the card's potential abundance and fertility in a doomed and useless waste. Saturn, the karma-lord, will ensure that every debt is calculated with compound interest.

Eight of Disks

Astrology: 21-30 Virgo, ruled by Venus   **Sephira:** Hod
Essential Dignity: upright Exaltation, Mercury in Virgo
Reversed Fall, Mercury in Pisces
Angelic Dignity: upright angel spelled HYY, spoken Haiyael
Reversed angel spelled MVM, spoken Mumiah

The Eight of Disks expresses the rhythm of creativity, with its alternating periods of labor and recreation. To express this pulse, four suns look out of the upright card, and four Moons arise on the reversal. Balancing intense concentration with periods of equally full distraction is the message of this card. When this Eight of Disks falls upright, you are encouraged to dive into your productions and get something fantastic accomplished. When it falls inverted, the suggestion is to put down your tools and find something entirely other to focus on. This is not so much about resting as it is about giving the project over to the unconscious, the dreamtime side of the self. This non-linear, non-verbal part of your genius will continue studying your goals, solving problems, and refining your ideas so that when you do get back to the workbench, your blocks to efficiency and productivity will be cleared.

The Eight of Disks is historically called "Works." In the fully illustrated packs, we often see the successful artisan spending long hours in his studio, hammering out the commissions he has attracted because of his skill. Generally this card refers to a Master. Such people are so enthusiastic about their work, and so skilled, that you can't drag them away from it. The joy of creation permeates the scene and beautiful accomplishments seem to just flow out naturally. Long practice had granted finesse, making the crafter's name synonymous with "best in class." His or her reputation is such that only the most prestigious commissions are accepted. The artist is rewarded with whatever he or she requests, and demand for more is never quite satisfied.

Robert Place's original *Alchemical Tarot* makes a delightful reference to "God the Potter" with this card, showing the Creator experimenting with matter in His heavenly workroom. There's a lot of merit to this visualization for the Eight of Disks. Without a spirit of experimentation and the willingness to fail, how would anybody, man or God, manage to build a vessel that holds water, literally and figuratively? One has to be willing to fail 99 times out of 100 in order to gain the skill it takes to make a masterpiece. Even more poignantly, one must hold out against the merely ordinary, through effort after effort, until the true work of genius finally emerges. Both the aesthetic conviction of Venus as well as the precision and attention to detail of Mercury in Virgo are needed to fulfill the demiurgic imagination.

At its Exaltation, when Mercury is at his peak in his high-summer home sign, the Eight of Disks manages to achieve an epiphany, the accomplishment of which sets a high bar for artists and visionaries of future generations. The whole concept of Exaltation implies making contact with something so essential and archetypal that it is able to lift us out of our normal state of existence and transfer us to a higher mode of being. Artists, musicians, trance-dancers and shamans have always had that power to sweep away the ordinary and assert a realm of archetypal forces, which both explain and resolve our mundane challenges. The power to usher his audience through inner awakenings has always been a gift of Mercury.

In the sign of his Detriment, on the late-winter side of the Zodiac in Pisces, Mercury doesn't find the great abundance of raw materials that abound in the harvest sign of Virgo. Therefore, he becomes a minimalist, an expert in frugality, a yogi, and an advocate of the poor. It is from this type that we are given the great saints of poverty like John the Baptist, Saint Frances of Assisi, Hildegarde von Bingham, or in the 20th century, Mahatma Ghandi and Mother Theresa. These hardy souls make a demand on their environments that, over time, evoke whole social movements and cultural institutions right out of thin air. The old folktale called Stone Soup helps us to understand the power of the well-placed suggestion, even in a climate of great poverty of imagination. When the stranger comes to the poor and dusty hamlet bearing a "magic stone," he is told the town is too poverty-struck to have a feast. But he has only to make a fire in the town square and set the magic stone to boil in a pot of plain water, to evoke the curiosity, and eventually the contributions, of all the kitchens in the village. The hitch is, one cannot have this blissful state of creative flow all the time.

The four Moons that show forth when the card falls reversed represent a necessary period away from being "the talent" in order to retain a well-rounded human life. This card in reverse suggests its receiver is buried in workaholism. Too easily one starts feeling indispensable, resisting help, and refusing to delegate any part of the project. Some fail to maintain order or prioritize, others have such high expectations they don't think anybody else will do a good enough job. All these people risk becoming so obsessed and identified that they can't let it go and move on.

It can even come to the point where a person is so identified as the creator of elegant objects that selfhood is eclipsed by the works themselves. This type

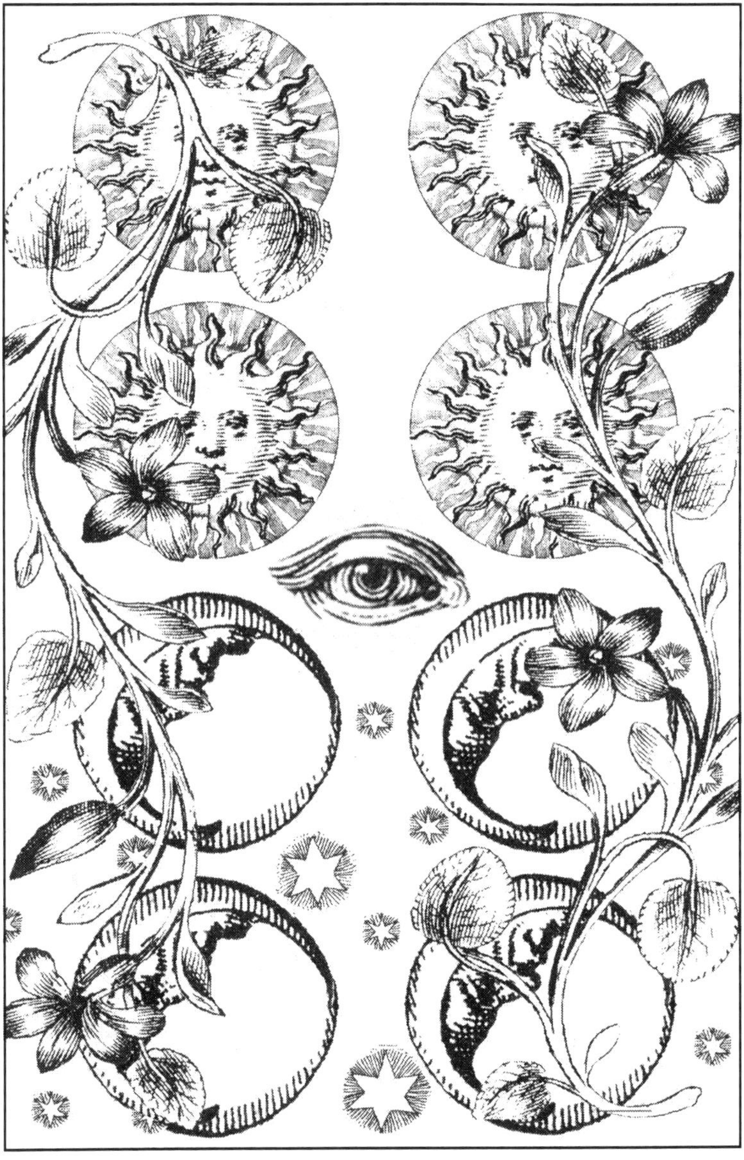

of person can feel owned by the work, even imprisoned by it, trapped in a love/hate relationship with the objects of his or her obsession. Enough time spent in this state puts the individual in danger of losing identity, becoming parasitized by the work.

Those who are over-enamored with their worldly role can also become alienated from their human life, afraid to take off the costume of their role and be naked with themselves. The truly obsessive can forget they have a body, or forget they have a family, or even forget to create any kind of life outside of the labor role.

Whether the card is upright or reversed, we have to question the programming that makes us take our work-oriented identity as the worth of our essence. We don't even remember that we have other options. It's time to think back to the intimate pleasures of the private life, the humble life, and the anonymous life. Becoming well known and successful can work against having a harmonious home life with its hang-loose time, friendships, and hobbies. So often the hard worker's family has a wonderful lifestyle, but the one who funds the fun is seldom present to enjoy it. This card lobbies for a balanced perspective so that the creator can live long as well as prosper.

Nine of Disks

Astrology: 1 - 10 Virgo, ruled by Mercury **Sephira:** Yesod
Essential Dignity: upright Domicile, Mercury in Virgo
Reversed Similar, Mercury in Gemini
Angelic Dignity: upright angel spelled AIO, spoken Eyael
Reversed angel spelled ChBV, spoken Habuhiah

Two cornucopias pour forth the fertility of the Earth at the feet of the royal lion. Green fields and plentiful water represent the terrestrial energies supporting this flourishing domain. From a nest made of this natural bounty, which seems to rest upon the lion's aura, the eagle takes flight into a cloudless sky illuminated by the radiant Sun. Disks representing the Lights and the higher Elements frame the scene (expressed in the Tattwa colors of green/red for Fire; orange/blue for Air; and astral violet/yellow for the "new Heaven and a new Earth"). The Lion represents the ideal of an enlightened social order that evolves to support the illuminated individual, figured by the rising eagle.

Across Tarot tradition, the Nine of Disks represents the joy and freedom available to one who has solved the survival challenge, and who lives well in relative ease and comfort as a result. This is a personal happiness card, and it indicates security, protection, and personal fulfillment. Here we move beyond the idea of rest after labor and enter a realm of free time, energy, and resources dedicated to one's unique interests. Among the Mantegna icons, this concept is illustrated at the halfway point of the Ranks of Man, standing between the Merchant and the Knight. Entitled Zintilomo (gentleman), the fortunate individual enjoys good nutrition, proper rest, creative leisure, and higher education. This is a lifestyle that many aspire to and few experience. Such grace is granted because the protagonist has found the "sweet spot" offered by his or her civilization and times.

To achieve the Nine of Disks, one's individual character and talents must offer something the current culture will generously support. Both lucky and astutely practical, such a person attracts a steady, trustworthy flow of resources in good times or bad. Whether the protagonist has arrived at this position by effort or by accident, the fact that he or she can hold it all together over time testifies to a well-seasoned and mature outlook.

A tradition of servants and loyal dependents accompanies the Nine of Disks. In mature societies, people who are materially secure understand that they have a duty to provide work in their homes and enterprises for the extra hands that might fall idle in the village. The Sufis refer to this trickle down with the image of plants outside the garden benefiting from the water that runs off from it. Masonic organizations also insist that their members own a business big enough to support several people outside of their immediate family. This is where the term "pillar of the community" comes from. The Nine of Disks person helps the less fortunate to earn through their labor some of the profits that have accrued through his or her success.

Traditional Nine of Disks keywords often point to fertility, pregnancy, happy birth, etc. This makes sense because for the majority of women in previous eras, healthy children and a cozy home were the ultimate measures of success and therefore happiness. A serene and well-ordered home life remains a hallmark of successful parturition and full intellectual development for both mother and child. Women have always multiplied the family riches through reproduction, although that is not by any means the only way it is done.

On the collective scale this card expands to cover any female-oriented or woman-led organization, from the nursery to the hospital, factory or farm. The world-of-women model was masterfully articulated in *The Treasure of the City of Ladies*, a 1405 treatise on the education and culture of medieval women written by Christine de Pizan. Taken in this light, the Nine of Disks can be associated with any organization that exists to support a minority or special interest population (like the Beguines, the Shriners, a civic group that sponsors refugees, and so on.) The lion and the eagle (or the Lady on the illustrated packs) are guardians at the entryway to a place of peace, grace, and order.

Thus the Nine of Disks represents the well-examined life that is truly worth living. The apparent ease displayed on this card is the end result of a long process of refinement. In such a realm the yearly cycle rolls out predictably across the decades allowing whole generations to experience the benefits of participating in a well-ordered enterprise. The virtues of an orderly society are proof positive of accumulating personal maturity building up throughout the community. A sustainable civilization inspires its outstanding individuals to focus their personal genius on advancing the cause of the whole. Naturally, the guardians of such a realm will rightly expect you to surrender to the existing order if you are to find a place here.

When this card is reversed, tension can arise from learned cultural guilt, which is one manifestation of Mercury in Virgo. The very presence of security and stability can make some people feel insecure and untrusting, fearful of being judged as wanting and left out of the bounty. Historically, pleasure is assigned a low value in the traditional Christian world. A spiritually dutiful soul was expected to suffer for their faith. (Never mind that this tension was more of

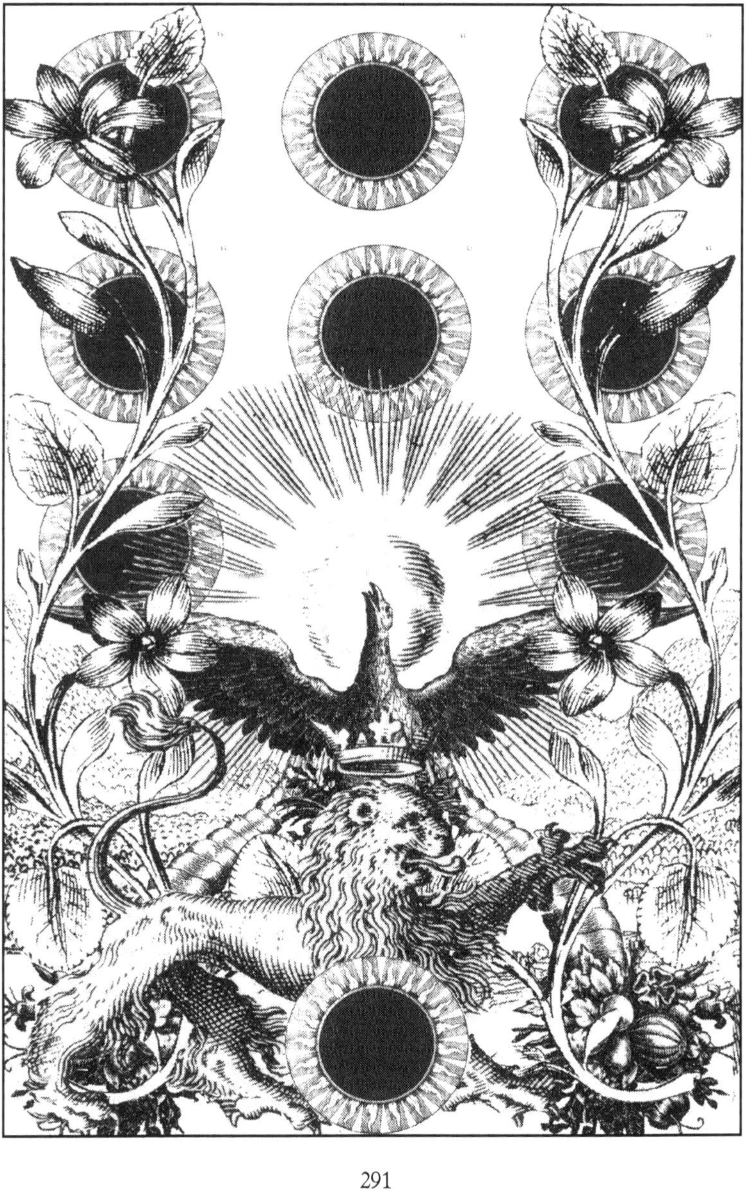

a social engineering construct of the Church than a stricture of Christianity.)

There are plenty of simple pleasures that aren't linked to guilt and shame, but those are often ignored because they lack the drama potential of the good-versus-evil narrative. In general, negative value has intentionally been attached to the kind of happiness that is found through the physical senses, whether that means play, sex, food, drugs, music, dancing, art, or leisure. This casts a broad swath of censure over those who are unwilling to restrain themselves within the narrow limits laid down by the monasteries and churches (Mercury in Gemini).

Wealth and leisure do permit some people to waste their time and life force on decadent distractions, as one might intuit with Mercury reversed in Gemini. Guilt and shame were also heaped on ownership of and interactions with money (Mercury in Virgo). Noble families of medieval Europe fell into poverty by failing to equip themselves with financial skills, but instead hiring out their accounting to better-educated immigrants from the Holy Land.

Ironically the Church meanwhile was deploying vast fortunes to build its cathedrals and support all of its political and economic enterprises, while at the same time decrying other organizations' attempt to do the same. This kind of double standard leaves the believing individual in the paradoxical position of always feeling vaguely insecure unless they are being singled out for punishment. Yet even that offers only a transitory feeling of atonement. This card's reversed appearance could be hinting at a culture of co-dependence like that found in a cult. This would be an economy based on the enslavement of Nature, plants, animals, and simple-hearted humans, all forced to pour out their substance and empty themselves regularly to benefit the few.

Ten of Disks

Astrology: Grand Trine in Earth
Capricorn, Taurus, and Virgo
Sephira: Malkhut

Here we are looking at a pre-Zoharic form of the Fallen Tree. Before the solidification of the so-called composite Tree in the latter half of the 1500s, multiple attempts were made to rationalize the consequences of the Fall on the interlacing path structure. What we see here is a projection of what's called the Tree of the Messiah, in this case laid over the two outer pillars and three horizontals of the Unfallen Tree. This Tree does not offer the lightning bolt path-pattern of the later Ari Tree. However, it does support the signs of the Zodiac on the diagonal paths, just as the Sefer Yetzirah originally dictated in the earliest Short Form. In this image each Sephira holds a symbol that points back to its traditionally associated planet. By entering the Heart-center, Tiferet, and then harmonizing all the surrounding Sephirot from that vantage, one can stabilize this pattern. We find this approach to be in harmony with Boehme's TheoSophia.

The Ten of Disks is long-associated with the word "castle." Built on a hill at the heart of the region, it offers a rampart of defense against enemies and a domicile big enough to shelter the whole community. We can see the Kabbalah Tree serving the same function for spiritually awake souls on the astral level. The Tree offers a collective blueprint for psychological and spiritual growth, putting us in contact with all the levels of reality that our body's inner and outer senses can be aware of. The Tree (like the castle) structures the collective flow of labor, energy, and aspiration according to patterns our spiritual ancestors mapped out for us. This model promises that when we lend our private energies into the collective organism, following the pathways that have been cut by prior generations, the larger metabolism (be it castle community or Tree) will in return host and succor us as one of its parts. One could say that the Tree is an earthly model of God's own castle into which humans are invited when we are mature enough to discover and occupy it.

The classic meaning of the Ten of Disks applies to the teachings of the Kabbalah just as easily as it does to the castle community. In both cases multiple generations of planning, labor, and refinement have culminated in a structure of such inherent stability and resilience that it can generate self-sufficient and entrepreneurial (self-actualizing and evolutionary) souls. Dynastic pride plays a role in the sense that there's a lineage of visionary (spiritually fertile) individuals who took it upon themselves to materialize the potential in the diagram and make something alive emerge from the initial blueprint. The long-term benefits of participation in the corporate body are strong enough to outweigh the inevitable pressure to conform, and to mitigate the harshness of living in close proximity to conflicting forces.

The world-view shared among the members imbues the emotional life of the realm with essential dignity and self-respect. Whether we are looking at the material economy of a wealthy land baron or the interior dynamics of the Hebrew ghetto, this Ten of Disks bears witness to a healthy, safe, and reasonably stable collective entity. The maturity and resilience of this society impacts the destiny of all the families who live in the shadow of this noble House (or Kabbalistic cabal), benefitting the full community down to the lowliest servants young and old, sick or well, family members and strangers.

Think of the Ten of Disks as the corporate identity that you belong to, something larger than yourself that enfolds your private life inside its larger destiny. Some Tarot authors emphasize the protective aspect to the castle, some the unchanging stamp of order and routine, but everybody recognizes the card as a sign of a self-sustaining system. The castle is so enduring that it claims its own place in the landscape; the stones of the castle watch over the generations, and the spirit of the people flows through its sturdy corridors. In the same way the spiritual teachings that nourished the persecuted populations of the Jews in Europe provided shelter and protection for those communities despite the harsh limits placed on their participation in Christian society. The endurance of this self-contained universe helps to smooth out the people's individual highs and lows, the lean times and the fat times, and the resulting team spirit gives character to the community.

The Ten of Disks is Malkhut of the Earth world, the very bottom spot on the lowest Tree in the unfolding chain of the Four Worlds. The Earth Element crystallizes under the invisible pressure of time and the cold hand of entropy, steadily fossilizing everything that doesn't crumble into dust. The Ten of Disks represents the point in the old myth when Creator turns around and retreats back into the Pleroma again, leaving humanity to its own devices. Thus we have reached the nadir of materialism, insensitivity, rigidity, and externalization. There is nowhere to go from here but to rise up the elemental chain again.

Unfortunately, there is a whole subset of the human race whose experience does not include intangible values, whether those invisibles touch on bonds of loyalty and affinity, invoke the strictures of morality and fairness, or pluck the

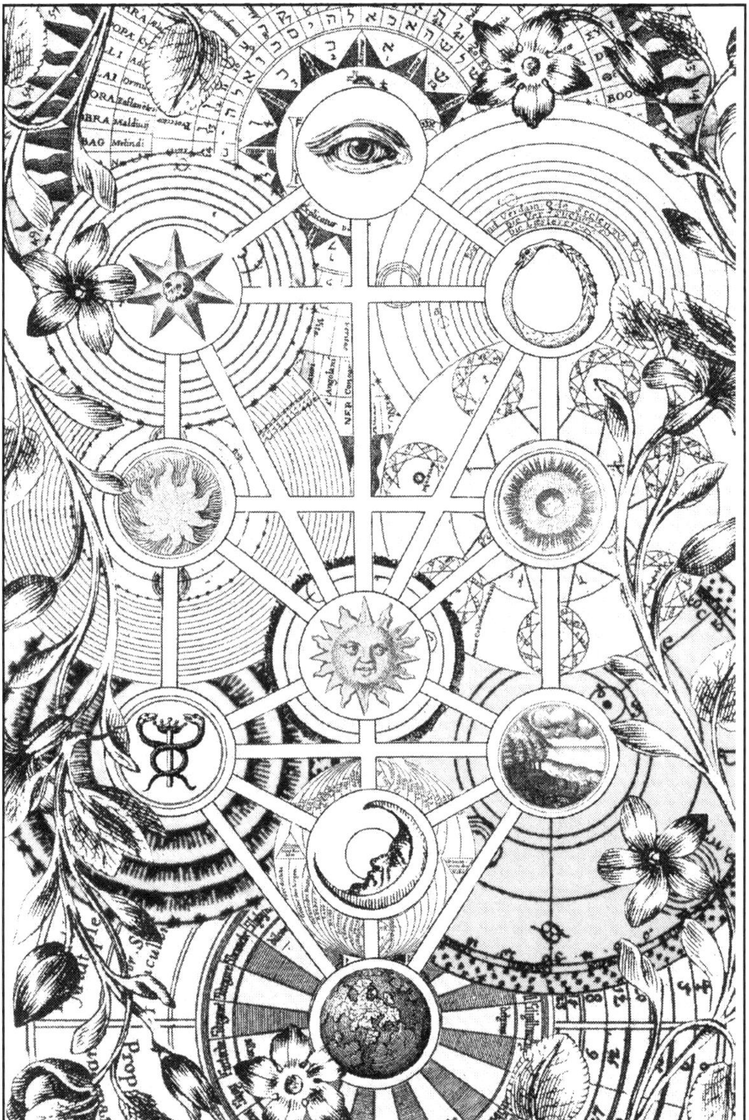

heartstrings of compassion and empathy. It is a terrible fall for a soul to reduce the world down to things that can be weighed and measured by the outer senses only; this attitude ultimately devalues everything it touches. Therefore, we have to worry when we see this card reversed. Take it as a sign that people need to get their priorities back in order, relinquish exploitive strategies, and give back (to the land, to the community) at least as much as they expect to receive in order for the exchange to be sustainable. Those who find themselves thinking in merely fiduciary terms about things like human lives, natural resources, cultural treasures, or the health of Nature are lost in the grips of poverty much greater than any lack of money could produce.

King of Disks
Taurus

The family of the King of Disks has deep roots in the land, being the country cousins of the other Royals (the Cups, Wands, and Swords). As befits his lineage, our King of Disks is well educated in the ways of the world, but he actually prefers the rural seat of his ancestral home to the court of the Emperor. He sees himself as the embodiment of his region, and he is supported in that idea by an army of very skilled survivalists, all sworn to rally to his cause. Living far out on the periphery of the region as this King does, his people have never left the "old ways"; they still live within the ancient rhythm of the Lunar cycles. The decades come and go while the fate of the region rests securely on the riches of this King's mines, forests, and fields. If he is doing his job correctly, one year is very like the next no matter what happens in the great population centers. This King of Disks is the dedicated shepherd of his people, and they in turn honor the lineage that sired him, their hereditary leader and guide.

His people regularly test the Disk King. They expect him to read Nature's signs like an ancient shaman and then lead accordingly. When traveling through the invisible worlds, he rides upon the alchemical eagle, which grants him the benefits of individuation, including far-sightedness and therefore the mastery of Time. One kingly foot rests upon the roots of his forest, the other on a Disk portraying the planetary metals growing in his underground mines, which are traditionally gold, silver, quicksilver, copper, iron, tin, and lead. The Septenary star on the disk marks a doorway to the underworld that only an initiate can enter, hence the death's-head center. In his hand is a shield showing links to the same seven entities, but in this case arranged as a star of six points with the Sun at the center. Behind his head is a traditional seal of the Element Earth. The King of Disks adeptly juggles these different unique but intersecting worldviews, adjusting their harmonies and ratios to enshrine the Pythagorean and Venusian ideal proportions.

What this King's court lacks in polish or glitter, it more than makes up for in sustainability and deep skills. The Disk people are responsible for managing the raw materials of the realm. They live in direct contact with Nature and are at the front lines when natural disasters strike. Like his people, this King is a hard worker and a hard partier, which suggests a habit of indulgence that could eventually lead to corpulence and gout. In general his illnesses are those of excess rather than insufficiency. Possessing a bottomless enjoyment of the pleasures of the senses, this King always knows where the best of every good thing is to be procured. However, despite his prodigious appetites, he is careful to be involved with only the real and the natural; the synthetic and the ersatz are anathema in this realm. The Disk King understands and oversees the traditional products of the four seasons, so he is not likely to be interested in paper markets or virtual currencies. This earthy practicality allows his region to ride out hard times better than those of his city cousins, whose substance gets swept up into politics, style, and drama rather than remaining focused on more fundamental considerations.

The King of Disks has deep understanding of his realm's ways and means. He has accomplished a lot in life, plus he has arranged his affairs to ensure that future generations will continue to benefit from his labors. It's inherent in his nature to know the price of everything to which his culture attributes value. This King possesses a practical genius that creates opportunity through affinity bonding. He loves building businesses with family and friends. For this reason his enterprises grow organically, just like families do. In fact, all of his businesses are "family values" enterprises, and he counts the health and prosperity of his workers as one of his products. This King's reputation is solid, and he makes generous deals with those who have proved their trustworthiness.

He has matured in his thinking to reflect values rather than just profits and power. In his more-evolved states, this King has figured out the exact worth of wealth and the taxes it rightfully extracts. The spiritual tax is the karmic responsibility for taking care that the engine of the people's destiny does not founder. The Disk King is responsible for many more people than himself and nothing can relieve him of that responsibility. The personal tax is that he must constantly fight becoming soft, flaccid, and addicted while being cocooned by the great abundance in his life. A wise King of Disks doesn't shirk a physical challenge; he isn't averse to pain and suffering. This makes him much less likely to succumb to the debilities and illnesses that others of his class too easily fall for. He understands that we can't afford to flout our innate design and nature, but must learn to work within it. The King of Disks has discovered that his people work for him, but he works for Nature.

It's true that the King of Disks has the power to make or break people financially, but he doesn't exert that power unless somebody is on track to do damage to the realm. Like a vigilant father, he is scrupulous in eradicating moral and social decay before it has the chance to invade the people's values. If this King's morals should decay, then he behaves more like the bull who is his astrological totem. He can absorb quite a bit of irritation before he is thrown

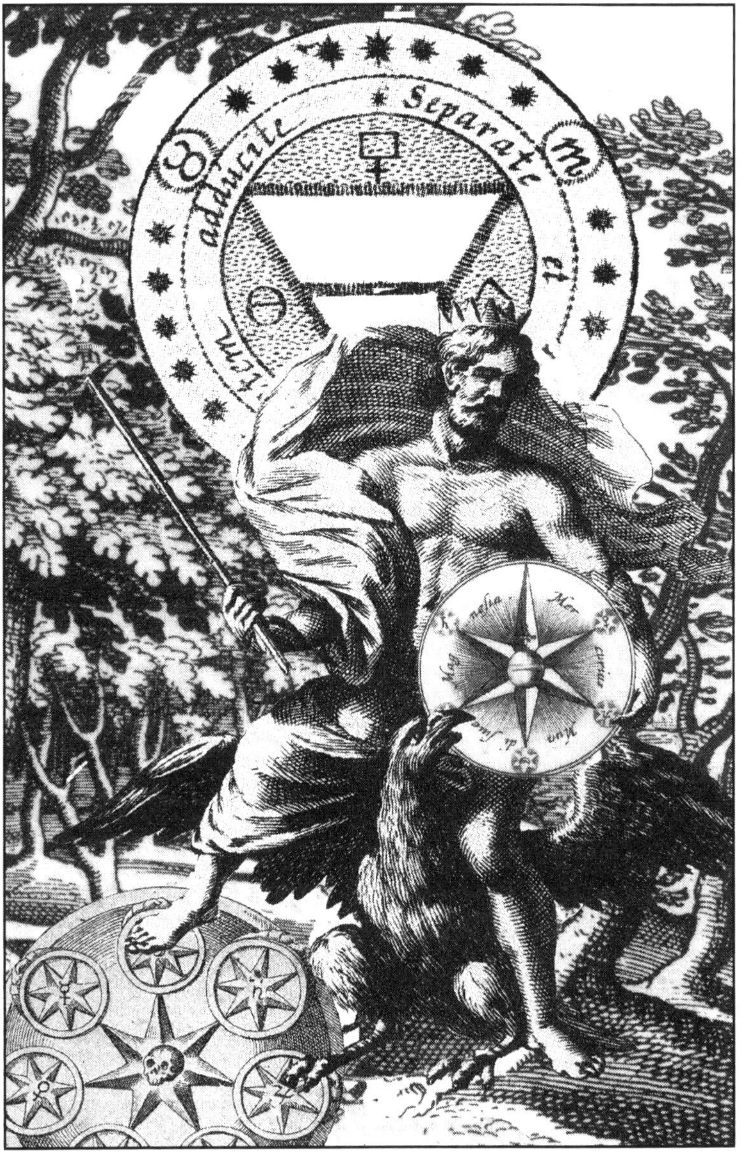
adducite
Separate

off his good nature, but once his equilibrium has been disturbed, the offender had better watch out. This King will quickly turn from tolerant to implacable, and his enemies come to rue the day that they raised his ire. When he appears in reversal, this King loses track of his family values and starts demanding more than he has any right to expect from everybody around him. When he's in this mood, he resents time with loved ones and only has eyes for business and profits. Like Midas of the old myth, everything he touches turns to gold until he loses his humanity entirely.

Another reference for the King of Disks reversed is the Minotaur in the labyrinth, who crushes everything and everyone he encounters, even those he thinks he loves. The demands of his bodily life are so imperative that he barely has time to question his impulses before he is overindulging them. Too headstrong to listen to others or admit the error of his ways, the reversed King of Disks learns the hard way about the drawbacks of looking at life through the lens of ownership. This is in fact the product of an inner emptiness, alchemically likened to an unslakable thirst.

Queen of Disks

Capricorn

The Queen of Disks is endowed with enormous good sense and problem solving energy. As the Queen of a wide and abundant realm, it is unseemly for her to labor in the fields or compete against her subjects in business. This leaves her free to watch, learn, and collect practical wisdom that the whole realm can benefit from. Her people use her as a sounding board, and she makes her counsel available to every level of the castle community equally. It is her special gift to advise, encourage, and empower her people, studying their problems with them and finding solutions. Neither a traditionalist nor a futurist, she is interested in what works, and she hates waste of any kind. She especially seeks out solutions that show the smallest ecological footprint married to the largest possible functionality, whether it's an antique technology, a 21st century invention, or some elegant hybrid in between.

In the history of Tarot, this Queen is the sibyl or oracle, perhaps a reader of one kind or another, whom the people have learned through experience to trust in times of need. She understands that the benefits that come to her through royal birth do not belong solely to her. She will spend freely of her time, energy, skills, and political capital, including redistributing her region's wealth for the benefit of her people. However, because she likes to work in an atmosphere of beauty, enjoyment, and abundance, she is sometimes misunderstood as being eccentric, self-indulgent, or even profligate. This is truly a false characterization of a trend that is both natural and useful to her. This Queen has excellent taste, loves to create beautiful scenes, knows how to orchestrate a really fun party, and is the wife of the King. Her area of expertise lies in accommodating situations where alliances can be formed and business that will enrich the kingdom will be planned and accomplished with grace.

The sign of Capricorn is the culmination point whence all of the goals, efforts, and fruits of this half of the year accumulate. As the Sun makes his transit from the warmth and brightness of Summer Solstice to the relative cold and dark of Winter Solstice, he crosses the realms of all Seven Planetary Governors. Hence this Queen presides over the furthest extenuation of the Dry Way, where the soul has supposedly grown to the stature that it no longer identifies one's individual best interests as being one iota different from "the greatest good for all." When we realize that the next cycle of descent on the Wet Way will start with the King of Swords, the very next sign of Aquarius, we can further see this Queen's sovereignty at the top of the wheel of life, wrapping up and summarizing the archetype of "the good life well lived" for both her family and her realm. Visitors from other realms would do better to look on and learn rather than hang back and doubt or resist her palpable charms.

One sterling virtue of this Queen is that she makes sure that even the little people of her realm experience the dignity of self-sufficiency. Everyone who comes in contact with her feels enriched by the obvious enjoyment she has in cultivating her realm, both its resources and its people. This can be a two-edged sword among the people. Because the Disk Queen is a happy and successful materialist, she assumes that everybody has the same fortunate DNA and vibrant health that she generally experiences. Her sense of empathy and charity have been many times honed by contact with "users," so she has a tendency to ration her attentions until claimants have proven that they are demonstrably following her excellent direction. In her less-charitable moments, she occasionally suspects that the people with the subtle setbacks, the hidden disabilities, and unusual attributes might just be grifters playing on her maternal instincts. (We know this is not true, but the thought plays about her mind sometimes.) It might also take her years to stop trying to organize everybody and everything into her idealized factory farm. She could be 60 or 70 before she matures to the point when she can simply put her hands in her lap and look around and witness the actual personhood of those who are around her.

Her cultural generosity goes a long way towards making up for her occasional chauvinism. This queen TENOFF fosters a climate of entrepreneurial opportunity in which all are encouraged to develop their skills and further themselves no matter how humble their start. She champions her subjects' right to a level playing field in life. This Queen fosters a gift-oriented barter economy, matching up those in need with those who can help maintain the castle economy without overemphasizing cash transactions. She knows the individual circumstances of the people in her region and envisions their mutual benefit. Before disputes harden into lawsuits, the Queen of Disks can diplomatically craft a solution both sides will accept. She ministers to the personality problems, the political snafus, and the acts of fate that impact the tribe through the seasons and years. Her organic and grounded intuition lubricates social relations throughout the tribe, providing a consistent and common presentation of cultural values.

At her most objective and psychologically transparent, this Queen is an earthly reflection of the Sophia principle, meaning that she has insight into the

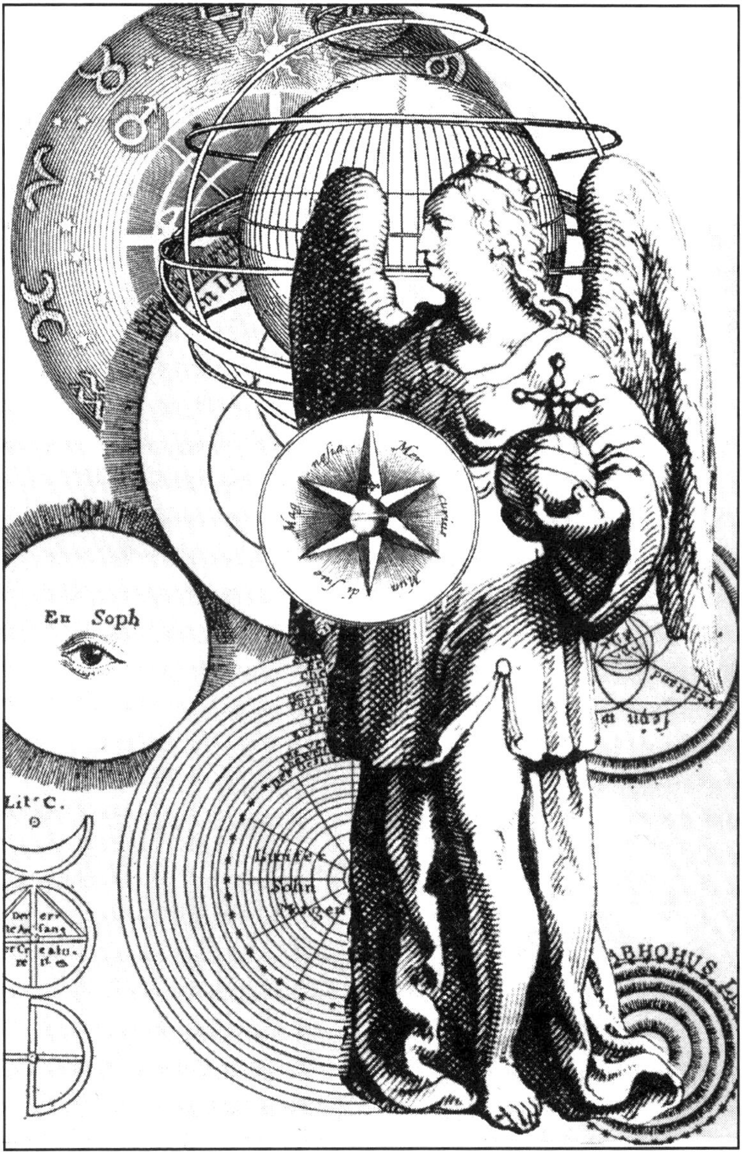
En Soph

Divine Design. She can help people find their places within the long cycles of the planets and stars. She has a special gift for translating the cosmic plan into terms her subjects can understand, allowing them to find stability, and even thrive, within the pre-ordained shapes of their individual fates. However, should this Queen be thrown off-center or emotionally upset by those with whom she is working, the things she foresees begin to shade towards liability and pessimism. Naturally she would prefer to reflect nothing but the best and brightest for all of her people, but like the faithful clay of her realm, her psyche dutifully reflects the imprint made by the individual in front of her. Because of this she has no tolerance for falsity, misrepresentation, or distortions of the truth and has no sympathy for sycophants or flatterers. All such people muddy up the honest, hardworking, entrepreneurial, and generous spirit of her city-state, which will therefore innately reject them. People who have won her favor find her the kindest and most caring of allies, but those who have failed her test experience her as cold, removed, uncaring, and judgmental. So be it. Like her ruling planet Saturn, this Capricorn Queen wastes no time with losers.

Knight of Disks

Virgo

The Knight of Disks is the most peace loving of the Knights, the overseer of fertility and growth. His period of greatest happiness is during the quiet times between conflicts when everybody can concentrate together on raising the collective standard of living. With his garden spade in hand and his alchemical shield's Tetractys map to instruct him, he ventures out into the fields and forests to study the land. Craggy mountains in the background represent the skeletal structure of the region, seeming to stare over his shoulder and speak into the back of his mind about the deep history of this place. The herbs and flowers in his hair serve as antennae, increasing his awareness of the breezes, birds, and weather changes. This Knight might seem like a simple countryman, but he is just as quick-witted, sensitive, and canny as the deer in the forest and the eagles in their rookery. Overhead shines the eternal astral Light representing the inner guidance of Spirit, his ally through the personality complications of human life. Meanwhile, at his feet the visible Sun and Moon mark out the steady pulse of the seasons, keeping him firmly anchored in the agricultural wheel of the year.

When this Knight is shown mounted, his horse is usually huge and thickset, more suitable for pulling a plow or sturdy farm wagon than for riding swiftly and nimbly into battle. The Disk Knight is always focused on responding to Nature and fulfilling her tasks. He wants to accomplish tangible labors that will ensure the survival of the people and improve the usefulness of the land for future harvest. Of all the Royals across the four Suits, this Knight is the most likely to strip off his armor and get dirty while laboring with his subjects. He loves engaging in worthy work that taxes his mind, heart, and will, as well as his muscles. A scientist as well as an environmentalist, he will use every tool available to move the fate of his region and his people forward. He is also an inventor whose agile mind excels at envisioning low-tech approaches to long-standing challenges. While others complain, he seeks solutions, be they found in the tribal memory, in the castle library, among his able bondsmen, or through his own cogitations. He honestly doesn't care who gets the credit, as long as the job is done well and he can glory in the feeling of participation in a truly noble task.

As the Mutable sign among the Disks, this Knight understands himself as undergoing continuous change in order to navigate the curved bias of Time. He knows very clearly that every "now" came from a previous cycle, which slips out of sight around the curve of the event horizon. He's also fully apprised that the present will soon give way to the inrushing future. A clock is ticking constantly in his head. Despite how solid and fixed the material plane appears, the Virgo Knight keenly realizes that the entire landscape is mutating around him. The longer, cooler nights tutor the plants to shift over from late summer metabolism to preparation for winter. In this harvest season, most plants are setting seed, building roots, and/or dying back after summer's riotous flowering and fruiting

Planning for the inevitable future, the Disk Knight doesn't allow momentary fads or fancies to distract him. One can feel his stability and dedication; he is totally responsible and even somewhat predictable in his dedication to the cycles of Nature. His personality is earthy and gentle, as simple and deep as the soil he tills and the herds he cultivates. Wherever he stands, there will always be food for his people and animals, the castle will be warm in winter, the markets will be well supplied, and the town's fortifications will remain in good condition. In his natural context, our Disk Knight is not proud, and he doesn't care how he looks to other people. He really wants to know that the subjects of his realm have the basics.

When he shows up in more urbane and decadent contexts, this Knight is sometimes associated with the banking profession. Quick to notice detail and profoundly intuitive the way all healthy animals are, he has excellent instincts about who is trustworthy and who is not. This Knight will tend to be on time with his payments and fully aware of others' outstanding obligations. He abhors waste and will immediately abandon the thought of doing projects with those who will not count the costs in advance. Do not disappoint this person in practical matters. He has a long memory, and he can easily arrange things such that you'll never be allowed to waste his time and energy again.

When reversed, this Knight is rootless, anxious, disempowered, dyspeptic, and riven by angry doubt. The techniques he has for managing Nature aren't as predictable in the political, ego-fueled jousting of court life. He becomes uncomfortable and untrusting, second-guessing everybody, neurotically latching onto every excuse for fear and unease. This Knight can show some of the qualities of a person with Asperger's syndrome: smart as a whip in his own element, but upset and ungrounded when he's pulled away from his natural environment. Whenever possible, leave this fellow alone to putter. He manages his time just fine and can attend to all of his variables better when people are not

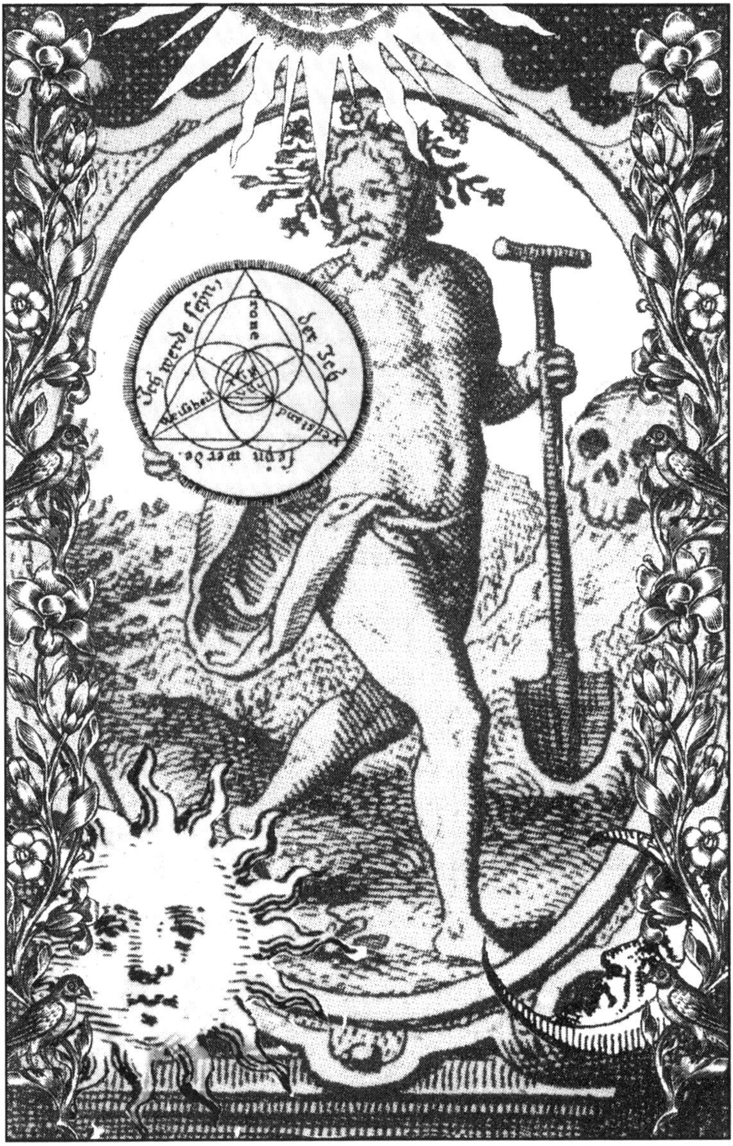
Ich werde seyn,
der Ich
seyn werde.
Krone
Weisheit

throwing competing agendas onto his plate. If you interrupt him in the middle of doing something complicated, his concentration will shatter like glass, making him so upset that he'll blame you for whatever bad thing happens next. He might not even realize how abrasive he actually is because his inner perfectionist is so fierce in criticism of his daily efforts, that he never cuts himself any slack either. He's still learning that it's important to regularly forgive God, life, and himself for the imperfections that abound in the material plane. Once he truly digests this essential bit of wisdom, his stomach can come out of its clench, and his heart will open in gratitude, like a flower under the sun.

Page of Disks

Winter Solstice

Appearing at the onset of the fourth quarter of the Zodiac, the Page of Disks announces the introverted testing season of winter. The rocky ribs of the landscape stand fully revealed, stripped of the soft green covering of the growing season. This Page has held himself in check all through the fertile cycle, but he is now ready to speak his piece. When he chants and beats on his shamanic drum, the vibrations cut through his bright but chilly landscape and shake the spirits awake. His song bouncing among the desiccated crags awakens the telluric dragon from his lair in the heart of the mountains. Signature landslides attend the Disk Page's utterance; his response to Full and New Moons is to crack the cliffs and send lahars rumbling into the valleys below. He carries Bruno's *Figure of the Quadrinity* on his drum, his voice is thunder, and his pineal is a lodestone. Whatever he gives voice to inevitably comes to pass.

Remembering that the four Pages represent roles more than individuals (being markers for the changing of the seasons), this Winter Page is the deliverer of natural consequences. Three seasons have passed since this cycle was inaugurated (by the Page of Wands). Those potentials, those opportunities that have been heretofore deferred or passed over must now either be seized or else relinquished. Nothing can be done to rewind the skein of Time, but the period of winter offers the opportunity to either come to closure, or prepare for a fresh start in the upcoming spring. This Page declares that there is no more time to waste; one must act now else lose the chance. His drumbeat demands that one "speak now or forever hold your peace."

Interestingly enough, the Disk Page has no attachment to results. Like the other Pages, he daily witnesses the full spectrum of his Element's effects as they emanate from and return back to the Queen's Cardinal throne. A person of any sign, gender, age, or natural temperament can play this role of servant or apprentice. However, those who accept the task of announcing and implementing the Royal will are obligated to lend their attributes to the Queen and serve her faithfully without inserting any of their personal agenda into the process. An upright Page needs to be read as a righteous agent of change, a sincere soul operating in good faith, representing the law of the land. Each Page is a catalyst of the natural changes brought by their seasonal stage of the cycle. The Disk Page is the announcer of endings, as in the final scene of a play or opera.

On the human scale, one might see this character in the position of the attendant or junior partner, but that is only his "plain brown wrapper," a costume that allows him to move around freely. As an ally of the Queen (figurehead of Winter Solstice), he is empowered to enact her will through any natural means available. This demeanor of humility and submissiveness provides camouflage for his subterranean potency. By studying the habits and beliefs of everyone around him, the Disk Page uses the natural tendencies of the overall situation to drive results without appearing to lift a finger. One could say he knows the odds in every situation. He also knows that time is his ally, bringing around every necessary development in right order. This Page doesn't have to chase his goals, pushing and prodding to get things done. His understanding of the people's appetites and cravings allows him to maintain many small trades throughout the Queen's domain. With the resources he is constantly redistributing, he creates an underground economy through which he can attract whatever is needed from the larger landscape. One could say he stands at the doorway through which resources and talent must pass to reach the Queen.

The Page of Disks is historically the student of abundance. This person's attention is focused on learning the natural laws that pertain to increase, multiplication, compounding, and all forms of growth. Whether the study is about farming and husbandry, the stock market, or culturing new medicines in the lab, this Page wants to understand the fundamental mechanism that supports the expansion of value. He asks cogent, penetrating questions that invariably reveal the blind spots yet to be illuminated. He is also a crack player of the trick-taking card games that were so popular in the early centuries of Tarot. He understands how to watch the odds and keep count of the moving pieces as the game goes along. It is not necessary to be a mathematician or a magician to follow the game, but only to possess a good enough memory to notice what cards have gone by and what is yet to be played. Through this subtle suggestion, we learn that our Page of Disks is an art-of-memory student who is developing a steel-trap mind trained to observe everything and retain the essence until it will be needed. Practical information of all kinds sticks to this Page and makes him a walking encyclopedia of little-known facts.

When reversed, this Page is often not taken seriously, which sours his attitude and causes him to feel rebellious and surly. He can lose track of what is practically possible, creating unrealistic expectations that eventually come back to haunt him. The resulting unpredictable behavior gets him in trouble. In some packs this Page is shown chained to a trunk that overflows with coins.

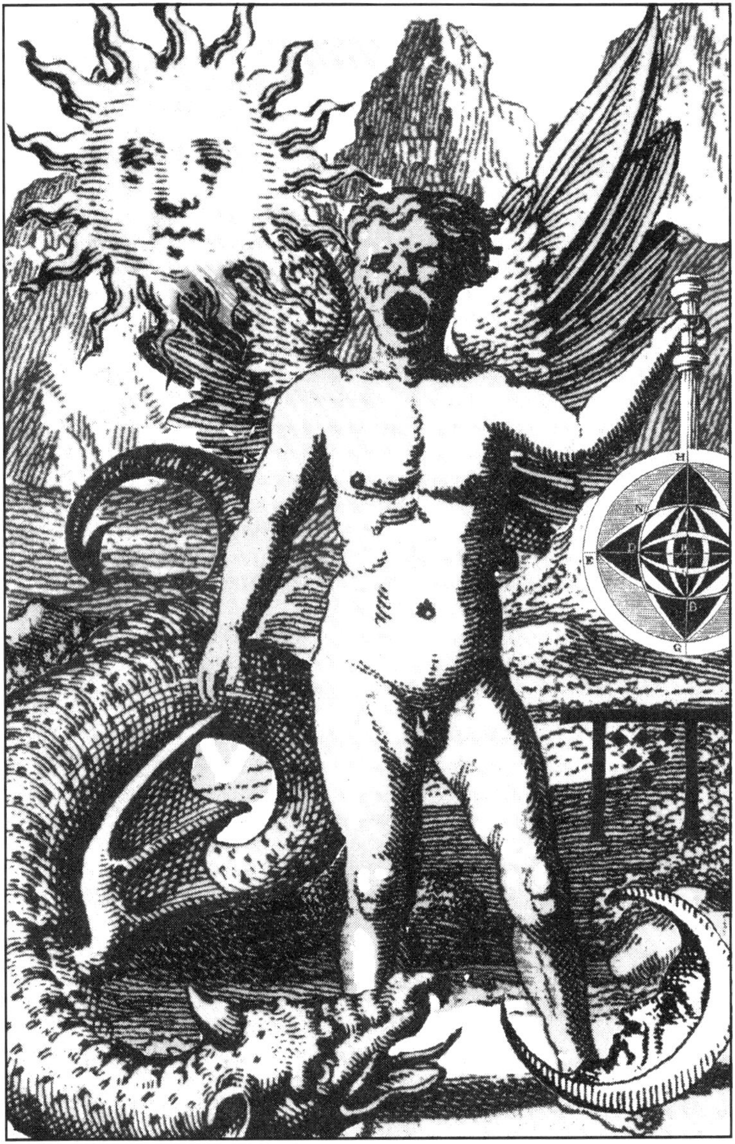

His punishment for being contentious (or just too smart for his peers) is to serve as a human guard dog over the castle treasure. In other contexts, this fellow has to hide his intelligence and possible high rank under the motley of a joker, entertaining the court by juggling on a unicycle, keeping his Disks aloft with expert sleight-of-hand. In many of the royal courts of old, the court jester was the only person who could speak truth to power, though so often that truth was veiled in comedy and delivered obliquely. Nobody ultimately knows where the Page of Disks comes from or what his story is because he plays his cards so close to the vest, showing only the poker face and laconic temperament of the natural gambler.

Chapter 6
Introduction to
The Major Arcana

The Trumps
Introduction to the Septenary Scheme

Tarot of the Holy Light's philosophy draws from the worldview shared by Astrology, Sacred Geometry, Alchemy, the theurgical arts, Kabbalah, music theory, and architecture. Individual cards represent the intersection-points of these different traditions in a condensed encapsulated form. Following the oldest packs, which place the Magus at the inception of an upward arc of development, the Trumps work their way through three rounds of seven stations to culminate at the cusp of transcendence signified by the Fool. This sequence of subjects quite self-consciously tracks an evolutionary course that starts with the inspired individual and ends with the humble but enlightened Fool for God.

Western esoteric tradition portrays the constitution of reality as (at minimum) three interpenetrating levels, planes, or frequencies ranging from subtle to dense. In *Tarot of the Holy Light*, the three levels are experienced as interpenetrating and mutually-completing, engaged in a continuous dance with each other. We picture them in this form:

- At the top the celestial or eternal reality reveals the radiant, expanding Word of Spirit (*fiat lux*), which appears as a descending triangle of Light. This energy informs the first three Trumps of each Septenary.
- In response, material reality undergoes a turbulent and chaotic upheaval represented by the rough, painful, and wrathful triangle of Fire. This energy informs the second three Trumps of each Septenary.
- From this interwoven dichotomy emerges the astral, harmonic, and psychic reality which awakens the Eye in the Heart and accomplishes the Tincture. This energy informs the seventh Trump of each Septenary and is summarized in the Fool.

The version of the Great Arcanum we are using comes from Abraham von Franckenberg's *Raphael, oder, Artzt-Engel* (1676, p. 22). The Light and Fire triangles overlap to form the six pointed star or hexagram also known as the Seal of Solomon. The seventh point at the exact center represents a unique psychological and vibrational reality that can only be realized when the ascending and descending energies find a balance. This seventh term opens a portal into what is known as the "astral plane," the invisible world of subtle energies meted out to the terrestrial Creation through the actions of the Lights, namely the Sun and the Moon.

Those who are familiar with alchemical ideas will recognize echoes of the Solar, Lunar, and Mercurial essences that are the prime materials for the Great Work. Astrologers also monitor their own version of this triplicity, expressed as the three modes that structure the internal unfolding of the seasons known as Cardinal, Fixed, and Mutable. All the great trinities of world religion are relevant here as well. The essential formula in every case is thesis/antithesis/ synthesis. But let us guard our minds from reductionism. What I'm actually saying is that to make up a single, cohesive "thing," one must posit a triangle of causes. Immediately a set of effects is unleashed carrying its own triple aspect reflected in form. To marry those two equals-and-opposites together such that they have a creative result requires the full seven-stage dialectic. This is the minimum possible number of stages required to convert untapped potential into a fertile and self-perpetuating reality.

The seven fold pattern of human experience has relevance beyond the personal life. In terms of the Trump sequence, there are at least three different scales of human significance being suggested: personal, socio-cultural, and spiritual. (The Fool might represent a fourth state, indicating the type of consciousness that is operative at all three levels at once.) In all the oldest packs, the Trumps seem to appear in nearly identical clumps of seven, even when we find them in a different numerical order than the way we now see them. This suggests that the Seven Planetary Governors, the Great Arcanum, or some other Septenary scheme has governed the Major Arcana since the first presentation of the 22 Trumps. Following that pattern, we will be dealing with the Trumps as three Great Arcana, made up of seven Trumps each, starting with Trump One the Magus and following through in what we now call Marseille order. The Hebrew alphabet takes its natural flow upon the Trumps, starting with Aleph on the Magus and ending with the Fool on the final letter, Tav.

This rhythm of crossing seven challenges to achieve a new grade or rank, repeated across three ascending levels, is found in the musical and geometric matrix of the alphabet, and also corresponds to the Masonic traditions inherited by Etteilla from the Masonic lodges of the 1700s. We read about a nearly-identical program of seven-step gradework with triple graduations as far back as Dante, using titles and correspondences that can be found on the faces of the Mantegna Icon series. This idea of nested worlds-within-worlds has come forward from our earliest religious literature and in the process has given rise to layered octaves of correspondences that include the ancient gods, the academic arts and their related crafts, the planets (and their rulerships within the Zodiac), musical keys, geometrical proportions and shapes, as well as a subordinate catalogue of colors, names, symbols, totems, and values. All this was assembled and available to the Renaissance world once Agrippa's *Three Books on Occult Philosophy* (1998) was published. In point of fact, an engaged student of magic would be able to derive a full set of correspondences to distribute upon his or her Tarot cards by simply acquiring this one volume. A second equally essential source, the *Sefer Yetzirah* (Kaplan, 1990), would confirm and flesh out anything that might have been left obscure by Agrippa.

The First Septenary

Within the First Septenary the initial three Trumps (Magus, Priestess, and Empress) represent the celestial impulse inspiring consciousness via direct cosmic Light pouring into us from Eternity. We regard these influences as being active, initiating interior changes in the upper frequencies of consciousness. The following three (Emperor, Hierophant, and Lovers) will represent the denser, more physical response from the sub-Lunar plane, analogous to a physical fire born of material friction. These influences are understood to be responsive or reflective (of the Divine Impulse), showing tangible proof of the Divine Hand stirring the world of matter. These Trumps point to the literal world including our body-wisdom and the knowledge that comes from our historic experiences. At the central point appears that clarified self-consciousness which is perfected by the union of spiritual energies and earthly forces. This resonant state of holistic consciousness is the goal for each Septenary, describing a state that transcends active and reactive states and exists beyond polarities, actualizing a flowing blend that pulses between the opposites.

Among the Protestant Sophianics, the radiant, initiating triangle was the Light pouring forth from the Supernal Triangle of the Kabbalah Tree. This is not the terrestrial "Air" as one might glibly suppose. The First Septenary is not aimed primarily at materialization but exists to illustrate the method by which Divine Light is stepped-down enough to condense into its physical reflection, Fire (or heat). It would not be amiss to say that this hexagram represents the operation of the Vast Face (the upper Septenary) of the Unfallen Tree, rather than the Small Face (lower Septenary) of the same Tree. Once this responsive Fire force begins to penetrate the sub-Lunar realms, then the awakening and activation of the other Elements Air, Water, and Earth are soon to follow.

Our illustration of the Great Arcanum (see p. 70) was gleaned from Franckenberg's writings published after Boehme's death. The younger

Franckenberg was Jacob Boehme's personal secretary during his developmental years; therefore, it seems fitting to recruit one of Franckenberg's primary symbols for a Tarot focused on Boehme's legacy. And let us also note that the Solar and Lunar figures at the center of this Great Arcanum are both parts of the same One Thing, which together represent the androgynous, bipolar, and hermaphroditic seventh term of the Septenary. We will read this syzygy just the same way one reads the bottom bar of the Hermetic Cosmos shown on page 68 (which stretches between Lunar-ruled Cancer and Solar-ruled Leo) as a single fused unit, the Lights, which together manage the day and night sides of the Zodiac. One can also visualize this union of opposites as a Sun/Moon conjunction happening at the cusp between Cancer and Leo. In essence it's the hinge or knot of the Solar System from which the entire Hermetic Cosmos model and Ladder of Lights unfolds.

It is essential for an individual to distinguish between active, responsive, and resonant modes of being in order to acquire any skill in the magical arts. These discriminations become the Tarot's focus in the first Septenary. For now let's assume that the word "active" refers to values that express through the highest and most subtle frequencies, while the word "responsive" designates values that answer the movements of Spirit in the denser frequencies of matter. What emerges between the two has qualities and characteristics of both. We call the third mode the resonant or harmonic state, being androgynous and holographic, able to communicate at every level simultaneously.

1 The Magus

Letter: Aleph = Air (between Heaven and Earth)
Path: Heart crossbar, Chesed to Gevurah
Quality: Breath, chest, respiration. Tongue of Balance

The Magus represents the imagination, site of one's genius and uniqueness. This is the communicating intelligence, Gichtel's "lifespirit," which employs planetary cycles to knit our random experiences into a coherent narrative of the self. Around him shimmers the energetic architecture of the higher planes towards which he is constantly striving. In the Sophianic Mysteries this is the scribe or aspirant to initiation who is coming awake to his true nature and seeks a path of return. He could also be viewed as the Christos, male half of the Christ/Sophia pair, who are each sent to redeem the world at different stages of the cosmic drama. We take this emanation of pure awareness as the first premise of our Trump sequence.

This Trump's original title and image, the Mountebank, shows him on the lowest step of the social hierarchy. At this stage he wore the cultural camouflage of a traveling salesman, juggler, magician, or tinker. Such a person lived a rootless life so his possessions would be meager. Later, as the archetype of the theurgical Magus emerged, the Magus evolved to represent the seeker of hidden truths and invisible powers. His tools came to symbolize the Four Elements: Fire and Water plus their two "children" Air and Earth.

Due to the personal freedom his lowly status grants, the Magus can respond to whatever unique opportunities arise. Freed from bondage to either fate or faith, the Magus follows the leading of Spirit through the Three Worlds. When functioning optimally, this individual has an innate form of self-discipline with which order and organization are evoked out of the chaos of life. The Magus advises to put oneself at cause, claiming the spiritual inheritance of a soul made in the image of God. We are witnessing the moment one awakens to a higher potential and sense of mission, initiating a ripple of action that will multiply across every subsequent Trump.

To serve the Creation in this way, one's immortal spark must willingly embrace enmeshment in the earthy (blood-red) sphere of embodied life. The Light body precipitates and concentrates around the lower Sephira. This evokes an upwelling of his animal vitality and egoist passion, gifts of the physical plane. The astrological Sun and Moon mark time in the physical sky, while the alchemical principals (Sun, Moon, and Mercury) anchor the Magus' spine in the Three Worlds, represented by the three circles of energy around his body. Inwardly and outwardly these great symbols educate the soul about its innate potentials. Such are the raw materials of incarnation that our Magus will subdue to fulfill his evolutionary mandate.

The Magus carries all the correspondences of the letter Aleph and the Element Air (mind). Blazing forth like a candle in the dark, his presence declares "Aha! Behold! Eureka!" Wings at his feet bear him into the pure sky of the imaginal, his natural element. Astrological and alchemical symbols of the Hermetic Cosmos circle his upper body. The peak of natural Fire supports and crowns him, while overhead the symbol of androgynous Mercury (Azoth) activates the caduceus in each hand. Thus armed with the tools of tradition, the soul of the Magus penetrates matter to arouse its latent potentials. He pledges to devote all the energies of his lower Sephirot to the actualization of his upper Sephirot. The awakened individual draws up from the animal/elemental self the resources needed to evolve towards eternal being.

Our Magus possesses a keen mind to pierce through the world of appearances and to connect with the Divine Idea that he embodies. The raw materials he is working with are his inborn nature and qualities, including any built-in limits or challenges. The caduceus in one hand represents his birth chart, his unique interior fixed points of reference. The caduceus in his other hand collects and transmits energies from the eternally changing dance traced in the sky by the moving planets. By staying in touch with both micro- and macrocosm, he witnesses and hosts the continuous play of creativity manifesting through his inner and outer senses. This Magus lives out an ongoing conversation with Spirit, and in response the world becomes increasingly ensouled, able to manifest ever-more sophisticated and resonant ideals.

The Magus doesn't simply allow ideas and impressions to flow through his mind unexamined the way a computer does. Instead s/he utilizes desire and attraction to point vitality towards the long-term goal of self-cultivation. His or her aura announces to the Three Worlds (celestial, astral, and terrestrial) that this person aspires to be tutored by the World Soul. Our Magus intends to become something more than just another body in the herd. He desires to evolve into a power center, a vortex of will, intention, focus, and drive, one who will assist the penetration of Spirit through matter. Stage by stage, the Magus becomes a vessel fit for the alchemical reconciliation of the opposites overcoming the opposites, overcoming the either/or dichotomy of the Zero-sum game. In the process the Magus will fulfill the full range of elemental potentials and

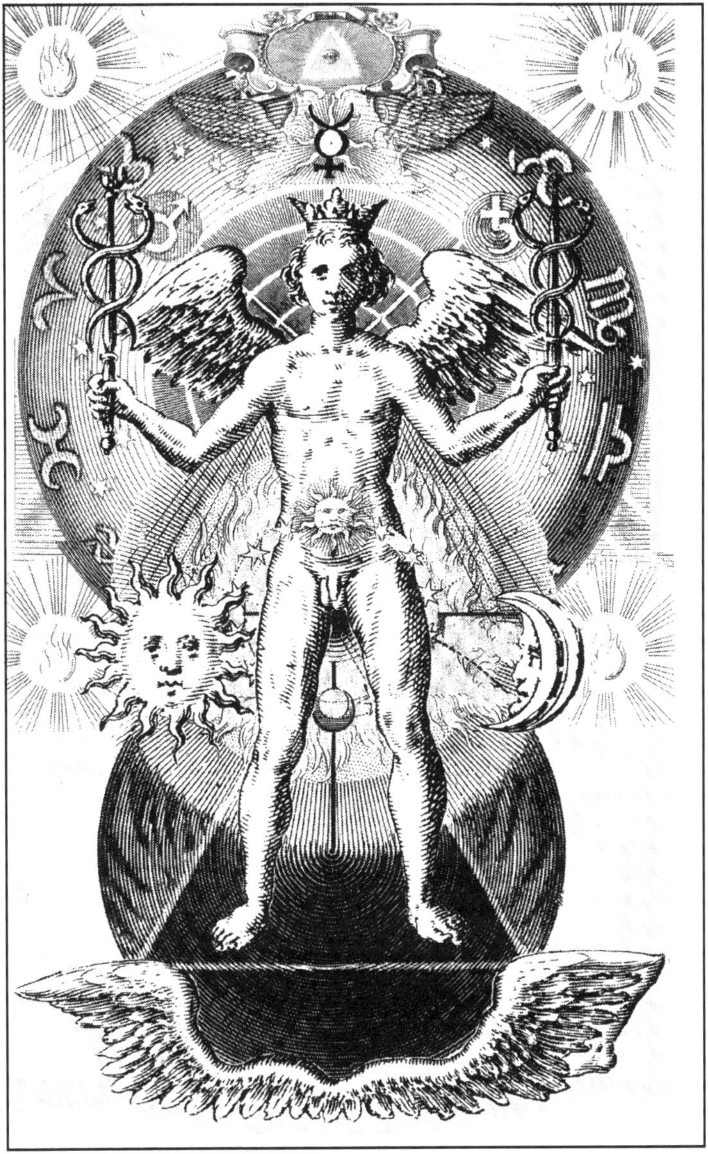

acquire every experience that evolution offers. Endowed with high hopes and all the best expectations, he or she brings a big heart and a wellspring of optimism to the Great Work.

At best the Magus shows us the active Holy Spirit calling forth a unique personality and creative impulse which can invent new patterns. However, one must constantly battle the forces of distortion, pretense, and egotistic fantasy, which continuously arise both within and without. The ancients said, "Know thyself." Without taking that essential inventory, including all flaws and weak points, there is no start-point for this journey of the soul.

There is another challenge for the Magus as well, which is endemic to his correspondence with the Element Air in the alphabet. The imaginal (the realm of the inner life), to which all shamans and magi point as the true location for their magical actions, isn't solidified in the way materialized things and beings are. In the mind's eye our apparitions are perfect and complete, untainted by the many compromises that Time/Space materialization forces onto the final product. Objects take the form of one's conjecture, and they can transform in a second based on the effects the mind is conjuring. Therefore, it is easy to become fooled about what can actually become real in material terms.

Because the letter Aleph sits on the Heart-bar of the Kabbalah Tree, it is the mediator between the chastening rain of sparks pouring down through the third eye (Shin/World) and the compassionate upwelling of empathy arising from the pelvic center (Mem/Death). Aleph represents the very first stroke Creator made to define the realm where the Creation could come to be. It places the Heart at dead center of the cosmos, labeled "Middle of the Balance and Tongue of Decree." Just so, each human life is lived at the intersection point between the Three Worlds – material, psychological, and energetic (or spiritual).

Therefore, whether this card falls upright or reversed, true success with the Magus depends on keeping one's balance, harmonizing all opposites instead of polarizing with one side against the other. One must open the mind to an inclusive and/and approach, because that is how Nature expresses herself, with everything interpenetrated rather than "this versus that." The Magus portrays that state of being in which one's gut, heart, and mind arrive at unity for an eternal moment. During this window out of time, a true view of reality can be gained, as long as we don't distract ourselves with fear, self-consciousness, or cynicism. Such moments are few and far between, so the Magus arranges both lifestyle and commitments to offer the best possible conditions for internal awareness and the natural self-adjustments that follow.

2 The Priestess

Letter: Bet = Moon
Path: Between Keter and Tiferet
Quality: Wisdom

The Priestess is the Virgin Sophia, first companion of Creator, who channels and conveys authentic Divine Love into the world. This is also the sensitive soul of the mystic (male or female) who, having entered the temple of the Heart, waits expectantly for a revelation of the goddess. We see the Priestess (or Papess) drawing life-force up her left side (the ascending Father Pillar), harmonizing it with cosmos around her crown, then pouring it out (along the descending Mother Pillar) through her right breast and hand, feeding the sub-Lunar realms with her heavenly Light. The two candlesticks with their twining vines demonstrate that all of Earth is the Priestess' altar, putting us in mind of Jakin and Boaz of the Hebrew Kabbalah Tree, later reproduced in Masonic temples. From antiquity this is Silence, spouse of Depth, first syzygy of the Valentinian Gnostics. She was present in the beginning and is the shaper of Divine Thought into individual things. As the personal guide and invisible lover of the scribe or aspirant (this is you, dear reader), she is also the Mistress of Books, foremost in the library. Boehme would call her the Noble Virgin of Divine Wisdom. Alchemically, she is the *Soror Mystica*, spiritual companion to the alchemist at work in the laboratory.

Major Arcanum 2, the Priestess, represents the antithesis-response which naturally develops in the Light after the appearance of the Magus. The rule is "if this, then that." Where he is outgoing, she turns inward. Where he is the Divine Word in action, she is Wisdom, witness to the truth that gives meaning to the Word. He balances across the breastbone, she plunges down the spine. Like night follows day, this Priestess is the vessel of the Magus' ideations.

As befits her association with the Hebrew letter Bet, the Priestess occupies the altar in the inner sanctum of the temple, enthroned between the two pillars of rising and falling energies that forever stir the cosmos. She represents the developed intuition, the ability to harmonize with Divine Will. Scripturally, Sophia is the name of God's Wisdom and first companion, called the Logos-cutter. She separates out the infinite potentials of God's mind and gives each thing its unique frequency for substantiation in matter. In Trump 2, she is the soul's tutor in the labor of contemplation, which requires conforming one's inner life to the archetypes. Under her title of Mistress of the Library, she has access to all of the teachings the ancestors distilled for our edification. She bears witness to pure potential, not yet committed to any particular manifestation but backed up by all the luminous intelligence shimmering forth from the vibratory universe. Whichever way she is named or portrayed, astral energy pours out of the Sophia's Heart into Creation at large.

Often we'll see the High Priestess represented as an oracle or a sibyl. She'll be veiled, and on her lap will rest the Torah, including sometimes a gold and silver key (keys to the inner sanctum, referencing Astrology and divination). Etteilla took a different tack and named her Eve. This title also emphasizes the intuition; Eve may be uncultivated and unsophisticated, but she is totally in touch with subtle currents both celestial and terrestrial. In any of these forms, she is a creature of the inner senses, the dreamtime fantasia of visualization and trance. This is the shadowy feminine figure that the Grail Knight follows both through his outer adventures and through his life of dreams and visions. She has various roles in his life: as sister, as guide, as lover, as corrector. But the one role she doesn't take is mother. (That is reserved for our next Trump, the Empress.)

Some religious philosophers interpret the symbol of Eve as the initiatrix of all future humanity. In this interpretation Eve's eating of the apple proffered by the serpent was necessary in order to open humanity's spiritual sight and awaken our capacity for discrimination. Her sacrificial act grants us some protection from false presentations and dissembling manipulators as we navigate this illusory world. We are to understand the "knowledge of good and evil" as being a good thing to possess, not a tragedy, but a growth stage to master. We have chosen to emphasize this reference with our Priestess of the Holy Light because it best illustrates the esoteric operation of this Arcanum.

This Priestess represents the keeper of all the esoteric arts, but such is her nature that she uses them only as a catalyst to open the mind towards higher states of consciousness. So whereas the Magus represents the will to awaken dawning in the individual ego, the Priestess represents Divine Consciousness looking in on us and out through us. This Priestess mediates awareness of the hidden realities that support the mundane world, spooling out the knowledge through the waxing and waning cycles of the Moon. Although the Priestess speaks all the languages of the mystery schools, her genius lies in synthesizing the teachings of tradition with the living presence of Spirit in the consciousness of the individual. She stimulates the awakening of intuitive inner voices, which become our guides and allies as we study the spiritual sciences.

The Priestess is all forms of sentience, bestowing a clarity that dawns from

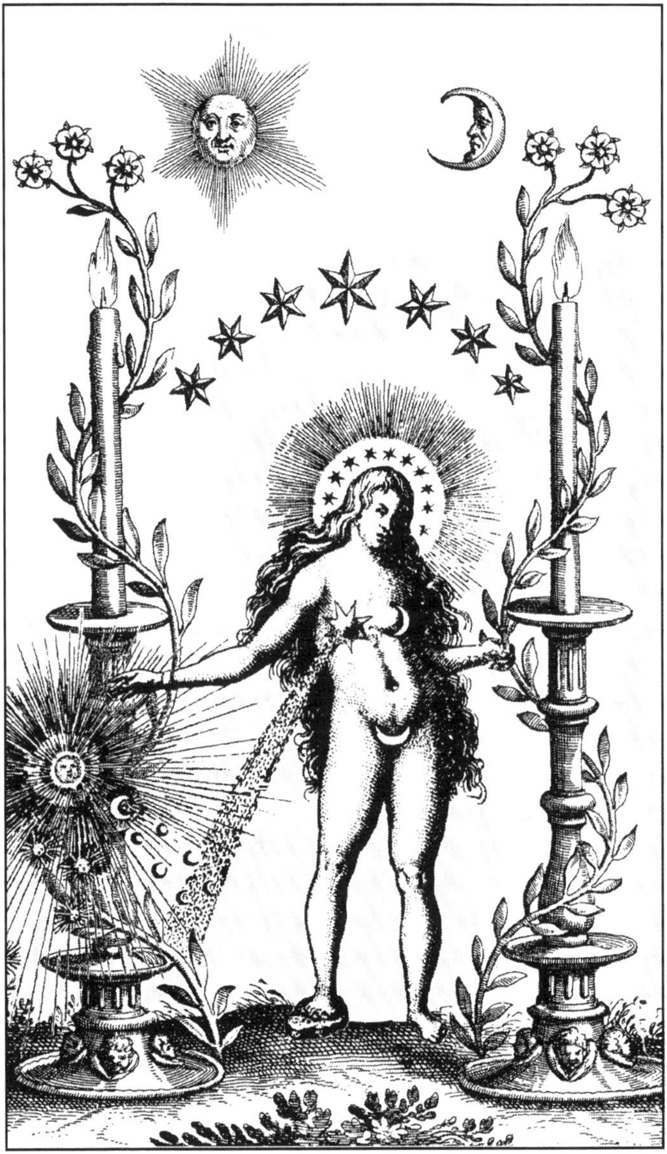

within. She teaches through the parables of the ancients, and there are multiple levels to her every word. With her help the voice of the personal Will is met by the even more compelling voice of Spirit. The Priestess is the first and last teacher, primary companion through the life of the mystic. She guards that inner sanctum within the self, where in her eloquent solitude we can relax and absorb the messages she writes on the mirror of the mind.

When the Priestess appears reversed, one might be facing a fear of silence and emptiness, including dread of one's unmediated thoughts and feelings. The Priestess imposes the discipline of external silence and stillness, whether this is wanted or not. She counsels that we go willingly into the most private places of our being and learn to still the endless jabbering of our self-talk. As we become increasingly transparent to the inward-looking eye of God, self-awareness increases until we willingly accede to the discipline of the Mistress of the Library.

In the inner sanctum we meet another attribute of the Priestess which some people are deathly afraid of, and that is the conscience. The sensation of an awakening conscience can feel like a ripping wound when it first dawns. For people who routinely choose their actions before consulting with their conscience, the presence of the Priestess is the worst form of punishment. As the letter Bet, the Moon neither rewards nor punishes. What she does is impose the clarity of Wisdom into worldly events, revealing the shadows we are casting and their effects on the things and beings around us. This gives us an opportunity to make changes and seek forgiveness, both within and without. The Priestess doesn't rescue anybody but allows us to experience the natural consequences of our actions, which is the only way humans manage to learn. She knows the truth of science, which is that any situation, circumstance, experiment, relationship, or unfolding event will begin to change as soon as it is being looked at by an outside source. The presence of Sophia/Priestess pouring through our mind's eye and illuminating our interior motives is the first step towards making the kind of positive, evolutionary changes that a true spiritual seeker wants to make.

Therefore, the smart individual takes the hint that suggests the Priestess' position in the sequence: Accept the burden of self-awareness. Find your true self and come into possession of your impact as a cause, not just a reactor, in your life. Realize the necessity of taking full responsibility for the self in relation to the vast otherness that fills the category of non-self. At this stage of the sequence, we don't know all of the details about who or what is "out there" looking in on us. It's only sensible to assume that the ego, the I, is not the only active agent present in the landscape. This is a simple lesson, one that all of

Nature teaches: There is always someone or something watching. Be aware of what they are witnessing about you. Modify your own behavior before an outside energy finds a way to use your lack of self-consciousness against you.

The Priestess in reversal only presses this point more firmly. All veiling we have wrapped around our secrets and hidden affairs is illuminated by her Moist Light. Our private bits are revealed, naked before the Priestess, stripped bare of all the rationalizations, subterfuge, and misdirection we have allowed to grow up around us. Will we fight off this bolt of clarity as if it were an enemy, or can we accept the Priestess' illuminating unmasking gracefully? The outcome of our choice will set the tone for everything that follows from this moment.

3 The Empress

Letter: G = Venus
Path: Between Chakhmah and Chesed
Quality: Wealth

The Empress is the compassionate and generous web of life envisioned by Godhead to provide vehicles for all the sparks that wish to enter the Creation. The principle of Venus is that of attraction, harmony, magnetism, charisma, and sympathetic resonance. Venus binds all souls and species together through mutual reliance and interlocking function. She is also the patient gardener of Eden, looking for the best conditions for every species. Therefore, she has been known as the Engine of Nature.

The Empress points to the Great Mother aspect of Sophia, wife of the King of the realm of Light. It is she who originally granted Anthropos the spark of divinity that animates him and shows forth his heavenly lineage. She sends a letter in the form of an eagle to her son who has forgotten himself and is slumbering in the world's distractions. This is the goddess of Nature and giver of life to all, without whom the seeker is lost. This would be the Mariological goddess of Paracelsus, the feminine side of the Father from whom the earthly Virgin Mary was reflected when it was time for Christ to be born.

Major Arcanum 3 provides the mediating third term for our first Trine of Light, supporting the creative and generative functions of the Magus in fertilizing the meditative stillness and sensitivity of the Priestess. The Empress balances these energies through her power of Love and Eros Magic, the attractive force that everywhere enlivens Nature. Boehme would call this quality "the magic of nature." The Empress evokes and nurtures life in the Earth plane; as the Holy Mother she sponsors every incarnation as microcosmic fractals of the One. She's the Mother of all the plants and animals, the inspiration for all the lifeforms on Earth, whose great magnetism attracts souls to occupy the bodies she calls forth from the mud. As the face of the planetary Goddess, she reveals herself through the vital and effulgent tissue of Earth, which sprouts infinite forms under her tender attentions. Once we accept her tutelage, we learn what each manifestation is intended for, what purpose each life-form serves in the overall fabric of Creation. The Empress powers the ecological web made of all the creatures that arise within it. She tends to the harmony, the interpenetration, the mutuality of the species as they hold each other in place. She does her work by evoking universal attraction, multidirectional brotherhood and sisterhood. Without the strong family bonds she forges between species, the web would fail. No individual consciousness, no matter how well-cultivated, can in any way affect the laws by which matter is structured. However, we can harness our growing understanding to what Nature herself already wants to accomplish. Paying attention to Nature's ways and responding to her requirements evokes the creative imagination out of which all of humanity's inventions and productions flow. Wherever she stands, the Empress organizes the lives around her according to her generous dictates of love and support, affinity and bonding, encouragement and opportunity. We have only to emulate the Empress to thrive.

Academic tradition tells that Venus is the patroness of the academic art of rhetoric because Venus is the most beautiful of the visible planets. Her visible brilliancy of aspect symbolizes the rhetorician's concern for style and taste, always presenting attractive combinations the same way poets labor to decorate their verse. But beauty for its own sake is not the issue with the Empress. In modern life the appearance of beauty can be simulated even in contexts where the traditional virtues are lacking. With the Empress we are beyond artifice and appearances, relying on direct insight granted by clairvoyance. Our Empress radiates an invisible emanation which awakens the internal memory of Divine Intention, instilled at the Creation of this world. This is the Light of "natural reason" by which humans perceive Wisdom even in this transitory realm of deceiving appearances. In the words of medieval exegete Guiseppe Mazzotta, "[Dante's] term, 'chiarezza'.., translates claritas, the light that St. Thomas Aquinas conceives to be the substance of beauty and the means of its disclosure" (Bloom, 1986, p. 189). He also suggests that "for Dante, memory is the visionary faculty, the imagination through which the poet can question the phenomena of natural existence and urge them to release their hidden secrets" (p. 193-4). In the Light of Venus (the Empress), the things of this world show themselves as they really are, allowing us access to their original ideal.

It is sometimes forgotten that the Empress not only gives life, but also eventually takes it back. Embodied life is temporal, meaning that it begins and ends; it is not perpetual in its fleshly aspect. Humanity's ambiguity on this point is expressed clearly in the two aspects of Venus among the Greeks. In antiquity it was not known that the stars called the "two sons of the dawn goddess Eos" were in fact a single planet, Venus. They named the morning star Eosphorus or Phosphorus (bearer of dawn or Light) and personified it as a male figure holding aloft a lit torch. They named the evening star Hesperus or Vesper (evening star, west, dusk) and this torchbearer holds his extinguished firebrand upside down. The father of Eosphorus was said to be one of the gods, but the father of Hesperus was said to be mortal. This gives us a hint that even so far back in time the influence of Venus was caught up in a human double standard.

In fact, the situation got worse for Venus when Christian translators got into the act. The Hebrew name for Venus is Helel, "son of dawn, the brilliant or shining one" (as found in the Hebrew version of Isaiah). This name was translated from the Hebrew in two ways: as Heosphorus in the Greek Septuagent, and as Lucifer in Jerome's Latin Vulgate. Lucifer means "Light bringer" in Latin, with exactly the same connotation that we see in the Greek Eosphorus or Phosphorus. But after an imaginative rewrite by St. Augustine during the 4th century, Venus (under the name Lucifer) was described as if "he" had raised "his" profile far beyond the status of an ordinary angel. In this telling Lucifer was the cherub annointed to create a starry covering to decorate the throne of God. Lucifer was also the angel chosen to rule over all the Earth until the creation of Adam was complete. Augustine acknowledges the angelic glory of Lucifer, but he does so only to contrast it with the depth of his ruin upon being banished from the celestial throne room, known as the "Fall from Heaven." This is the device by which Venus' more ambivalent evening appearance became identified as the disgraced and fallen archangel Satan, personification of unbalanced narcissistic forces that fatefully distort the Light-bringer's self-esteem. (This banishment echoes the gnostic myth of Sophia whose trajectory also includes a Fall from Heaven, though for slightly different reasons.)

How easy it is for one culture to appropriate a figure from the mythology of another, applying a makeover that obliterates most of the original archetype. This is the first time we see this rebellious, self-centered, enraged archangel of Christian repute identified with overweening pride and egoic greed, who aspired to the status of a god but could not maintain the necessary humility. Though stripped of his title as Morning Star/Lucifer (an appellation subsequently given to Christ), Satan's still-angelic countenance continues to lead the unwary to spiritual harm as collective attention remains riveted on "his" spectacular Fall.

What a paradox for benevolent Venus to be cast in this Satanic role. We can see the implications this split mythos has upon the reversal of this card. With the two aspects of the single Venus so polarized in the mythological imagination of humanity, it is no wonder the people can become afraid of love and their creative urges, afraid of their feelings of attraction and magnetism. Many people fear allowing their true desires to become conscious whatever their reasons. Others cringe away from the results of their creative passions. Why?

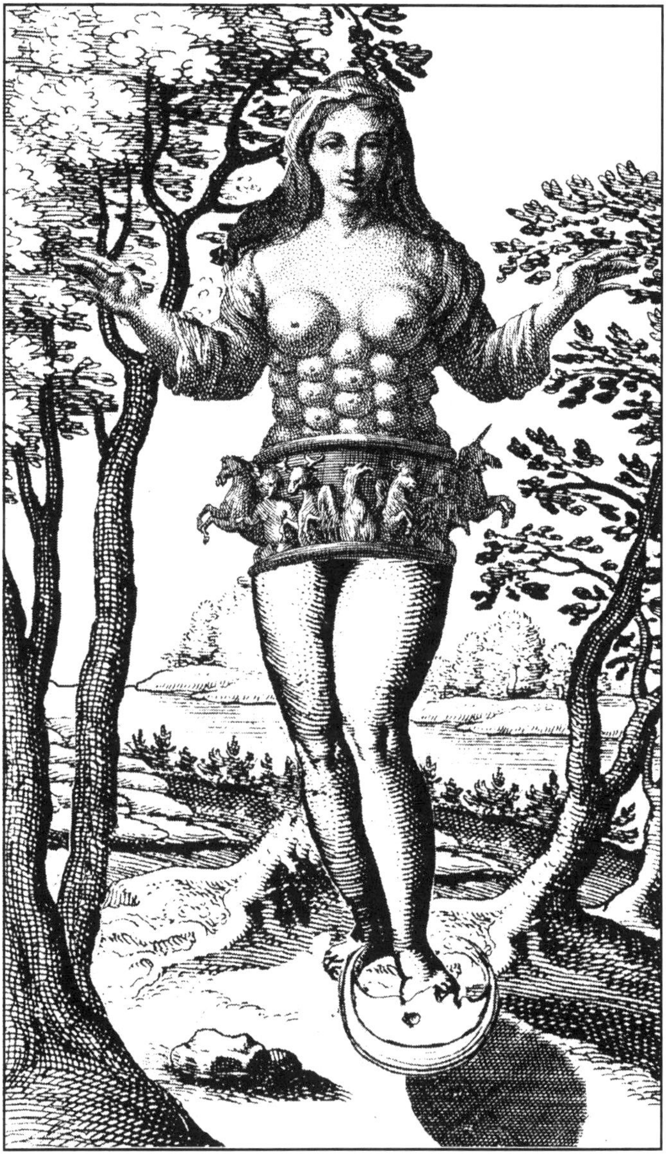

Let us remember again that Venus is reputed to show things in the light of their own true essences. If, as Mazzotta says, "knowledge is made available by and through the light of natural reason" (p. 191) then the least we should do is learn to stand in that beam and see what is present. We have nothing to fear from the Light of Venus and much yet to learn.

Summary of the First Descending Trine of Light

As we have seen, the Magus represents the awakened aspiration that strides onto the spiritual stage saying, "I'm ready to assume my higher identity." The instant response of Spirit to that idealistic self-assertion is to impose a period of meditation to help the newly-awakened Magus discover the original pattern underlying the ego's urge to conquer new territory. The Priestess teaches discrimination, encouraging reflection upon the heavenly plan and our own part within it. Her insight provides a blueprint for the Empress, who provides a middle ground where self and other, the explicit and the implicit, work together to manifest the sensory world of things and beings. Time/Space matter of the type we live in guarantees that violations of Nature's limits will fail to attract enough substance to maintain a physical form. Only those developments which possess a natural place in this Creation will be sponsored by the Empress.

This first luminous Trine represents consciousness awakening to the laws of manifestation. Going forward as self-awareness solidifies at the ground of being, the seeker learns to arrange his or her attitude in a way that respects heavenly leading. Success must first be achieved in the realm of self-discipline, laying the groundwork for a sensitive yet sensible stance that communicates with the invisible while maintaining effectiveness in the outer world. Only then can we proceed with some confidence that we are not adrift in a hostile universe. In these first three Trumps stimulation from higher frequencies enlivens the inspired soul who willingly accepts the necessary limits required to host these rarefied energies in flesh.

The ascending Trine of Fire personifies those complementary factors inherent in Time/Space, in our animal natures, and the manifest world, which support the mystical quest from the earthly side. One could say that these three Trumps express matter's great excitement at being held and shaped by Spirit. These three Trumps are responsive in relation to Spirit, though they will seem active in relation to matter. Trumps 4, 5, and 6 picture forth matter's reflection of the invisible magnet created by the collusion of the first three Trumps. A self-perpetuating vortex is starting to form, and as a result, the individual begins to see its interior condition reflected in outer circumstances.

For those who have access to Papus' book *Tarot of the Bohemians* (1958), one finds there an exposition on the Septenary scheme of the 22 Trumps from the early 20th century (starting with chapter X). There is quite a bit to be learned about 18th and 19th century Tarot esotericism through exposure to Papus' catalogue of writings, so I highly recommend investigating anything one can find in print. (Now that Kessinger has picked up his works for reproduction, there is actually quite a bit to examine.) We have not chosen to follow Papus in every detail for *Tarot of the Holy Light*. The synthesis offered by Papus represents Tarot on the cusp of the 20th century, whereas *Tarot of the Holy Light* represents a mode of thought that made itself known in the middle 1600s.

4 The Emperor

Letter: D = Jupiter
Path: Between Binah and Gevurah
Quality: Seed

In Valentinian terms the Emperor is the King of Heaven, Bythos, the original Source of the Pleroma, archetype of all father gods, such as Zeus or Yahweh. This Emperor exudes nobility of purpose from every pore. As Jupiter, he identifies with expansion and multiplication of all kinds; his optimism and generosity keep a door open for a better future to appear. At the human level the Emperor is the icon of personal sovereignty in that his individual history becomes the destiny of his lands and peoples. Knowing this, he lives his life with full commitment, accepting the mandate of Heaven. In the Greek pantheon, it was Jupiter who was given lordship over the Earth after the death of Uranus. But despite his utter and complete power, our Emperor humbly remembers himself as the head servant of the realm, the fortunate son of destiny. He truly understands that the same fate that empowers him now will eventually bring the doom to which he must also obediently submit.

While he occupies the throne, the Emperor's empowerment as leader and figurehead causes all to bow to the inevitability of his vision. His desires and attractions provoke the first stage of this responsive Trine; his thesis is the appetite body awakening in matter. Trump 4 is passionate and avid about his involvement with matter, his body, and his "place" in Time and Space. He consumes and dominates his realm, yes, but he does so because he enjoys the experience of its administration so much. It pleases him to be engaged with the various parts of his extended domain: He revels in being the husbandman, lord, and master of all he surveys. Whether things go well or not, he's always there like a good father, steering the course of the ship of state with mind and heart fully engaged.

As the scion of a royal family that traces back to semi-mythical ancestors, the Emperor's very presence exposes linear Time/Space to a touch of Eternity. His aura billows and spreads around him like the clouds of Heaven. The holy blood of his lineage has the power to heal his subjects; like Samson, there is power in all of his parts, even (or most especially) his hair. All the lives in his realm are subject to his will and dependent on his grace. He even has treaties with the laws of Nature, affecting the formative functions that the Elements usually render unconsciously. When he's in tune with the Creation, the four winds and the directions happily respond to his inclinations, bringing fair weather and full harvests.

The Emperor abounds in human will and libidinal drive, which is Earth's answer to the spiritual awakening of the Magus. Energy courses through the Emperor's body as the desire to innovate, the will to lead, and the boldness to break with the past if doing so will advance the well-being of his empire. There is no need to fear this force unless one is trying to contain it. The Emperor brooks no opposition and deals forcefully with those who think to inhibit his self-expression.

We could see this Emperor as a social scientist involved in an experiment of civic evolution. His enterprises are almost always fortunate. By encouraging his people to do what they are best at, he nurtures a local economy that is diverse enough to support his empire, even reaching beyond the borders of his region. His court is like a business incubator, attracting a wide range of creative individuals who possess the boldness to form associations and undertake increasingly sophisticated challenges. The natural gravity of his personality builds up the metropolis and increases the reputation of the realm.

The Emperor's quest to find better ways to meet his people's needs acts like a catalyst, permeating the environment with his enthusiastic and progressive expectations. This is the inspired man of destiny who puts his signature upon the landscape and upon his times. In the era of Tarot's first appearance, there were many little city-states all over Italy, and each one was a culture-center with its own form of government, its own traditions, and its own style of art, music, and Tarot. This Emperor can be seen as a culture King and performance artist, personally embodying his realm with a signature ethos that magnetizes and attracts talent of all kinds to his court.

The eagle standing in a bed of flames atop the Emperor's shield amplifies the meaning of this Trump. According to *A Dictionary of Symbols* (Cirlot, 1962, p. 87-89):

> The eagle is a bird living in the full light of the Sun and it is therefore considered to be luminous in its essence, and to share in the Elements of Air and Fire....Since it is identified with the idea of male activity which fertilizes female Nature, the eagle also symbolizes the father. It is further characterized by its daring flight, its speed, its close association with thunder and fire. It signifies, therefore, the "rhythm" of heroic nobility. From the Far East to northern Europe, the eagle is the bird associated with the gods of power and war....[I]n Christianity,

the eagle plays the role of a messenger from Heaven. Theodoret compared the eagle to the spirit of prophecy; in general, it has also been identified...with prayer rising to the Lord, and grace descending upon mortal man. According to St. Jerome, the eagle is the emblem of the Ascension and of prayer....As Jupiter's bird it is the theomorphic storm, the "storm bird" of remotest antiquity....On Roman coins it occurs as the emblem of imperial power and of the legions....Dante even calls the eagle the bird of God.

With this totem as a sign, we know that our Emperor is a powerful actor on the world stage for the fulfillment of Divine Will. He knows his life is not an ordinary one, and he does not begrudge the fate that makes him a figurehead. Possessing the full courage of his convictions, he challenges himself and all of his subjects to live up to their highest potentials, to reach for the heights in all that they do.

When reversed, the Emperor appears to be an unrepentant narcissist. He certainly accepts no correction, and like Alexander of old, he precociously takes more than is freely given. The level of inspiration and entitlement that are available to this larger-than-life ego can certainly border on mania and madness. But for those who fall under his patriarchal rule, his status as benevolent dictator remains uncontested. Those who find themselves in a tussle with the Emperor should double-check their expectations. There is such a thing as "losing by winning" and the reversed Emperor will take pains to ensure that his adversary experiences this lesson to the fullest.

Another difficulty that can appear with the Emperor reversed is the syndrome of "too much of a good thing." The Emperor, being Jupiter, honestly believes that more is better, whether that is in fact true or not (usually not). The temptation to overtalk, overreach, overeat, overspend, and overkill is this Emperor's pitfall. The best of everything comes to him, and he loves to indulge in it all. For this reason he is prone to all the ailments of excess: inflammatory syndrome, cancer, addiction, hoarding, and related issues.

The suggestion to supersize our appetites and expectations comes at us from every direction in our current culture as well. The wisest course for Jupiter in his progress through the mine-field of temptations is, whether working or playing, exerting or resting, to keep a pace and style that is humane and healthy to all participants, young and old. Whatever the goal, work is best done "family style," with proper breaks and holidays to balance the heroic projects this Emperor loves to undertake. You are doing it right if you still have time for play, for love, for sleep, for hobbies, and for simply "doing nothing."

337

With Jupiter's slow orbit longevity is one of his gifts to humanity. People who know how to titrate their cycles of indulgence and austerity will be much better equipped to thrive in whatever climate and conditions Nature dishes out over the years. Remember the biblical Joseph, advisor to the King of Egypt, who put away grain for seven years of famine during the time that his country was experiencing seven years of plenty. There is no rule of mutual exclusion between having a good life and being sensible, at least not in this Emperor's domain. His goal is to see his friends, family, and subjects living a full and meaningful life. He knows that if he can provide peace and opportunity for all, he will always command the people's loyalty and affection.

5 The Hierophant

Letter: Heh (E) = Aries
Path: Between Keter and Chakhmah
Quality: House of Life

Trump 5 is the High Priest of every lineage, the master of the Doctrine of Correspondences. He is also the headmaster of the temple university, setting the curriculum and choosing the students. He wears the triple crown and enacts the role of Hermes/Mercurius (the Philosopher's Stone), separating out the ascending, expanding influences (Sun, Mars, and Venus, with Elements Fire and Air, thumbs up) from the descending, consolidating influences (Moon, Jupiter, and Saturn, with Elements Water and Earth, thumbs down). Hierophant is the role for which the soul is being prepared and tutored by Sophia. The person who wears the mitre assumes political and administrative responsibilities of a cosmic nature.

As antithesis to the Emperor's thesis in this fiery responsive Trine, the Hierophant departs from the sensuality and worldliness of the court to establish the medieval institution of the "holy hill": a cathedral with a monastery, a bookbinding operation, and a university attached. This High Priest or Pope transmits the Mysteries, opening his students to a new dimension of awareness. His position in the receptive Trine is analogous to that of the High Priestess in the active Trine; but instead of working with consciousness born from the pure interior life, his gift is the consciousness generated from studies of the historical Mysteries. She uses her time at the altar to cement her communion with God, but the Hierophant is more attached to the symbols of the Arcana: the letters and numbers, the charts and glyphs of Astrology, the alchemical and Kabbalistic concepts. Where the Popess occupies the inner sanctum, attuning her consciousness to the harmonic proportions of the holy shrine, the High Priest faces the outer temple, seeking those who could become initiates and inviting them to the Mysteries.

The Hierophant faces down the test of technical transmission every day. The intelligence of the body is a pristine gift of Nature, but it is largely unconscious and inarticulate. The Hierophant trains people to penetrate that obscurity and bring the unconscious into consciousness. Having gained voluntary control over his bodily energies, this Pope can shift his life force at will, from interior to exterior, active to receptive at need. This is why he is associated with the sign Aries: He has been reborn through the mystery teachings to live simultaneously in both worlds, the temporal and the eternal. He uses the Doctrine of Correspondences to work the energy world like a Taoist or a martial artist, simultaneously tracking subtle energies while operating on multiple realities.

This Trump provides the Magus with his first formal teacher, who administers the program of established tradition impartially. His school is a boot camp of sorts, but in this case the goal is to awaken the spiritual faculties. The Hierophant winnows out the psychically-gifted from those whose mentality or emotionality interfere with their intuition. As he comes to understand the strengths and special gifts of his students, the Hierophant will reassign the natural empaths for further tutoring with the High Priestess. Those who are intuitively denser and less transparent will stay with him to fill out the functional ranks of the outer church. Such people keep the temple running and administer the social services that churches have historically provided.

The Heirophant performs this sorting and sifting process under our gaze. At the top of the image in the Hierophant's astral laboratory, he separates the subtle from the gross. Wearing Hermes' triple crown, he balances the Lights around the summer signs. I mean this literally: Mercury who is Hermes (ruler of Gemini/Virgo) balances the Lights (Moon/Cancer and Sun/Leo) around the Summer Solstice. These are the most active times of the year for the alchemical work. The Elemental Dignities system embedded in the Ladder of Lights assures that the influence of the alchemical triplicity saturates through the whole Zodiac via the extended relationships these special three maintain with the remaining signs.

The Hierophant's right hand approves Sol's influence on Mars and Venus, the rulers of the spring (Aries/Taurus) and fall (Libra/Scorpio) signs. By this he indicates that these transitional seasons also have their usefulness in the alchemical labor. The Moon, on the literal "other hand," languishes with the rulers of the slower, colder, and more internal signs of the year. These signs prevail during the dark months of the northern hemisphere's winter (Sagittarius, Capricorn, Aquarius, Pisces), hence the thumbs-down signal. One cannot commence any new projects in this period because seeds won't sprout, trees are bare, and the life force has retreated underground. Further, the two crossed orbs (containing these combinations) under the Hierophant's feet demonstrate that each grouping comprises its own realm and climate (or temperament) and serves its own function in the metabolism of Nature. This whole suite of visual ideas illustrates that the system moves forward only when powered by solar energies and falls into hibernation when the Lunar-lit winter

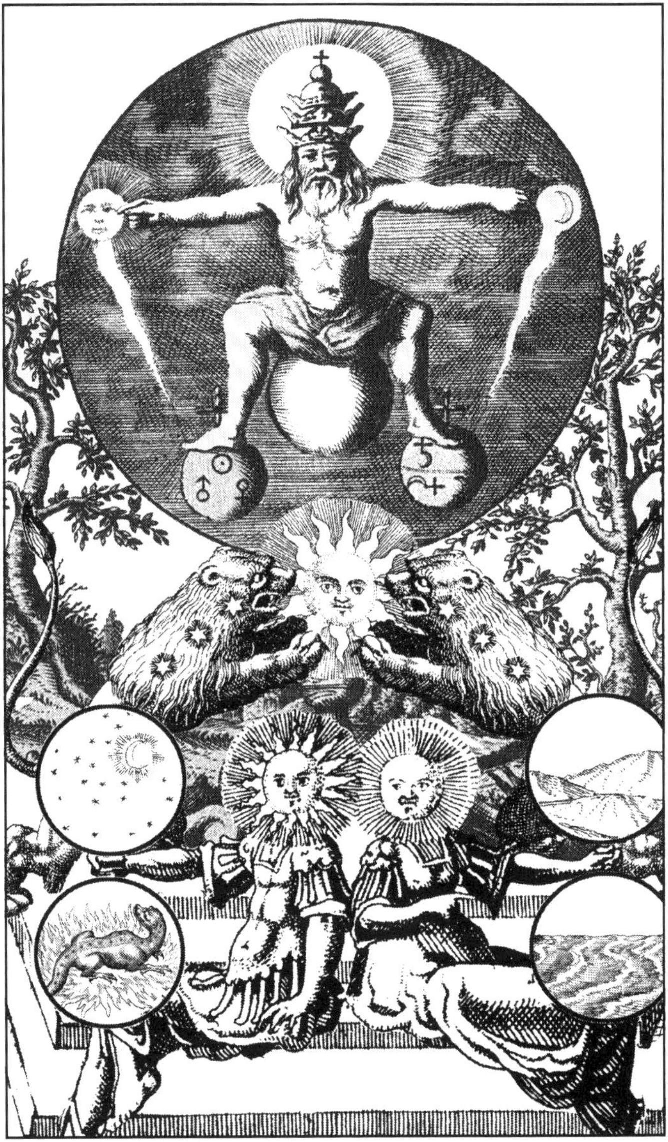

grouping is ascendant.

Moving down the diagram, the celestial bears (ancient symbolism of the North Pole) represent the physical Sun's relationship with the galactic center across the vast, slow cycle of the world ages. Meanwhile, on the steps below the Hierophant's immortal circle, the mundane operations of the transiting Sun and Moon work through the Four Elements to ensure the stability of the seasons, including weather and fertility cycles. Worldwide the priesthoods traditionally retain the necessary knowledge and calculations to reestablish the calendar and the clock, whether civilizations should rise or fall. Despite pole shifts, cultural cataclysms, or the slow but ceaseless precession of the equinoxes, the Hierophant continues to calculate the calendar and administer the Mysteries. His personal experience is enhanced by the magical boost of priestly affiliation, which extends far back and far forward in Time.

Tradition holds that once a soul has accepted initiation in any lifetime, it will be marked for service in all lifetimes. This is a mystery that only a soul who feels an authentic calling understands. The Hierophant has only to open the door and his students will find their way to him. His enhanced aura catalyzes the initiate's encounter between the limited self and the unlimited universe. The Hierophant also stands by to buffer that wave of shock and awe that hits the soul newly faced with the All-One. In this sense the Hierophant is the modern equivalent of the shaman, healing those among the tribe whose bodies are suffering from soul-sickness. He does this by tossing their stuck and boxed-in souls out of their bodies and into the cosmos, forcing them to discover new dimensions and giving them a taste of their immortality before death.

In the world of medieval Europe, all of the original universities were associated with religious communities. This gave Hierophant his pick from the smartest students of each generation. In fact, the High Priest holds the keys to the magical techniques, which are the high arts and sciences of his culture. Whoever he selects and trains will join the charmed circle around the Emperor as advisors and functionaries. This is the basis of his reputation as the power behind the throne.

As an Aries the Hierophant arouses and communicates a great attraction to the spiritual sciences. He is passionate about literacy, numeracy, and psychic development the exact same way an artists are passionate about their media. He wants to create priests who can heal, bishops who can talk to the elementals and help direct the weather, and bardic cardinals who can change the spiritual fate of whole cities with a single sermon. The Hierophant wants to see his students be skillful in all Three Worlds. Even as the right brain can communicate directly with the Spirit world, the left brain can calculate with the Arcana of letters and numbers, synthesize the spiritual meanings in play, and pull out a remedy that will fuse body and soul into a new and more integrated synthesis. Moderns tend to think that "books on the shelf" translates instantly into knowledge and skill. Far from it. This Hierophant's mission is to ensure the students' mental ambidexterity in the theurgical arts.

In reversal the Hierophant desperately makes up edicts and persecutes charismatic individuals to cover up for his lack of capability in the mantic and theurgic arts. The same syndrome takes hold in government and industry when people in authority rise beyond their true capacity. Such people are dangerous to associate with because they have no personal loyalties nor spiritual ethics. Even the individual with the title of Head Primate can't rescue the ship of state when the corporate body allows predators to mingle with the flock. When this card appears reversed, Light needs to penetrate into the backroom deals and behind-the-scenes abuses that are corrupting the community. Only full transparency will address the trust issues that make the reversed Hierophant's claim to legitimacy absurd and tragically farcical.

6 The Lovers

Letter: Vav (W) = Taurus
Path: Between Keter and Binah
Quality: House of Property

Trump 6 the Lovers points to the charged eros-magical field that springs up between the Lover and the Beloved. In this field new lives are created, gestated, and brought to birth. Unanticipated worlds come into existence evoked by the charisma between the charmed opposites. Trump 6 presents Sophia as Lover and personal tutor of the scribe, who opens the path to success and riches but only if she is valued over all other offers.

The final antithesis card in this responsive fiery group of Trumps is usually called The Lovers. But in Tarot's early days the title refers directly to Love, meaning the discipline of eros-magic, which is a branch of sympathetic magic. Trump 6 actually signifies the energy running between the Lovers (be they infernal, human, or supernal), highlighting the magnetic, irresistible field of mutual attraction. This was traditionally symbolized by a cherub with a bow and arrow aimed at one or the other of the charmed couple. The language of Eros Magic is replete with images of Love's dart piercing the Lover's heart and stealing attention away to the Beloved. There is something fateful, some kismet or karmic gravity operating beyond the will of the individuals involved, which brings the opposites together to complete their mutual fate.

The Lovers is one of the most variable Trumps of the pageant, showing a number of different aspects over the centuries. An early version shows one or more couples meeting, strolling, and dancing in a public place, playing out local courtship rituals under the watching gaze of the community (or at least the community's proxies, the Lovers' personal Pages). In the decks bearing this image, the Lovers seek a union that benefits the blending bloodlines, one that will solidify village prosperity, being sanctified in the local religious context.

Another early Lovers image shows a "meeting at the crossroads" theme. In this case the Lovers' paths only cross in a place that's at some distance from either one's natural domain. Arriving from entirely different realms, the Lovers meet as in the traditional Scottish song "Comin' Through the Rye." Venturing forth from the safety of their known worlds, opposites attract and the loving couple celebrate their attraction "in the rye." The issue in this case in not about choosing one path over the other. Rather, what we have here is the symbol of fate leading two unique destinies away from their self-created spheres into a neutral space that is safe for their private union. (Think of the Lovers in the Cary-Yale Visconti pack where we see the loving couple standing in front of a lavishly-appointed marriage bed, whence they will repair, draw the curtains, and take their leisure.)

After the mid-1600s this card begins to show the image of a youth stopped at a split in the road forced to choose between two very different paths. The difference between the two directions is usually cast as a choice to follow carnal appetites and the animal sensibilities on one side (seduction), contrasted against accepting a spiritual assignment and cultivating the inner senses along the other path (self-discipline). The Magus has to be very self-knowing and wise at this juncture in order to make a choice that he can live with for the future as well as the present. The fundamental question posed at this crossroads is "Shall I go with my instincts or shall I follow reason's guidance?" There's actually no wrong answer to make at this crossroads, which appears so often in a person's life. However, by answering this question in either possible way, fateful developments determine future relationships to everyone and everything.

Trump 6 of *Tarot of the Holy Light* shows balanced opposites in a willing union. The chivalric Alchemy of Boehme teaches that the best results arise when the fiery forces of ego are put in service to the illumined forces of Spirit. This orientation allows for magical results. As in our Great Arcanum, celestial Light (active) and terrestrial Fire (responsive) are inherently entwined with each other. But remember, Boehme's followers were not subscribers to the old male-dominated, patriarchal philosophies. In the thinking of Paracelsus and Boehme, the excessively harsh Wrathful father-force requires a soothing, quenching immersion in Sophia, the Holy Spirit. Spirit's sensitive understanding of the gap between the heavenly ideal and the compromised real introduces healing to the roiling chaos of Jehovah's demanding intensity, allowing him to reveal his Heart, the Son/Sun. It's a match made in Heaven, symbolically and literally (referring to the 13-times-a-year renewal that happens every new Moon).

The Lover's conjunction allows the self to be completed by the other, even if that "other" is the invisible Sophia, companion to the mystic. The left and right hands, like the left and right hemispheres of the brain, find each other across the midline and start to coordinate. The dynamic cosmic radiator and the absorptive, nurturing receiver form a strong creative union that evolves the material plane and produces opportunities for growth in all participants. As we can see, the firmament of Heaven and the depths of embodied Earth truly desire each other; they are meant to be brought together and complete each other. Between them shimmers the field of attraction that is the true identity of this Trump.

The reversal of the Lovers might suggest a circumstance where people act like magnets presenting like poles to each other. In this case the Lovers could repel with the very same force that attracts them when they are lined up correctly. For every instance of sympathy one experiences, there will be another experience marked by antipathy. It is important to be aware of one's natural responses to life and be authentic in our responses despite the opinions of others. The Taurus correspondence reminds us that everything happens in its proper season. Until all of the individual preconditions are met and all the cosmic forces are in alignment, the ancient triangle of the Lover, the Beloved, and Love cannot manifest in flesh.

Remember, the lack of an outer partner does not preclude having a significant relationship with Sophia, the invisible companion of the Grail Quest and Soror Mystica of Alchemy. The best protection against cynicism and emotional damage is to have an ideal upon which you can rest your love and devotion, whether or not the human world is offering a physical avenue for its expression. And when one is in relationship with Sophia, (for example, as the Priestess living within the imagination), then even challenging situations and unfulfilling human relations become useful lessons and grist for the mill. Nothing is lost and all experiences are metabolized towards the goal of Wisdom.

At the fulfillment of this manifestational Trine, we have an alchemical union of inner and outer opposites sanctioned by the secular leadership of the Emperor as well as the esoteric blessings of the Hierophant. This willing union can represent the harmonizing of any two opposed forces, be it a loving relationship between two strong individuals, the conjoining of two businesses, or treaty-making between nations. In every case the message is union and mutual completion. This is the higher meaning of the Lovers card, to heal and resolve those inherited dichotomies that entrap us into a too-small, self-dominated worldview. Here we see the opposites lovingly engaging each other's differentness without canceling each other out or losing their individual identities. The card suggests that we can create room within ourselves (and in our lives) for a fertile union of opposites where spiritual intelligence quickens the inherent potentials of matter. When we can achieve this intimate union within our private, internal contrarieties (inside the watery cave), then we can start to bring this supportive and trustworthy energy out into our manifested human relations, eventually healing the whole community (the prospering city).

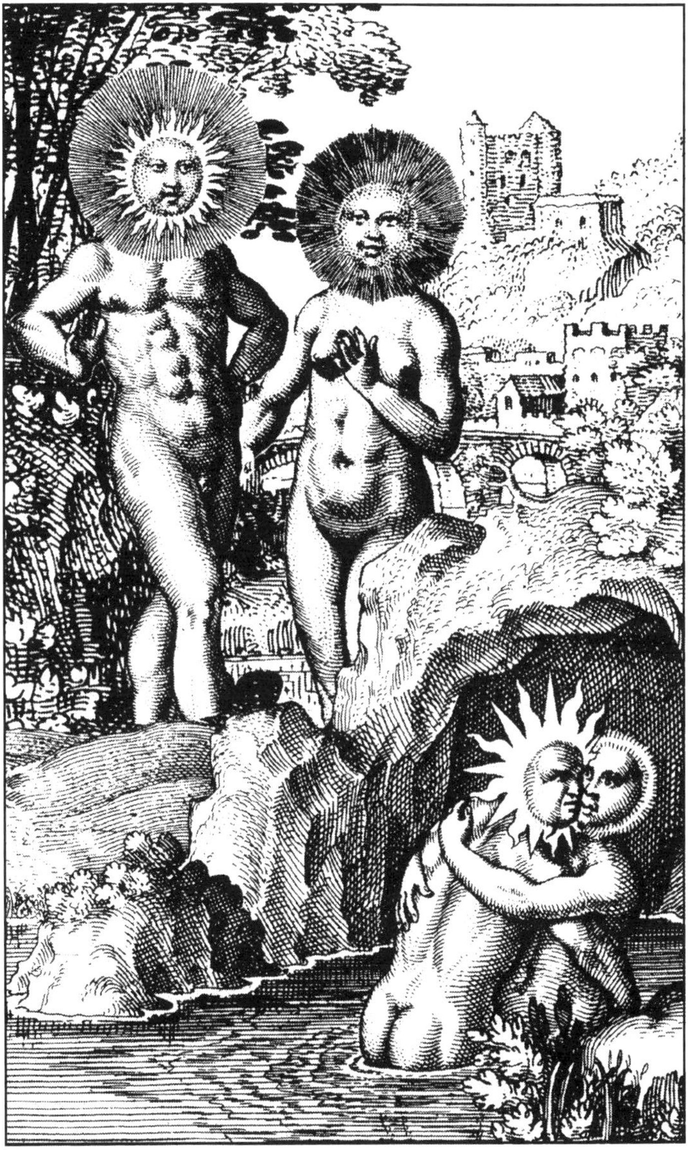

7 The Chariot

Letter: Zayin (Tz) = Gemini
Path: Between Chakhmah and Tiferet
Quality: House of Attraction

The Chariot represents the principle of perpetual motion, meaning the eternal circulation of Light and sound frequencies that compound invisible energies into tangible matter. The awakened human, that heavenly animal, becomes attuned to the voice of Spirit. Sound is the vehicle of Sophia immanent in the human world, traveling across all cultural, temporal, and religious boundaries, seeking an abode among the children of men.

The Chariot card, capstone of the first Septenary, represents polarity in co-operation or integrated frequencies. The individual who entered upon the self-cultivation path in the Magus card has reached the first synthesis. The Fixed throne of matter is now animated, moved by one dark and one light horse. These two steeds (sometimes sphinxes) show that all polarities are harnessed to their common denominator working towards a mutual goal. Individually, the horses are each very distinct in their own nature but function best in harmony with their equal-and-opposite partner. By harnessing the body's great passion and libido (dark horse looking backward) to the clarity of an awakening consciousness (white horse looking forward), the pair can influence each other's evolution over time. This is the sign of the yogi, the meditator, and the martial artist, exposing a duality that transcends the either/or paradigm.

The state the Chariot represents is more than the sum of the previous six Trumps. We now have a vehicle that responds to the witness in consciousness. Our charioteer has won the first level of Hermetic androgyny by bringing the physical body (original referent for the Cube of Space) into harmony, balancing its cosmic and terrestrial attributes around its astral center. In Trump 7 contending opposites no longer have power to take the driver off the chosen road (which was determined in Trump 6). The charioteer has outgrown the pose of victim of circumstances. Nevermore will she be pulled in one direction by intuition and in the other direction by reason or acculturation. Having yoked and directed both opposites onto the spiritual path, she is ready to claim the first evolutionary victory, that of self-mastery and self-unification.

Our female charioteer's armor signals her awakened left brain. The Medusa head on her shield suggests this dynamic lady is Athena, bearing gifts derived from the reasoning mind. This points us back to the Wisdom Tradition again, the cumulative inheritance of our literate ancestors. This Gemini Charioteer can be likened to Sophia in the Chariot of our ancestors. She aligns her goals to Divine Will, as signaled by the course of the planets overhead. The inner vision of her mind's eye directs her horses and keeps her wheels on the road. When this card is at its best, the planets, the body's energies, and the mind's eye are functioning as one.

Another quality that the Chariot card refers to is ambidexterity, a brain so well-balanced and cross-wired that either hand can be rallied for action at any time. So often in life we find ourselves building up with one hand and tearing down with the other, and it happens right under our own noses. Cross-coordination (of thought, at very least) is a signal accomplishment. Those who harbor internal inconsistencies can't get their ego, will, and spiritual vision focused on the same project at the same time. Society takes advantage of this unfortunate situation because humans make better herd animals when our internal balance is repeatedly upset. Those who wish to achieve higher than average levels of integration have to expand their capacities across the centerline and develop their weak side, however that might manifest. This is a vital aspect of the traditional symbol of androgyny.

The implications of having a feminine figure driving the Chariot reach into the astral plane and stimulate theological ideas. The Protestant Theosophers were all ardent spiritual feminists, self-chosen servants of the Holy Spirit. This Trump implies that the Chariot of the body is being cultivated by Sophia, the comforter or Paraclete. This suggests a life associated with the inner leadings of Spirit, instead of being guided by the more ego-bound aspect of the worldly personality. Seen from this point of view, even the acculturated ego is part of the body, being a product of the time-bound outer layer of matter that encases the soul. Whenever a Chariot card shows a feminine charioteer, we are to envision Sophia enthroned within the psyche of one who is blending Light and matter, ascending and descending forces. The Chariot archetype also points to an alchemical image called "The Triumphal Chariot of Antimony" (de Rolla, 1988, p. 227). The pictured Chariot is not a war-chariot, but a classic triumphal parade wagon studded with symbolic references. In Valentine's illustration two traditional planetary pairings (Mars and Venus, Saturn and Moon) collectively pull while Jupiter (with Thor's hammer tucked into his belt) holds the reins. Mercury and Antimony are the celebrated couple grasping each other's hands within a suspended hoop or ring. The ring is held aloft by the wreathed angel representing the Sun, hoisting a flaming torch. This image announces, "Let all who witness understand: With the spagyric preparation of Antimony, Paracelsus has achieved the homeopathic creation of chemical medicines." The male-androgyny of Mercury is hereby completed by the female-androgyny of Antimony as if to boost the Planetary Governors from the visible seven up to the gnostic Ogdoad.

Metallic Antimony is known as far back as 3000 BC in Chaldea and Egypt, but this word is most often found in connection with kohl, the ubiquitous eye-blackening cosmetic used in many civilizations since the most ancient times. Kohl is the oily smudge coagulated from the fumes of multiple medicinal substances that are combined and burned together under a brass bowl. The result was daubed around the eyes to protect against blindness, communicable diseases, the evil eye, and the intense brightness of the Sun. Meanwhile, mineral Antimony was considered by the alchemists to be a higher octave of mineral Mercury, more potent for healing purposes and closer to the "quintessence" (the most refined and complete form of matter). Yet this same ore has poisonous qualities that have caused its name to be translated in the popular etymologies as "monk-killer." Paracelsus became famous specifically because of his ability to tincture such venomous substances into healing remedies.

Valentinus relates that Antimony is produced in the course of an interaction among the Four Elements. Through a complex "Spiritual Sidereal Transmutation" (a day/night process), earthy water is evaporated and then precipitated (like dew or manna). As it ripens, the Antimony demonstrates attributes that bridge the gap between gold and Mercury. The alchemical terms for the threefold states of matter are Salt (hardness or fixity), Mercury (not the metal, but the style of manifestation that is mercurial, flowing, liquid), and Sulfur (heat, the "spark of life"). Valentinus' analysis of Antimony shows her to be on a continuum with gold and Mercury: having more Salt (hardness) than metallic Mercury, and more heat than metallic gold. The essence of this solidified vapor (kohl) safeguards physical vision and wards off the malevolent glances of others. I am certain that our Protestant Theosophical alchemists would consider Antimony a fit symbol for the gift of clairvoyance as well, characteristic of visionaries and those who possess "second sight." Antimony's symbol in Alchemy is a circle with a cross on top, the reversed Venus symbol. That makes it the two-dimensional equivalent of the orb of sovereignty in the hand of the Emperor. We can condense these ideas together to suggest the Chariot stands for the person with a cultivated and trained energy-body demonstrating all of its natural qualities and attributes.

Looked at from an exterior perspective, the Chariot appears to grant access to the larger world, providing mobility in the realms of culture, time, and space. But the cost to win these privileges is high; Sophia, rather than the

351

worldly ego, is put firmly in mastery. The Chariot symbolizes a personality that is no longer ruled by self-referenced motives. Instead it works to fulfill Spirit's directives, in particular the aspiration towards the most pure spiritual subjectivity, which is to say "not my will but Thine be done." By subduing worldly assertiveness and innate intelligence through submission to a Higher Power, all the self-serving fragments of the ego come under one master. What results is a synthesis of Spirit, human, animal, and machine, all working together to convey consciousness to the next higher plane. Receiving the Chariot card in a spread represents a graduation diploma for achieving the first grade of the initiate. And if this card should come up reversed, it's back to the drawing board to learn from your failures and engineer yourself into a more worthy Chariot. Remember, nothing ventured, nothing gained. While you still have a body, the path to self-mastery remains open before you.

Summary of the First Septenary

This concludes our tour of the first Great Arcanum of the Trumps, that of the personal sphere. The process of the first Septenary, spoken in Tarot terms, goes like this: The imagination (Magus) is a luminous seed of heavenly inspiration. As that soul quickens within the pristine consciousness of the Priestess (Sophia, Wisdom), the lovelight switches on inside the Empress (Venus), and her generative signal is sent out into matter. Meanwhile, the Emperor is building his castle according to the design that the Hierophant proposes in order to provide the best possible environment for the consummation of the Lovers. The result of this fortuitous multidimensional union is the Chariot, a living vehicle for the Magus's further explorations. This Chariot is the awakened human animal body, vehicle, and vessel piloted by Sophia.

It must be understood that all of the moving parts of this Septenary are provided by one's own personal qualities. In other words, this first set of Trumps interact to form your unique internal dialogue, motives, and beliefs. Every station of this Septenary is occupied by your own attributes and awareness. You are the Great Arcanum. And this is every day more true as you become more aware of the internal conversations going on between your various psychic "organs," which are themselves being moved and stirred by the moving planets overhead. We know this metaphorical language is meant to be taken literally, not just figuratively, because the Great Arcanum is derived from and anchored in the Kabbalah Tree, which is, after all, the Western chakra model. This model is by no means arbitrary but was instead put together with great sagacity as a guide to self-development and the Restitution of the soul.

To embark on the evolutionary program of the Trumps, this collection of ideas has to be integrated, organized, and set to work within the private life. Over time these interlocking energies will start to wear down any pre-set karmic blocks and build up one's capacity to function as a power-center. Remember that the planets/Sephirot (as defined on the Tree) correspond to organs and organ systems that fulfill the energy frequencies of each node in the Grand Arcanum. This model teaches that our daily experience and characteristics are all natural consequences of these seven functions. Attending to the smooth interaction of these centers over time is the primary occupation of the Magus. When the inner machine of selfhood is well-oiled and functioning efficiently, all of life is experienced in a more optimistic and compassionate light.

It is not an easy victory to achieve the integration of these first seven Trumps, but it can be managed within the will of a focused individual without having to depend too much upon the cooperation of external circumstances. Up to this point the seeker is cultivating the personal sphere. We take it as a given that all drives and desires that arise in the private psyche express the tension between the urges of the flesh and the urges of the Spirit. Now that we've seen that those things can be harmonized and are not necessarily mutually exclusive, the work for the seeker is to find the center where all those first six Major Arcana balance and harmonize with each other to produce the stance, attitude, and worldview of the Chariot.

A look at the inherent geometry of the Septenary will help us realize how many relationships are actually operative within the Star of David or Great Hexegram. The whole Tree of Life is structured on a honeycomb (sexugesimal) grid, which is the mathematical visualization used by the Babylonian astronomers of antiquity. To become aware of our participation in this ancient model, we open ourselves first to the descending "Moist Light" of Spirit, allowing the innate inheritance from our celestial Source to inform consciousness and awaken the seeds of consciousness within. As a result the fiery responsive Trine begins to fulminate, stirring the denser structures of our animal nature and ego-oriented personality in ways that shape our outer reality commensurate with the urgings of Spirit now active within.

Some of the Trump concepts may seem rarefied compared to our materialistic culture. Practice of the cultivated memory arts was more current in the Middle Ages, Renaissance, and Reformation than they are now. But if we can learn to identify those aspects of ourselves that correspond to the Trumps, we can make order in our personalities. This puts us on the path to acquiring the Chariot both as an astral signature in the aura and as a literal "self-conscious vehicle" to carry us through life. (And yes, for those who are aware of this concept, the Chariot in

Tarot makes a direct reference to the Merkabah of Hebrew mysticism.) We are invited to recognize ourselves in the various roles and activities of the first seven Trumps, to catch ourselves in the act, so to speak. Each Trump offers a platform or role model to help us organize our natural, inherent preconditioned essence. As we learn to discriminate among these Trumps individually, they will interlock and sync up with each other the same way we see them functioning in the Great Hexagram. This is the traditional formula for producing self-transformation in the spiritual quest as expressed through the Tarot.

There are two more such Septenaries yet to traverse before the world is attained. But in each case the formula is identical: $(3x2)+1$. From this we see that the thesis/antithesis/synthesis model has to happen twice, the first one in an expansive space-generating mode symbolized as a rain of Sophianic Light. The second triplicity manifests as a contracting, time-generating shift among the forms, symbolized by burning flames. The Light and the flames forge a new product, the multi-modal and multidimensional seventh term, which exists in Three Worlds. If one were to analogize the Great Hexagram as a human organ, as our Protestant Theosophers were prone to do, we could experience the two interpenetrating Trines as systole and diastole, the double-stroke beat of a balanced and healthy heart.

Naturally, there's a paradox to this seventh position, as well as the 14th and 21st positions which follow in their octaves. The moment one has attained a Septenary pinnacle, the response from Nature is to immediately unleash the next round of lessons. The second Septenary provides a whole new set of challenges that offer more stumbling blocks per Arcanum than this first set of seven. To this point we have worked on our inner lives, not yet looking outward to the widening circles of relationships, work, community, or world. Going forward into the second Septenary addresses the manifested universe at the level of human politics and cultural change, unleashing a broader spectrum of variables and factors that could seduce you off the path, steer you wrong, and set you back. The road ahead is a steeper uphill grade, but at least the individual is now prepared, spiritually and literally. Like a traditional yogi of any school, the student of Tarot takes responsibility for his or her spiritual and psychic constitution first and foremost.

Introduction to the Second Septenary

The orientation of the Tarot embraces a broad range of alchemical, astrological, and spiritual arts and sciences which teach us about the path of self-transformation and evolution. One could think of it as a flash-card system for teaching the yoga of Western civilization. The first seven Trumps encourage a holism that makes us more unified and coherent, less easily derailed into either/or thinking (male/female; love/hate; virtue/vice; right/wrong). Once that dilemma is stilled and reformed, we can turn our attention to the outer world where human institutions and collective experiences dominate. At this new level we learn to sublimate our personal instincts and preferences in order to fully participate in the development of culture and human relations.

Examined within the structure of the Great Arcanum, this second Septenary of Trumps continues the dialectic of thesis/antithesis/synthesis in each of the two triangles. First we see the enlightening impulses of Spirit raining down "from above" through Trumps 8, 9, and 10 (Justice, Hermit, Wheel of Fortune). Then we see the heated pulse of consolidating matter rising up in response through Trumps 11, 12, and 13 (Strength, Hanged Man, and Death). Finally these balanced opposites interlock to create the Temperance icon, which is the sign and seal of the second Septenary.

8 Justice

Letter: H (Chet) = Cancer
Path: Between Binah and Tiferet
Quality: House of Ancestors

Trump 8 Justice shows the principle of analysis, that piercing vision which cuts to the heart of things. She weighs and measures all the parts of the process until the balance-point is revealed. This is Sophia as a figure of Law, Torah, Nomos. In this form she is the possessor of shrewdness in statecraft and the scribal profession. She is also the symbol of intellectual Light, the "Mistress of Science." She embodies the canon of weights and measures.

The Justice card is the first step out of the inward focus of self-cultivation, which makes internal resources available to society and fosters the transformation of consciousness at a collective level. We are immediately confronted with a symbol of the law, both natural and human-made. Core concepts associated with Justice are balance, equilibrium, fair measure, and the challenge of being weighed against collective norms. Justice adjudicates the commonweal in the collective assembly, ensuring the sustainability of the culture despite the tendency of individuals to take advantage or tilt the playing field.

We tend to be familiar with the image of blind justice with scales in one hand and the sword of truth in the other. This is the classic posture of the Greek goddess Themis. Hers is the ancient justice principle that theoretically sorts out human relations in the cultural marketplace, the realm of trading and social exchanges. I emphasize this point because in our materialistic society we have lost track of the greater good, tending instead to look for opportunities to take advantage rather than opportunities to further the well-being of the whole. The modern lust for profit is part of the cultural myth of manifest destiny and marketplace determinism. But these values are not suitable for human relations or spiritual development. So the feminine Divine must unsheathe the two-edged sword of truth and prune away all hyperbole, dissembling, and excuses. This Justice will measure every corner by those exacting standards of impartiality and equity by which she measures herself. Each person who comes before her in the community court will have their "story" examined for every shred of accountability. In this sense Aleister Crowley was inspired when he changed the traditional name of this Trump to Adjustment for his personal Tarot.

Our Justice is of the type to speak truthfully to the needs of the innocent, the helpless, all those who have no individual voice and who therefore cannot defend themselves. Tending to the welfare of the least among us is one of the highest ideals of the Rosicrucian movement, but humanity is still struggling to find the best ways of realizing that dream in practice. To fill in the gap, Major Arcanum 8 offers the image of the wise and disciplined mother who is at pains to balance out the needs of her individual family members while still advancing the general well-being of the whole. She knows how to make all of the products of wild Nature into food, comfort, and remedies. Rather than living in an either/or universe of "bad and good," Justice figures out what is useful and appropriate about every circumstance she examines. She understands the constant recombination of the four-season, four-Element wheel of changes, and from this format she is able to anticipate and provide for the needs of her people as they arise. Justice also knows how to distribute the goods of the family (or of society) equitably, ensuring that the largest number of her subjects get the benefits, instead of the most powerful few commandeering all the resources.

Another very powerful image of Justice is seldom seen in modern packs. In this version we see Solomon ready to resolve a problem that would vex a lesser man. A case is presented at his court by two neighboring women, each of whom has recently given birth. Sadly, on this day one mother woke up to a dead baby. But instead of accepting that her infant was gone, this woman accused her neighbor of slipping a corpse into her bed and stealing her live infant. How could the true mother of the living child prove that it was hers? Solomon knew that one of the mothers was lying, so his proposal was to cut the live baby in half and give each mother half. The real mother was horrified and protested, "Give the child to my neighbor. It will break my heart, but at least then I'll get to see him grow up." On the other hand, the mother of the dead baby said "Yes, cut it in half, at least then we'll both be even." It might sound savage and arbitrary for Solomon to make a judgment like his; we have to remember that the event happened millennia ago in a culture very different from our own. But we can see the wisdom required to find the perfect strategy that would reveal the motives of each mother, exposing which woman showed the maturity to properly value this new life. This illustrates a poignant challenge that constantly faces the Justice card: to ignore the sway of appearances or established convention but fearlessly test appearances until they reveal their true underpinnings.

Further, since it is the four-Elements, four-seasons grid (the Elemental Dignities) that is at the basis of all alchemical cures, the Justice principle is intimately involved in the year-round work of creating and administering energetic medicines. We see her here, weighing out the balance between Fire and Water, or any two opposites that we might find in the world, as a precursor to making the medicine in the course of this second Septenary (which culminates in Temperance, the alchemist). At this stage Justice (adjustment) assays all the ingredients meant for the alchemical (social, spiritual) medicine and ensures the purity of each ingredient separately. Holding the finished recipe in mind from the earliest steps in the process, Justice deconstructs the formula, weighs out the newly-purified ingredients, and hones her own sensitivity to the subtleties of each step in the process. All through the work, she holds herself back from making judgments based on preference or popularity, opinion or reputation. She is single-mindedly interested in discovering what works, what will truly and sustainably serve the need.

In her fine-tuned precision and attention to detail, Justice represents a traditional feminine gift that is being rediscovered in the 21st century. This generally-feminine icon defends as well as administers. Her keen blade and exacting scales will not allow counterfeits or impurities to enter her aura unchallenged. Nor will she be tempted or swayed by an over- romantic fantasizing of Nature. This wise mother has truly "been there and back," qualifying her as a keen judge of character. Her Cancer influence gives her the dauntless heart and spiritual passion of all mothers. Justice fights for the Creation as a whole, even when this involves disciplining her individual creatures.

Another aspect of Justice is that she's administering the karma of the community; her fearless accountability reveals who has to accept limitation versus who gets that extra helping. In this way Justice is adjudicating the social and economic flow as it plays out through the community's transactions. Justice sets the standards, then holds her subjects to the letter of the law. Individuals can forget that there are spiritual principles that demand our participation, but Justice always remembers and exacts her due. It is the Justice principle that fosters us when we give freely and take only at need. This same Justice undermines us when we attempt to dissemble, make excuses for our greed, and do things in the margins that we wouldn't want shown in the light of day. Without intending to be punitive, Justice is an enforcer: She sees to it that those individuals who want to grant themselves shortcuts or misrepresent their needs or help themselves when they haven't yet contributed their share will eventually be corrected in an appropriate way for their development and growth. Nor is Justice dramatic or theatrical; her style is to support the inevitability of natural consequences. Ultimately Justice gives us the motivation to adjust our stance to the needs of society rather than demand that society adjust to us.

PHILOSOPHIÆ
SVLPHVR
FEVER.
ERDT.
VIRTVTES.
ANTIMONIVM.
WISMATT

In the second Septenary we're moving away from internal work and towards work in the world at large. A prerequisite for earning the right to affect other people's lives is our willingness to consider their feelings and their reality as being of equal magnitude and importance as our own. We can't move on until we learn the lesson of Justice, which is to put ourselves in the shoes of everyone whose lives our decisions might impact. This Trump and the next two comprise the radiantly active Trine of Light in the second Septenary. This trinity represents formative forces working invisibly to channel and adjust the world of matter from the celestial plane. Justice lays down the law, thereby creating the context in which the Hermit will cultivate himself in service to the greater good.

Justice reversed displays the same characteristics as it does upright, only less mercifully and more implacably. The concept of blind justice means that no attempt to curry favor or claim special privilege will avail at the time of this fierce accounting. Both our internal motivatiuons and our ultimate actions will come under rigorous scrutiny, publically revealed in the bright light of the collective judgement. In the course of this exposure, those whose values are self-centered or in some manner exclusivist will likely find themselves deprived of the compassion and understanding they crave in their time of need. The Justice avatar's relationship to karma is mirrored in her commitment to natural consequlences: We will all eventually wind up eating our words and sulffering the treatment we have meted out to others. Her sword, raised and ready to cleave reminds us not to attempt to tip the scales or fudge our testimony. For the sake of the good of the whole, Jusice has no compunction about correcting the community's errant members. In this Trump we see the natural foundation for all bodies of law, including the customary punishments for antisocial tendencies. Her reversed presence reminds that we can do whatever we want, but there will be no evading the consequences of our choices.

9 The Hermit

Letter: T = Leo
Path: Between Tiferet and Chesed
Quality: House of Descendants

The Hermit, the possessor of gnosis, not only has the Light, but is a Light and guide for others. This natural shaman is a self-initiated Priest of the Order of Melchizedek. Having abandoned all false paths, the Hermit lives intimately with Nature and Sophia. Hence this Trump points to the aspect of Sophia that makes her teachings available at the gateways and the crossroads, calling out from the ramparts of the city and appearing in the liminal places "between the worlds." This is Hecate, Trivia, her shrine placed at the meeting point of the Three Worlds or three paths guarding the place of their linkage. The Hermit highlights Sophia's link with prophets and diviners, whose calling it is to interpret the oracles.

Trump 9 represents the second (antithesis) point in the Light triangle, following mastery of the first Septenary. While Justice stands in the marketplace accessible to all, the Hermit occupies a location accessible only to the intrepid. Historical allusions to the Hermit's identity have ranged far and wide: the planet Saturn, the angel Melancholia, the philosopher Diogenes, St. Francis of Assisi, Father Time, the agricultural god Kronos, one of the Desert Fathers, or as here, the mythical Hermes Trismigistus. His title means "thrice born," implying true continuity of consciousness maintained across multiple lifetimes. This Hermit has found the key to humanity's eternal potential and has shaped his life accordingly. He is an accomplished yogi, a devoted eros magician, and a dedicated life-extension strategist, having achieved functional immortality without having to drop his body, a coveted accomplishment.

The apparent maturity of the Hermit is as much a symbol as it is a state. At any age the Hermit arranges daily life to avoid unnecessary worldly demands so as to protect the privacy necessary to maintain a deep immersion in Nature. Having left cultural time, he is participating in worlds that operate by laws of being instead of becoming. Though shown with his feet encircled by the terrestrial leviathan (water serpent of material time), our Hermit has realized that his only connection to Eternity is his consciously-directed imagination. A life of self-discipline imbues the environment with a preternatural calm and lucidity. The traditional lamp in his hand has become a mini-sun with which to banish the spiritual darkness of the reflexive reptile brain. The pontifical shepherd's crook is not only there to support this wise elder, but also to serve as a magical wand, fixing and subduing the restless leviathan at his feet. The entire landscape is in communion with the Hermit's point of focus, which is to still the fearful fight-or-flight reflexes and thereby release consciousness to its higher destiny.

Overhead the Hermit's inner practice is laid bare. Knowing that consciousness exists both within and outside the body, the Hermit seeks experiences that exceed the coarse material senses. The higher mind's all-seeing eye blazes through the cosmos, following the lead of the Holy Spirit. The whole operation is protected and guarded by the cosmic mate of the earthy leviathan. This cosmic serpent, the Teli or pole Serpent that circles around the balance-point of Heaven, organizes the eternal Light that forever emanates from the invisible higher world. These two serpents demonstrate the Hermit's control over his electro-magnetic presence, both in the Time/Space world and beyond it. This opening in the fabric of Time/Space is mediated by a sub-sonic harmonic hum emanating from the Hermit's throat (a reference to Daat, the salvation of those who struggle in the Fallen Tree of the Kabbalah). This tuning device helps strengthen the vibrational platform that allows the Hermit to expand his temporal consciousness past the ring-pass-not into Eternity.

Our Hermit exemplifies the natural royalty of the individuated human soul, one who has outgrown every role that culture defines. A person in this role is no longer beholden to parents, spouse, family, commerce, culture, or legacy for a sense of identity. Self-motivated and self-created, this Hermit demonstrates the attributes and attitudes of Leo, the Fixed Fire sign that is the natural home of the Sun. The Hermit is alone in a magical landscape much of the time, following inner Lights, not answering to outside sources. Having long ago solved the problem of survival, the Hermit lives entirely on personal terms, as if high on the holy mountain. For the Hermit the superficials of cultural reality become insubstantial and fade away. S/he has moved from clock-time to natural time, from sophistication to simplicity, and from a declining stage of life to ageless immortality. Staying true to inner currents, the Hermit takes refuge in an austere-seeming lifestyle that opens into the vast richness of the inner life. When you see a Hermit card dressed in the "plain brown wrapper" standard monk's robes, this is the implication.

Notice the obvious link between philosophical Hermeticism, the myth of Hermes Trismegistus, and the Hermit. Hermes is the Greek god of intelligence and Mercury is his Roman form. He is the master of communication and crafty

363

solutions whose gift with languages facilitates all forms of exchange, especially across cultural boundaries. Hermes was considered to be the inventor of numbers and letters, therefore the denominator of the Hermetic Cosmos with its 12/7/3 pattern (mirrored in the alphabet and the Trumps). Hermes' traditional presentation with an astrolabe in one hand and the other hand pointing to Earth ("as above so below") is meant to remind us of his ability to navigate around both macrocosmos and microcosmos.

This portrayal of Hermes in oriental robes and tall, squash-shaped headgear teaching Astrology and the Alchemy of long life represents a standard visual trope for Trismigistus by the late 1400s and early 1500s. Due to his reputed sagacity, Trismegistus came to symbolize the emergent observational method of science. Following this approach (first employed by Paracelsus), one studies phenomena objectively (without preconceptions) and tabulates natural developments without interfering. The idea is to learn the norms before attempting to address deviations. This is where the Hermit acquires the more modern implication of silent witness: the canny observer who can fathom the subtleties of a situation without directly entering into it.

Our Hermit has collected such a wide range of exposures and experiences that s/he only has to look within to accurately diagnose the dilemmas that arise in the environment. For some this level of insight appears to operate by magic. For this reason the Hermit archetype arouses suspicion in the Roman Church, creating situations in which the solitary individual could become a distrusted and suspect figure. The city-based clergy understood that if the people were getting their needs for healing and spiritual guidance met by a charismatic local figure like a village shaman, they would not turn to priests and deacons. An even greater threat was that the people might encounter the gnostic heresy of reincarnation. How could a stark Heaven-or-Hell confrontation staged during a single short lifetime ever compete with the idea of multiple incarnations? Trismegistus gave Europe a new kind of cultural hero, an ordinary human (or so they thought) who could penetrate so far into the Divine Mind as to recover knowledge stored in the world soul from previous lives. To the mystics after Paracelsus caught up in a Rosicrucian fervor, Hermes Trismegistus offered an alternate model for spiritual growth.

Among the alchemical illustrations, one can see the Hermit conversing with the Serpent of Genesis, even following it through the landscape. This is a reminder that one is to look beyond the human world for models of creative evolution. Through befriending and studying humanity's old adversary, the Hermit learns those wise secrets that Nature holds. The serpent at the Hermit's feet handily symbolizes our collective not-quite-tamed human instincts. When this card is reversed, it represents a constant undertow, buffeting human civilization with sub-conscious and regressive pressure, ready to drag us down into fears and phobias whenever we are stressed. The upright Hermit can separate himself from the grip of the hive mind, can distill his consciousness out of the collective trance of self-absorbed subjectivity. By learning from Mother Nature how the whole ecology is interwoven, the Hermit acquires perspective on humanity as a species and comes to understand our intergenerational planetary destiny.

The Hermit studies the strategies that the Divine Intelligence apportioned among the plants and animals to create their unique technologies for life. Modern humanity desperately needs this wisdom. Like Aesop, Pythagoras, and Paracelsus, our Hermit extracts remedies from the living thoughts of Nature. The highest discoveries are made by taking the position of the fly on the wall, witnessing the mind of God at play. From this vantage point the Hermit has access to all Three Worlds: manifest Nature here on Mother Earth with all of her themes and variations; human nature as it is revealed in the psychological and socio-cultural world; and finally, celestial Nature, meaning the astronomical developments continuously descending from on high.

10 The Wheel of Fortune

Letter: Yud (I/J) = Virgo
Path: Between Tiferet and Gevurah
Quality: House of Health

In the Wheel of Fortune, we have a representation of the circular and cyclical metabolism of Time as a bubble within Eternity. Fast or slow, the Wheel never stops and it never retraces its steps, despite rhythmic fractal reflections. Creation is forever carried along via the Wheel's interlocking cycles, though at the macrocosmic level nothing ever changes. In Sophiology this is God's providence or Pronoia, the gift of seeing forward through time, understanding the cyclic dynamics that mediate the outworking of the macrocosmic ideal. Pronoia refers to God's "providential koine" expressed as heavenly governance through what may at the moment seem to be chaos.

After the Justice card presents the thesis in the Light Trine, and the Hermit card gives the antithesis, we move to the Wheel of Fortune, representing the synthesis of this radiant triangle of Light. The Wheel of Fortune evokes the law of karma, which simply stated means that "reality is round." Whatever we put out there will eventually come back to us, bringing its consequences along as well. One cannot escape one's widening wake, and there is no relief for the repetitious nature of daily life. Each one of us is married to our unique daily track, whether the personal sphere is tiny or huge. The nervous system plays its tape-loops over and over again. One must eat, sleep, wash, and make order, and every day it's all to be tackled anew. Some find this repetitiveness comforting and safe; some find it appalling to the point of rebellion and even self-harm. All who exist within a human body are subject to the mill-wheel of time, which, as has been said, grinds slow and exceedingly fine. The pre-Christian world called this cosmic mechanism Heimarmene, the personification of fate.

The historical Wheel of Fortune is a very sophisticated image in that it combines a number of allusions in its details. Sometimes at the bottom of the picture we see a small and fragile moon-shaped boat bearing a giant Wheel in the place of sails. This little craft floats upon the turbulent ocean of the subconscious, reminding us how dependent fate is on accident and synchronicity. Sometimes a wheel of eight spokes recalls the Wheel of the Year or the compass-rose of the mapmakers and navigators. Other times the wheel shows only six spokes, which references the Great Arcanum of the Hebrews. On the left you see the descending path of those who are abandoning Eternity to come into materialization and incarnation. On the right side ascends the avatar of those who are evolving beyond the merely human, whose aim is to return to their point of origin in the invisible. This is the mythic World Mill, the wheel of Time/Space that brings us into these bodies for our personal schooling and the evolution of our inner life. As each of us dives onto matter, we become that reptile creature of the descending side, avidly embracing sensation, ego, and entrapment in matter. This path of descent is seen in spiritual teachings as a Fall of sorts: from the purity of immortal life into this dense flesh that is locked and limited to temporally and hormonally dominated modes of thought.

The soul that chooses to follow the path of return, longing to extract itself from the terrestrial bog, is symbolized by that ambiguously gendered human-headed creature climbing the right side of the Wheel. This illustrates the effort needed to move out of entrapment in the flesh towards the higher self and away from the realm of attachments and addictions. At the top of the Wheel, we see an alchemical hybrid (sometimes a phoenix), which in this case is a blend of an angelic human, a lion, and an eagle. This creature suggests the fused Fire/Air/Water intelligence that defines our fulfilled being according to the three Mother Letters, the three modes of astro-Alchemy, and the Trinity of Jehova/Christ/Sophia according to Boehme and his followers.

The sideways 8 (lemniscate) on the Wheel refers to the greater whole, consisting of the visible and invisible worlds intertwined. This twisted circle describes the two sides of reality, the known and the ever-unknowable. These Compliments feed into each other, providing an early visualization of a perpetual-motion machine. Their relationship expresses a dynamic rather than a static exchange. In a static polarity you have two things that withdraw from each other because they're so opposite as to be mutually exclusive. But in a dynamic polarity you have two halves that catalyze and attract each other as they chase each other around the circle (like the Taoist Great Ultimate, the yin/yang symbol). The lemniscate also testifies that the visible is the mirror of the invisible, an essential insight. As J. E. Circlot reminds us in the excellent *A Dictionary of Symbols,* "The ouroboros biting its own tail is symbolic of self-fecundation, or the primitive idea of a self-sufficient Nature - a Nature... which...continually returns, within a cyclic pattern, to its own beginning" (p. 235).

At its simplest level the Wheel signifies Nature embracing all of us in the cycles of life, that of the Moon or the seasons of the year. Everybody reading this is caught up in the karma of our planet Earth and the material world. In order to succeed and thrive, we need to stop fighting our relationship to this Creation, symbolized by the four Suits/Elements. This card challenges us to start cooperating with the energies that comprise our substrate, including the autonomic processes that are built into our bodies and our psyches. This means getting to know our birth charts and the movements of the planets and Lights overhead. Without this essential knowledge, we will continue to be caught by surprise and cast down by the Wheel of Fortune, subject to excess ups and downs that waste our energy and break up the continuity of our spiritual cultivation.

The Wheel is a tester, challenging us to see ourselves in context and surrender to those forces that are larger than ourselves. We must learn to trust that all immediate manifestations are temporary and natural; they are each flowing one after the other according to the larger cycles of Nature. The Wheel suggests that we integrate ourselves with the flow and go with it instead of fighting it. We do not have to experience ourselves as being mowed down and run over by the process of Time. Instead we can learn to roll with the Wheel, learn to work with the tenor of the seasons and the planets in the sky.

The basic premise of Alchemy is that we are made of sensitive material which is responsive to the cosmic clock and the movement of the planets in their great procession around the Sun. The Wheel says that once we understand our place in the larger mosaic of Time and Space and find that channel of flow that governs our destiny, we can then ride the Wheel, become the sphinx, and skip being beat up by the ins and outs of impersonal fate. This includes those challenges over which we will never gain complete control. When this understanding is achieved, you wear the crown of gnosis, are lifted by the wings of angels, and your individuation is "Fixed" for Eternity (the Lion's head). The two hands hold the sign of the lily, or fleur de lis, which Boehme took as a symbol of the coming age of the Holy Spirit, come to quell the turbulence of the human ego. This is the gift available to those who make the effort to still their own churning and find their balance. Esoteric study teaches that we can be intentional about where we fit on the Wheel of Time. The more equilibrium we can manifest, the more we can allow the flow of Nature's plan to move through us and carry us along.

For people who are still learning the lesson of the Wheel, this dizzying churning expresses our day-to-day adventures here in the human world. One could think of it as the great washing machine of life: You get thrown in, tossed around up and down, put through your changes, and are finally spun dry. By the end you've had the opportunity to see what sort of substance you're made of, what the real fabric of your being is. Those few who are organized to flow within Nature's cycles, who understand the workings of the planets and

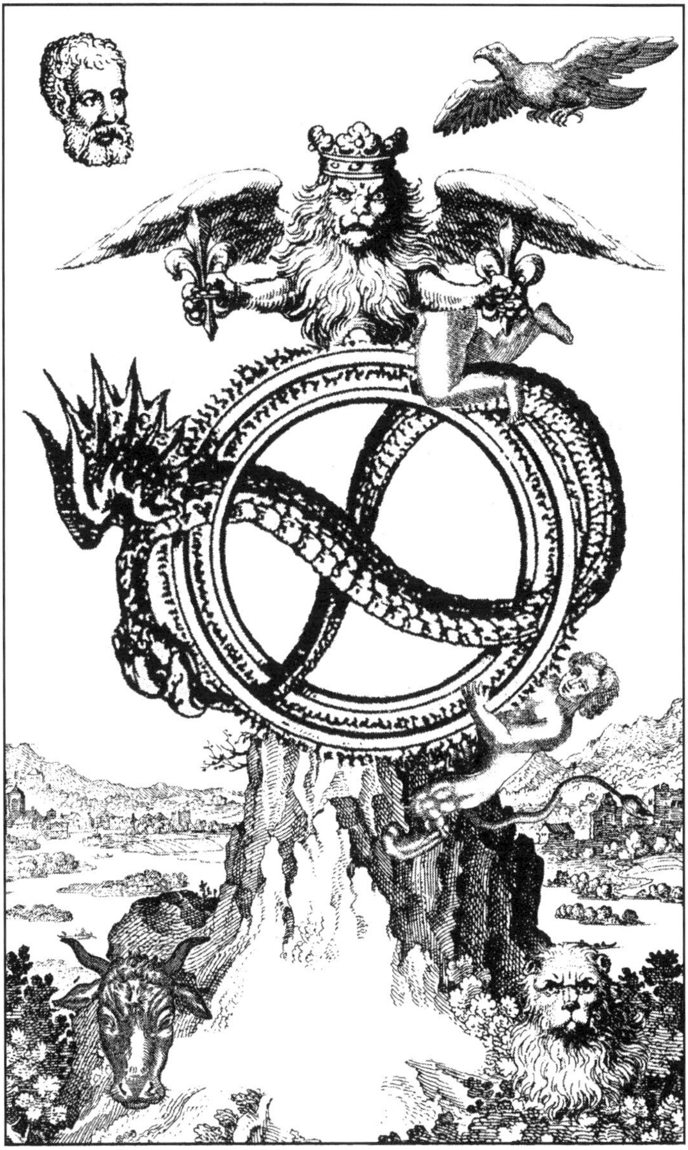

Elements in the Zodiac, can identify with the sphinx and not be distressed by all the changes that happen in a seemingly chaotic fashion. The truth is most of us are still overfocused on the reversed qualities of the Wheel, bemoaning the fragility of our point-of-perspective as we struggle to navigate the choppy waters of the subconscious. Completing the Light Trine requires learning to wield Justice from our active side while holding the wisdom of the Hermit (that inner insight of the Serpent) close to the heart on the responsive side. Only then with those forces in place can one finally learn to balance within the Wheel's cycles, cultivating a resonant integrity that will endure through the changes, adjust with Nature, and partner with the flow that has us all in its grip.

11 Strength

Letter: Kaf = Mars
Path: Between Chesed and Netzach
Quality: Life, vitality

The Strength card channels the immutable strength and relentlessness of wild Nature, which is only ever temporarily tamed. The power that allows us to live and thrive can also recycle us at a moment's notice. The only control we truly possess is self-control, which needs constant renewal through fresh acts of self-discipline. In Sophianic terms this is the taming and refining power of Love working through Wisdom to harmonize Creation and organize the animal, vegetable, and mineral world for humanity's sake. Here we see Harmozousa, the universal technician who arranges or structures things, putting them together in the appropriate manner and seeing to it that they maintain mutually-supportive relations.

Some might be surprised to find a feminine face upon a card representing Mars, but this is absolutely not an anomaly. In another variant of the Continental family packs, the branch emanating from Spanish esoteric currents, one can see Mars attached to the Empress card, leaving Venus to occupy the Strength icon.

As a rule gender images within the sequence of the Trumps are not to be interpreted in a physiological manner as if these forces were actually burdened with inflexible either/or limits. The ancient Hebrews who developed the alphabet as an astronomical and astrological tool didn't suffer from the same gender expectations that we moderns do. It was common to find the women in charge of running the household dealing with practical issues like food, children, livestock, and the domestic economy. Masculine preoccupations (beyond survival tasks) were focused on studying scripture, embracing mystical explorations along the lines of yoga and/or meditation, and writing extensive scholarly commentaries on the ancient teachings. The basic construct by which the Kabbalah Tree emerges from its invisible Source is that the Father force of expansive Space (Fire) pours out and emanates into matter, which precipitates the condensing force of Time (Water) in the Mother as a response. On the Tree, Mars is the middle Sephira on the descending Pillar corresponding to the right hand in the body. This is the point in the materialization process at which an empowered individual begins to gain some personal capability, some sense of traction and leverage for implementing one's will. One could explain the attribution of dominance to this Trump by realizing that the Strength icon represents the intention to prevail, irrespective of the momentary goal.

Having completed the Light Trine of celestial motivation, we now enter into the Fire Trine of emotional and intuitive responsiveness. This triangle registers the descending forces of the previous three Trumps as they impact upon matter, which in response starts to seethe and give birth to new forms engendered by the Light. The first term of our "dark Fire" Trine is Trump 11, called Strength or Force. This Trump has a revolutionary implication, which is summed up in the phrase "entering into the Wrath-Fire unafraid." Unlike the Fool, who stumbles into his situation unpremeditated, the Strength icon shows us the courage and fearlessness that comes from engaging with one's challenges head-on, openhearted, and ready to respond with full energy. Such is the virtue of feminine force that her passionate suasion empowers the most noble and radical of our Divine Elements.

When this representative of Spirit appears, the usual clanging chaos among the Elements subsides. For love of her, the unregenerate instincts of Nature feel moved to conform themselves to a higher power, of which this lady is the representative. Even the king of beasts cannot resist this prodigy of nonverbal engagement. The persuasiveness of this expression of Martian vitality is fulfilled perfectly by Mulder's amazing image:

> The hair of Lady Alchimia is Fire. Her eyes are Sun and Moon, the twin Principles - Mercury and Sulphur - of the Work. Her breath is Air and the influx carried in the shape of rays by light. The three Stars on her forehead are the three Works, and the milk flowing from her generous breasts is Lac Virginis, the Virgin's Milk which nourishes the Stone... (de Rola, p. 307).

In the esoteric system that connected with the Marseille-style Tarots, the Strength angel embodies the most attractive, constructive, and creative aspects of the planet Mars. Nevertheless, this Lady Alchimia is a fully ambiguous figure, somewhat monstrous upon close inspection. Her deviations are also apt: As a symbol of ambition, drive, desire, aggression, and the appetites, Mars is not above the occasional confrontation or conflict demanded in order to win the fulfillment of our visions and desires. In this context the lion symbolizes the restrained yet still feral side of the Martian force. The humanesque figure in this Trump (which is most often shown as feminine, sometimes androgynous, very occasionally masculine) is with no apparent effort stilling the fierceness of this

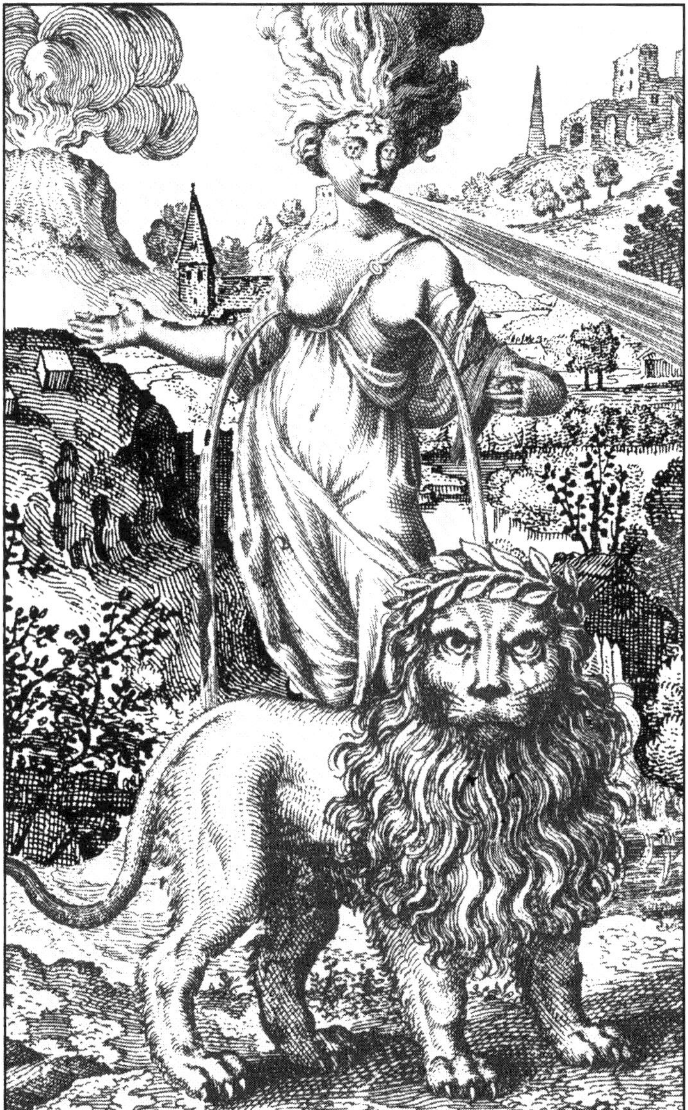

lion and silently encouraging it to take a protective but not aggressive stance. Despite the title Force, this is clearly not the strength of muscles and brawn (although we do occasionally see the image of Hercules or Samson as Strength in some older Tarots as discussed below).

According to historical usage, this card represents a spiritual force. It's a strength of heart, a strength of principles, of inner conviction and integrity in relationship with the Spirit world. The Strength angel knows that nothing in this material world is going to hurt her or him. She comes forward as a sibling to all of Creation with no known enemies. Revealed to be a servant of the collective need, the only goal is to bring harmony and respect among the different life forms and among the Elements going into the alchemical cauldron. In this case this extraordinary goddess is telepathically communicating with the lion to still the passionate ego-bound temperament. She's transmitting that there is no need for the adversarial paradigm; we are all equal parts of the Divine Intelligence that Nature has woven together like a web, each designed to support the other. There is no "us versus them" in the planetary mind; it is therefore our responsibility to recognize our kinship and relatedness and to cease engaging with ideas that cause us to take adversarial stances against each other.

The goal is to let go of personal interest or human acculturation at this point in order to defend and befriend Creation in a guileless and openhearted way. This feminine form of Strength is motivated by compassion, acting from empathy and sensitivity. A feminine Strength also accepts the special case instead of defaulting to averages (which are therefore insufficient in every case). The Strength angel asserts, "We are brother and sister. There is no contest. We have no reason to fight or squabble with each other. Our responsibility right now is to acknowledge our kinship, to solve mutual problems, and to expand the field of our understanding so it includes the whole web of life." All this is done, let it be noted, without words or "reason" with its confounding overlay of rationalizations and excuses. Strength communicates nonverbally but is never misunderstood. Her assertive aura does all the talking.

A deck that shows the Hercules or Samson image offers a flip side to the refining power of Lady Alchemy. Historically the male hero's strength exists to wrestle his people away from their animalistic instincts, to conquer the beast within. Self-control is the primary focus in case of a deck that makes a masculine reference with the emphasis on struggle and overcoming resistance. This is certainly an important part of the Strength card, pointed towards overcoming internal resistance to personal growth and maturation. But when we see it with a feminine or angelic actor, emphasis falls on the use of non-violent, voluntary, and loving means to corral and refine (rather than crush and dominate) the wilder impulses. Persuasion and the power of attraction provide more trustworthy motivation for the lion (ego) to come into alignment with the angelic program. This form of Strength employs personal charisma, moral force, and social conditioning to uphold right action in situations when no laws, rhetoric, or luck can be enforced. Mutual agreement asserts an invisible constraint that guides behavior even in circumstances when impulse would otherwise rule.

The key to the Strength arcanum reversed is an exaggeration of "the intention to prevail." We have all been in circumstances where conflict between potential leaders steals away the energy that was gathered to accomplish a worthy goal. We have also known individuals whose motives and ideas might be fine but their methods are too forceful and aggressive to attract cooperation from others. People who haven't put enough thought into their passionate positions often discover the hard way how unwilling their friends and loved ones are to follow through unprotestingly. Those who actually push their personal agenda all the way to compelling obedience through intimidation usually produce longstanding resentments and eventual rejection. Wisdom enjoins us to temper our forcefulness with sensitivity to others if we are ever going to find our allies and create circumstances that are conducive to collective progress.

One might also associate the reversed Strength card to the retrograde manifestation of Mars, which occurs every other year for a few months. This seems to cause a radial deflation of everybody's will power for the duration of the retrograde period. Forward progress comes at such a high price that most enterprises end up circling and dog-paddling until the transit resolves. If this card comes up reversed, it might be pointing to an ennervated state of exhaustion that is undermining the usual and expected daily dose of productive energy. This is the corollary of the phrase "Where there is a will, there's a way." In this case the reciprocal is "No will? No way!"

12 The Hanged Man

Letter: Lamed = Libra
Path: Between Chesed and Yesod
Quality: House of Coition

The Hanged Man is upended, suspended, and undefended, a willing sacrifice to the principle of non-resistance. With hands, arms, and heart open, the soul enters into the problem, embraces the opposites, and quenches their contrariety. In the ancient Hymn of the Pearl, this is the prince who must redeem himself before he can recapture the pearl and return to the world of Light; this is also the Christ/Sophia, both of whom self-sacrificially descend to the lowest level of Creation to harvest the Fallen and dormant soul-sparks before making the turn-around to begin the ascent again. In Tarot, Trump 12 symbolizes Metanoia, the spiritual turn-around point, which marks the end of the Fall and the beginning of the upward path.

The second, antithetical term of our responsive Fire Trine presents Trump 12, the card of the martyr. This idea evokes many cruel and horrific associations because of the layers of pagan, gnostic, and Judeo-Christian spiritual politics that have become attached to it. In its purest form, however, the Hanged Man represents an initiatory exercise, a personal sacrifice undertaken by an individual at a certain level of spiritual development. In this Trump the commitment is supreme: It will be an ordeal and there is no way to avoid the bodily and/or psychological agony involved. Through the extremity of the ordeal, the aspirants are driven out of their ordinary perspective of reality, which transforms the entire body of socio-cultural programming, turning their worldview upside down and inside-out. The Hanged Man views the world through the inner or Third Eye from this awkward and helpless position.

This Trump doesn't always involve torture and martyrdom by any means, although that aspect is sometimes present. Better to see Trump 12 as the talisman of a voluntary awakening that involves upending one's perspective by putting the consciousness of the crown chakra at the feet and putting the consciousness of the root chakra at the crown. This is the idea of the Shaman's Tree from deep antiquity, which has always served as a vehicle for moving between the worlds.

Part of the value of this type of experience is that we must face the fact that communion with Spirit demands a sacrifice. Some of your personal comfort, trust, and feeling of safety will be sweated out in the process of having this experience. Now that one has passed the previous Trump's test by overcoming fears of the outer world, the next challenge emerges. The reciprocal fear of certain upsetting and unbalancing internal experiences is now under examination. This means overcoming the aversion to being shamed or made to look bad in the collective judgment. It means overcoming the fear of revealing any personal emotions that might pour out while upended and suspended. It means overcoming the fear of pain or debility, as well as any fear or dread around the inevitable loss. This Trump counsels a total willingness to endure whatever it takes to serve the group good. Remember, the second Septenary addresses the collective consciousness, and this triangle within the Septenary relates to Earth's response to a wave of incoming Light. Therefore, this Trump exemplifies the willing sacrifice of matter to Spirit, the turned cheek and the soft answer, poured out into the Wrath to still its restlessness. In the process the seeker becomes a contributing member of a corps of self-evolving individuals who collectively devote themselves to raising the consciousness of humanity.

Selflessness is the watchword here, doing the right thing just because it's the right thing to do. The Hanged Man lets go of personal interests and devotes his vitality and energies to the causes that the Universe will dictate. If he's got his attitudes straight, he is willing to go through the process of relinquishment or even humiliation to advance the cause for the larger whole. Generally speaking, one cannot fight the role even though it means hanging on the martyr's tree and letting the grapes of Wrath be distilled within your character. Often times these situations utterly transcend what is "fair" or "deserved" from the individual point of view. What the person who is hanging has to remember is that they are atoning for collective sins, and only when the mass guilt is expiated will they be taken down from their cross. Each one of us will be called to take our place on the hanging tree over the course of a lifetime, so there is no shame in being recruited for this role. If you participate in this world, you will find yourself hanging on this tree at some point; it is simply inevitable.

What the icon represents is the individual who is willing to leap into the breach to highlight a matter of principle, which in the process awakens the collective consciousness. It doesn't matter that this action undermines the individual good in the sense of security, health, or physical safety. From the point of view of reincarnation, all sacrifice is temporary. That's what makes this sacrifice voluntary; the soul understands that it isn't a waste but an honor to use one's incarnation in defense of a principle. When the sacrifice is timed appropriately according to the need of the situation, it can make all the difference to the cause going forward. The martyr doesn't have to outlive the revolution; he's not angling to become a bureaucrat or politician. The Hanged Man's significance and his impact stem from his willingness to put his flesh on the line for the cause where and when it can do the most good. There is no strategy involved. Often the whole drama is a debacle from the start, but once the passion play starts, the Hanged One submits and wholeheartedly plays his/her allotted part wherever it might lead.

One of the things that you regularly see in this card is that the Hanged Man is suspended between the two outer Pillars, which are either (depending upon your point of view) the two Pillars of the Kabbalah Tree or the two halves of the Zodiac (as we see in the Hermetic Cosmos diagram). In either case, the individual suspends normal *modus operandi* and reverses his point of view. This is done for the opportunity to enact a timeless sacrificial ritual that will (in theory) reduce the community's karmic load, as well as cleanse the practitioner of her or his individual sins of omission or commission.

If there is a paradox here to meditate on, it is that fate designates certain individuals (who are seemingly mere creatures of the moment) to provoke collective awakenings that produce timeless results. One may or may not be a Christian, but the story of Christ's sacrifice has galvanized people of every era and culture for two thousand years. What lifts a person up to arouse such a response through personal sacrifice? The Jungians would explain that the collective psyche was ripe, and it called forth its chosen Hanged Man. The Hanged Man is an icon of how the supernal plan can seize upon an individual as if s/he were a straw or a siphon, reaching out of Eternity and into time, demanding sacrifice but in the process resolving our collective guilt. This is why we sometimes see the Hanged Man surrounded by a vineyard or hanging from a grape arbor. The exquisitely poignant imagery of Christ's blood transubstantiating in the pomegranate grail cup only extends the analogy between Christ and the grapes in the wine press. This is the offering of the mundane self for the sake of creating a higher octave of consciousness through which the distilled wine of the Spirit can be shared out through the collective mind in a sacramental way. When upright this is not a symbol of wasted martyrdom, useless bloodshed, or self-sacrifice that fails to make any impression. At best this is an intelligent act of self dedication to preserve what is highest in the human makeup and relinquish those ego-centered motives that only impede the progress of humanity's maturation. No attempt to activate an archetype in Space/Time will be perfect; but at least when the card falls upright, it suggests that there is value is making a sacrifice for the sake of future humanity.

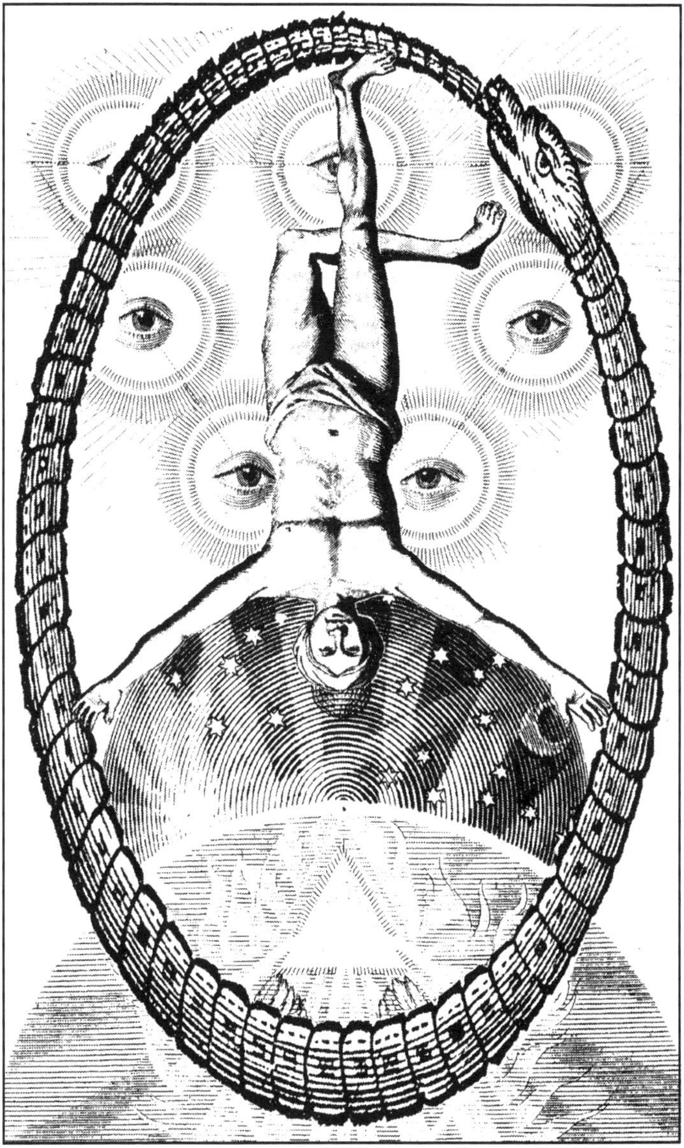

13 Death

Letter: Mem = Water (distilled from Earth)
Path: Pelvic crossbar, between Netzach and Hod
Quality: Dissolving, surrender. Pan of Merit, Time

Death portrays the realm of dissolution and surcease, where all structure and differentiation collapse into a seemingly lifeless substrate. The totality of the transformation forces the soul to precipitate and quit the body, whether temporarily or permanently. The Earth then hungrily devours the nutrients released by the abandoned structures, the bones, and the ashes of the past. The Kabbalists say the letter Mem drives compassion and mercy up the Father Pillar away from the realm of matter and into consciousness (to Chokhmah, the Left Eye of Witness). We can only attain Divine Forgiveness when all ego ties to the past have been severed. Fascinatingly, Death represents the relative dormancy of the eternal soul while still embedded in the flesh and serving out its incarnated time. An ancient homily holds that an angel cries every time a human is born and rejoices every time one dies. This expresses the relative spiritual oblivion of incarnation compared to the harmony and peace of the Pleroma.

Death marks the third term of our Fire triangle of the Septenary, bringing a synthesis between the two previous Trumps. This is one of the most controversial cards in the Trump sequence, at least in terms of exciting the individual's superstition. When this card comes up in a reading, people tend to panic. This is not because it always means a literal death but because of the much more real and frightening possibility of radical and permanent change with no going back. The Death icon presents the necessity to absolutely abandon the past and all of its attachments in order to become worthy of the future that is yet to come. What a paradox for the lower nature: becoming willing to die to the self in order to go forward in the chain of incarnations.

Part of the drama of this card comes because it belongs to the responsive Fire triangle, where we no longer have the perspective of the type that we learned in the Light Trine (by which I mean detachment, rationality, learned wisdom, freedom from instinct's and superstition's chokehold, plus an understanding of how to use the wheel of destiny through making sensible choices). In the responsive triangle one is thrown back on one's personal cultivation to date, where the individual's unique evolution and innate responses make all the difference in how things turn out. With the Death card we experience intimately the breakdown that makes the alchemical recombination possible. What I mean is, without undergoing the "separation of the quick and the dead" in Trump 13, it is not possible to purify and evolve our "lead" (the lower attributes that make up the denser, more material aspects of the self) into "gold" (which historically symbolizes the highest, most radiant and most integrated of substances).

Now that we understand more directly the ways the alchemical system references astrological and Kabbalistic processes, it becomes clearer that the Death card signals the alchemical furnace of transmutation. After we have run the gamut of stock responses and solutions derived from the past, nothing will serve but to recycle ourselves. In this process everything (our patterns, our attitudes, even our very ground of being) cries out to be rendered back to its constituent parts and recast with a new goal in mind. Death is the third of three worldly effects of the responsive Trumps within this collective Septenary, coming after Strength (defending what's worth preserving) and the Hanged Man (rectifying one's attitude towards suffering). Now in Trump 13 we're ready to release everything that made it possible for us to exist in the old context, even up to being obliterated from the known Universe. This does not mean that there is no life on the other side of this passage, only that it is necessary to completely reframe our understanding of ourselves, our potentials, even our very purpose for living. Life as we've known it is gone. Now what will we do with ourselves?

This Death card means utterly dissolving in the compost heap or the melting pot, willingly enduring all the hard parts and sources of resistance inside. There is no worldly cause so compelling, no tie or bond so profound that Death has no sway over it. This means giving up all hope and allowing even one's very body to be stripped away. Death is the cosmic pruner, who like the winter wind wields the scythe of Saturn. For this cycle your time is up. Just as pre-school children encounter a certain day when they have to go off to public school, and the college student has to finally graduate and look for a job, at every stage of life we must outgrow what we've known about the self of the past in order to experience a new identity at a higher order of reality.

Death is also the path of the phoenix or firebird in the sense of the old Greek myth of the eons. This cosmic bird flies for 500 to 1000 years. It then reaches a point of exhaustion, falls to Earth, bursts into flame, and self-immolates to incubate the egg within. As the flames die down, the bird of the new age rises up out of ashes and flies again for another world age. This is a very ancient myth about the precession of the equinoxes, but it's very strongly tied to this pivotal stage in the relationship between the soul and body at which point we must finally drop the old pretenses and either mutate or die. Any move to a higher order is accompanied by relinquishing the dear peculiarities of the old self, which is often harder to do than one would expect. With the Death card we finally merge with the forces that will liberate the eternal Light from the clay.

When the Death card comes up reversed, you might be facing the paradox of being rejected by the pruner's hook. All those around you have been felled (or have transcended), but amazingly somehow you remain. This can leave one feeling hollow, full of ghosts, even riddled with survivor guilt and wordless shame. Even if the incoming change is absolutely necessary and healthy right now, some people will still become riveted by grief and loss, finding it difficult to let go and move forward into life again. Clinging to a devitalized past leaves one empty and exhausted, stripped of the motivation and identity from which to build a future.

As would be natural with the Element Water, our best strategy is to surrender like the man wrapped in the green snake lying in the grave. He offers no resistance as he willingly enters the fatal embrace. No protest mars his demeanor, nor does he attempt to bargain with his captor as his head tips back for the kiss of death. The coils of the serpent's body remind us of the windings of Time as the planets move around the Sun. This accords with the Kabbalistic understanding that the letter Mem (and the Element Water) represents the flow of Time in the life of manifested creatures. There is a time to be born and a time to die.

It is possible that only in the presence of Death can we live a life of authenticity. When we forget about the very thin veil that separates us from the invisibles, we begin to become heedless and sloppy, putting off until tomorrow what we should be attending to today. The Death icon presents the archetype of the true deadline beyond which the old manner of being, the old arrangement, is no longer viable.

It is also wise to remember that in situations where no healing is possible, a good death can be the very best outcome. The Death card can be paradoxical in that sometimes a termination will represent the best outcome for all concerned. A situation that cannot be redeemed in its fullness can at least be disassembled and/or recycled, leaving any useful parts to go forward to new applications.

The law of conservation of energy and mass assures us that in a closed system nothing is essentially lost, no matter how many changes of form or state are undergone. When ending-points are reached, every soul contemplates the choice of whether to go down with the ship (like the man melting into his grave), or whether to somehow survive and start over from scratch (like the woman feeding the dead bodies to the funeral pyre). In either case nothing will ever be the same again; one is tasked with finding new reasons to go on.

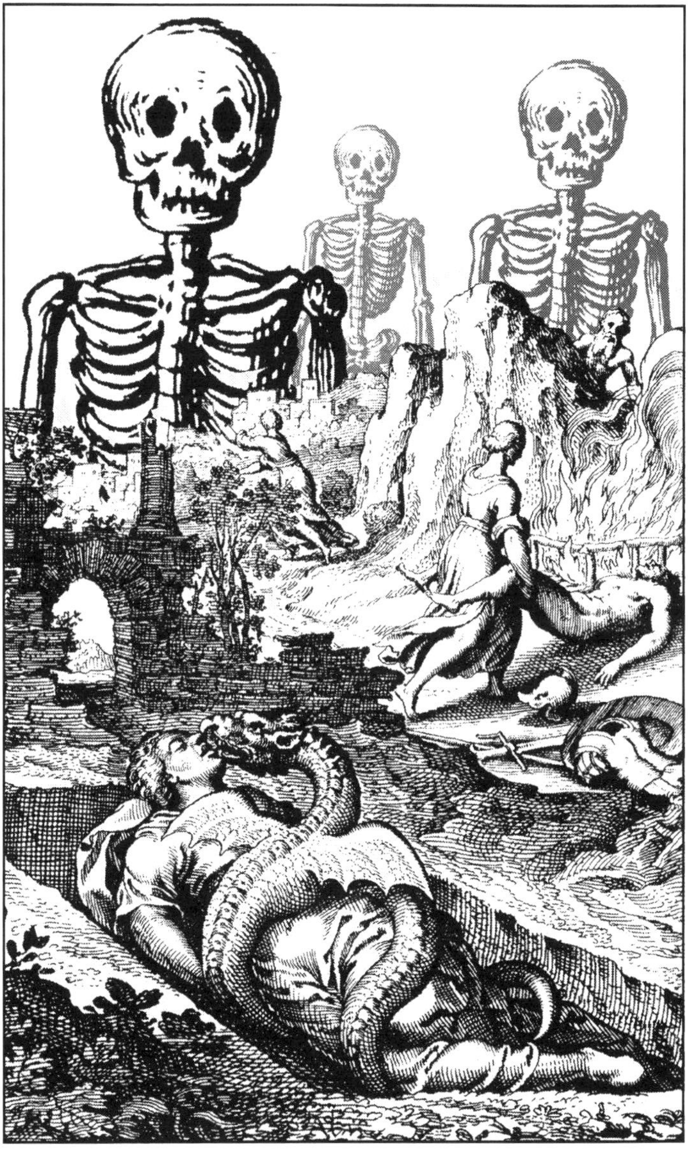

The wonder and glory hidden in this zone of tragedy is the discovery that there is always something new growing out of the carcass of the old. The yearly flooding of the Nile is a perfect model of this process as it refreshes the dead and exhausted soil of its delta, leaving behind enough fertility to feed a nation for another year. Just so, the compassionate waters of Mem (the flow of Time) will eventually dissolve and wash away the evidence of the present suffering and loss. Those who are observant are likely to discover sprouting seeds of future possibilities springing up as a result. We have only to cultivate them while remaining open to the mystery of life.

14 Temperance

Letter: N = Scorpio
Path: Between Gevurah and Yesod
Quality: House of Death

Directly following the Trump traditionally entitled Death, we encounter the Trump that corresponds with Scorpio, the Zodiacal sign that has been known as "the House of Death" since ancient times. Attention now shifts from the process of dissolution (the astral Waters of Mem; the flux of time that separates the soul from Eternity) to the process of transformation as it is lived in consciousness by one who is undergoing it. This period of intensification is symbolized by the subtle agitation communicated to the mutating substance by the Temperance angel. This angel's mission is to awaken the immortal soul from its dormancy within matter, using whatever methods are required. On the Kabbalah Tree, the path of Temperance is mirrored by that of 12, the Hanged Man, both of them leading down from the base of the Heart Triangle into Yesod, the pelvic center.

In this Arcanum the angel of Alchemy distills out the Spirit that has been inhabiting matter, separating the dross from the pure essence and tincturing the attendant poisons into healing medicines. This purification process greatly reduces the bulk of the matter but exponentially increases the concentration and quality of what remains. Trump 14 represents the alchemist at work, transforming both the baptist (soul healer) and the Tincture (meaning the fusion of Father, Son, and Sophia according to Boehme's followers). The dove, symbol of Sophia and Holy Spirit, is the unique bearer of the germ of soul. The dove moves in all directions between the heavenly and earthly planes, mimicking the shaman's role of effecting communication between the worlds. Also signifying election, the dove marks the initiated soul for immortality.

In Trump 14 we are finally brought to the end of our second Septenary to win the prize that awaits those who have integrated the previous six Trumps. The Temperance concept has correspondence to the angel Raphael, the healer in the celestial pantheon. Raphael was sent over this Earth to monitor the ecology, to balance the forces, to bring about the experiences (historically, socially, politically, culturally) that are designed to temper our species, forcing us to grow into our higher potential as a collective. Temperance literally refers to the tempering of metal in the very manner by which iron becomes steel. Alchemi-Kabbalistically, the Wrath-Fire of the Father-force is attenuated in the fountain of compassion that is the Mother-force, during which the angel mediates a medicinal blending of the opposites.

We saw in the Chariot card the two opposites of yin and yang yoked together to pull the same vehicle. Now we see those polarized forces actually being poured together to make the elixir of life. The elixir is to be distributed through Nature and into the terrestrial world as a balm or a healing essence. Such medicine can ease the pain of our struggles as we attempt to interface inner life and outer life, the personal ego and the collective life, mortal forces and the immortal quest. Temperance means finding a living balance, a liquid balance, a flexible balance of mediated opposites that supports life beyond the ministry of the Reaper. In the Paracelsian style, Temperance seeks to modify, blend, and dilute life's poisons into medicines and agents of awakening. Temperance indicates a level of consciousness that no longer lives in a dualistic universe. The ego is beginning to realize that all value-systems are relative to the level of consciousness their believer has attained. The Creation begins to show itself as an infinite ladder of steps ascending towards higher and higher orders of wisdom and integration. At this stage all dependence on either/or thinking evaporates to be replaced by the infinite question, "What is this (situation, thing, experience) good for? How does it serve the larger Creation? What can I learn from it?"

When the opposites are brought together, there can be quite a storm; but when they find their balance they provide a creative matrix out of which the new format of selfhood can be born. We shouldn't be surprised that Temperance follows the Death card: Trump 14 illustrates the soul as it exists outside the envelope of Time and Space. Everything that ties the soul to materiality has been etherealized to reveal the medicine. In order to move to that new state of reality that survives the tempering crucible and outlasts the stresses and strains of this purification process, one has to identify solely and completely with one's quotient of Light. This is the highest of the world's magical disciplines: to bring together the Light Trine and the Fire Trine of the Great Hexegram without annihilating either of them. Each triangle's potencies are brought to bear upon the other, sparking a fertile union from which something new emerges on the scene of human consciousness. At Trump 14 that newly emergent gift is the angelic consciousness that earns the possessor the right of passage into the next realm, meaning cosmic consciousness (the final Septenary of Trumps numbered 15 through 21, followed by the Fool).

With the appearance of the dove, we can also read the Annunciation into this image. Our Protestant Theosophers would recall the Baptism of Jesus

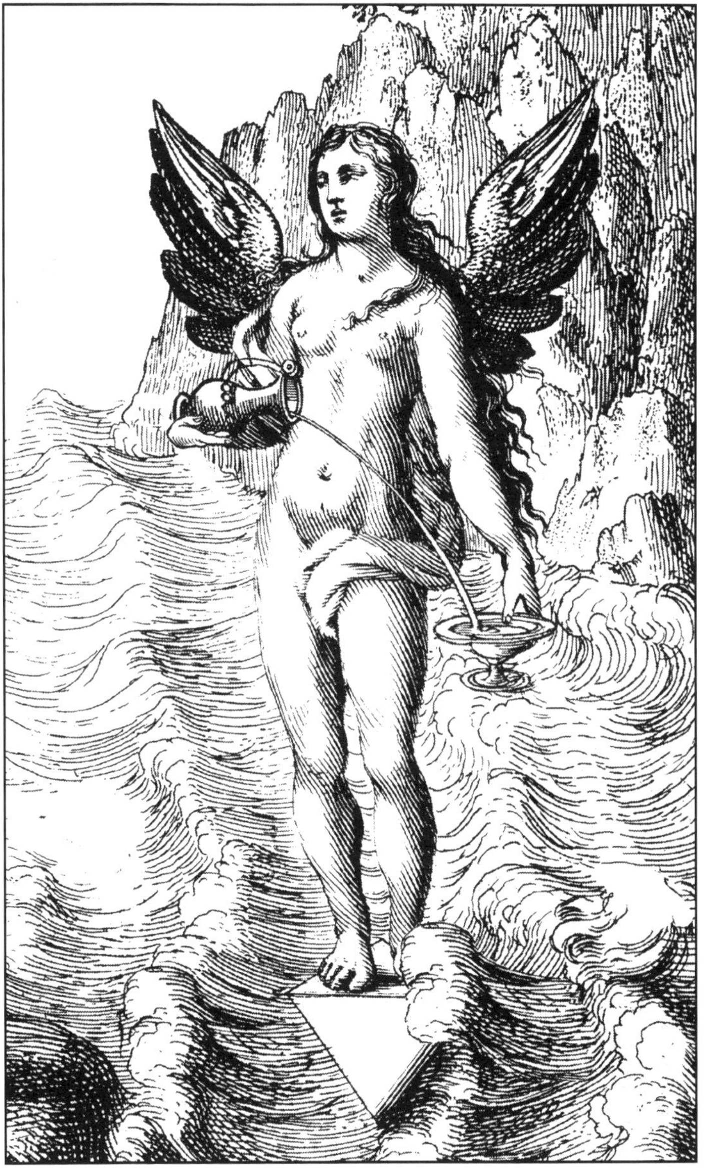

by John and the dove that descended to ensoul the Christ and complete the Incarnation. In terms of the individual psyche, this would represent the moment when one finally realizes that the "I" of our self-referencing is not the body nor the ego nor the emotions nor the mind, but the immortal soul, the spark of Light within, which is indeed "made in the Image of God." This is the seat of identity and the key to our ultimate transcendence.

The Temperance cards from several of the original Etteilla Tarots show the angel navigating a somewhat tippy perch. A thick triangular stone block is under one foot (suitable for being the head corner stone of a pointed arch), while the other foot rests on a stone orb or ball. This is yet another suggestion about the mediation of opposites. There are any number of ways one might read this (rough-hewn vs. polished; the one vs. its infinite geometric facets; the plane vs. the sphere) depending on the circumstance. Maybe the angel isn't actually standing at all but is only hovering over these objects to unite them. These geometric shapes could also be understood in reference to their known significance within Sacred Geometry, architecture, music, and the other architectonic arts.

One could also consider the dichotomy that was often faced in early medicine, which is the question of whether the remedy could be found among the "simples" (single-herb remedies), or whether true healing will require a more sophisticated combination approach. A future researcher who is better schooled in Masonic and Rosicrucian symbolism will eventually point out the very parable or ritual that informs this symbolism. We can, meanwhile, rest assured that though the stone and the sphere might appear very different in their physical form, their internal geometrical proportions are ruled by the same governing law. In our version of Temperance, we merge the significance of these objects into a single inverted triangle symbolizing the descending Light-triangle of Spirit colored with the passionate red of the holy Wrath-Fire. Like the dove, this ruby platform of purified passion suggests a successful fusion between opposites, providing another vehicle for the soul to move between worlds.

Correspondingly, should this card fall upside down in a spread, one must allow the diamond-sharp tip of this fiery triangle to pierce directly into the hidden truth that sets us free. This is the moment when all superficials are washed away. The remains of the past are lost forever and irredeemable, submerged by the ocean of time. Now we must finally stop attributing the accidents of life to outside causes; we must stand alone and naked in the deep psyche, revealed to Heaven and all of Nature. Only in Scorpio in this pressure-cooker atmosphere can we convert our ancient karmic poisons and deficits into the medicine of spiritual rebirth. Only after we've been melted down, rendered, poured out, and recast many hundreds of times (through who knows how many lifetimes) do we finally become pure and self-aware enough to realize that this distillation and concentration process is, in fact, the very experience we came into matter to undergo. Finally we learn to stop fighting with ourselves, stop the resistance to the forces of growth and change, and willingly accept the correction that awaits us. It's time to surrender to the forces that have always been right there, trying to guide and educate us through our life's lessons, but which we were resisting and rebelling against for whatever reasons. What remains after having burned out and eroded away every previous stance and worldview is our original Nature, that pure essence of Spirit which has been with us all along.

Summary of the Second Septenary

To this point the Trumps have been focusing on human values, in particular the virtues and skills required to knit together and maintain one's local community. The issues on display take into account physical nature in her terrestrial form and human nature in its social and intellectual forms. But after the Temperance card we have the birth of Divine Consciousness in the individual and an awakening perspective that sees beyond the life of the individual or a unique incarnation. From this point on, we learn to operate from the perspective of Eternity and to take responsibility for our place in the celestial order.

The goal of self-initiation in the Hermetic scheme is to outgrow being a happy animal in Eden, to move past becoming a successful person in the social world in order to become eligible for cosmic citizenship. The goal is to graduate from the world of Time and Space, things and beings, and move on to a firm focus of eternal identity. This coming range of Trumps will allow the soul to leave behind time, gravity, and all of the material laws, a dear childhood fantasy of many. But in exchange the soul is burdened with an increasing reawakening of the immortal perspective, the evolution that's been spread throughout all of our incarnations or through all of our life experiences. It doesn't really matter whether one thinks of this process as happening over multiple lifetimes or in the present lifetime. Progress assumes an expansion of consciousness that moves beyond just self development or integration into the world, to aim the individual soul towards cosmic participation and the realization of a higher level of destiny.

It's not until we graduate from both schools (the school of self-development that culminates in the Chariot and the school of social and intellectual development that culminates in the Temperance card) that we actually come into range of ideals like eternal life or cosmic citizenship. The challenge here is to avoid jumping the gun by assuming that after the Temperance fusion, one has completed the Great Work. So far we have merely crossed the ground that brings one up to the door of entry into the Mysteries (symbolized in the final Septenary of the completed the Great Work). Amongst historical gnostics of whatever stripe, whether Hermetic, Hebrew, Arabic, or Christian, it's taken for granted that more than one lifetime of working with this symbolism is required to come to a fullness with it. It's understood that the Tarot Arcana, the astrological sciences, Kabbalah, Sacred Numerology, and Alchemy comprise a quest that informs a number of lifetimes. Only by taking the long view is it possible for the individual to slowly distill those higher qualities and rise up from being an animal to being a human, and then rise again to our ultimate exalted state. The Tarot presents this process through a staged set of initiations, each with its own observances and with its own time frame, that has to be lived out day by day.

One can generally trust that the average adult will have experienced Trumps 1-14 before they even encounter the Tarot. Life in any era simply demands that we rise to the occasion, and these first 14 archetypes represent a spectrum of considerations that have to be met to be taken seriously in this world. To move on into the final Septenary, all of those previous issues must be grappled into place so they provide a stable platform of consciousness underfoot. Without this being accomplished, one cannot be equal to the archetypes of the later Arcana. The final Trumps may come up in your readings, but their reality will remain abstract, mysterious, and possibly frightening until the wobbly ego is recast by Temperance into a coherent, unified lodestone that can guide the soul back home. Full understanding of the final Septenary is earned, not simply given. One can be standing up to one's earlobes in spiritual issues, but if one is not even ready to acknowledge the work of Spirit in one's direct experience, then the chances are low that the true facts of the case will penetrate.

We pause with the Temperance to acknowledge the Hermetic image of human maturity, meaning the developmental ripeness of an adult who has actualized his or her human potential. To bring those qualities into focus, we must learn the reality of justice and wisdom as found in Nature. This grants us the flexibility to adapt and adjust as the wheel churns up our karma, individually and collectively. With the Light Trine functioning for us, we possess the spiritual strength that keeps us facing forward despite resistance and threats to our status. Like the Hanged Man, we will put our own safety on the line to take a stand that embodies right action. This allows us to operate without fear of Death in trust that whatever happens, we are all growing into a higher level of reality. The momentum of these accomplishments delivers us to the realm of Temperance, the angelic healer who accomplishes the Tincture (fusion of the

Trinity, however named or configured) within the soul.

Now we proceed to the last and third school within the planetary circuit. We point ourselves ever-upward to arrive at last to the Edenic state that was our ancient origin and remains our future destiny. Going forward, we climb the frequency-ladder with all our might during our return back to the Pleroma in the form of self-conscious Light.

Introduction to the Third Septenary

In the third Septenary we are facing the biggest challenges that the Tarot offers an individual soul. This is so because the stakes are cosmic citizenship or immortality, which is only won through paying the ultimate price. One has to already have conquered and assimilated the first and second Septenary before being capable of comprehending this third Septenary at any level beyond the superficial. The lessons of the third Septenary take many revisitations before we fully comprehend what they mean in our unique private experience. The best one can do when encountering any of the cards in this final grouping is to surrender immediately and rearrange one's mind to the most optimistic attitude one can achieve. Any attempt to fight against the forces these cards represent will result in extensive losses and personal damage to the self-esteem and perhaps the estate of the receiver.

One consideration that's worth remembering with this final Septenary is that any card of this set could represent a completion in terms of the ascending cycle of the Trumps. Not every person perfects every step of the long and winding journey described by the Trumps. Accomplishing the lessons contained by any one of these final Trumps could be a life's work. At this point each position in the Great Arcanum has been reiterated three times, meaning that each of these seven cards comprises a triple composite. Hence, the Devil card is not just itself, but is also a synthesis of the Chariot and Temperance. The Tower is not just itself, but is also supported by the Priestess and Justice, and so on.

15 The Devil

Letter: S = Sagittarius
Path: Between Yesod and Netzach
Quality: House of Sleep (and other altered states)

In this Devil we witness the display of the Peacock Angel, Alchemy's fleeting but revelatory experience, a sign of suppressed goddess energies reawakening. The writing on the arms of the rebus testifies to the two repeating stages of the alchemical work expressed as the breakdown of attachment to the body (Solve) and the strengthening of attachment to the soul (Coagula).

The first step into the Septenary of celestial reality is taken with the deeply ambivalent Trump 15, known as the Devil. We have retained the title and traditional associations that belong to this Trump but have discarded the camouflage that defaces this card via the goat mask and legs. Our Protestant Theosophers would have probably taken a harsher stand towards this Trump than we have. We took this liberty because even our leading thinkers were not in total harmony about the ultimate fate of Satan or the Devil upon the Restitution. Some of Boehme's followers, most notably Jane Leade, felt that the Devil would ultimately be rehabilitated along with all the rest of Creation. Gichtel felt the Devil was banished here to the Earth and punished by being locked into his own negative world-view forever. Boehme felt that it was Satan's lot to represent "the shadow" eternally and provide contrast to the Light. According to Roob's commentary on Figure VIII of Frehrer's 13 Figures, "The two S's, Sophia and Satan, are the two contrary snakes of the staff of Mercury (Caduceus) and must be united" (Roob, p. 171). Each of us has to decide for ourself how to handle the energy of Trump 15. We will catalogue some of the considerations involved so the reader can draw his or her own conclusions.

In the Eros Magic event pictured on the Devil from *Tarot of Holy Light*, both sides of the self are so illumined and attuned that they dissolve out of their individual separateness and coagulate in the heart of the other, fusing into a mutual "yes." The opposites which have been purified are now reunited at a higher order of functionality. Two-headed Lucifer, the Light-bringer or Daystar, provides the meeting-ground for the reborn animus and anima. Implications include shedding acculturation, awakening of the suppressed self, shamanic shape-shifting, and renewed libido. Trump 15 grants the return of the parts of one's innate being that have been tabooed, scapegoated, attacked, and castigated. We discover what we have been missing and seeking within ourselves after all.

The letter Samekh also carries with it tremendous energy from antiquity for several reasons. The very shape of the Hebrew letter is that of a snake with its tail in its mouth, a veritable high-sign for gnostic ideations. Some also suggest that this symbol was used as a graphic representation of opening of the vagina, the ultimate female sexual symbol. In many ancient societies including the early Hebrews, the spiritual implications involved with women's fertility cycles were an important preoccupation due to masculine fears of being "polluted," unmanned, and disempowered by contact with menstrual blood. These additional vectors of meaning help us understand how the Devil has accumulated such a fascinating and frustrating set of correspondences across the centuries.

The earliest pictured cards we have show the composite demon named Legion in the Old Testament with the faces of its constituent demons at every prominent spot on its body. In the 1660s the Devil suddenly morphs into the prototype of the card we have become used to in present time: the Baphomet figure. When this Templar title is taken apart using the Kabbalistic art of gematria, we discover that Baphomet spells out the word "Sophia" in the Hebrew atbash cypher (Schonfield, Appendix A). This revelation aligns the Devil with other early Creation stories in which Creator always manifested as a male/female pair, known among the gnostics as a syzygy (two-in-one). Unmasked and put in theological terms, this would be Christ/Sophia, the united co-redeemer syzygy who rescue and complete each other while immersed in the material Creation. Once this syzygy forms, matter and Time/Space begin the process of Reintegration with the Pleroma. The presence of this magical "white hole" reveals itself through its powerful magnetism in the material plane, even before the scapegoat costume is discarded. What makes the letter S (Samekh) so magically and magnetically attractive is in fact the magician's secret well of materialization.

The Protestant Sophianics never gave any indication that they knew the atbash transliteration of the word Baphomet. The reality behind the Devil has taken such a terrible beating over the last two thousand years of religious and metaphysical overwriting that we need to reach all the way back to the earliest linguistic roots to demonstrate this Arcanum at its primary level. Sophia is a Greek noun meaning wisdom (spelled sigma-omicron-phi-iota with the acute accent-alpha) that was appropriated and transliterated by the Hebrews ("sofih") to refer to the feminine half of the celestial creativity. The rabbis of the Alexandrian synthesis could have simply stayed with their native Shekhinah and appended the attribute of "wisdom" to her, but apparently they felt that the Greek Sophia deserved Her own word and spelling in the lexicon. Sophia found her way into the Christian scriptures through the Old Testament.

Boehme's students and friends were aware of alternate interpretations of the serpent of Genesis. According to the Ophites (an early sect of Gnostic Christians), Sophia grants the Moist Light that is latent within the human soul. Our remembrance of this Light constitutes our awakening. The serpent (Ophis, anagram of Sophia) was sent to Adam and Eve to awaken them to their immortal quotient and show them the way past the Archons (the planets), who keep them enchained to the wheel of incarnation (i.e., stuck inside the Time/Space of our birthcharts). Further, upon the banishment of Adam and Eve from the garden of Eden, Sophia (whose Wisdom had made possible all the manifestations of this world) accompanied Her children into the Fallen world to look after Creation and foster our kind. Contrary to the portrayal of the Serpent as a tempter, the Serpent is our educator and role model, as we also see in the stories related to Moses and the Serpent. (There is more on this theme in the section on the Ten of Wands.) This ancient gnostic insight might help to explain the female-headed Serpents in the early alchemical manuals.

Think of the implications of this: The Mother of Creation is ejected from Heaven through her own choice, preferring life in the "lower worlds" to co-habitation with the wrathful Jehovah. She has further been demonized as the tempter in the garden and as the Devil in Tarot. Now recall our Kabbalistic alchemists' stubborn insistence that they were personally espoused to and married with Sophia. Boehme's followers were committed to having a direct relationship with the imminent (everywhere-accessible, materialized) Feminine Divine, even though the normative Christian world was scapegoating the same principle as Lucifer, Satan, and the Devil, accessory to the Fall and source of all temptation. This helps us understand more fully why Boehme received such fierce and unflagging resistance from his Lutheran pastor. By collecting all traces of Sophia across multicultural scriptures, these religious alchemists were reawakening the feminine face of the Holy Spirit. There was even sympathy for the idea of Restitution for some or all of the Fallen angels after the Resurrection, not to mention the issue of the Christian Eros Magic they were practicing with Sophia through their prayers and visualizations. How could all this be reconciled with the Protestantism of Boehme's day?

To the Lutheran Gnostics following Boehme, who looked at the wrathful triple-masculine God of the normative Christians with dismay, a passionate longing for Sophia made uncomplicated and natural good sense. These warriors of Love made it their passion to re-establish relations between the

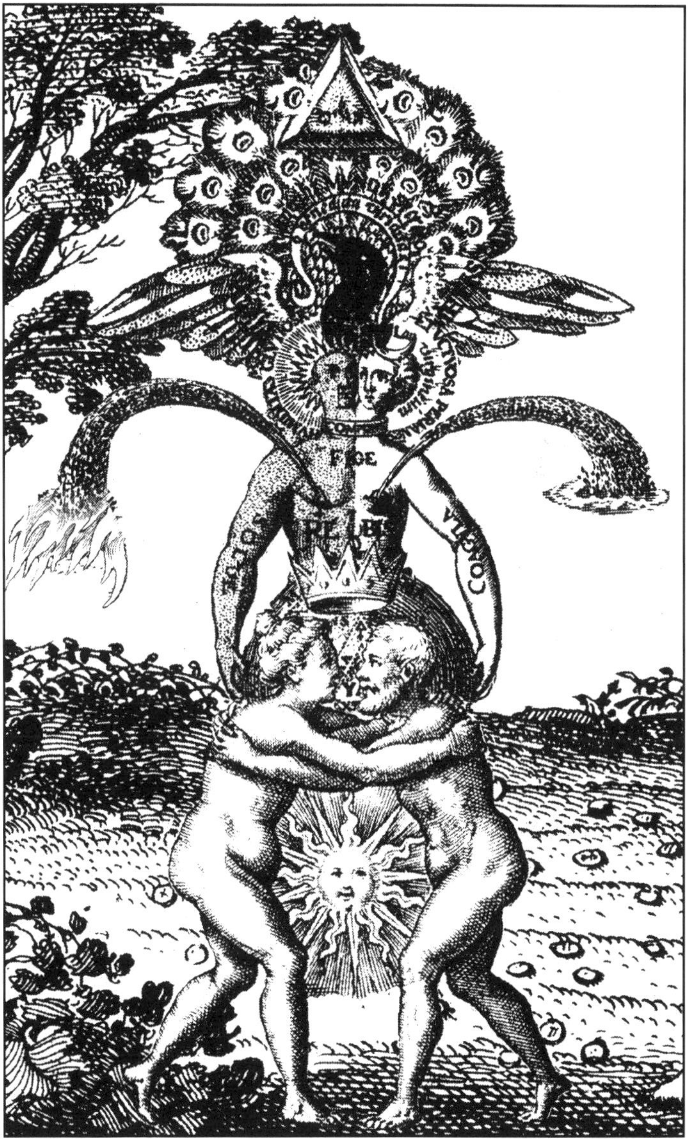
FIGE
REBIS

angry God and the healing Goddess in hopes of stilling the chaos of life as we know it, and to inaugurate the thousand years of peace promised in Scripture. Remember that in the full Creation myth, the first default was attributed to the Christian interpretation of Lucifer because the beauty and radiance that Venus contributes to God's throne was seen as rivaling the glory of God "himself." (Note our ancestors' paradoxical reaction to Venus and Nature's mechanism of attraction.) The overwhelming evidence suggests that the Christian Devil (Samekh) is actually, esoterically, the cast-out and scapegoated Sophia, whom the patriarchal culture of the Western Church had been busy neutering (renaming her Logos) since they first translated the Hebrew scriptures into Greek. The final evidence of success in this matter is apparent in the ignorance of modern Christians regarding who, or what, the Holy Spirit of their faith actually represents.

Settled research has confirmed that the goat head on the Devil card appears partially to demonize Pan, the Greek god of Nature and the wilderness. In the era that produced the Trumps, this was an obvious and natural reference to Eros. Pantheism, the religion that holds that Nature is one of many material forms of God, was another anathematized belief that the Christians persecuted unto oblivion. This represents a second level of taboo laid over this card's original referent via scapegoating, another part of the long, slow conspiracy of the Judeo-Christian tradition to reduce the West's access to the feminine (read: Venusian) Mysteries.

Although this card has been left to languish under the myth of the rejected feminine, there is plenty of other content here to be explored. The Hebrew letter Samekh (an image of the fertile void that links the Serpent with feminine genitalia) points out the magical aspect of expectant Nature. Here is a very broad hint about a power that is essentially feminine and "negative" (in the sense of seeming externally passive and receptive), but which nevertheless evokes from the father or the patriarchy both attraction and irritation. This spectrum of responses is collectively very hard to resist. Whereas Jehovah decrees "Don't eat that apple!", Sophia responds with "Why not eat the apple?" and the never-ending dialectic begins. (Boehme reduces the entire eternal struggle down to the strife between the "no" and the "yes," the stern and wrathful descending force versus the warm and nurturing ascending force, which together eternally turn the wheel around Tiferet.)

In the archetypal script the Goddess initiates and provokes by retreating and entreating. Meanwhile, God is undone by his irresistible desire to discipline her and fulfill his inchoate Wrath (and sexual attraction). Before long the two are locked in a tantric embrace. Now Sophia has Him where She wants

Him, and soon enough She will wring the inevitable lightning-bolt out of Him (analogous to the *fiat lux* which created the world). In the course of this flowery battle (a Taoist term for sexual co-meditation), She melts Him down and floods Him with yin, thereby neutralizing and eliminating His excessive force and bluster. Meanwhile, He will fertilize Her, from which She will create more bodies for life to occupy. As this goes on over our heads and all through our lives and psyches, earthly humanity discovers our heavenly origin and destiny, and Sophia continuously invites us to follow the "Serpent's path" back up the Kabbalah Tree and return to the Pleroma.

It is also known that the Protestant Sophianics were well aware of the Hindu concept of kundalini with its various manifestations and cultivation methods. We have to figure all of this into our thinking when we look at the Devil card. Something very primordial is being evoked by the alchemical couple who are merging under the gaze of the rebus and the peacock angel. In all of its forms, the Devil card takes its stand outside of the official Christian canon and yet attracts a huge amount of ecclesiastical energy all the same.

Samekh's correspondence with the Zodiac sign Sagittarius also points towards the power of desire which, when focused on the material plane, is said to be unstoppable and irresistible. When grounded in her natural Elements, Water and Earth, and backed by the pregnant void's insistence to be filled, Baphomet/Sophia has tremendous evocative power wherever She casts her charm and weaves Her spell. This impassioned and literally inspired (Spirit-filled) arousal is something every settled church greatly fears. When in the "charmed" state of spiritual excitement and enchantment, a person has a huge amount of charisma, especially if the inspired individual starts literally "speaking for the Spirits." One who can bring forth the voices of the ancestors, of the Elements, or the daemons (what we call "channeling" in modern times) is particularly threatening to an institution that claims to have the sole conduit to God. The uncontrollable wildness of a prophet (like John the Baptist) is incompatible with the legalistic and materialistic edifice that Catholicism (and later Protestantism) has become. This is another reason why Sophia has to be veiled and scapegoated: to muzzle Her communications with the people. Fossilized hierarchical religious teachings that restrain all experience to the limits of the past inhibit our autonomy to follow our own intuition, imposing strictures that control us through "orthodoxy," whether or not it fits with our God-given conscience.

In truth the charisma, spontaneity, and passion associated with this card are not a product of either good or evil; they come right up from the unfiltered life force of the individual, which is why you will often see a caduceus on the belly of the Devil card. The energy that animates this Devil, this magnet of desire and natural attraction, represents the heightened aura of the individual who is focused on his or her strongest attractions. This is the astral vortex, or *tourbillion*, that we set loose into the world with our vitalized appetites. There is no doubt that a great deal of focus, will power, and individuation are necessary to handle this power without becoming victim to its multiple seductions. The Devil represents everything that you desire and lust after. Who can discipline our desire for the things we naturally find most attractive?

The caduceus of Hermes brings with it the challenge of communication and interpretation. This refers to both our overt acts of linguistics and symbolism as well as our covert acts of interior image and dialogue. Powered by the charged and conscious wand of the Magus, the Devil is urgent to consummate what the Magus could only imagine. This empowered and androgynous rebus is also urgent to broadcast her intentions invisibly, seeking a receptive audience from among those who haven't already neutered their imaginations. Naturally, no one is comfortable in the presence of this type of intensity unless it feeds his or her own desires. As befits this ultimate Eros Magic icon, the agenda of Trump 15 draws the individual by his or her own likes and dislikes into a more powerful area of self development. The Devil challenges the ego to rise above its long-suppressed fears about knowing and acting on its true desires and goals. And, truth be told, we aren't really safe until we learn to surrender to the Divine Desire. We need to stop scapegoating Venus, the power of attraction, or else we are going to be forever lopsided, constantly running in circles because we permit ourselves to use the right-handed (dexter) logical self, but we don't permit ourselves to use the left-handed (sinister) intuition and the enlightened instincts that come along with it.

Patriarchal Christianity sees in the Devil the passions, desires, addictions, disturbances, and distractions imposed upon the soul by incarnation and embodiment. Among the dualist gnostics, the Devil symbolizes the demiurge, creator of earthly bodies and enslaver of the souls trapped within them, the wrathful and controlling ruler of Time and Space. Diablos means "the one who sows discord," that which destroys order and promotes devolution. Obviously, the Christian apologists felt the need for a bright white line to be drawn between the Divine design and the forces of uninhibited recombination. Unfortunately the body and its inborn polymorphous-perverse proclivities fell on the wrong side of that line.

One must be careful when reading this card in a spread to remind the querant and oneself that the energies associated with the Devil card are perfectly natural for humans, but every culture chooses to name and train those forces differently. It does no good to attack natural energies or try to eradicate them. The best that we can do is channel them via will-power after an investment of time and attention. This focus on will and self-cultivation to sublimate undisciplined appetites harmonizes with the highest teachings of all spiritual paths. The goal is not to extinguish the life force, but to cultivate it towards its highest expression. In some cases this can indicate a lifestyle of solitude, austerity, and/or celibacy to foster concentration on a burning passion.

Thus there is a broad spectrum of things to consider when the Devil comes up reversed. Depending on the context, it could represent everything the more superstitious Christians have feared about human self-centeredness and narcissism. Alternately, there is a case to be made that hubris is inflating one's judgment to such a degree that it puts one out of touch with reality. In this sense the Devil consolidates all of our temptations into a possessing delusion of having no limits, as if an endless stream of power and pleasure could be had with no long-term negative consequences. The Devil reversed could also represent the unspoken taboo against self-fulfillment and enlightenment, possibly threatening consequences for the person who strays beyond the socially-approved bounds. Meanwhile, it might be time to investigate one's judgmental reactivity in the face of other's innate and natural inclinations. In reversal, Trump 15 is the theological night-star (Venus' nighttime visage) highlighting our flaws, lack of evolution, and feet of clay. Then again, it might also be time to lift the scapegoat mask off the face of Sophia and look deeply into our inborn, God-given, natural, and innocent characteristics, uneven and tragically flawed though they might seem on the surface.

16 The Tower

Letter: O = Capricorn
Path: Between Yesod and Hod
Quality: House of Wrath, anger; The Lightning

In the Tower card we face the shock of the unforeseen, plus the losses and their close-following accusations occasioned by the sudden failure. As is evident, the precious medicine combining in the sealed and suspended vessel is vitalized by the electrical bolt, suggesting that the forthcoming liberation will prove to have been worth the shock. In theosophical terms Sophia is companion to the prisoner, both of the worldly regime and of the bodily incarnation. She is the architect of release from the "sleep" of the incarnated soul and the savior of the endangered individual. This is accomplished through the progressive heating of the soul in the alchemical furnace until every atom of its gross and astral "matter" is shattered, releasing its locked-in Light. This Trump also points to the Lightning Bolt that cracks the Heart in the Boehmian synthesis. At this point all the hardness, dryness, fixity, resistance, and immovability of the Father are pulverized, liberating the soul from its embeddedness in Time/Space and form. This forces a sudden re-prioritization of the soul's focus. Some might see this as the Lighting Bolt that ejected Lucifer (the Daystar) out of Heaven and Adam and Eve from the garden, in the myth of the Fall. That lightning is the punishment for hubris or excessive self-esteem.

Let's assume that the Devil has explored as far as possible the potency of its own desires, concentrating a huge vortex of charisma around the ego's center. Nature's way of restoring balance will be to unleash the lightning and blow that power-center to smithereens, releasing all the condensed energy and distributing it around again to seed the next wave of results. What goes up must come down. This illustrates the shift from Sagittarius Fire (expansion) to Capricorn Earth (contraction). To the extent that the Devil has become puffed-up and full of self-importance, overweeningly consuming and decadent in its indulgence, the situation begs for a response from Nature to restore a more peaceful and balanced state again. Remarks we find in the Martinist literature (some of the inheritors of the Boehmian worldview and praxis) make it clear that in literal, bodily terms, the Devil represents a state of sexual excitation, and the Tower is the inevitable release that follows. Does it get any clearer than this?

One now has to inquire: Is the lightning that blasts the Tower a normal, natural event, or is it the punishment for evildoing? The answer to this question will color one's interpretation of this card in a spread. In this pair of cards, we run into a huge theological issue that has never been and will never be resolved. The orthodox Christian will look at the faces of these two cards and read the story of Lucifer's Fall and punishment. Meanwhile a theosophical Christian might see the liberation of Sophia from her demonic scapegoating and the ending of the patriarchal regime. Someone from outside the Judeo-Christian discussion might further see the release of Nature from under the enslaving hand of man. Who is to say what is the "correct" interpretation? The lightning has been known to descend even at times when the innate self-pleasure principle (the Devil) hasn't done anything particularly wrong. Sometimes just being the nail that sticks out beyond the rest is enough to attract attention and therefore correction. There are, of course, karmic reasons why at certain points in life one is treated to the electro-shock therapy of the lightning, but normative Christianity doesn't allow for any speculation along those lines other than guilt and atonement (which we have already seen in the Hanged Man). With Trump 16 one can feel punished or one can feel liberated by a celestial absolution, but the net effect in either case is a total restructuring of one's relationship with the manifested world.

A more direct esoteric statement is being made with this Trump in the alchemically-inflected *Jaques Vieville Tarot*. In this Trump 16 a young blond shepherd is grazing his flocks under a large tree which is suddenly illuminated by a radiance emerging from a bank of clouds. A shower of brilliant red, gold, and white sparks descends from on high, lighting up or possibly inflaming the canopy of the tree. Has this unwitting shepherd stumbled upon the Burning Bush? Jean-Claude Flornoy's reproduction of this card shows the young man wearing a white apron and gloves with his right hand raised as if in surprise and the left hand hitched up behind his back holding a sticklike tool. The apron, gloves, and tool could be the guild tools of a practicing mason, as this pack was produced in the era before Masonry shifted over from a practical to a speculative endeavor. But the most mysterious aspect of the imagery is the lit-up tree with the many sparks flying around under a fulminating, red-rimmed sun. This image gives us a sense of the Light and energy resident in this card when the magical landscape of Trump 16 is relieved of the Tower construct altogether.

The solidity of the stony structure that so often appears in the picture causes us to forget that the active force in the card is natural electricity. When the Tower of the alchemists appears, we are observing a carefully-crafted experiment for collecting and grounding the ambient Wrath (friction, irritation, static) that accumulates in the landscape. This Tower serves as a lightning-rod, sited and set up to attract the lightning and channel it through the sealed vessel and into the ground. By its very nature, lightning cannot be tamed or called or controlled. One can only construct the conditions that are conducive to provoking it and then be patient.

With the Tower we are in the antithesis stage of the descending Trine of this Septenary. Life experience, education, self-development, spiritual evolution, and higher mind unfoldment have together accumulated a solid and evolved edifice around the individual ego. Over time the Tower densifies and solidifies until it encases the mystery of the peacock angel in a thick, rigid containment vessel. We think we "know something" now, and we think that what we know is "it," the final word. We get this impression because while we were in the (inflated, exalted) Devil state, we lost all perspective on the trough at the other end of the high. The soul that hasn't learned the lesson of willing self-limitation will eventually careen off course, stray off of its center of gravity, and be subject to Nature's correction. Earthy Capricorn's ruler Saturn, the karma lord, will bring on the lightning to blow off the inflation and restore balance to the Creation.

The original myth for this icon is the story of the Tower of Babel. A persistent fantasy of humans is of a Tower or ladder that can be built up to Heaven, providing a short-cut that allows the clever few to artificially possess the advantage of higher ground (spiritually, culturally, morally, etc.) while leaving the goodhearted masses behind. The Ladder of Lights is more than just a symbol; we have explained it as the inherent structure of the Zodiac's interior family dynamics. Some civilizations have used this Ladder to justify high expectations from humanity, where other societies used the Ladder to stratify a social hierarchy that distorts human relationships (just as true for the so-called winners as it is for the losers). Exalted feelings of specialness, immunity, entitlement, and superiority actually hasten the inevitable comeuppance, comprising a cosmic "kick me" sign in the aura. One well-placed lightning bolt, accident of fate, or blindside blow from an unknown quarter radically challenges the integrity of one's edifice. The lightning confronts one's ego-construct with its irresistible weakness, forcing it to surrender its elevation and let gravity bring it down to its lowest common denominator again.

In *Tarot of the Holy Light*, when the process in the flask has matured, the lightning penetrates the veil between worlds and delivers the spark of life to the alchemical vessel. When this happens, something from the larger life of all humanity takes form in collective consciousness. It is an exalting moment but also

403

humbling in the extreme. Now we must face the fact that at the cosmic level we tiny human individuals are helpless, useless, complete creatures of luck and circumstances. Nature is no respecter of individuals. If we have not contributed to the larger labor of human evolution, all the steps that have gone before Trump 16 avail us nothing. Our greatest individual accomplishments can be wiped out in the blink of an eye without a second's notice right out of the blue. The Great Work is utterly impersonal, so much so that it repels all those who have failed to purge the "I-me-mine" out of their thinking. Only the radical enlightenment delivered by the lightning can pierce the veil between the worlds and liberate the Divine Seed in matter. (The Egyptian-style Tarots show people being shaken off the sides of a pyramid, which they tried to scale as interlopers instead of earning their welcome and entering through the official channels.)

Those who can survive that cosmic bolt out of the blue and come through the experience whole are few and far between. Most folk fight tooth and nail against this insight; 95 per cent of the things humans stay busy with amounts to little more than a pile of stacked stones, which a stray lighting bolt from the Divine can upend in one shot. Finding the Devil, signifier of great inflation, immediately followed by the Tower, signifier of punishment from the Divine, delivers a very strong message. In fact, you can develop yourself into the greatest magician, greatest seducer, greatest redeemer, or whatever else seems powerful to you, and Spirit will not interfere with you. However, if in the process you accumulate an intense ego-charge and inflated sense of self-importance, you are courting disaster.

Self-importance marks the soul as ripe for the lightning, the sure remedy that puts the overgrown ego to rout. Until we have graduated from this planetary incarnation, we will be repeatedly tested regarding our distorted idea that any one of us can accomplish anything alone. Without the whole tribe, even the whole species, pooling our resources and sharing the wisdom gained from hard experience, we will lack the open-minded understanding to grow towards a sustainable future. Seeming to be the "top dog" in a militaristic hierarchy might look good from some society's point of view; but spiritually and culturally it's a disaster, and that's what this card is speaking about and confronting in the individual ego.

When the Tower appears in a spread, it signifies the emotional or cultural equivalent of an electrical storm crashing through your neighborhood. This is a violent and destructive episode in the short term, but in the long term it allows the over-concentrated energies to discharge and in the process inseminate the landscape with fresh potentials. There is no knowing in advance whether this will be a grand tragedy or a quickly-passing dance with fate. Generally, whatever is not either well-grounded or deeply buried is fair game for the lightning, also known as the Finger of God. When the card is reversed, it might imply the ivory tower of detached theory and educated speculation with no practical experience. It might also point to the Tower of the renunciate or recluse who walls himself in to impose spiritual discipline and exclude worldliness. The reversal of this card could also reference the Tower of imprisonment and liberty's loss. At minimum there is always an experience of shock with this card, which sets us back a minute and requires that we reorient our point of focus closer to our gravity center.

17 The Star

Letter: P = Mercury
Path: Between Gevurah and Hod
Quality: Dominance, wisdom, skill with language

In the Star we see the newly-awakened soul freshly in possession of the purified (astral) body beginning to explore the new Heaven and Earth that are revealed all around. She is bathing in the astral Light, exquisitely sensitized to the invisible world, while blessing the Earth and the Waters. All the veils separating the soul from its eternal identity have been lifted, and the purpose for this incarnation is understood anew. The Star card symbolizes the eighth or starry sphere beyond the visible planets, the final limit of human experience (according to antiquity) verging on the borders of Heaven. The enlightened soul is shown dispensing the Moist Light of Sophia, which the terrestrial waters will circulate throughout the Earth. Possession of this Light identifies the individual as an immortal. This Light also illuminates and aligns the astral chakras (microcosmic cognates of the planets of the Solar System), freeing the soul from compulsion on the wheel of Time.

Now that the soul is finally disentangled from its illusions and delusions, the Star reveals what the ego would never be able to find on its own. We have reached the third point of Light on the final descending triangle, or more rightly put, the third amplification of the impulse of Light showering into matter, in response to which the next three Trumps will emerge. The Star card portrays the virgin psyche, the infinite potential of the intuitive inner self. This represents the personal, subjective "feminine" side of human experience personified as the anima. Research in the early iconography of Alchemy shows that, following Hermetic premises, the earliest alchemical texts described and illustrated the "Philosophic Mercury" in feminine form, while the "Philosophic Sulphur" would be envisioned in the masculine form. It was from the varying admixture of these polarized substances that the alchemical metals were thought to emerge. (The third term, Salt, was named, described, and integrated as a "medicine" by Paracelsus.)

In Trump 17 the Mercurial soul is freed from the strange attractors of the previous two Trumps: the demon of desire and the prison of karma. As is often the case, the greatest of spiritual liberations can only follow after some kind of breakdown process. When we are finally knocked off our pedestal and the ivory tower falls, we are thereby liberated from both our excesses and our deficiencies. Unburdened from the accumulated results of past cycles, this anima figure is free to bond with life and respond to the moment without any preconceived program. It's as if the slate of memory had been wiped clean, but the wisdom and maturity gained through eons of human experience remain available. The individual self is in remission, and the transpersonal self has taken over, bringing her quicksilver power of mythic reinterpretation, which in an instant can change the destiny of any mere mortal.

In this eternal moment the virgin immortal Spirit stands forth from the bindings of Time/Space. Historically the Star figure (who is sometimes an angel) has the same two (Solar and Lunar) vessels in hand that we first witnessed in Trump 14. Temperance assembles the Tincture or the alchemical medicine, whereas the Star typically pours the medicine out onto the Earth and into the Water, initiating a transformation in the bodily and psychic life. This Trump shows the soul working its way towards a true healing of the wounds caused by its incarnations, achieving the re-integration of the personal heart with the immortal soul.

In this image we are to see the purified and distilled alchemical trinity (Sun, Moon, and Mercury) finding a new balance within the Creation, therefore allowing a new order of manifestation to commence. The paired elixirs of Light which Mercury dispenses will address both the ecology and the psyche, in essence healing the World Spirit at all levels simultaneously. As a side-effect these elixirs re-empower the parts of the self that are worth reviving after the shock and devastation of the Tower card. The shell of the ego has indeed been cracked by the Lighting Bolt from above. Nevertheless, the celestial energies vitalized by the lightning are now being dispensed by the liberated and timeless anima. Finally, our past accomplishments and identifications no longer "protect" us from the opportunity for true spiritual growth.

The alchemical stork watching over the soul makes a reference to chastity, attentive care, and peace. In Hebrew the stork's name literally means kindness, referring especially to the stork's tender nurture of its young. Their migratory habit allows them to symbolize harbingers of another world along the lines of the ibis or crane. This stork is the soul's guardian, guide to the future evolution of Mercury up the planes of consciousness. Spirit sends the stork to Mercury for a protector and as recompense for having outgrown ordinary reality and the preoccupations of her own kind. Its posture suggests an immanent ascension, poised to spring into flight.

Tarot of the Holy Light fills the sky of Trump 17 with the Pleiades or Seven Sisters of Greek mythology: an open star cluster at the end of the constellation of Taurus, which was associated with the Spring Equinox in Babylon of the 23rd century BCE. Regarding the Pleiades, Cirlot says, "Both Hebrew and Hindu traditions see in these stars the image of the Septenary as applied to space, to sound, and to action" (p. 248). He refers here to the light and sound spectrum, both of which express in repeating cycles of seven, with the eighth term or octave note being a restatement of the first at a faster or slower frequency. Traditionally, Taurus is associated with the harmonic sequence, music, and the throat-chakra in astro-anatomy. Mercury, of course, is associated with speech, tone, note, and word. When we realize how important this combination of ideas is for motivating invisible energies into manifestation, these remarks take on extra weight and poignancy.

Meanwhile, shining through the Pleiades from the opposite side of the galaxy is the (invisible) Spiritual Sun or galactic center. This design for the Star card symbolically links our current moment in time with the spiritual renewal foretold for this era by the Maya, the Vedas, Islam, and the Egyptians (Jenkins, 2002).

Our Solar System's current passage through this macrocosmic alignment is aptly compared to the Devil-Tower-Star sequence in the Trumps. Humanity having arrived at the place of uttermost materiality (the iron age or Kali Yuga according to ancient myth), this alignment signals a reversal of consciousness after which the souls who have forgotten their origins in the Light will be lifted again with the onset of the next 13,000-year cycle. This cosmic drama is playing out in the private life of every conscious creature embodied during this pivotal era (roughly from 1975 to around 2021). With every breath, we collectively carry humanity across this period of transition. I have no doubt that every soul presently incarnated is using this experience to complete lifetimes of self-development work.

Note that our Lady Mercury is out in the wilderness doing her work for the planetary order itself. She doesn't ask for recognition or any attention from the human arena. She's dealing directly with the aura of the Earth. At this stage she doesn't work through the collective mind anymore; her attainment authorizes her to function as an independent agent. Finally, halfway through the final Septenary, we experience the true freedom of liberation from the bindings of ego with the awakening of the higher mind, communicating and receiving purely without filters, immersed in higher frequencies. In this magical landscape she is unburdened of all physical and psychological defenses, free to stand forth naked in Eternity, purified of the need for veils, armor, or inhibitions.

409

In the situation of the Star reversed, it might be best to consider the bone-deep vulnerability of this tender soul in the magical landscape. The soul's arrival at this point of consciousness can only be won by successive divestiture from all false identifications and inhibiting structures. Like a chick stepping out of the shell that encased it, she must learn to discriminate everything anew as if for the first time. Her only protections are the impeccable Star in her aura and the stork of Spirit. This Mercury figure calmly holds her center despite a condition of total transparency, even under the scrutiny of every celestial eye. Nakedness in ancient symbolism means "nothing to hide"; therefore, having all of her upper chakras open to the sky declares her psychic condition of utter surrender to the Divine Impulse. How many of us can fully open ourselves to the urgings of life with no blocks and no denial to limit the scope of the engagement? Because she brings no ego-agenda, her entire body is awake to the cosmic situation, pulsing with the cosmic alignment of our times. No part of her private self interrupts her communication and communion with the entire Creation. One cannot know where this renewal of spiritual orientation will lead, but one can at least strive to handle one's part in the outworking of destiny with grace.

18 The Moon

Letter: Ts = Aquarius
Path: Between Netzach and Malkhut
Quality: House of Taste, discernment

The Moon represents the twilight, the magical crepuscule, the luminous darkness that is the doorway to the dreamtime where we are instructed by the voice of instinct and imagination. The sub-Lunar realm is the realm of the Pips, which represent the laws of matter that govern events on the surface of the Earth. In the gathering darkness, instinct battles intuition, and our more civilized aspects must either spontaneously combust or wash away in the rising tide of feelings and sensitivities. Only a person who is conscious in his or her unconsciousness can navigate here. The Moon rules the Elemental sphere immediately surrounding the Earth and is the feminine Compliment of Saturn, the Old Testament Jehovah of Wrath and control.

At this point the Trumps move on to the fiery trinity of earthly manifestation that rises in response to the incoming Light. This final trinity of Trumps exhibits the forms of matter that reveal the Divine Hand at work. The descending triangle (Devil, Tower, Star) has stripped the soul of all its defenses and revealed its innermost thoughts, forcing the aspirant to conquer his or her fear of the inner demon, fear of worldly collapse, and fear of nakedness before the Eye of God. Now at this first step of the ascending responsive triangle, the sub-Lunar realm or unconsciousness (Moon) struggles to contain and reflect the Eonic radiance without shaking apart from the inadequacy of matter to express the dictates of Spirit.

The Moon has been the Earth's spiritual Mother all of human memory, being our first heavenly guide and constant companion, our local center for interplanetary communication according to ancient tradition. The Moon's job is to gather in the energies of the Solar System as a whole, then render the result down (as from a baby-food grinder) and spoon it out to us gradually. According to astral legend, she digests the "raw" energies of the signs and planets, giving us a chance to work them into our psyches through the waxing and waning cycles she provides for us.

Jacob Boehme elevated the Moon's importance to the highest degree by associating it with the Seventh Property, quality, or Source Spirit. Luna's pairing with Saturn and her station in the sequence demonstrates that the Moon locates the goal of the Sophianic mission to fully ensoul the world with the Holy Spirit.

The Septenary star upon the castle to the right tells us that those who have cultivated their inner balance are protected and safe despite the seeming chaos outside the walls. This is the memory castle of the Western esoteric master within which has been gathered all of the Wisdom imparted by the Holy Spirit since the Incarnation. Those seekers who take refuge in the castle will find a thriving hive with the Priestess as their queen.

As in most oft-repeated versions of the Moon, we see no human protagonist. We simply see the Moon herself, full and occult, calling the tides, and dripping with mystical Light. In the landscape stand two castles with towers, one of which seems to be abandoned and crumbling, the other standing tall and whole. A path or road between the opposites leads into the distance. Meanwhile, in the foreground a bay or inlet fills up at high tide, and a crab crawls out of the waters. Two fighting dogs struggle for dominance, signifying the tension between the wild animal nature versus domestic servility. Those with copies of the oldest packs might also see drops of "celestial dew" falling (or rising) in response to the Moon, another hint about its power to stir the waters and move the Creation through the collective dreamtime.

All references to "moving the waters" carry a double meaning because behind them stands the Hebrew doctrine of the Tzimtzum. This refers to the time before Creation when the unmanifest world was still hidden in the void of the deep. In order to open an arena wherein Creation could take place, God had to exit the void and carve out a realm that would become the cosmos. This process is manifested for humanity in the Kabbalah Tree, said to be the pattern that God inscribed through a series of emanations. When the process of emanation was complete, out of compassion for humanity's nascent free will, God retreated and left us in possession of a neutral, un-impinged Creation. What becomes of it now is left up to us. This is the essence of the Tzimtzum. Now we can better understand the drops rising towards the Moon in the oldest cards: These drops symbolize not only the Moon drawing the earthly tides, but also the pull-back of the Divine Radiance to make space for human development. Just like the parents of a nearly-grown child need to offer space and refrain from overshadowing the child's growth, so too does God take a hands-off approach. This is not because we have been abandoned. It is a grace, a mercy, in order to give us some space in which to make our own mistakes.

In the meantime, let us not miss the theosophical pun that is built into this card because of its name and its correspondence to the Hebrew letter for Aquarius. Remember, Boehme's Seventh Property is the Moon, and its developmental arc is the longest of all of them. Traced sunwise, it covers from the sign Cancer to the sign Aquarius, bracketing the entire summer/fall arc of its partner the Sun. Boehme tells us that we won't find anything new in the Seventh Property; rather it represents the "ensouled matter" of the material cosmos after Sophia has fulfilled her wish to penetrate it all with the Moist Light of her celestial dew. In short, once the Star (the Great Hexegram) has appeared in a person's aura, that person can rest assured in his or her immortality, meaning that soul will be "going home to God" when this incarnation is over. One's primary relationship is no longer with Earth, but is instead with Eternity. This is not to make the sub-Lunar realm (our earthy world) wrong or inferior or infernal, only that it represents the human incubator for immortality: We came here to hatch and fly on, not to stay here forever and identify with it perpetually. The Moon in the Tarot as well as in Boehme's system provides the reset mechanism for the eternally-rotating sweep of the planets to return the soul to its original estate once the lessons of incarnation have been gained.

The truth is any given individual consciousness can only hold so much of the intuitive pool of communal knowledge that is associated with this Lunar flow. The Moon card makes available to us whatever we can handle. It also marks out a path that carries us through the parts we can't make sense of. The signals of dramatic extremes in the situation (e.g., high tides, creepy-crawlies, haunted towers, and fighting dogs) all have to be bypassed and avoided if we want to keep our composure and make progress. Any tendencies we have to revert to a feral mentality and lose control, to beg for rescue or howl in fear, have to be stilled to navigate this territory. The Moon illuminates the road between the extremes, but only those who know the look-out signs and have a strong inner compass will make the passage. The haunted landscape and darkened forest provide the perfect analogue to the soul when it's out-of-body and between the worlds. One must learn to navigate the astral planes while still unsure of one's own boundaries and without fully understanding the significance of incoming perceptions.

The existential loneliness of the soul is the biggest test of all the Trumps. This very loneliness is what stops us from claiming our immortality as a birthright, as individuals, and as a species. We cringe away from the arid austerity of those dark heights and the depth of space facing us, while we suffer from crushing doubt about how our private, individual experience could possibly matter to the vast cosmic plan. The people who thrive in this environment are true argonauts of consciousness. Only the special soul who has no fear of Eternity can embrace the Moon's opportunity for open-ended being despite the lack of guarantees or safety nets. Many fears and bogeyman fantasies have been projected onto the Moon card, but those serve to weed out the souls who lack the courage of their convictions. Until the soul is able to hold up its own spiritual autonomy no matter what the environment is doing, it cannot be included in the larger psychic and spiritual projects needed by the Moon. We can only be carried by Spirit to the extent that we are yielding and receptive, like obedient white blood cells, going where we are sent. At this stage the soul needs to have outgrown every tendency to default back to control urges, automatic resistance, or adrenal drama. To become truly helpful in life, we leave behind the need for constant reassurance and approval from a consensus reality (which mostly only dumbs us down to the lowest common denominators of our collective-mind assumptions).

As a species we have little hope to achieve a settled higher consciousness until we individuals learn to bear our true spiritual autonomy, our unfettered image-of-godhood, without falling into anomie, disaffection, agnosia, and terrible loneliness. Until we can feel joy and confidence in our unique one-of-a-kind nature, we will be trapped under the untrustworthy reflected light of this Moon. This mere fraction of true sunlight triggers our worst instincts, our fight-or-flight reflexes, encouraging a dog-pack culture burdened with crustacean conservatism. As a species we won't be ready to leave this terrestrial nursery school until we can understand and fully train our animal natures: our impulses, instincts, and inherent paranoia. All of these operate far faster than the mind will ever comprehend. Without a full vetting of everything we keep below the threshold of consciousness, locked in our so-called anxiety closet, we are not fit to face the world of unknowns out there beyond the Earth's aura. Spending time under this Moon will call forth your full catalogue of interior demons for review. If somewhere on the inner planes there is a boot camp for aspiring cosmic citizens, this Moon card is your invitation to attend.

In this sense the Moon card reversed would signify a landscape deprived of the Light of God, a truly agnostic realm where impulse and instinct fight for dominance. In this landscape the soul who lacks an interior Light to guide and orient him or her will devolve into an animal and come unstrung. In such a condition Trump 18 is attributed the siren song of Nature, the call of the wild, as in *Lord of the Flies*. Here we meet the final test of the Trumps, the test of one's self-rulership in the absence of outside intervention. Many sources will refer to this episode as the dark night of the soul. This type of experience stimulates our childhood fear of parental abandonment. In this case the fear is existential, focused on our relationship to God. The soul raves through the landscape like these agitated dogs, hovering at the fringes of consciousness, feeling lost and riveted by an ignorant fear of the dark. We feel alone and forsaken

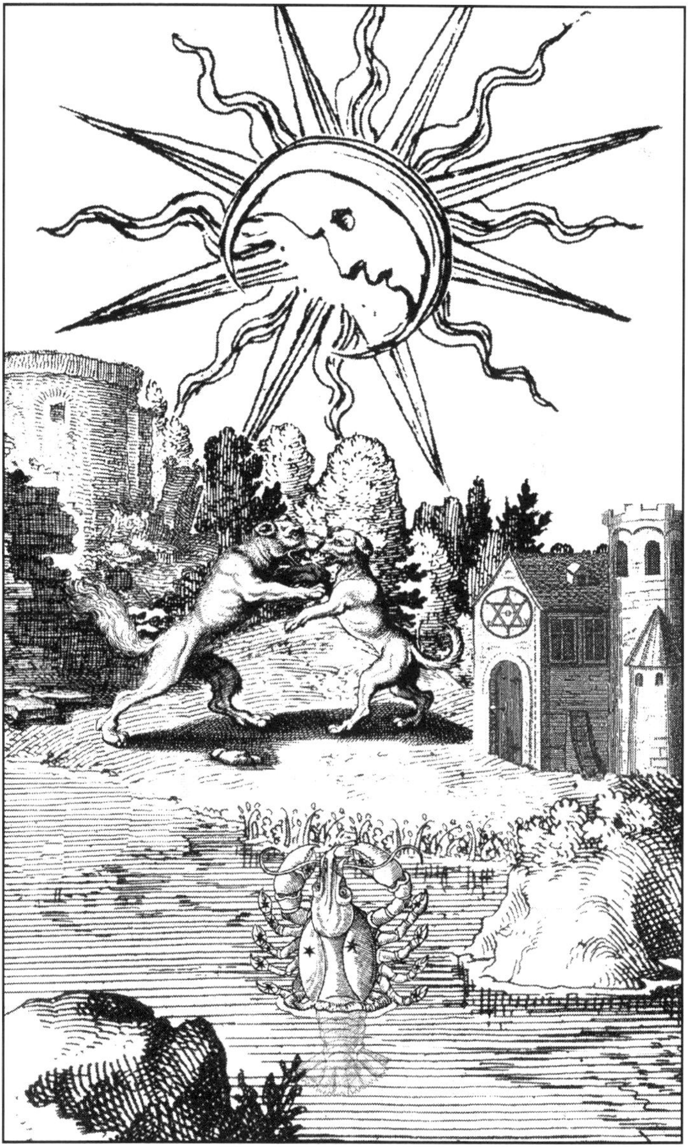

in an alien landscape where even familiar guideposts seem to mutate in the unstable light. The Moon card signals childhood's end for the soul and the quintessential gnostic dilemma. This is the message for the mature and fully-formed soul: Do not seek the Light from your environment, but become a Light unto your environment.

19 The Sun

Letter: K (Q) = Pisces
Path: Between Hod and Malkhut
Quality: House of Laughter

In the Sun card we meet Apollo, the Sun as the figurehead of the planetary corps and leader of the Muses. Light and sound being Appolo's domain, he can pass freely through the underworld (Twelfh House) with ease, armed with nothing but laughter and music. Here is the symbol of the Solar System as a whole and of the ego that is backed by its astral constitution as portrayed in the astrological birthchart. Sol's presence presages the fulfillment of our individual dreams.

In the second stage of the responsive triangle, the Sun provides the joyful counterpart to the Moon's dark but fertile matrix. The union of these two accomplishes the bonding of the Hermetic androgyny inside the self. In the Trump sequence this is the final union of the opposites within one's nature. Some packs emphasize the idea of a meeting of soulmates. This might have romantic connotations (as we see in *Tarot of the Holy Light*), but that is by no means always the issue.

The ancient myth that Plato put in the mouth of Aristophanes relates that when the world was formed and humanity first appeared, people were double gendered and they came in three arrangements: male/male, female/female, and male/female (androgynous). These creatures were very powerful; so when they started to make the gods feel at risk, Zeus disempowered them by splitting them in half. Forever after the human individual has felt incomplete, longing for its missing other half that the instincts testify to. The story of soul-fragments being sent out into separate incarnations to eventually find themselves in each other and re-unite is also the extra-biblical story of Sophia and Christ.

Like all gnostics, Boehme feels keenly the loss of his feminine side, his personal Sophia, who withdraws from the individual when he or she clings to an external gender-identification for the sake of attracting sexual activity. This is the very technical sense in which Boehme and the Protestant Sophianics used the term "virgin": They mean the state of being androgynous, undivided, male/female simultaneously. This state emphasizes the angelic quality of the immortal soul over any degree of identification with the world's cliches of sexual expression. Like a spontaneous priesthood, most of the Protestant

Theosophers came to their faith at a point in their lives when they were ready to lay all of their gender acculturation down. We would now describe the state they were aspiring to as "whole brained" in contrast to the "split brained" state. Plenty of documentation exists about the brain patterns of meditators and athletes to help us understand the union going on in the background of Trump 19. This Trump can be representative of the unified heart and mind, the dream self, and outer-world self, or the Mother and Father Pillars in the energy-body. They stand for the resolution of all personal dichotomies in a full acceptance and celebration of our personal uniqueness and multidimensionality.

What the Sun Arcanum represents is the first fruits of initiation, the realization of true, conscious freedom in the individual soul. This is not the dark and unconscious freedom of chaos that built itself up into an anxiety of Divine Wrath in order to boil its way into being. No, this is the self-aware freedom of the resolved and tinctured Light that offers immunity from guilt, fear, and the existential dread that haunts every unawakened individual. With Trump 19 the seeker leaves behind the worldview of limitedness, which includes submitting to the confines of any externally-defined construct whether sexual, social, or religious. In this newly-unified state the soul sees and participates in Eden directly, acquiring its own evidence of the restored Garden, at least insofar as his or her body's constitution can support. The Sun emanates a surge of prana, life-force, or kundalini into the body-mind, often shown as cosmic drops raining down from the sky.

Trump 19 represents that passage where the soul stops being a creature of temporality, having its existence purely in Time and Space. Now it graduates into an incorruptible state of unity and wholeness that resembles gold in its shining purity. No longer in danger of breaking down into a lesser by-product, the soul completes its androgynous integrity. The Sun also points to states of mind that resemble lucid dreaming, in that the dreamtime and ordinary self-awareness are literally conscious of each other without the experience of oppositeness. This erases our ancient cultural programming that taught us to live within an either/or worldview, left brain or right brain, but never both at once. The Sun fuses the dream self and the lucid waking self at three levels: in the world of things and beings, at the psychic level of the inner life, and in relation to Eternity.

Historical Tarots show different images. Often there is either a single golden-haired child, or the Gemini twins riding the white horse of the Divine Nature and carrying the Sun. At other times the two children play in a garden protected by a secure wall while being bathed in the Solar effluent. These two represent humanity's future, destined to fulfill the promise that Adam and Eve

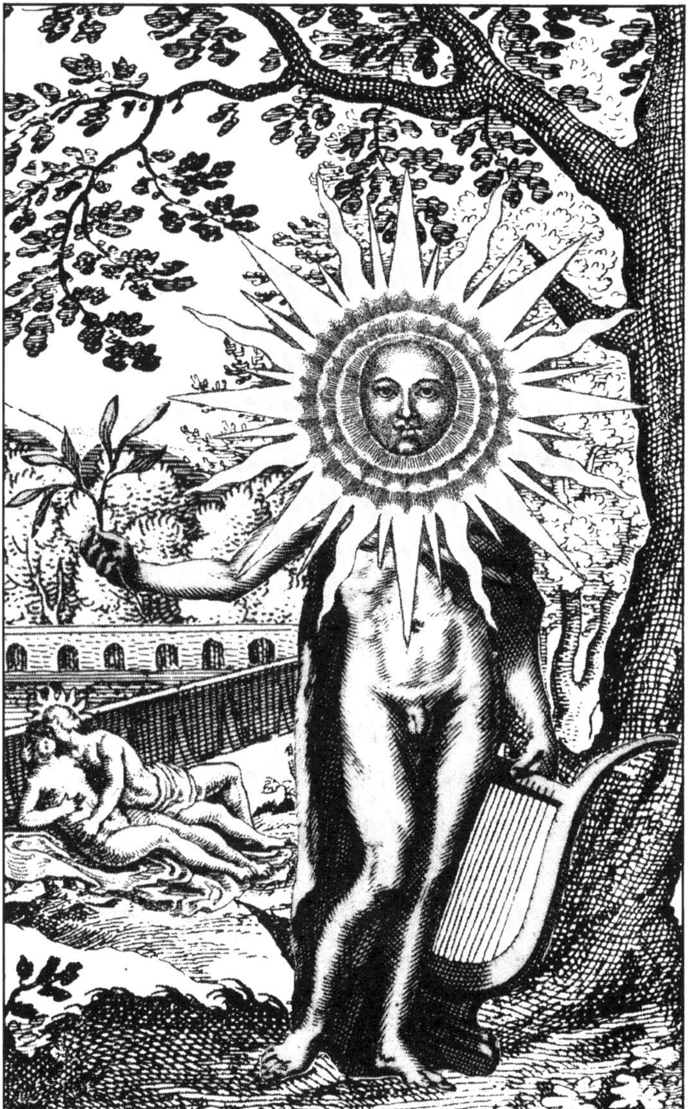

supposedly abdicated. Other packs show the two as mature man and woman, raising the possibility of alchemical tantra, wherein all the lifetimes as a feminine soul and a masculine soul finally merge together into full conscious within the individual. In *Tarot of the Holy Light,* we represent this idea by showing the sacred couple embracing outside Paradise, while Apollo moves freely through the landscape purifying everything his searchlight beams touch. Even as the previous year's leaves crackle underfoot (this is the sign of Pisces after all), Apollo causes the new growth of spring to burgeon all around.

The challenge that accompanies this card is our ego's fear of our soul's true vastness, glory, beauty, truth, and responsibility to the Creation. No matter how mature, old, or wise we might become, there is always more to learn and master. In an expanding universe we will be continuously tasked to increase our capacity for response. If we have passed the Moon card, then we know there is no "oblivion" we can hide in. It is not permitted for any soul to remain stuck within the ego's self-referencing worldview forever. In truth, arriving at this androgynous Light is not an ending of anything; in fact, it's the beginning of a whole new mode of living. With Trump 19 one moves beyond just managing the private ego and balancing out the daily stresses of incarnation. Imagine gaining access to the wisdom of all of one's incarnations, all of one's sins: The weight of such knowledge would be awesome if not crushing. Only an awakened soul can laugh and sing past the graveyard of human folly, becoming fully reconciled with all the pain, suffering, grief, horror, and oblivion that we impose upon each other as we grow in self-awareness. Hence we have put Apollo in the foreground and outside the Paradise fence. Let him serve as a sign of release from limited, programmed thinking, signifying freedom from victimhood and the forgiveness of sins.

20 Judgement

Letter: R = Saturn
Path: Between Tiferet and Yesod
Quality: Peace

Judgement illustrates the sounding of the Divine Word into matter: the Call. Here we see the dove of election appearing over the globe, embracing all the world in its wingspan. This is also the descent of Sophia into the world. Her eagle of speech provokes the prince (the immortal soul) to awaken from its sleep in the grave of incarnation. The soul separates itself from matter in response to the Eonic announcement. Releasing all focus on the transitory field of Time, the soul climbs and then casts aside the Ladder of Lights to discover its eternal identity. The self, the soul, the Call, and the angel are one.

In the Judgement Arcanum, which I like to call Resurrection, we see the completion of the responsive, fiery, materializing Trine. The achievements stabilized with the Moon and the Sun Trumps allow the individual to solidify a platform of consciousness that was only hinted at in the cards preceding this moment. This Trump marks the activation of the throat chakra, the energy that the Kabbalists call Daat, otherwise known as gnosis. In the Fallen Tree, Daat is keyed to Saturn and holds the reality-tester function of demanding direct experiential knowledge. But in the (mythological) era before the Fall, Daat was a property of the whole Middle Pillar (encompassing all the chakras along the spine); and Saturn occupied Malkut, the material Kingdom that is the footstool of Yesod, the Moon. In those "Fallen Tree" outlines that don't explicitly delineate Daat, one sees Saturn shunted off to a holding pattern at Binah. But for the Protestant Sophianics, Saturn clearly belongs on the Middle Pillar/central axis, holding his part of the planetary wheel around the Sun and paired with the Moon.

At this point we can fully survey the heavenly forces alive within the power of desire (the Star of David described by all six Trumps of this sequence). That desire has now evolved through the whole descending Trine and is in the third stage of the responsive Trine, finally settling into the fully-balanced pattern of the Star of David. Judgement grants the awakening of the power of the Word, the (often internal) magical voice. This signifies the individual achieving control of his or her vibrational frequency, which supports ever-more-subtle attunement and true change in the expression of matter. Trump 20 is a revelation of the resonant magical power of the Logos, which in the traditional biblical story is the sonic weapon used to win the Battle of Jericho.

Here the soul comes into a set of capabilities that is commonly considered to be beyond human ability. This whole final Septenary introduces energies that transcend the world we are accustomed to. Bad becomes good, Exaltation leads to a terrible Fall, then we wake up naked in the cosmic night. The void sucks at our soul until we pop and disclose our own interior Light, perhaps for the first time. Only after we have resolved all of our opposites, have identified with every error, and have forgiven all transgressions can we finally face the opening of the throat chakra and the release of the living Word. With Trump 20 we finally reveal to ourselves whether we are truly "made in the Image of God," capable of fulfilling the mandate from the Divine, or whether we have let go of that seed of the soul and are no longer responsive to the Call of Eternity.

Jacob Boehme was, for his time, extremely sensitive to the force of Saturn, both as the paternal Source of eternal strength and support and as the potentially crushing force of karma that binds the soul in Time. It all depends on the way we use our choices in our lifetimes. In Boehme's understanding, Saturn stands for the uncreated Wrath of the Father-force boiling out of the unmanifest, which unleashes the rest of the Source Spirits and manifests the Creation as we currently experience it. Saturn is a condensing force like gravity, like entropy, which slows down and crystalizes energy into the forms of matter. When this Word is unleashed in the landscape of the Judgement card, those souls that are still in debt to the karma-lord are unable to slip out of their material shells (the oblivion of incarnation) and follow the Call. Those souls that have become fully mature, on the other hand, will have the innate development to hear the Call and the cumulative self-cultivation to respond appropriately.

To state this more plainly, Saturn's effect is to rip through the astral ground-of-being with a super-low frequency like that of an earthquake. In the process he shakes apart those structures that are used up, flimsy, or non-sustainable. This releases the Light that has been trapped in the transitory forms of matter, liberating it for return to the Monad. Saturn is no respecter of individuals, nor can one bargain with one's karmic debts. When the trumpet blows, we each are revealed for who we truly are.

This Trump is traditionally clothed in many of the trappings of the biblical Last Judgement, including the angel of the apocalypse. Gabriel comes down from the sky and blows the proverbial trumpet, unleashing the Judgement with a blast of his horn. This discorporates everything that has a limited Time/Space identity. (Hence the Kabbalistic attribute of "peace" for Saturn; discordant energies are shattered and dissolved, after which a single harmonic-rich tone pervades the scene.) Despite its seeming destructiveness (for the unready),

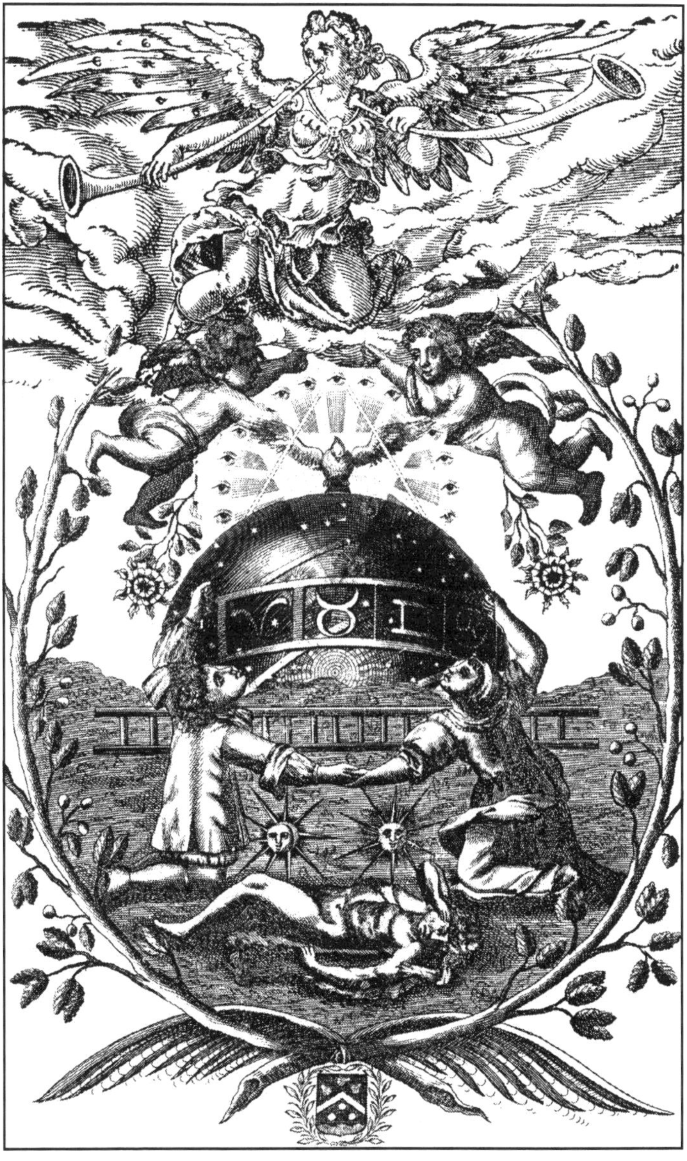

the Call attracts and elevates those whose energies are compatible with the eternal OM. In this way the sheep are separated from the goats, so to speak: The devolutionary or materially-bound souls are separated from those who are ready to rise beyond the Ladder of Lights and become citizens of a larger and more enlightened cosmos.

At this stage of the process, those individuals who are eligible for Eternity have such a strong basis of psychic integrity that they are unafraid to allow their repressed and hidden subconscious factors to come out and show their full colors. This is part of the significance of the soul's awakening from the tomb: One is released from all the socio-cultural inhibitions that were imposed just to make us more easily manipulated, more tractable by external forces. As the individual soul opens up to its natural power to wield the Logos, the Holy Word, all the hidden potentials of the human species, all our secret powers that have been slumbering in the collective consciousness, come back online and make themselves available to us.

Once this Call has been sounded, the soul has permission to preempt any material reality that holds it back or inhibits it from the fullest expression of its Divine potentials. From this location in consciousness, every form of Resurrection that you can imagine is possible: making up for lost time, reawakening of faculties that have fallen into disuse, the return of past and future life memories, even the abolishment of Time and Space itself. As the soul ascends into this wide-open firmament, it is restored to its eternal identity. This is what the Zen masters mean by seeing "the face you had before you were born." Transcending all previous identifications, we effortlessly flow into alignment with the heavenly invitation. In some Judgement cards you actually see the whole world bathed in the violet ray (or the unique energies of galactic center). Somehow the Solar System (or, mesocosmically, the astral body) achieves a state that is at one with the Heart of Creation. This is the glyph of our Resurrection as individuals and a species, becoming conscious again of the planetary organism within the larger body of the cosmos. The soul is finally redeeming the inheritance connected with our Divine Nature from the vault of matter.

In reversal, the concern is that the price of responding to this Call may be to lose your former self. Anything less than full commitment is inappropriate given the opportunity being offered. What stands to be gained is more worthy than what would be lost in the larger scheme of things. If you can't give a "yes" to this energy when it appears, then be truthful with yourself and let it go completely. The greatest sin in response to Judgement stems not from foregoing the Call, but from being oblivious to it.

21 The World

Letter: Shin (Sh) = Fire
Path: Cranial (third eye) crossbar, Chakhmah to Binah
Quality: Contrast, awareness of imperfection
Pan of Liability, Space

In the World card we see the celestial Sophia's immanence within the manifested Creation. We know Sophia as Harmozouza who decorates Creation with all the things and beings found within the Divine Imagination. The Sun, the Earth, and the planets are all parts of her construct; there is even room made for the shadow. Sophia is the glue, the bond of the Universe, who holds Creation within God's plan. Therefore, Sophia permeates Space, ensuring the limitlessness of consciousness and holding up the arch of Heaven under which all lives are lived. In her vast and timeless witnessing (Third Eye), all opposites are reconciled, all extremes are swallowed up, and in their place comes understanding, the true insight that purifies everything it touches, even as it consumes and recycles Time. Sophia's presence spans the vastness between "above" and "below." In this final card of the Septenary scheme, the World shows the fullest realization of all the Sophianic aspects brought together in manifestational mode. Her catalytic power is symbolized by the letter Shin and the Element cosmic Fire.

The Kabbalists taught that the fierce and fiery letter Shin drives downwards along the Mother Pillar expressing as extreme contrast with the goal of redeeming Malkhut from oblivion. Malkhut is our Earth, the "Fallen" matter that was expelled from the Pleroma (followed by Sophia) when Lucifer staged (or was provoked into) his famous abdication and banishment. Not every Christian denomination felt that this rupture, or even the subsequent enchaining of the Devil in Hell, was meant to last eternally. This card holds out hope for all compromised souls at every level.

The letter Shin, the essence of fiery awakening, sends Logos (meaning Reason and Order) down upon the chaos of matter with instructions for Creation to evolve and become more conscious. Logos is one name for undescended Sophia, God's Light, co-Redeemer (with Christ) of all Time/Space. With the World card we reach the goal and claim Sophia's final victory, which is to mediate the awaking of that heavenly Spirit within every form and every molecule of matter. This fulfills the infinitely recombinant celestial Virgin of the World (*Kore`Kosmou*), Bride of Christ in Eternity, the platonic *anima* *mundi*, the World Soul, our Mother Earth.

She is the Harmozousa or technician who structures and arranges Time/Space according to the ideas present in the Imagination of God. Scripture tells us Sophia/Wisdom was present at the beginning, the *Arche* in Greek, which makes Her the co-creator of the archetypes, the prototypes, or "first forms" of matter. Because of Her exalted station as the mirror of God's Wisdom, She becomes the goal and teacher of the seeker or Magus. Her legacy comprises all of the sacred arts and sciences catalogued in the *Mantegna* icons, which were also symbolically condensed into the Tarot Trumps through their association with the Hebrew alphabet.

Here on Earth the seeker craves knowledge of and communion with the Virgin of the World. The longing, desire, and attraction of the Magus evokes the warming, arousing potency of Sophia (the Moist Light) to fully saturate him or her and by extension this Earth. Over time the re-virginized soul internally resurrects the latent state of original, unhindered Divine Nature, this being the ultimate goal of the mystical quest. The symbolism in this card often refers directly to the Cube of Space in the Kabbalah Tree, showing the four angels of the apocalypse ranged in the cosmic directions outside of the wreath (or ouroboros) surrounding the Virgin of the World.

In the *El Gran Tarot Esoterico* World card (this is the pack that shows Gichtel's "Endarkened Man" as the Magus), there is a hermaphrodite with breasts and penis at the center of the wreath, making another reference to holistic functioning. Sophia is present at the middle of all extremes, facilitating a collapse of the opposites into the androgynization of consciousness. This pulse between the All and the One was first described as the *coincidentia oppositorum* by Heraclitus, a pre-Socratic Greek philosopher. The term was later revived by Nicholas of Cusa, who used it to explain his "doctrine of learned ignorance" in the spiritual life of the Holy Fool. We see many instances of the same idea playing out in the art and practice of Alchemy.

Here at the next-to-last station of the Trump sequence, at the culmination of the third and highest Septenary, we come to understand that Sophia is shorthand for the sum total of ascending and descending activity that makes up the grand metabolism of this Creation. All the forces we witnessed making a fiery descent on the Mother Pillar eventually penetrate the path Tav (the Fool), where they bounce off the nadir of the evolutionary arc (Malkuth) and begin to ascend again. Seeking souls encounter the *anima mundi* at the deep heart of the Earth, supporting the root chakra of our flesh bodies. Sophia provides the perpetual-energy wellspring that fuels our eternal quest, strengthening our inner Nature, and connecting us (even in this descended state) with cosmic

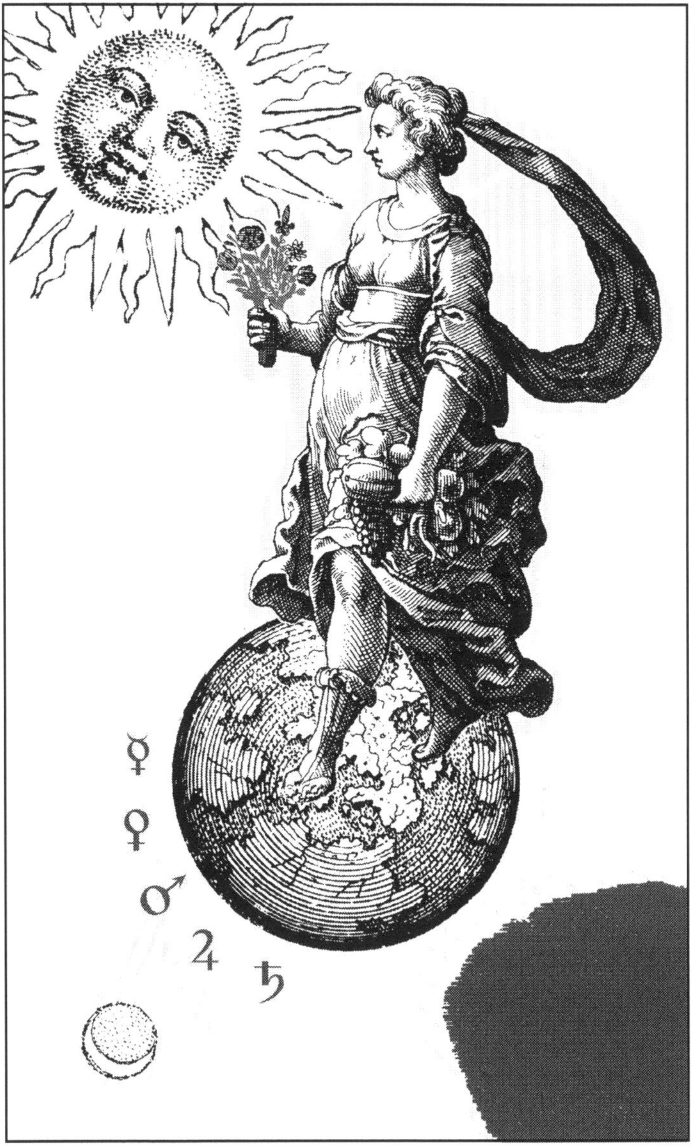

Space and cosmic reality. The Virgin of the World embodies the reunion-in-consciousness of all the separated particles, just the same as her celestial function represents the emergence of those same particles from the Divine Mind. Sophia's grasp on the process of manifestation transcends any limits of consecutive time, psychological history, or collective evolution. As She puts us through our paces, we increase in self-knowledge and knowledge of the whole until we finally awaken to the unlimited field supporting the sacred, intuitive interior life of the soul.

The World is cast in the feminine form because that signifies a high order of intuition and responsiveness to the probings of Spirit. In this Trump cosmic citizenship is not only attained but enjoyed. Now we see the individual soul having passed the tests of Saturn, therefore eligible to shed the accumulated karmas of the past and move up the ladder of consciousness. Trump 21, the World, represents a full revelation of our spiritual purpose, origin, and root power of manifestation. In short, this is the Monad healed and restored from the realm of the opposites by harmonizing all individualistic frequencies into a single grand and glorious living chord. One could think of this as the common denominator that links and interweaves the frequencies of Light and sound with the slower, denser frequencies that qualify matter.

In Tarot terms the World provides a perfect example of the *coincidentia oppositorum*. Looking across the whole scope of the Trumps, the unfolding plot represents a climb from humanity buried in its karmas, up through all 20 subsequent levels of development to culminate in these final Trumps, Sophia and the Holy Fool. Yet, when we correspond the Trump numbers to their cognate letters in the Hebrew alphabet, the Trumps lead us downward towards materialization relative to the Kabbalah Tree. The alphabet descends stage by stage from the head of the Tree (Keter) to the foot of the Tree (Malkuth). This means there is a dual circulation always happening in the Trumps: The Magus climbs "up" while Sophia climbs "down." Better said, even as the soul evolves "up" the ladder of lessons described by the Trumps, Spirit penetrates "down" the Tree, precipitated as drops of heavenly dew and manna, from the celestial state to the terrestrial state. Humanity ascends the microcosmic socio-cultural ladder while the Light descends the macrocosmic steps of the Ladder of Lights. The two impulses, both moving along the vertical axis between Heaven and Earth, meet here in the World card, in the "Divine Body" of the Virgin of the World.

The goal of the Western esoteric Magus, just like the goal of Buddhist enlightenment, is to evolve into a point of unity and synthesis despite the teeming multiplicity of manifested reality. From the microcosmic intercellular self to the macrocosmic interstellar self, the same operative principles are at work providing harmony, alignment, and synchronization; this is the way the seamless unity of the whole Creation is maintained. Often we see the Serpent of Time wrapped around the *anima mundi*, thus reminding us that Sophia is the arbiter of all beginnings and endings. The Virgin of the World encompasses the integrated pulses of the earthly, astral, and celestial planes comprising the eternal symphony of manifestation. Since we are "made in the image of God" and therefore reflective of God in the same way Sophia is, Trump 21 implies that the form of human consciousness arising at this epicenter awakens and consolidates all the labors of the whole species and the entire planetary evolution to date.

This is, of course, what the Tarot has always purported to do: to give us a map of consciousness by which we might route our evolution and encounter our highest self in a staged and sane process. At each step of the way, we are granted the guidance of deep historical wisdom and spiritual insight that challenges us to live up to our opportunities. This body of teachings illustrates the meaning and value offered by the twists and turns of fate, especially during those times in our lives when we cannot control what is happening to us. What we can control is ourselves, our reactivity, our stuck thinking. If we study Sophia and watch her ways closely, we can render and recast our human experience in the mold of the Virgin of the World. And I pray, dear reader, that this happens for all of us in our lifetimes because with this transformation at a personal level comes transformation at a planetary and species level as well.

If the upright World card represents the reunion of Heaven and Earth, the reversed card could signify the lack of this healing convergence. Trump 21 reversed might point to a failure to awaken, the negative spiral of addiction and denial, or being thrown back onto the wheel of incarnation with imbalances unresolved. One might feel trapped within implacable attachments and the ring-pass-not of "no." *Spiritus mundi* is Boehme's name for the wrathful and consuming force of the old-Testament Jehovah, the "great constellative world-spirit" that entraps us in our natural consequences. This is the father of Nature, Boehme's Abgrund, also known as the Mysterium Magnum, the magical Fire-eye of ardent Wrath/Love. (Think of the consuming rage of the two-year-old trying to get Mommy to do what it wants.) One could also identify the reversed World with the Turba or astral *tourbillion*, also known as God's finger of correction, which moves like a hurricane through this world disrupting whatever it touches. The World card reversed is the devouring and possessive graspingness of matter and the senses, source of endless appetites, which drags the soul into another incarnation and the creation of further consequences ad infinitum.

0 The Fool

Letter: Th (tav, tau) = Sun
Path: Between Yesod and Malkhut
Quality: Grace

In our Fool card we see Freher's presentation of the Holy Fool or Fool for God, the redeemed and awakened seeker who has used the "doctrine of learned ignorance" to contain and diminish the Hell realms within himself. This Fool may be "enlightened" (filled with Solar, Lunar, and Stellar Light), yet he orients his energies towards this unfinished world to serve as a protective and healing influence, illuminating the path of the seeker with Sophia's Moist Light.

The Sun (Heart chakra) is seen by Boehme and his students as half blasting and wrathful when facing "up" the Tree towards the Father forces in the head. The other half of the Heart is warm and loving when facing "down" the Tree towards the Mother forces in the pelvis. This teaching reminds us that we must never scorn the lower functions in the body. The Sun/Son's mediating Light, when realized within the awakened individual, creates a divisor or boundary between the descending Old World (Jehovah, God of Wrath and anguish) and the rising New World (Sophia, fulfillment of Light and Love).

As we know from the planetary Properties that Boehme revealed, these things are just flip sides of the same planetary pair (Saturn and Moon in this case). But what a difference we experience depending on which face of this *coincidentia oppositorum* is dominant at the moment. It is easy to see on the Kabbalah Tree, whether Fallen or Unfallen, that the Sun, Moon, and Saturn have a special relationship along the Middle Pillar. What is easy to forget is that there are two other such opposite pairs that the Fool/Sun manages to unify as well: that's Jupiter/Mercury and Mars/Venus. Both of these pairs cross the Kabbalah Tree's Middle Pillar along diagonal lines that connect the Mother Pillar to the Father Pillar.

Among the Continental Tarots, only Etteilla puts the Fool in the final place, assigns it to the letter Tav, and gives it the astrological Sun. This represents one of the three unique subgenera of the Continental Tarots, Etteilla's model being clearly identified with the Hermetic/Greek application of the alphabet. Alternately, there are Continental packs from the early 1900s that follow the Gra form of the Sefer Yetzirah (Aryeh Kaplan, 1990) and put the Fool at 21, corresponding to Shin, primal Fire (I call this the Spanish school).

Meanwhile, the French school variant promoted by Christian, Levi, Papus, Wirth, Haich, Sadhu, and Gad makes the Fool the penultimate card, granting it the cypher 0 and the letter Shin, primal Fire (leaving the World for last and granting it the astrological Sun). Each one of these variations has its natural interior logic and thus its adherents, but the only arrangement that remains consistent when carried over onto the Kabbalah Tree into the astro-alchemical medicine formulas and back to the ancient Astrology is the pattern that Etteilla passed along. Therefore, Etteilla's esoteric correspondences guide our choices in *Tarot of the Holy Light*.

As becomes obvious when one studies the worldwide phenomenon of shamanism, a certain domain of human consciousness is devoted to experiencing reality outside of our Time-Space references. What to call it and what meaning to attribute to it is reinterpreted for every society, but the core phenomena remain. Those who develop their subtle sensitivities can actually construct a point of view that transcends both linear time and psychological time. This platform of consciousness aligns us with all realities simultaneously so that a move made in one world (whether it's the terrestrial world, the intellectual world, or the celestial world) is a move made in all worlds; and a realization accomplished at one level is accomplished at all levels. This is the domain occupied by the Fool for God, who bears the Sun and symbolizes the soul standing outside of Time, contemplating its options.

In the excellent testament to the Tarot written by Harriette and Homer Curtiss there is a systematic presentation made that addresses the interrelated symbols of the Zero, the circle, and the Sun. The Curtiss' books are devoted to the interior esoteric structure of the packs that follow the Gra order of the number-letters onto the Tarot as we see in *El Gran Tarot Esoterico* and its cognates (again, the Spanish group of Continental packs). Therefore, the individual Trumps as delineated by Curtiss show the switch between Mars/Venus and Jupiter/Sun that I have mentioned as part of their unique approach.

> The serpent therefore represents the cosmic Great Creative Force which manifests as sex-force only when focused in the sex organs. The Great Creative Force is The Christ-Force or that fructifying and vivifying power through whose action all things are brought into manifestation, not out of nothing but out of the [circle] or great storehouse of potential energy which awaits only the creative activity of "the Lord God"(the Law of Good) to bring forth. In the biblical allegory we have the Godhead manifesting in its positive (man) and negative (woman) aspects with the magnetic attraction of the Creative Force

(serpent-power) uniting them and forming His likeness or the expression of the Trinity on earth (Curtiss, *Key to the Universe*, p. 30).

Remember that the Fool in his earliest historical manifestation had no number whatsoever, meaning that we have to look at the relatively-modern Zero as an overlay on the older archetype. Our Fool is the Spiritual Franciscan's Fool for God, the Holy Fool who, like a member of Gichtel's Angelic Brethren, lives exclusively in and for the Holy Spirit. This Fool has access to the entire eternal storehouse of infinite potential, but that is only possible because he does not abuse his position by unduly squandering it in meaningless action. Standing within the wheel of Time portrayed as a Mobius strip containing the Zodiac, the Fool averts his eyes and allows his Mother Pillar chakras to rest. The "naughting" that he represents is his refusal to donate energy to the chaos of the manifested Universe. The Fool confines all of his acting and reacting to the interior world of his own consciousness, his own mythic imaginal. The outer world plays around him, the hellfires seethe, the Lights and planets come and go overhead, and the barking dog of daily concerns nips at his ankles. But the Fool remains focused on the interior Eden, taking his cues from the Father, Son, and Sophia that have constellated within his energy-field as a result of his yielding attitude.

Thus Trump 0 demonstrates the soul in its reborn innocence and untrammeled divinity, meditating on its option to descend into matter and set loose a chain of consequences that will drive it through another round of the Trump sequence. The Fool stands at the threshold of incarnation with the best of motives, but it also realizes that stepping into Time and Space puts it at immediate risk of losing consciousness to the worldly ego and thus forgetting its original mission.

The Fool represents a mystery that is at once the end and the beginning. The Trumps represent a cycle, each one stemming from the last and leading on to the next. Therefore, the fact that we have arrived at an end is merely an appearance; in fact, this card links the World to the Magus. Because of this the Fool represents the state of "in between," the pause between acts of the play, so to speak. One could imagine that this Fool represents a vast expanded field (like the gravity-body of the Sun) that contains all the other ingredients of the Solar System (the signs, planets, and Elements, meaning all the other Trumps) within its aura and orb of influence.

In microcosm the *Tarot of the Holy Light* Fool is a Western yogi caught in a moment of contemplation, looking to the Solar System within. He has achieved the Tincture (of androgyny) and has constellated the Trinity within

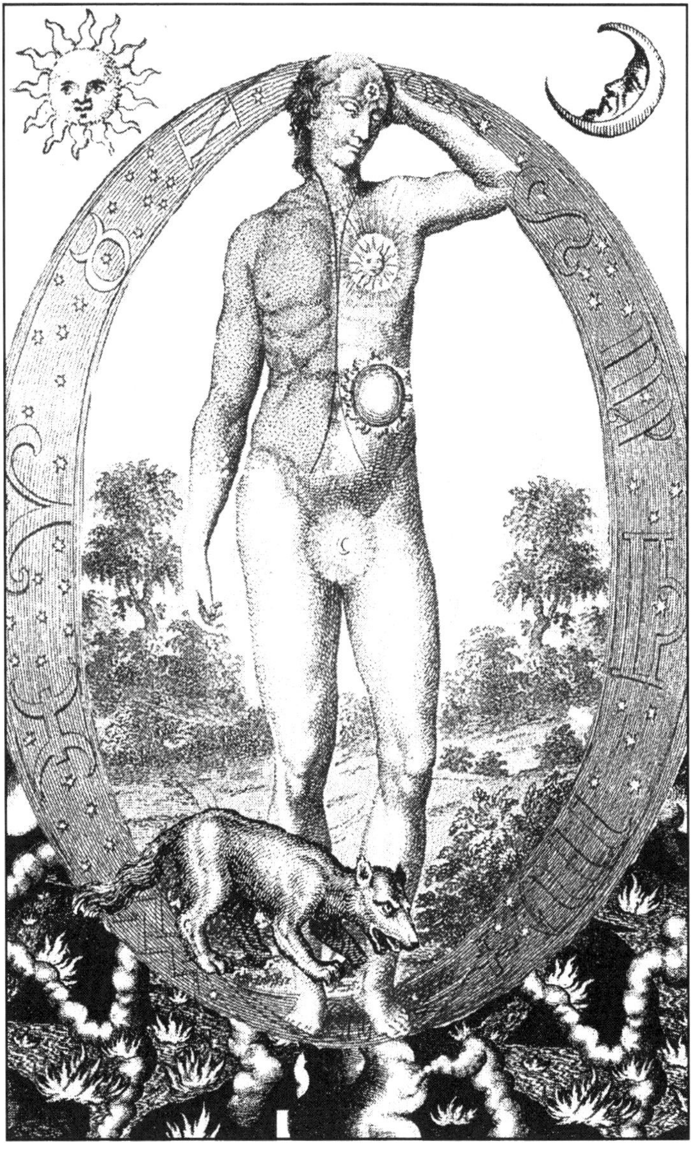

the three centers: creative speech (Mars/Venus), central regulator (Mercury/Jupiter), and root (Saturn/Moon). His right side that would direct ego-centered action in the world is dormant, meaning that he has surrendered to the powers of Wrath and ceased defending or offending. He agrees to work within what Divine Will manifests and to devote all care and attention to the labor of healing the world and returning Love back to Deity.

The Fool's only aspiration is to serve, share, and perform his practices in humble gratitude for Love's sake only. His self-cultivation ceaselessly lifts up the Fallen ones with the power of Sophianic compassion and understanding. His immediate surroundings demonstrate the temperament, complexion, and natural climate that he creates with his own thoughts. Understanding himself to be a microcosmos within the world, he exercises his resemblance to God by enclosing his outer senses and opening his Third Eye (with the Jupiter symbol on it). Despite the churning that ceaselessly rises from the unfinished nature of the temporal Creation, the Fool is no longer prone to mistake the outer world for the plane of causality. Like a seed waiting to sprout, he is now a representative of Eternity on Earth. So he waits and listens and only moves when he is shown the opening by Sophia. This keeps him free to follow his inner Lights, whether he is guided to re-enter the throng of the vast human hive, or find another position within the great web of life.

Appendix 1
The Horoscope Spread

Zodiac Spread

East — West

1. Self, Life, All Beginnings
2. Wealth & Value
3. Siblings & Communications
4. Parents, Home & Family
5. Pleasure, Children, & Self Expression
6. Health, Hygiene, & Nutrition
7. Partnerships, Groups, Long-term Relationships
8. Death, Rebirth & Reincarnation
9. Philosophy, Culture & Long Journeys
10. Ambition, Contribution, Social Status
11. Friendship, Associations
12. Seclusion, Retreat, The Shadow

Zodiac Spread

This layout is modeled after the 12 Houses of the astrological horoscope. It makes a general survey of the classic 12 categories of life without any kind of weighting or prioritization to strengthen one position over any other. Each House position has deep associations with a specific set of planets, signs, and Elements; one can certainly include these in your interpretation if you know them. For ease of use with Tarot, we will simply note each House's primary characteristics and most predictable contingent relationships. Some might find that these Houses become more meaningful and evocative when they are visualized in association with the same-numbered Trumps.

After the shuffled and cut cards have been dealt into the spread, you can investigate the House that most closely approaches your question. Don't forget to read and study the related Houses that might impinge or have an influence on your issue. In effect you have 12 small readings of up to eight cards each (if you follow every contingency). This approach allows for a customized interpretation as short or as in-depth as you wish. You can also use this spread to provide an overview and current commentary on your birth chart, either as a substitute for, or in company with, your astrological transits.

When reading the lists of contingent Houses, here are a few hints to help you assimilate the messages you find:

Strong support cards can be trusted and depended upon. They are your most potent allies outside of the card in your chosen House; they favor your immediate cause.

Cooperative cards are energies that are inherent in the circumstance that could prove helpful. You can't expect personal involvement from them, and you have no sway over their choices; but by nature they can assist you in the course of their inherent action.

Conflicting forces are people and things that are going to jump out from the margins to steal your energy and derail your goals. Expect interference as a natural part of any project, and don't let such incidents ruin your mood or make you feel victimized. Self-disciplined creativity will help you turn stress and competing agendas into more positive forms, such as humor, understanding, and leadership.

Opposing energies will confront you directly; at first they might even seem to have the power to stop you. You must find a mutual accommodation with this force before you can fulfill your goal. Life is very seldom as simplistic and clear-cut as winning or losing (as in a sports event or military conflict). Instead of looking for a quick fix, use this card to help you broaden your view of the options available to you. Consider this card your worthy adversary and trainer, and be respectful of its part in this situation. Once you become equal to this energy, having mastered your reactivity and found a creative response, then the designated opposition-energy becomes your ally, or at least another dependable thread in your safety net.

A note on reversed cards:

First of all, relax. Reversals do not mean you are doomed. The physical nature of most Tarot cards is that they appear binary, with a "top" and a "bottom." The mind wants to jump to the conclusion that an upright card is "good" and a reversed card is "bad." By holding to this reflexive superstition, we miss all the shades of meaning in-between. However a card should fall, it is still only itself, still working through the same range of issues. Try to take the attitude of the Taoists with their yin/yang understanding: All opposites are interpreted as the bright side of the hill and the dark side of the hill. It's the same hill, just a matter of where the light is falling right now.

It is wiser to think through all the possible manifestations of each card no matter which direction it lands. Interpret each card as a continuum, with the designated upright and reversed meanings at the furthest extremes of a spectrum with a rich middle range of and/and possibilities. A card in reversed position is asking you to study it a little more deeply, investigate and examine your assumptions regarding the position the card has fallen in, and just generally bring more consciousness to the indicated areas of life. Reversed cards are not necessarily the enemy, nor is the universe out to get you in some malevolent way. More likely they represent aspects of life that have temporarily fallen into the shade of inattention. Reversals invite you to shine more wattage from your inner Light upon them so they can show you their full range of implications.

First House: House of Self, of Life, of All Beginnings

This is the place one looks when dealing with issues of identity. What was I born to do? What makes me different from the people around me? How is it that certain circumstances seem to happen over and over around me? What is my archetype, my traditional role, and my standard operating procedure? What do I characteristically want and consistently seek no matter what the circumstances? Questions like these can only be answered by setting all outside influences aside and taking the measure of your own deep self-knowledge. The card that falls in this position gives you a mini self-portrait of your energy-body, your motivation, and the effects you are having on your environment.

> Strong support can be found in Houses 5 and 9.
> Cooperative forces come from Houses 3 and 11.
> Conflicting forces are in Houses 4 and 9.
> Opposing force comes from House 7.

Second House: House of Wealth and Value

This House represents the raw materials that you find essential and indispensable for your daily quality of life, including your body, your money, your living space, and your possessions. The ideal Second House environment supports your natural inclinations, whether that takes the form of a little plot of land to grow your own veggies, a self-owned and -operated business, or even a position of power and responsibility in your community. Second House resources give you grounding; they stabilize your roots at the foundation, demonstrating in material terms your essential values. Most people are motivated to work hard and invest both hope and pride in providing for their Second House needs. The card in this position offers a resource you currently have in abundance, right use of which can support your well-being. This card wants to firm up and become solid around you, to provide the security of stability.

> Strong support can be found in Houses 6 and 10.
> Cooperative forces are in Houses 4 and 12.
> Conflicting forces are in Houses 5 and 11.
> Opposing force comes from House 8.

Third House: House of Siblings and Communications

This House addresses your connections with friends, siblings, classmates, and people of your same rank. This is the House for finding allies among the people in your age-related social peer-group. Our primary learning and common sense are acquired in this House, including the folk wisdom and family knowledge that comes to us through our roots. We also look here for developmental issues taken on in early youth, when we were still impressionable and unguarded. The imprints made in our psyche from this era of life stay with us forever, both the traumas and the inspirations. Our instincts for fair play, trust, open-mindedness, and optimism are grounded in this House, which is the natural realm of the magical inner child.

> Strong support can be found in Houses 7 and 11.
> Cooperative forces are in Houses 5 and 1.
> Conflicting forces are in Houses 6 and 12.
> Opposing force comes from House 9.

Fourth House: House of Parents, Family, and Home

The Fourth House represents the maternal seat, the belly and the breast, the nest and its protected zone around the Mother. The altar of the Heart is in the Fourth House, providing the archetype of loving nurturance and unconditional Love. In the Fourth House we encounter the river of feelings that links us to life itself, the subconscious emotional and psychic stream, which feeds the mystical and imaginative side of life. This House puts us in touch with our most intimate dependence upon the bosom of the Divine, be it Mother Nature, the inner guide, the guardian angel, or any other manifestation that we can contact and take nurturance from. The Fourth House is where we retreat when we are weak and tired; this is where we go to restore ourselves when we are used up and empty. Whatever trust or confidence we can have in the web of life and our place within it is renewed and rewoven through our Fourth House experiences.

> Strong support can be found in Houses 8 and 12.
> Cooperative forces are in Houses 2 and 6.
> Conflicting forces are in Houses 1 and 7.
> Opposing force comes from House 10.

Fifth House: House of Pleasure, Children, and Self-Expression

The Fifth House is the domain of all creative and visionary activities, whether that involves a torrid love affair or the sustained concentration required to produce deathless art. In this House we feel free to experiment, testing our capacities to reach beyond our previous limits and demonstrate our inspired genius. This kind of environment produces works of true innovation because it is stimulating in a recreational way, providing the safety and support to "let our hair down" and lose our inhibitions. Even if competition is present, it is handled playfully in a spirit of fun and learning. The whole climate of this House rewards us for stepping out of the cultural lockstep and showing something of our true colors. This stimulating and encouraging climate brings the best out of us. We can feel at our most strong and beautiful, at the peak of our abilities, and most fully representing our inner archetype when visiting the Fifth House. For this reason, it is important for every person to make time for creative play that stirs his or her pot, tickling the imagination into action.

> Strong support can be found in Houses 1 and 9.
> Cooperative forces are in Houses 3 and 7.
> Conflicting forces are in Houses 2 and 8.
> Opposing force comes from House 11.

Sixth House: House of Health, Hygiene, Nutrition, and Necessary Duties

The Sixth House is the realm where we learn to take proper care of our bodies, where we learn to make the choices that lead to well-being. In general it's about keeping a healthy lifestyle, which includes nutrition, exercise, sleep, positive attitude, and attention to our special needs. But beyond the basics, Sixth House energies seek to imbue their whole realm with therapeutic, restorative, and remedial qualities. The Sixth House ethos is one of self-cultivation and discipline in pursuit of higher values. The long-term goal in the Sixth House is longevity and sustainability. Here one strives to achieve a state of "functional immortality," where the body ages very slowly and advancing years are not an affliction. Sixth House people work towards orderly, integral systems that cycle through productive and self-renewing stages. Whether the focus is the ecosystem of the digestion or of the global oceans, Sixth House energies mimic Nature in promoting optimum diversity within a harmonious whole. The good habits supported by this House lead to love of life, optimism, resilience, and mental clarity.

> Strong support can be found in Houses 2 and 10.
> Cooperative forces are in Houses 4 and 8.
> Conflicting forces are in Houses 3 and 9.
> Opposing force comes from House 12.

Seventh House: House of Partnerships, Groups, and Long-term Relationships

It is in the Seventh House that we reach outside our habitual comfort zone and try to connect with people who are truly different from us. Here is where we discover what we love and are attracted to in others, whether the bond is of the romantic, friendship, or professional persuasion. This House holds long-term connections we make with people, bonds that have the potential to last for many years. Here is where we find the people whose advice we can trust, even if it comes through long-dead role models or long-distance virtual connections. Any person who has made a lasting impression on our imaginations remains part of our Seventh House community, affecting us subtly no matter how many years it might be after the fact. The Fourth House is the traditional location of our genetic family, but the Seventh House is the place where we collect our intentional family, the people with whom we are related by choice over time. It is also possible to form relationships with service professionals that end up being just as intimate and longstanding as any friendship or love affair.

> Strong support can be found in Houses 3 and 11.
> Cooperative forces are in Houses 5 and 9.
> Conflicting forces are in Houses 4 and 10.
> Opposing force comes from House 1.

Eighth House: House of Death and Rebirth, Reincarnation

This is the House where we ponder life's mysteries. We have come to the end of "believing," being finally strong enough to learn the truth. One might feel an upwelling of great exhaustion, disaffection, alienation, or aversion, making it clear that something needs to change. Often people feel an essential loneliness around their Eighth House issues, despite our appearances to the contrary. The persona by which you are known to others suddenly feels like a stranger to you. An inner, deeper, more mysterious part of the self calls out for attention, demanding that you leave your worldly ego at the door. This is the House where we find the sobering truths that explain the camouflaged surfaces of our relationships. We can finally see through those broken promises (the ones we made, the ones others made) and discover what they really meant. If there is a discrepancy between rhetoric and reality, the card that falls here will shine a spotlight on it. This is also the avenue by which our karma from previous lives and earlier stages of the present life can find us. If we have been harboring a blind spot, we will be called to this House to illuminate it.

> Strong support can be found in Houses 4 and 12.
> Cooperative forces are in Houses 6 and 10.
> Conflicting forces are in Houses 5 and 11.
> Opposing force comes from House 2.

Ninth House: House of Philosophy and Culture, Long Journeys

The Ninth House introduces us to the wide world of human expression and inspiration, encouraging both physical and mental travel to foreign shores and far-off times. The energies of this House foster religious vision and philosophical enlightenment, expanding personal awakenings into cultural and historical movements that raise the bar for human potential. Multicultural exposures allow us to grow in directions that our birth environment might never have offered. Education raises our point of view so we can witness the breadth of human achievement. We embark upon a quest for a higher and more authentic life, one that carries us past the parochial views that used to limited our outlook and goals.

> Strong support can be found in Houses 1 and 5.
> Cooperative forces are in Houses 7 and 11.
> Conflicting forces are in Houses 6 and 12.
> Opposing force comes from House 3.

Tenth House: House of Ambition, Contribution, and Social Status

In this House we create and uphold our reputation, crafting our contribution to history and leaving our imprint on the stream of Time. For some it's all about success and riches, but for others there is the deeper motive at work. All the ancient wonders of the world are Capricorn accomplishments, bending natural resources into prodigies of human vision that demand persistence, daring, and hard physical labor. Accomplishments of this type are built to last. Even just living through historic times will leave a mark on all those who participate.

This card illuminates your place within the collective goals and struggles of your generation, your tribe, or your field.

> Strong Support can be found in Houses 2 and 6.
> Cooperative forces are in Houses 8 and 12.
> Conflicting forces are in Houses1 and 7.
> Opposing force comes from House 12

Eleventh House: House of Friendship, Associations

The ancient world gave this House to the realm of voluntary associations, those relationships and connections that are exclusively based on affinity without consideration for role, age, wealth or its lack, gender, family affiliation, or partisan stances. This is where we seek out people and situations purely to fulfill our personal interests, to take refreshment among birds of a feather. In this House we seek freedom of mind, the chance to explore and investigate truly new ground regardless of convention. It takes courage and stamina to individuate, to outgrow all of the cultural stamps that have been imposed upon us and discover our innate and natural being. In this House we get our rewards for bearing up and patiently outsmarting life's distractions, which constantly threaten to drain the energy we reserve for our private joys.

> Strong support can be found in Houses 3 and 7.
> Cooperative forces are in Houses 9 and 1.
> Conflicting forces are in Houses 2 and 8.
> Opposing force comes from House 5.

Twelfth House: House of Seclusion, Retreat, Self-Undoing. The Shadow.

This is the House of endings, small or large, quick or slow, planned or accidental. Sometimes the completion comes easily, being simply a matter of natural timing and agreed-upon boundaries. At other times it will represent the emotion-laden loss of persons, situations, trends, or institutions. Everything that has a beginning also has an ending. This House protects the incipient future from being cannibalized by the leftovers of the past. To use an agricultural example, the Twelfth House separates the annuals from the perennials, the quick from the dead. Whatever we might lose as we pass through this realm (or period of time), the result is usually for our own good. Like a late-winter haircut, our Twelfth House losses lighten our load, granting a fresh start in the next House, where the cycle starts over again from scratch.

> Strong support can be found in Houses 4 and 8.
> Cooperative forces are in Houses 10 and 2.
> Conflicting forces are in Houses 3 and 9.
> Opposing force comes from House 6.

Appendix 2
The Celtic Cross Spread

Celtic Cross Spread

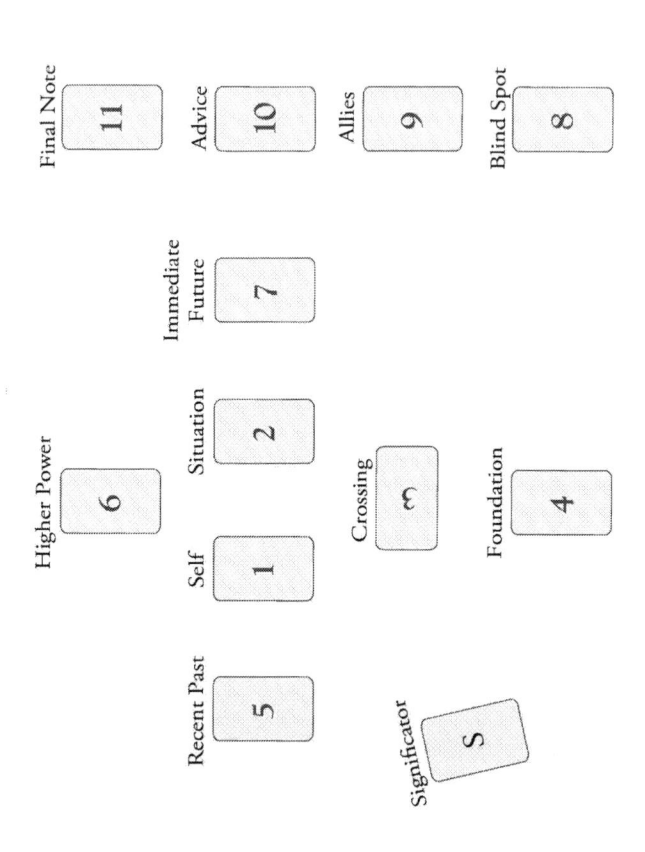

1	Self
2	Situation
3	Crossing
4	Foundation
5	Recent Past
6	Higher Power
7	Immediate Future
8	Blind Spot
9	Allies
10	Advice
11	Final Note
S	Significator

The Celtic Cross Spread

The Celtic Spread is the modern Tarot world's go-to spread. Made up of three sections, it addresses current events from multiple angles. With 11 positions, there is room for three cards that focus on the immediate moment, four cards that put current events in context with a four-directions wheel surrounding the previous three, and four final cards that move the action forward into the possible future.

The user can imagine the first 11 Trumps in the outline of the spread to make the position numbers and relationships clear. I find that the positional meanings take on added depth when the Trump sequence is envisioned as a subconscious backdrop to the cards that appear in these stations during a spread.

We are including an extra position as a way of linking us back to the world of medieval magic. Traditionally a Magus learns how to read both inner and outer events as an interpenetrating network of spiritual signs and signifiers. Like windows into the invisible world, such signs have the potential to reveal the Divine Hand at work behind the opaque surfaces of life. The Significator position (labeled S) will indicate a symbol, sign, or signature that the questioner can focus on during the events described by the spread. It repesents both an active force in external events and an inner current affecting the psyche. The S position stands outside the numeric sequence of the formal Celtic spread, so one can pick a Significator any time it feels appropriate. One can also use different segments of this spread as a model for making "quickie" spreads of fewer cards:

1) The first three numbered positions give us a classic approach to the "thesis, antithesis, synthesis" formula.

2) Alternately, one can use a Significator to replace the first three (representing "here now"), following with the four cards that define the cross. These illuminate three dimensions of time (past, present, future) and the three levels of consciousness (subconscious, conscious, super-conscious).

3) Another shorthand approach could be to simply use position one followed by positions seven through 11 as a way of scanning the near and unfolding future.

1) The Self Card

This is a mini-portrait of the self, whether that is the person who has shuffled the cards, or the person for whom the cards have been dealt. Older Tarot practice would have the reader select a carad according to age, gender, and physical appearance, or else from the question at hand. But modern usage allows for the shuffled cards to reveal a Self card that is unique to the situation. Whatever the card is, whether upright or reversed, this is how you are currently viewed through the lens of Tarot.

2) Situation

As befits the number two, we now face the first expression of our "issue." Because it's being defined through contrast with the first card, there is always a slight tension inherent in the difference-value between the two. If there is a tendency towards dualistic thinking, this card will bring it out. However, this is by no means always a problem card. It is better to read it as an important aspect of the Significator's immediate circumstance and setting that requires greater focus. This tells us more about the topic the spread is addressing.

3) Crossing

Typically this position forms a bridge or fulcrum between cards one and two. Like the crossbar of a scales, it can offer a way to harmonize the potential for conflict between the self and the situation. But this position can also be the sticky-wicket or stumbling block card, which explains why card one can't be entirely comfortable with card two. This position challenges the stability of numbers one and two by highlighting a moving element that escapes control and introduces variables that the initial cards might have been ignoring. Even in a great situation, it presents a balance challenge.

4) Foundation

The card that falls here represents the historical roots of the current situation, both temporally and psychologically. It is literally the bedrock or fundament, the "ground of being" upon which the moment's manifestation stands. Look for karmic patterns and ancient, unquestioned assumptions here, but also look for long-established strengths and strategies. It can represent the family, workplace, religious, or cultural matrix in which current events are playing out. Whatever card falls here, its influence is long-held and probably inherited, imbued by one's background and origins. It might so happen that questioning the unspoken implicits will begin to unlock the energies of the situation.

5) Recent Past

This position has two functions. Firstly, it represents the precipitating cause of the reading, the event, or condition that spurred the idea of seeking counsel from the Tarot. Thus the card in this position will point to the immediately preceding developments that created the "now" of the Significator, the one who is receiving this reading. Simultaneously, this position recognizes the card's impulse as declining, waning, becoming spent and drained of power, losing impact with every passing hour. So even as we recognize the seminal importance of the influence shown here, we can also know that it is expired and done with, like a popped balloon, a mere chimera of its former self. Those energies will never have such a large influence on you again. This card occupies the beginning of a past-present-future cycle that shows itself across the horizontal axis of positions five, three, and seven.

6) Higher Power

This represents the perspective of the higher self, oversoul, conscience, or ideal. The card that appears in this position offers a more complete overview, a broader perspective that transcends self-interest and suggests a larger world of meaning. Sitting at the top of the column of cards made up of numbers four, one, two, and six, it represents a Light that shines from one's own highest intuitions, penetrating the present story of the self (positions one and two), even shining into the depths of the unconscious (position four). The card in this position puts one's private experience in context of the larger moving front of human evolution.

7) Immediate Future

Following the momentum of cards five and three, the future card illustrates the natural consequences of the previous actions and influences. Every revelation exposed by cards one through six must funnel through position seven to reach the future and those final four positions. Use the card that falls in position seven to make the best possible use of the inherent natural consequences suggested by the previous six. Think of position seven as a doorway that you want to move through gracefully on the way to your appointment with destiny.

8) Blind Spot or Achilles' Heel

This is by no means always a negative position, but what it does do is bring attention to the part of the story that one might otherwise tend to overlook. Nobody has 360° vision, so this position allows for a signal from the unspoken depths. Consider the card that falls here as a report from your inner-opposite or invisible twin, which is sometimes the angelic inner child, and sometimes a clever trickster. Your "other half" knows what you don't. So let the card that falls here signify this essential information, and take it to heart.

9) Allies and Loved Ones

Here is where to look for outside threads of the safety net, including people, places, and things that build one up and inspire one's best work. Here we'll find our friends and family, role models, teammates, supporters, and coaches. These are all people who have your best interests in mind and are happy to lend a hand or give a kind word towards the fulfillment of your goals. The card that appears here says the indicated resources are available in the immediate environment, ready to be utilized.

10) Advice

This is the best position to focus on when answering the question, "What do I do now?" Try to read it as a suggestion you could follow to move the action along in a positive direction. This card offers possibilities that you can say yes to, including strategies that have a chance to reduce any chaos or confusion, bringing more coherent energies into play. Even if you aren't in a position to immediately resolve all the challenges inherent in the spread, at least this card offers a ray of hope for your personal experience. Be open to this idea.

11) Final Note

Some consider this an outcome card, but in fact it equally represents the beginning of the next cycle that will take over once the momentum of this reading is exhausted. Think of it as a goal to work towards, or a light at the end of the tunnel. If the implications are ominous or the card is showing its darker side, read it as fair warning of a challenge that will soon have to be addressed.

Appendix 3
Tarot Deck Citations

Tarot Deck Citations in Chronological Order

All members of the Marseille family of Tarots: Mentioned is the *Tarot Jacques Vieville*. Published in Paris circa 1650, republished by U.S. Games Systems in 1991.

The *Mantegna* series of classical icons. Several reprints in Tarot format by different publishers are available.

The 78-card packs conforming to *The Book of Thoth / Etteilla Tarot*. The Grimaud edition first appeared in Paris around 1800. Modern reprints are available of the several packs attributed to Etteilla's students.

Tarot Balbi by Domenico Balbi. Published by U.S. Games Systems in 1978.

El Gran Tarot Esoterico, created by Luis Pena Longo and Marixtu Erlanz du Guler. Published by Fournier in 1978.

Neuzeit-Tarot / New Age Tarot by Walter Wegmuller. Published by AGM AGMuller in 1982.

Knapp-Hall Tarot, a reprint of the original *Knapp Tarot* first published in 1929. Reproduced by U.S. Games Systems in 1985.

Ibis Tarot by Josef Machynka. Published by U.S. Games Systems in 1988.

Tarot de Euskalherria by Marixtu Erlanz de Guler. Published by Fournier in 1990.

Alchemical Tarot (boxed set), art by Robert Place, writing by Rosemary E. Guiley. Published by Thorsons in 1995.

Royal Fez Moroccan Tarot by Stewart Kaplan. Published by U.S. Games Systems in 1996.

Medieval Scapini Tarot by Luigi Scapini. Published by U.S. Games Systems in 2005.

Dali Universal Tarot, created by Juan Larch, Salvador Dali. Published by U.S. Games Systems in 2012.

Magdalene Legacy Tarot by Casey DuHamel and D. L. Shutek-Jackson. Published by Grail Quest Press in 2014.

Appendix 4
Graph of Minor Arcana Values

Suit of Wands	Degrees	Sign & Decanate Rulers	Sephirot
Ace of Wands	1-10 Aries	Mars in Aries	Keter
Two of Wands	11-20 Aries	Sun in Aries	Chakhmah
Three of Wands	21 - 30 Aries	Jupiter in Aries	Binah
Four of Wands	11-20 Leo	Jupiter in Leo	Chesed
Five of Wands	21 - 30 Leo	Mars in Leo	Gevurah
Six of Wands	1 - 10 Leo	Sun in Leo	Tiferet
Seven of Wands	11-20 Sagittarius	Mars in Sagittarius	Netzach
Eight of Wands	21 - 30 Sagittarius	Sun in Sagittarius	Hod
Nine of Wands	1 - 10 Sagittarius	Jupiter in Sagittarius	Yesod
Ten of Wands	Grand Trine in Fire	Mars/Sun/Jupiter Conjunct	Malkhut
King of Wands	Leo	Sun	Fixed Fire
Queen of Wands	Aries	Mars	Cardinal Fire
Knight of Wands	Sagittarius	Jupiter	Mutable Fire
Page of Wands	Spring	—	—

	Upright Sympathies	**Essential Dignities**	**Reversed Antipathies**
Ace	Mars in Aries	Domicile/Similar	Mars in Scorpio
Two	Mars in Taurus	Compliment/Detriment	Mars in Libra
Three	Mars in Capricorn	Exaltation/Fall	Mars in Cancer
Four	Sun in Capricorn	Compliment/Detriment	Sun in Aquarius
Five	Sun in Aries	Exaltation/Fall	Sun in Libra
Six	Sun in Leo	Domicile/Similar	Sun in Cancer
Seven	Jupiter in Virgo	Compliment/Detriment	Jupiter in Gemini
Eight	Jupiter in Cancer	Exaltation/Fall	Jupiter in Capricorn
Ten	Jupiter in Sagittarius	Domicile/Similar	Jupiter in Pisces

Suit of Cups	Degrees	Sign & Decanate Rulers	Sephirot
Ace of Cups	1 - 10 Cancer	Moon in Cancer	Keter
Two of Cups	11 - 20 Cancer	Mars in Cancer	Chakhmah
Three of Cups	21 - 30 Cancer	Jupiter in Cancer	Binah
Four of Cups	11 - 20 Scorpio	Jupiter in Scorpio	Chesed
Five of Cups	21 - 30 Scorpio	Moon in Scorpio	Gevurah
Six of Cups	1 - 10 Scorpio	Mars in Scorpio	Tiferet
Seven of Cups	11 - 20 Pisces	Moon in Pisces	Netzach
Eight of Cups	21 - 30 Pisces	Mars in Pisces	Hod
Nine of Cups	1 - 10 Pisces	Jupiter in Pisces	Yesod
Ten of Cups	Grand Trine in Water	Moon/Mars/Jupiter Conjunct	Malkhut
King of Cups	Scorpio	Mars	Fixed Water
Queen of Cups	Cancer	Moon	Cardinal Water
Knight of Cups	Pisces	Jupiter	Mutable Water
Page	Summer		

	Upright Sympathies	**Essential Dignities**	**Reversed Antipathies**
Ace	Moon in Cancer	Domicile/Similar	Moon in Leo
Two	Moon in Aquarius	Compliment/Detriment	Moon in Capricorn
Three	Moon in Taurus	Exaltation/Fall	Moon in Scorpio
Four	Mars in Libra	Compliment/Detriment	Mars in Taurus
Five	Mars in Capricorn	Exaltation/Fall	Mars in Cancer
Six	Mars in Scorpio	Domicile/Similar	Mars in Aries
Seven	Jupiter in Gemini	Compliment/Detriment	Jupiter in Virgo
Eight	Jupiter in Cancer	Exaltation/Fall	Jupiter in Capricorn
Nine	Jupiter in Pisces	Domicile/Similar	Jupiter in Sagittarius

Suit of Swords	Degrees	Sign & Decanate Rulers	Sephirot
Ace of Swords	1 - 10 Libra	Venus in Libra	Keter
Two of Swords	11 - 20 Libra	Saturn in Libra	Chakhmah
Three of Swords	21 - 30 Libra	Mercury in Libra	Binah
Four of Swords	11- 20 Aquarius	Mercury in Aquarius	Chesed
Five of Swords	21 - 30 Aquarius	Venus in Aquarius	Gevurah
Six of Swords	1 - 10 Aquarius	Saturn in Aquarius	Tiferet
Seven of Swords	11 - 20 Gemini	Venus in Gemini	Netzach
Eight of Swords	21 - 30 Gemini	Saturn in Gemini	Hod
Nine of Swords	1 - 10 Gemini	Mercury in Gemini	Yesod
Ten of Swords	Grand Trine in Air	Venus/Saturn/Mercury Conjunct	Malkhut
King of Swords	Aquarius	Saturn	Fixed Air
Queen of Swords	Libra	Venus	Cardinal Air
Knight of Swords	Gemini	Mercury	Mutable Air
Page of Swords	Fall		

	Upright Sympathies	Essential Dignities	Reversed Antipathies
Ace	Venus in Libra	Domicile/Similar	Venus in Taurus
Two	Venus in Scorpio	Compliment/Detriment	Venus in Aries
Three	Venus in Pisces	Exaltation/Fall	Venus in Virgo
Four	Saturn in Cancer	Compliment/Detriment	Saturn in Leo
Five	Saturn in Libra	Exaltation/Fall	Saturn in Aries
Six	Saturn in Aquarius	Domicile/Similar	Saturn in Capricorn
Seven	Mercury in Pisces	Compliment/Detriment	Mercury in Sagittarius
Eight	Mercury in Virgo	Exaltation/Fall	Mercury in Pisces
Nine	Mercury in Gemini	Domicile/Similar	Mercury in Virgo

Suit of Disks	Degrees	Sign & Decanate Rulers	Sephirot
Ace of Disks	1-10 Capricorn	Saturn in Capricorn	Keter
Two of Disks	11 - 20 Capricorn	Venus in Capricorn	Chakhmah
Three of Disks	21 - 30 Capricorn	Mercury in Capricorn	Binah
Four of Disks	11 - 20 Taurus	Mercury in Taurus	Chesed
Five of Disks	21 - 30 Taurus	Saturn in Taurus	Gevurah
Six of Disks	1 - 10 Taurus	Venus in Taurus	Tiferet
Seven of Disks	11 - 20 Virgo	Saturn in Virgo	Netzach
Eight of Disks	21 - 30 Virgo	Venus in Virgo	Hod
Nine of Disks	1 - 10 Virgo	Mercury in Virgo	Yesod
Ten of Disks	Grand Trine in Earth	Saturn/Moon/Mercury Conjunct	Malkhut
King of Disks	Taurus	Venus	Fixed Earth
			Cardinal
Queen of Disks	Capricorn	Saturn	Air
			Mutable
Knight of Disks	Virgo	Mercury	Air
Page of Disks	Winter		

	Upright Sympathies	**Essential Dignities**	**Reversed Antipathies**
Ace	Saturn in Capricorn	Domicile/Similar	Saturn in Aquarius
Two	Saturn in Leo	Compliment/Detriment	Saturn in Cancer
Three	Saturn in Libra	Exaltation/Fall	Saturn in Aries
Four	Venus in Aries	Compliment/Detriment	Venus in Scorpio
Five	Venus in Pisces	Exaltation/Fall	Venus in Virgo
Six	Venus in Taurus	Domicile/Similar	Venus in Libra
Seven	Mercury in Sagittarius	Compliment/Detriment	Mercury in Pisces
Eight	Mercury in Virgo	Exaltation/Fall	Mercury in Pisces
Nine	Mercury in Virgo	Domicile/Similar	Mercury in Gemini

Appendix 5
Graph of Major Arcana Values

English Letter		A	B	G	D	H	V	Z	Ch
Greek Letter		α	β	γ	δ	ε	ς	ζ	η
Hebrew Letter (Continental use of Hebrew)		א	ב	ג	ד	ה	ו	ז	ח
Arcana Names	Fool	Magus	Priestess	Empress	Emperor	Pope	Lovers	Chariot	Justice
Arcana Number	0	1	2	3	4	5	6	7	8
Gra version SephirYetzirah – From ~1800 B.C. El Gran Tarot Esoterico, Tarot of the Ages		🜁	☾	♂	☉	♈	♉	♊	♋
Old Alexandrian, 600 B.C. – Hermetic Etteilla, Falconnier Tarot		🜁	☾	♀	♃	♈	♉	♊	♋
Continental Tarots ~1880 A.D. Levi, Wirth, Papus		🜁	☾	♀	♃	♈	♉	♊	♋
Marseilles, Spanish Tarot Maxwell's correspondences	Fool △	☉	☾	♀	♃	☿	♐	♂	♎
Pierre Piobb, 1908 A.D. – Spanish Variant #1 Dali, Euskalherria	Fool ♏	☉	☾	Earth (♁)	♃	☿	♍	♐	♎
Balbi, Spanish Variant #2	Fool ♅ ♏	☉	☾	☿	♃	♉	♍	♊	♎

Heb	Letter	Symbol	Tarot	#	Col A	Col B	Col C	Col D	Col E	Col F
T	⊕	⅁	Hermit	9	♋︎	♋︎	♋︎	✱	♊︎	♊︎
I	⌐	ʳ	Wheel	10	♍︎	♍︎	♍︎	♈︎	♈︎	♈︎
C	κ	∩	Strength	11	♌︎	♌︎	♌︎	♋︎	♋︎	♋︎
L	⋋	⌐	Hanged Man	12	♒︎	♒︎	♒︎	♉︎	♊︎	✱
M	μ	⊓	Death	13	▽	▽	▽	♐︎	♐︎	♐︎
N	ν	⌐	Temperance	14	♏︎	♏︎	♏︎	♒︎	♒︎	♒︎
S	ʆ	◘	Devil	15	♐︎	♐︎	♐︎	♑︎	♑︎	♑︎
Ayn	○	⅄	Tower	16	♂︎	♂︎	♂︎	⚴♎︎	↑	↑
P	π	◘	Star	17	☿	☿	☿	♒︎	♌︎	♌︎
Ts	φ	⋈	Moon	18	♒︎	♒︎	♒︎	♋︎	♋︎	♋︎
Qk	ρ	⌐	Sun	19	✱	✱	✱	♊︎	♊︎	♉︎
R	σ	⌐	Judgement	20	♐︎	♐︎	♐︎	♏︎	✱	⋎
Sch	τ	⅁		21	Fool △	World △	Fool △#0	World ♍	World ♉	
Th	⊃	⌐		22	World ♃	Fool ☉	World ☉ #21			World ♀

Appendix 6
Graph of the Shem Angels

Degrees	Sign	Letters	Spoken Name	Ruler	Card
1-5	Aries	VHU	Vehuiah	Mars	Ace Wands
6 - 10		YLY	Jeliel	"	rx
11-15		SIT	Sitael	Sun	Two Wands
16-20		OLM	Elemiah	"	rx
21 - 25		MHSh	Mahasiah	Jupiter	Three Wands
26 - 30		LLH	Lelahel	"	rx
1-5	Taurus	VMB	Umabel	Venus	Six Disks
6-10		IHH	Iah-hel	"	rx
11-15		ONV	Anauel	Mercury	Four Disks
16-20		MChI	Mehiel	"	rx
21 - 25		DMB	Damabiah	Saturn	Five Disks
26 - 30		MNQ	Manakel	"	rx
1-5	Gemini	VHV	Vehuel	Mercury	Nine Swords
6 - 10		DNY	Daniel	"	rx
11-15		HChSh	Hahasiah	Venus	Seven Swords
16-20		OMM	Imamiah	"	rx

Degrees	Sign	Letters	Spoken Name	Ruler	Card
21-25		NNA	Nanael	Saturn	Eight Swords
26-30		NITh	Nithael	"	rx
1-5	Cancer	LVV	Leuviah	Moon	Ace Cups
6 - 10		PHL	Pahaliah	"	rx
11-15		NLK	Nelchael	Mars	Two Cups
16-20		YYY	Yeiayel	"	rx
21 - 25		MLH	Melahel	Jupiter	Three Cups
26 - 30		ChHV	Haheuiah	"	rx
1-5	Leo	AKA	Achaiah	Sun	Six Wands
6 - 10		KHTh	Cahetel	"	rx
11-15		HZI	Haziel	Jupiter	Four Wands
16-20		ALD	Aladiah	"	rx
21 - 25		LAV	Lauviah	Mars	Five Wands
26 - 30		HHO	Hahaiah	"	rx

Degrees	Sign	Letters	Spoken Name	Ruler	Card
1 - 5	Virgo	AIO	Eyael	Mercury	Nine Disks
6 - 10		ChBV	Habuhiah	"	rx
11-15		RAH	Rochel	Saturn	Seven Disks
16-20		IBM	Jabamiah	"	rx
21 - 25		HYY	Haiyael	Venus	Eight Disks
26 - 30		MVM	Mumiah	"	rx
1-5	Libra	ANI	Aniel	Venus	Ace Swords
6 - 10		ChOM	Haamiah	"	rx
11-15		RHO	Rehael	Saturn	Two Swords
16-20		YYZ	Yeiazel	"	rx
21 - 25		HHH	Hahahel	Mercury	Three Swords
26 - 30		MIK	Mikael	"	rx
1-5	Scorpio	NThH	Nith-haiah	Mars	Six Cups
6 - 10		HAA	Haaiah	"	rx
11-15		YRTh	Yeratel	Jupiter	Four Cups
16-20		ShAH	Seheiah	"	rx
21 - 25		RYY	Reiyel	Moon	Five Cups

474

Degrees	Sign	Letters	Spoken Name	Ruler	Card
26 - 30		AUM	Omael	"	rx
1-5	Sagittarius	IZL	Yezalel	Jupiter	Nine Wands
6 - 10		MBH	Mebahel	"	rx
11-15		HRI	Hariel	Mars	Seven Wands
16-20		HQM	Hakamiah	"	rx
21 - 25		LAV	Laviah	Sun	Eight Wands
26 - 30		KLI	Caliel	"	rx
1-5	Capricorn	MBH	Mebahiah	Saturn	Ace Disks
6 - 10		PVI	Poyel	"	rx
11-15		NMM	Nemamiah	Venus	Two Disks
16-20		YYL	Yeialel	"	rx
21 - 25		HRCh	Harahel	Mercury	Three Disks
26 - 30		MTzR	Mitzrael	"	rx
1-5	Aquarius	VVL	Veuliah	Saturn	Six Swords
6 - 10		YLH	Yelahiah	"	rx
11-15		SAL	Sehaliah	Mercury	Four Swords

Degrees	Sign	Letters	Spoken Name	Ruler	Card
16-20		ORI	Ariel	"	rx
21 - 25		OShL	Asaliah	Venus	Five Swords
26 - 30		MIH	Mihael	"	rx
1-5	Pisces	LKB	Lecabel	Jupiter	Nine Cups
6 - 10		VShR	Vasariah	"	rx
11-15		YChV	Yehuiah	Moon	Seven Cups
16-20		LHCh	Lehahiah	"	rx
21 - 25		KVQ	Chavakiah	Mars	Eight Cups
26 - 30		MND	Menadel	"	rx

Appendix 7
Bibliography

Bibliography

From the personal collection of Christine Payne-Towler

Agrippa, Henry Cornelius. *Three Books of Occult Philosophy*. Translated by James Freake, edited and annotated by Donald Tyson. Saint Paul, MN: Llewellyn Publications, 1998.

The Bahir. Translated by Aryeh Kaplan. York Beach, ME: Samuel Weiser, Inc., 1990.

Bamford, Christopher, ed. *Rediscovering Sacred Science*. Edinburgh: Floris Books, 1994.

Begg, Ean. *The Cult of the Black Virgin*. London: Arkana, 1985.

Benjamine, Elbert (CC Zain). *The Sacred Tarot, vol. VI*. Los Angeles: The Brotherhood of Light, 1935.

Berdyaev, N. A. "Studies Concerning Jacob Boehme: Etude 1, The Teaching About the Ungrund and Freedom." *Journal Put'*, no. 20 (Feb. 1930): p. 47-79. www.berdyaev.com/berdiaev/berd_lib/1930_349.html (accessed Feb. 2015)

――――――. "Studies Concerning Jacob Boehme: Etude 2, The Teaching About Sophia and the Androgyne: J. Boehme and the Russian Sophiological Current." *Journal Put'*, no. 21 (Apr. 1930): p. 34-62. www.berdyaev.com/berdiaev/berd_lib/1930_351.html (accessed Feb. 2015)

Blau, Joseph Leon. *The Christian Interpretation of the Cabala in the Renaissance*. New York: Columbia University Press, 1944.

Bloom, Harold, ed. *Dante: Modern Critical Views*. New York: Chealsea House Publishers, 1986.

――――――. *Omens of Millennium: The Gnosis of Angels, Dreams, and Resurrection*. New York: Riverhead Books, 1996.

Boehme, Jacob. *The Way to Christ*. Translated by William Law (English Edition. London, 1764) including "Heiroglyphica Sacra, or Divine Emblems" by D. A. Freher. www.jacobboehmeonline.com (William Law tab) (accessed

Feb. 2015)

Cavendish, Richard. *The Tarot.* London: Chancellor Press, 1975.

Churton, Tobias. *Gnostic Philosophy: From Ancient Persia to Modern Times.* Rochester, VT: Inner Traditions, 2005.

Cirlot, J. E. *A Dictionary of Symbols.* Translated by Jack Sage. New York: Philosophical Library, 1962.

Codex Rosae Crucis, D.O.M.A: A Rare and Curious Manuscript of Rosicrucian Interest. Introduction and Commentary by Manly P. Hall. Los Angeles: Philosophical Research Society, Inc., 1971.

Cohn, Norman. *The Pursuit of the Millennium: Revolutionary Millenarians and Mystical Anarchists of the Middle Ages.* New York: Oxford University Press, 1970.

Comte de St.-Germain. *The Most Holy Trinosophia.* Introduction, Commentary, and Forward by Manly P. Hall. Los Angeles: The Philosophical Research Society, Inc., 1983.

Cooper-Oakley, Isabel. *Masonry and Medieval Mysticism: Traces of a Hidden Tradition.* Whitefield, MT: Kessinger Publishing, 1996.

Corbin, Henry. *Swedenborg and Esoteric Islam.* Translated by Leonard Fox. West Chester, PA: Swedenborg Foundation, 1995.

Couliano, Ioan P. *Eros and Magic in the Renaissance.* Translated by Margaret Cook. Chicago and London: University of Chicago Press, 1987.

_____. *The Tree of Gnosis: Gnostic Mythology from Early Christianity to Modern Nihilism.* Translated by H. S. Wiesner. New York: Harper Collins, 1990.

_____. *Out of This World: Otherworldly Journeys from Gilgamesh to Albert Einstein.* Boston and London: Shambhala Publications, 1991.

Curtiss, Harriette A. and F. Homer. *The Key to the Universe or a Spiritual Interpretation of Numbers and Symbols.* North Hollywood: Newcastle Publishing Company, Inc., 1983.

_____. *The Key of Destiny: Sequel to "The Key to the Universe."* North Hollywood: Newcastle Publishing Company, Inc., 1983.

d'Olivet, Fabre. *The Hebraic Tongue Restored: And the True Meaning of the Hebrew Words Re-established and Proved by Their Radical Analysis.* Translated by Louise Redfield Nayan. York Beach, ME: Samuel Weiser, Inc., 1991.

Daineilou, Alain. *Music and the Power of Sound: The Influence of Tuning and Interval on Consciousness.* Rochester, VT: Inner Traditions, 1995.

de Jong, H. M. E. *Michael Maier's Atalanta Fugiens: Sources of an Alchemical Book of Emblems.* York Beach, ME: Nicolas-Hays, Inc., 2002.

De Pizan, Christine. *The Treasure of the City of Ladies.* Translated with an Introduction and Notes by Sarah Lawson. New York: Penguin Books, 2003.

de Rola, Stanislas K. *The Golden Game: Alchemical Engravings of the Seventeenth Century.* London: Thames and Hudson, Ltd., 1988.

Decker, Ronald. *The Esoteric Tarot: Ancient Sources Rediscovered in Hermeticism and Cabala.* Wheaton, IL: Quest Books, 2013.

Dee, John. *The Heiroglyphic Monad.* Translated by J. W. Hamilton-Jones. New York: Samuel Weiser, Inc., 1975.

_____. *Secrets of Doctor John Dee: Being His Alchemical, Astrological, Qabalistic, and Rosicrucian Arcana.* Introduction and Commentary by Gordon James. Edmonds, WA: Holms Publishing Group, 1995.

Doczi, Gyorgy. *The Power of Limits: Proportional Harmonies in Nature, Art, and Architecture.* Boston: Shambhala Publications, 1994.

Dubois, Jenevieve. *Fulcanelli and the Alchemical Revival: The Man Behind the Mystery of the Cathedrals.* Rochester, VT: Destiny Books, 2006.

Evola, Julius and the UR Group. *The Hermetic Tradition: Symbols and Teachings of the Royal Art.* Translated by E. E. Rehmus. Rochester, VT: Inner Traditions, 1995.

_____. *Introduction to Magic: Rituals and Practical Techniques for the Magus.* Translated by Guido Stucco. Rochester, VT: Inner Traditions, 2001.

Fabricius, Johannes. *Alchemy: The Medieval Alchemists and Their Royal Art.* Wellingborough, England: The Aquarian Press, 1989.

Faivre, Antoine. *Theosophy, Imagination, Tradition: Studies in Western Esotericism.* Translated by Christine Rhone. Albany: State University of New York Press, 2000.

Faivre, Antoine, and Wouter J. Hanegraaff, eds. *Western Esotericism and the Science of Religion.* Leuven, Belgium: Peeters, 1998.

Faivre, Antoine, and Jacob Needleman, eds. *Modern Esoteric Spirituality.* New York: Crossroad Publishing Company, 1995.

Fanger, Claire, ed. *Conjuring Spirits: Texts and Traditions of Medieval Ritual Magic.* University Park: The Pennsylvania State University Press, 1998.

Faulks, Philippa and Robert L. D. Cooper. *The Masonic Magician: The Life and Death of Count Cagliostro and His Egyptian Rite.* London: Watkins Publishing, 2008.

Feldman, Daniel H. *Qabalah: The Mystical Heritage of the Children of Abraham.* Santa Cruz, CA: Work of the Chariot, 2001.

Fideler, David, ed. *Alexandria V.* Grand Rapids, MI: Phanes Press, 2000.

Fideler, David. *Jesus Christ, Sun of God: Ancient Cosmology and Early Christian Symbolism.* Wheaton, IL: Quest Books, 1993.

Filoramo, Giovanni. *A History of Gnosticism.* Translated by Anthony Alcock. Cambridge, MA: Blackwell, 1992.

Flint, Valerie I. J. *The Rise of Magic in Early Medieval Europe.* Princeton: Princeton University Press, 1991.

Forshaw, Peter J. *The Early Alchemical Reception of John Dee's Monas Hieroglyphica. AMBIX*, vol. 52, no. 3 (Nov. 2005): 247-269. www.ac.uk/english/tbs/ForshawAmbixDee2005.pdf (accessed February 2015)

Fournier, Felix Alfaro. *Playing Cards: General History from Their Creation to the Present Day.* Vittoria, Spain: Heraclio Fournier, S.A., 1982.

Freher, D. A. *The "Key" of Jacob Boehme.* Translated by William Law. Grand Rapids, MI: Phanes Press, 1991.

Fulcanelli. *Le Mystère des Cathédrales: Esoteric Interpretation of the Hermetic Symbols of the Great Work.* Translated by Mary Sworder. Las Vegas: Brotherhood of Life, 1984.

Gabay, Alfred J. *The Covert Enlightenment: Eighteenth-Century Counterculture and Its Aftermath.* Westchester, PA: Swedenborg Foundation Publishers, 2005.

Gad, Irene. *Tarot and Individuation: Correspondences with Cabala and Alchemy.* York Beach, ME: Nicolas-Hays, Inc., 1994.

Garin, Eugenio. *Astrology in the Renaissance: The Zodiac of Life.* Translated by Carolyn Jackson and June Allen. London: Arkana, 1983.

Gettings, Fred. *The Book of Tarot.* London: Triune Books, 1973.

_____. *Secret Symbolism in Occult Art.* New York: Harmony Books, 1987.

Gichtel, Johann G. *Awakening to Divine Wisdom: Christian Initiation into Three Worlds.* Translated by Arthur Versluis. St. Paul, MN: New Grail Publishing, 2004.

Godwin, Joscelyn, ed. *The Harmony of the Spheres: A Sourcebook of the Pythagorean Tradition in Music.* Rochester, VT: Inner Traditions International, 1993.

_____, ed. et al. *The Hermetic Brotherhood of Luxor: Initiatic and Historical Documents on an Order of Practical Occultism.* York Beach, ME: Samuel Weiser, Inc., 1995.

Godwin, Joscelyn. *Athanasius Kircher: A Renaissance Man and the Quest for Lost Knowledge.* London: Thames and Hudson, Ltd., 1979.

_____. *Music, Mysticism and Magic: A Sourcebook.* New York:

Arkana, 1987.

_____. *Robert Fludd: Hemetic Philosopher and Surveyor of Two Worlds.* Grand Rapids, MI: Phanes Press, 1991.

_____. *The Theosophical Enlightenment.* Albany: State University of New York Press, 1994.

_____. *Music and the Occult: French Musical Philosophies 1750 – 1950.* Rochester, NY: University of Rochester Press, 1995.

Goodrick-Clarke, Nicholas. *The Western Esoteric Traditions: A Historical Introduction.* New York: Oxford University Press, 2008.

Greer, Mary K. *The Complete Book of Tarot Reversals.* St. Paul, MN: Llewellyn Publications, 2002.

Haich, Elisabeth. *Wisdom of the Tarot.* Translated by D. Q. Stephenson. New York: Aurora Press, 1975.

Halevi, Z'ev ben Shimon. *Kabbalah: Tradition of Hidden Knowledge.* London: Thames and Hudson, Ltd., 1979.

Hall, Manley P. *Freemasonry of the Ancient Egyptians.* Los Angeles: Philosophical Research Society, Inc., 1965.

Hames, Harvey J. *The Art of Conversion: Christianity and Kabbalah in the Thirteenth Century.* Leiden, The Netherlands: Brill, 2000.

Hanegraaff, Wouter J. and Ruud M. Bouthoorn. *New Age Religion and Western Culture: Esotericism in the Mirror of Secular Thought.* Albany: State University of New York Press, 1988.

_____. *Lodovico Lazzarelli (1447-1500): The Hermetic Writings and Related Documents.* Tempe: Arizona Center for Medieval and Renaissance Studies, 2005.

_____, ed. *Dictionary of Gnosis and Western Esotericism.* Leiden, The Netherlands: Brill, 2006.

Hartnup, Karen, ed. *On the Beliefs of the Greeks: Leo Allatois and Popular*

Orthodoxy. Leiden, The Netherlands: Koninklijke, Brill, 2004.

Hogan, Timothy W. *The Alchemical Keys to Masonic Ritual*, 2007. www.Lulu.com i.d.: 1516561 (accessed Feb. 2015)

Huson, Paul. *Mystical Origins of the Tarot: From Ancient Roots to Modern Usage*. Rochester, VT: Destiny Book, 2004.

Iamblichus, attributed to. *The Theology of Arithmetic: On the Mystical, Mathematical and Cosmological Symbolism of the First Ten Numbers*. Translated by Robin Waterfield. Grand Rapids, MI: Phanes Press, 1988.

_____. *Egyptian Mysteries: An Account of an Initiation*. York Beach, ME: Samuel Weiser, Inc., 1993.

Jenkins, John Major. *Galactic Alignment: The Transformation of Consciousness According to Mayan, Egyptian and Vedic Tradition*. Rochester, VT: Bear and Company, 2002.

Kaplan, Aryeh. *Meditation and Kabbalah*. York Beach, ME: Samuel Weiser, Inc., 1982.

_____. *Sephir Yetzirah: The Book of Creation*. York Beach, ME: Samuel Weiser, Inc., 1990.

Kaplan, Stuart R. *The Encyclopedia of Tarot*, vols. I and II. Stamford, CT: U.S. Games Systems, Inc., 1994.

Klossowski de Rola, Stanislas. The Golden Game: Alchemical Engravings of the Seventeenth Century. London: Thames and Hudson, Ltd., 1988.

Kuntz, Marion and Paul, eds. *Jacob's Ladder and the Tree of Life: Concepts of Hierarchy and the Great Chain of Being*. Washington D.C.: American University Studies, 1987.

Kuntz, Marion Leathers. "Hebrew and the 'Other Sister' Arabic: The Language of Adam as a Paradigm for the Restitution Omnium in the Thought of G. Postel." *Quademi di Studi Arabi*, vol. 15 (1997): p. 21-44.

_____. "Gender, Kabbalah and the Reformation: The Mystical Theology of G. Postel." *Renaissance Quareterly*, vol. 58, no. 3 (Fall 2005): p. 958-960.

Lawlor, Robert. *Sacred Geometry: Philosophy and Practice.* London: Thames and Hudson, Ltd., 1982.

Lehrich, Christopher I. *The Language of Demons and Angels: Cornelius Agrippa's Occult Philosophy.* Leiden, The Netherlands: Brill, 2003.

Lévi, Eliphas. *Transcendental Magic: Its Doctrine and Ritual.* Translated by Arthur Edward Waite. York Beach, ME: Samuel Weiser, Inc., 1968.

Leviton, Richard. *The Imagination of Pentecost: Rudolph Steiner and Contemporary Spirituality.* Hudson, NY: Anthroposiphic Press, 1994.

Lubell, Winifred Milius. *The Metamorphosis of Baubo: Myths of Women's Sexual Energy.* Nashville and London: Vanderbilt University Press, 1994.

The Magical Calendar: A Synthesis of Magical Symbolism from the Seventeenth-Century Renaissance of Medieval Occultism. Translated by Adam McLean. Grand Rapids, MI: Phanes Press, 1994.

Mancuso, Piergabriele. *Shabbatai Donnolo's Sefer Hakhmoni; Introduction, Critical Text, and Annotated English Translation.* Edited by Tirosh-Samuelson and Veltri. Leiden and Boston: Brill, 2010.

Matthews, Caitlin. *Sophia, Goddess of Wisdom: The Divine Feminine from Black Goddess to World-Soul.* London: Thorsons, 1992.

McClain, Earnest G. T *The Pythagorean Plato: Prelude to the Song Itself.* York Beach, ME: Nicolas-Hays, Inc., 1978.

_____. *The Myth of Invariance: The Origin of the Gods, Mathematics and Music from the Rg Veda to Plato.* York Beach, ME: Nicolas-Hays, Inc., 1984.

McLean, Adam, ed. *A Treatise on Angel Magic: Being a Complete Transcription of Ms. Harley 6482 in the British Library.* Grand Rapids, MI: Phanes Press, 1989.

Merkur, Dan. *Gnosis: An Esoteric Tradition of Mystical Visions and Unions.* Albany: State University of New York Press, 1993.

Newman, William R., and Anthony Grafton, eds. *Secrets of Nature:*

Astrology and Alchemy in Early Modern Europe. Cambridge: The MIT Press, 2006.

Nicolescu, Basarab. *Science, Meaning and Evolution: The Cosmology of Jacob Boehme.* Translated by Rob Baker. New York: Parabola Books, 1991.

Pagels, Elaine. *The Origin of Satan.* New York: Vintage Books, 1996.

Papus (Gerard Encausse). *The Tarot of the Bohemians.* New York: Arcanum Books, 1958.

_____. *Astrology for Initiates: Astrological Secrets of the Western Mystery Tradition.* Translated by J. Lee Lehman. York Beach, ME: Samuel Weiser, Inc., 1996.

_____. *The Qabalah: Secret Tradition of the West.* York Beach, ME: Samuel Weiser, Inc., 2000.

Patai, Raphael. *The Hebrew Goddess.* Detroit: Wayne State University Press, 1990.

_____. *The Jewish Alchemists: A History and Sourcebook.* Princeton: Princeton University Press, 1994.

Payne-Towler, Christine. *The Underground Stream: Esoteric Tarot Revealed.* Eugene, OR: Noreah Press, 1999. www.tarot.com/about-tarot/library/essays/minorarcana (accessed Feb. 2015) www.tarot.com/about-tarot/library/essays/confluence (accessed Feb. 2015)

Pennick, Nigel. *Sacred Geometry: Symbolism and Purpose in Religious Structure.* Wellingborough, Northamptonshire, UK: Turnstone Press, 1980.

Penny, Edward Burton, ed. and trans. *Theosophic Correspondence Between Louis Claude de Saint-Martin and Kirchberger, Baron de Liebistorf.* Covina, CA: Theosophical University Press, 1949.

Reuchelin, Johann. *On the Art of the Kabbalah.* Translated by Martin and Sarah Goodman. Lincoln and London: University of Nebraska Press, 1983.

Roob, Alexander. *The Hermetic Museum: Alchemy and Mysticism.* Cologne, Germany: Taschen, 2001.

Sadhu, Mouni. *The Tarot: A Contemporary Course of the Quintessence of Hermetic Occultism.* Hollywood: Wilshire Book Company, 1962.

Scholem, Gershom. *Kabbalah.* New York: New American Library, 1978.

_____. *Alchemy and Kabbalah.* Translated by Claus Ottmann. Putnam, CT: Spring Publications, Inc., 2006.

Schonfield, Hugh. *The Essene Odyssey.* Rockport, MA: Element, Inc., 1993.

Schuchard, Marsha Kieth. *Restoring the Temple of Vision: Kabalistic Freemasonry and Steward Culture.* Leiden, The Netherlands: Brill, 2002.

_____. *Emanuel Swedenborg, Secret Agent on Earth and in Heaven: Jacobites, Jews and Freemasons in Early Modern Sweden.* Leiden, The Netherlands: Brill, 2012.

Segal, Robert A., ed. *The Allure of Gnosticism: The Gnostic Experience in Jungian Psychology and Contemporary Culture.* Chicago: Open Court, 1995.

Silberer, Herbert. *Hidden Symbolism of Alchemy and the Occult Arts.* Translated by Ely Jeliffe Smith. New York: Dover Publications, Inc., 1971.

Smoley, Richard. *Forbidden Faith: The Secret History of Gnosticism.* New York: Harper Collins, 2006.

Sullivan, Lawrence E., ed. *Death, Afterlife and the Soul*, "Ascension," Ioan Couliano (p. 107-116). New York: McMillan Publishing Company, 1987.

Szonyi, Gyorgy E. *John Dee's Occultism: Magical Exaltation Through Powerful Signs.* Albany: State University of New York Press, 2004.

Tarnas, Richard. *Cosmos and Psyche: Intimations of a New World View.* New York: Plume, A Division of Penguin Group, 2007.

Thomas, Heath. *Religion and the Decline of Magic: Studies in Popular Beliefs in Sixteenth and Seventeenth Century England.* New York: Oxford University Press, 1997.

Underhill, Evelyn. *Mysticism: A Study in the Nature and Development of Man's Spiritual Consciousness.* New York: E. P. Dutton and Company, Inc., 1961.

van den Broek, Roelof and Wouter Hanegraaff, eds. *Gnosis and Hermeticism from Antiquity to Modern Times*. Albany: State University of New York Press, 1998.

van der Toorn, Karel, Bob Becking, and Pieter W. van der Horst, eds. *A Dictionary of Deities and Demons in the Bible*. Grand Rapids, MI: William B. Eerdmans Publishing Company, 1999.

Versluis, Arthur, ed. *Wisdom's Book: The Sophia Anthology*. Saint Paul, MI: Paragon House, 2000.

_____, ed. et al. *Esotericism, Art and Imagination*. East Lansing: Michigan State University Press, 2008.

Versluis, Arthur. *TheoSophia: Hidden Dimensions of Christianity*. New York: Lindisfarne Press, 1994.

_____. *Wisdom's Children: A Christian Esoteric Tradition*. Albany: State University of New York Press, 1999.

_____. *Restoring Paradise: Western Esotericism, Literature, Art and Consciousness*. Albany: State University of New York Press, 2004.

_____. *Magic and Mysticism: An Introduction to Western Esotericism*. Lanham, Maryland: Roman and Littlefield Publishers, Inc., 2007.

_____. *The Secret History of Sexual Western Mysticism: Sacred Practices and Spiritual Marriage*. Rochester, VT: Destiny Books, 2008.

von Franckenberg, Abraham. *Raphael, oder, Artzt-Engel*. Amsterdam, 1676. http://diglib.hab.de/wdb.php?dir=drucke/xb-2820 (accessed Feb. 2015)

von Stuckrad, Kocku. *Western Esotericism: A Brief History of Secret Knowledge*. London: Equinox Publishing, Ltd., 2005.

Wasserman, James. *Art and Symbols of the Occult: Images of Power and Wisdom*. Rochester, VT: Destiny Books, 1993.

Waterfield, Robin, ed. *Western Esoteric Masters Series: Jacob Boehme*. Berkeley, CA: North Atlantic Books, 2001.

Wescott, W. Wynn. *The Occult Power of Numbers.* North Hollywood, CA: Newcastle Publishing Company, Inc., 1984.

White, Ralph, ed. *The Rosicrucian Enlightenment Revisited.* Hudson, NY: Lindisfarne Books, 1999.

Wilkinson, Lynn R. *The Dream of an Absolute Language: Emanuel Swedenborg and French Literary Culture.* Albany: State University of New York Press, 1996.

Williams, Thomas A. *Eliphas Lévi: Master of the Cabala, the Tarot and the Secret Doctrines.* Savannah, GA: Venture Press, 2003.

Wirth, Oswald. *The Tarot of the Magicians.* York Beach, ME: Samuel Weiser, Inc., 1985.

Yates, Frances A. *The Art of Memory.* Chicago: The University of Chicago Press, 1966.

_____. *The Rosicrucian Enlightenment.* Boulder, CO: Shambhala Publications, 1978.

_____. *The Occult Philosophy in the Elizabethan Age.* Boston: Routledge and Kegan Paul, Ltd., 1979.

_____. *The French Academies of the Sixteenth Century.* New York: Routeledge, Chapman and Hall, Inc., 1988.

About the Author

Christine Payne-Towler has been a Pacific Northwest presence since the 1970s. In 1997-8 she wrote the core interpretive Tarot text that launched the seminal and ever-popular website www.tarot.com. At the same time, her first book was released entitled *The Underground Stream: Esoteric Tarot Revealed*. In 2005 she began her blog site at www.tarotarkletters.com where she has been sharing her research articles and astrological analysis ever since. In 2011 she and artist Michael Dowers released *Tarot of the Holy Light*, which was voted the sixth best deck of 2011 at the international Tarot forum Aeclectic Tarot (www.aeclectic.net/tarot). Companion volumes for that deck are entitled *Tarot of the Holy Light: A Continental Esoteric Tarot* and *Foundations of the Esoteric Tradition*. Christine is also featured in a Time Monk Radio Network series under the title "AstroTheology: The Thin Spindle of Necessity."

Praise for *Tarot of the Holy Light*:
A Continental Esoteric Tarot

"If you want to know where someone like me turns to for card meanings, it's this book. What the *THL* companion book does expertly that I haven't seen any other contemporary Tarot text do quite as well is address the esoteric and magical interior architecture of Tarot. The book can be read independent from the deck. It will add new dimensions to what you thought you knew about the 78 cards."

Benebell Wen, author
Holistic Tarot

"This is a very unique work, impressive in content and very audacious, since it poses a challenge to the established beliefs surrounding the history of Tarot, as well as the magical, astrological, alchemical, and cabalistic interpretations given to the cards, the Hebrew letters, their position and energies along the Tree of Life, as well as the qualities and movements of the various Planets and how these impact our own energies and chakras."

Yolanda Robertson, Ph.D
The Revised New Art Tarot

"If you are seeking to deeply understand how this moment in your life illuminates, in a real and practical way, the mystery of life itself, as described by esoteric, astrological, and psychological considerations, you will find astonishing treasures in the pages of this book."

Frances Hatsfield, Ph.D, LMFT
Jungian Analyst

"*Tarot of the Holy Light* is the deck I use when doing readings for myself or for another familiar with the Tarot."

Cynthia Tedesco, author
PSC: The Novel

Made in the USA
Middletown, DE
27 November 2021